What Makes People Click: Advertising on the Web

WHAT MAKES PEOPLE CLICK: ADVERTISING ON THE WEB

Written by Jim Sterne

What Makes People Click: Advertising on the Web

Library of Congress Catalog No.: 97-68666

ISBN: 0-7897-1235-0

00   6 5

Interpretation of the printing code: the rightmost double-digit number is the year of the book's printing; the rightmost single-digit number, the number of the book's printing. For example, a printing code of 97-1 shows that the first printing of the book occurred in 1997.

Contents at a Glance

Table of Contents

7 What Makes People Click?   257

Credits

PRESIDENT
Roland Elgey

SENIOR VICE PRESIDENT /PUBLISHING
Don Fowley

PUBLISHER
Stacy Hiquet

GENERAL MANAGER
Joe Muldoon

MANAGER OF PUBLISHING OPERATIONS
Linda H. Buehler

PUBLISHING MANAGER
Tim Ryan

EDITORIAL SERVICES DIRECTOR
Carla Hall

EDITORS
Sean Dixon
Patrick Kanouse

MANAGING EDITOR
Patrick Kanouse

DIRECTOR OF ACQUISITIONS
Cheryl D. Willoughby

ACQUISITIONS EDITOR
Tim Ryan

PRODUCT DIRECTOR
Jácquelyn Mosley Eley

PRODUCTION EDITOR
Tonya Maddox

PRODUCT MARKETING MANAGER
Kourtnaye Sturgeon

ASSISTANT PRODUCT MARKETING MANAGER
Gretchen Schlesinger

SOFTWARE SPECIALIST
Adam Swetnam

SOFTWARE RELATIONS COORDINATOR
Andrea Duvall

EDITORIAL ASSISTANT
Jennifer L. Chisholm
Travis Bartlett

BOOK DESIGNER
Ruth Harvey

COVER DESIGNER
Ruth Harvey

PRODUCTION TEAM
Melissa Coffey
DiMonique Ford
Brian Grossman
Anjy Perry

INDEXER
Tim Tate

Composed in *Century Old Style* and *ITC Franklin Gothic* by Que Corporation.

This book is dedicated to Colleen

About the Author

Jim Sterne is an Internet marketing strategy consultant and international public speaker with 16 years of sales and marketing experience. Since 1994, he has been looking beyond the hype to find the business value of the World Wide Web. This is his third book after *World Wide Web Marketing* and *Customer Service on the Internet*, which were mostly written on the road, away from his home in Santa Barbara, California, where he co-founded an Internet access provider. Sterne has helped create Internet plans for such companies such as Sears, Sun Microsystems, Pfizer Pharmaceutical, and IBM, and has delineated the benefits of a Web site for small businesses while trekking through the jungles of Thailand on an elephant.

Acknowledgments

There are many people who lent a hand, provided an insight, offered moral support, corrected my thinking, lifted my spirits, acted as a shining example, performed a valuable service, or bought me lunch. Without going into pages of detail, I'd just like to recognize a few of them. . . and say thank you.

Kim Bayne, wolfBayne Communications

Mark Gibbs, Gibbs & Associates

Cliff Kurtzman, Tenagra Corporation

Mark Grimes, Eyescream

Mellanie Hills, Knowledgies

Rob Raisch, Internautics

Ron Richards, ResultsLab

Lew Rose, Esq., Arent, Fox

Steve Roth, Thunderlizard Productions

Tim Ryan, Macmillan Computer Publishing

Karl & Connie Sterne

Dave Taylor, Intuitive Systems

Eric Ward, Netpost

Peter Rip, Infoseek Network

Mark J. Welch, Esq.

Kristin Zhivago, Marketing Technology

Special thanks to Chryss Yost, able assistant and Internet Sleuth.

We'd Like to Hear from You!

As part of our continuing effort to produce books of the highest possible quality, Que would like to hear your comments. To stay competitive, we *really* want you, as a computer book reader and user, to let us know what you like or dislike most about this book or other Que products.

You can mail comments, ideas, or suggestions for improving future editions to the address below, or send us a fax at (317) 581-4663. For the online inclined, Macmillan Computer Publishing has a forum on CompuServe (type **GO QUEBOOKS** at any prompt) through which our staff and authors are available for questions and comments. The address of our Internet site is **http://www.quecorp.com** (World Wide Web).

In addition to exploring our forum, please feel free to contact me personally to discuss your opinions of this book: I'm **jeley@que.mcp.com** on the Internet.

Thanks in advance—your comments will help us to continue publishing the best books available on computer topics in today's market.

Jácquelyn Mosley Eley
Product Development Specialist
Que Corporation
201 W. 103rd Street
Indianapolis, Indiana 46290
USA

Introduction

The trouble is all inside your head, you realize.
The answer is easy if you stop to analyze.
I'd like to help you in your need to advertise.
There must be fifty ways to leave your message.

An advertisement is intended to intrude
Furthermore, you hope your meaning
won't be lost or misconstrued.
So I'll repeat myself, at the risk of being booed.
There must be fifty ways to leave your message.

Just put up a site, Mike; list in Yahoo!, Sue;
But don't ever use spam, Sam. You listen to me.
Hop on the Web, Fred; you know that it's widespread.
Just get on the screen, Jean, and get yourself seen.

(With apologies to Paul Simon)

Advertising has a new playground. Most of the rules are the same. A lot of the rules are new. If you have a Web site and want to draw people to it, if you have a brand and want to build it, if you have a product and want people to order it, advertising on the Internet may be the way to go.

No, this is not about marketing. It's not about building Web sites. For that, you can look to my first book, *World Wide Web Marketing, Integrating the Internet Into Your Marketing Strategy* (John Wiley & Sons, 1995). This book is about advertising.

Ads. Commercials. Spots. Billboards. On the Internet, this means banners and sponsorships. It also means big business.

Enough people are logging on to the Internet now that it has caught the attention of some of the world's largest companies. Of course, IBM and Digital are buying ad space out there. Naturally, Microsoft is spending giga-bucks on banners. Yes, AT&T wants you to know they are running with the wolves of high tech. But companies like Toyota, Proctor & Gamble, and Disney feel it's a good place for some of their advertising budgets as well.

When button-down, middle-of-the-road, take-no-risks P&G starts floating banners in Cyberspace, it's time for a serious look. That's what you'll find here. The descriptions, the definitions, the examples, and the results. How to think about it, how to plan for it, and how to excel at it.

The rules for Internet advertising are much the same as other forms of advertising and, in some way, much, much different. They are not as strict or nearly as widely known as the rules for bridge or canasta, nor are they as arbitrary as the rules for Calvin Ball. (You may remember Calvin & Hobbes playing a combination of football, rugby, hide-and-seek, and global thermonuclear warfare, where the only rule was the one you called out at the moment.) There's a *little* more structure to the Internet advertising game than that, and it's starting to actually settle down just a bit.

Think of this book as the program. You'll get to know the players. You'll get a feel for the ups and downs of the action, the types of balls in play, the kinds of pads you should wear, and which teams are leading the field.

An entire industry is growing up around creating online ads, delivering them, measuring the results, and auditing the players. It's time to get a handle on what all the excitement is about. ▩

What's In It for You?

You have competition headaches. You have budget dilemmas. You have production snafus. You have media planning nightmares, agency creative disagreements, Web site ROI controversies, and market segmentation disputes. When are you going to find time to learn about advertising on the World Wide Web?

If you're a marketing or advertising executive, you'll find more of your colleagues, more of your staff, and more of the media reps knocking on your door talking about buying banners. The time to learn is upon you.

If you are responsible for managing a campaign, rolling out a new product, shepherding a brand, or making a business unit successful, you need some ground-level intelligence about what is possible and what it takes to make Internet advertising work.

If you're a media rep, it's past time to figure out how to add the online arrow to your quiver. When clients start asking about a Web-based ad strategy, you have to have the answers at the ready. "I'll get back to you on that," simply doesn't cut it anymore.

If you plan on selling banner space on your Web site in order to pay the bills and feed the kids, you might want to read this book tonight. The majority of this tome is from the buyer's perspective and it serves you well in trying to discover, clinch, and keep advertising clients.

If you're like me and are fascinated by the possibilities, this book offers a look at a whole new world of advertising. It answers the questions about the activity, the viability, and the future of promotions on the World Wide Web.

With this book in hand, you'll be able to hold your own in a conversation with your peers, create a meaningful online advertising plan, and see a little bit into the misty future of advertising. You'll be prepared. More important, you'll even know what questions to ask.

Is There Life on the Web?

The first question every advertising or marketing executive asks when looking at the Internet is, "Who is looking back?"

You know that it took radio 28 years before there were 50 million listeners. It took television 13 years. It's only taken the Internet five years. Yes, 37% of the American population has home computers. Yes, 46% of those are online.

But you want to know if your prospective customers are out there where they might see your ad. You want to know if they are out there in quantities sufficient to make it worth your while.

The answer comes in two forms. First, depending on the survey you read, there are anywhere from 18 million to 50 million people surfing the Web. What's newsworthy is that that group's makeup is starting to look like your average cross-section of the population. That means you're looking at a huge collection of people and some of them are going to be your marketplace.

Okay, so if you sell shoes and gloves to peasants in the Yunnan Province of China, it's going to be a few years before your customers are online. But if you think selling Medicare augmentation plans to seniors is out of line, think again. That growing portion of our population with more time on their hands and less time on their feet is going online.

If you don't normally place ads in *Life* magazine to promote your nuclear decontamination consulting services, you won't be buying banners on Yahoo!, either. But you do place the occasional ad in *Nuclear New*s. So you should think about buying a banner on their Web site. You should think about sponsoring a section on the American Nuclear Society Web site.

Where Does It Fit?

The next question on your mind is how the Internet fits into the rest of your marketing plans. In an article called "Marketers Overlooking the Obvious in Advertising Age's Net Marketing" (**www.netb2b.com/cgi-bin/cgi_article/monthly/96/11/01/article.8**), Bernadette Tracy, President of NetSmart, did a pretty good job of putting Web site marketing in perspective:

Let's step back a moment and think about the benefits TV, magazines, newspapers and radio offer.

> *–TV creates awareness and impressions. ("I've heard of that brand.")*

> *–Magazine print ads supply the details. ("I didn't know that.")*

> *–Newspapers and radio drive the traffic to local dealers. ("I think I'll stop in and look.")*

Now, what role does the Internet play? Where does it fit in the overall media plan? And, most importantly, where should the budget come from?

> *–The Internet can generate pre-sold prospects. ("By the time I am ready to buy, I will know what I want.")*

Now that there are enough people on the Web to make advertising viable, the benefits of the Internet equate to all of the elements Tracy mentions. It can create awareness, make impressions, supply details, drive store traffic, and generate pre-sold prospects.

The Web has more flexibility than any other medium. You can create a short-run, one-off, highly-targeted promotion. You can run a long-term, high-concept, wide-ranging branding program. You can sponsor Web programming with a totally exclusive, competition-tormenting, image-enhancing contract. Your only limits are your imagination and your budget.

And one other thing. Don't think about using e-mail as a broadcast medium without recipients' permission. Just say no.

Deadly Mistakes

Do not send unsolicited e-mail. Got that?

"But Jim. It's so easy. It's so cheap. Even if I only get a hundredth of a percent of a response, the payback is enormous."

No sir. Not on your life.

There are a number of ways not to advertise on the Internet. Some are expensive. Some are illegal. Some get people so mad at you they will find ways of harming your public image, not to mention your mail servers.

Unsolicited e-mail and the irresponsible posting of ads to newsgroups are the two cardinal sins of the Internet. If you're not sure you agree, there are healthy portions of Chapter 2, "Before the Banner," you should read.

That's not to mean e-mail and the newsgroups can never be used for advertising. Don't get me wrong. But understanding netiquette and knowing the rules and following them keeps you out of harm's way.

E-mail, newsgroups, lists, games, newsletters, classified ads—there are lots of ways to do it right and they are well worth pursuing. But there are dangerous ways to spread the word on the Web and I take my role as Web advertising cartographer seriously and loudly proclaim, "Here there be dragons."

Just say no.

Banner Alternatives

If bringing people to your Web site is your goal, you may not even have to pay for banners. There are a lot of sites that would willingly point to yours because it's cool. Hopefully, they'll point to your site because it's interesting and useful, but in a pinch, "kewl" (as Californians say) still works a little.

One full page may do you more good than a thousand banners if it's on the right site. Think of it as a mini-site within somebody else's site. In the right spot, this can get your message delivered to just the right person at just the right time.

But why stop there? If you want people to come to your site, how about putting your banner on a mousepad. A mousepad? Check out the end of Chapter 2, "Before the Banner," for that one.

Sponsorships are becoming very worthwhile, especially for branding. But that's in Chapter 4, "Beyond the Banner." The real light that's shining on the Net these days is focused on the banner. For that, there's Chapter 3, "The Buck Spangled Banner."

A Banner Year

Banners are those rectangular graphic distractions at the top of Web pages. They are the 30-second commercial, the four-color ad, and the billboard of the Web. They are the center of attention because they seem to have taken over the role of the standard ad format. They're easy to create. They are easy to transmit. They are easy to place on multiple sites because they are slowly but surely getting standardized. Okay, so there are some 275 different banner sizes out there at the moment. Heck, the industry is you. But there is a great deal of effort being put into standardization which will benefit both the advertiser and the content creators whose Web sites host the ads.

To increase the visibility of their banners, many are resorting to animation. All the studies point to movement in a banner as the best way to attract the eye. But does it attract prospective customers? Depends on what you're selling.

So banners are getting more sophisticated. They are engaging the audience, instead of simply distracting the audience. They are getting interactive. Heck, some of them are taking the order without the need to leave the page.

The temptation to create really cool, really cutting-edge banners is strong. So strong that I come across at least one each week that does not display, does not display properly, kills Netscape, or brings my whole system down. Somehow these advertisers are not compelling me to buy their products. If they're so willing to disrespect my desire to avoid rebooting, then heaven knows how they'll treat me after they safely have my money.

Other Ways to Make Them Salute

You can raise a banner and see how many salute. That's what most are doing. There are some, however, who are striking off in another direction. They're trying to apply old models and finding out the old methods seem to work. Some are willing to stretch this new medium in ways that would break others.

Radio and television taught us about sponsorships. Now it's become a successful Web advertising method as well. "Brought to you by Nabisco" is as valid on Saturday morning TV as it is on the computer screen.

Sweepstakes and contests have always been favorite ways to garner attention and gather names and addresses. It's the same online. Only now, the games can be played at the moment instead of mailing and waiting. Games can be played against the computer. Games can even be played against other contestants in real time.

The closest we've come to television commercials on the Web take the form of *interstitial* pages that pop up between page one and page two. Reading an article, the next page is the equivalent of a magazine double-spread you have to click past to continue. Waiting for a search engine to find what you're looking for? While you're waiting, here's something you might be interested in. Playing a game? We pause for a word from our sponsor.

Another common approach to getting your name in front of people is the tried-and-true product placement routine. Show the character drinking the soda. Have the good guys driving the car. Have soccer mom stop at the drive-through between chauffeur sessions. Works just the same on the Web. With lots of advertising-supported *content sites* popping up (destination sites), there are lots of creative people looking to find new ways to get the cash to flow. That means ample opportunities for advertisers to be creative as well.

Then, there are old ads on even newer technologies. Chat sessions offer lengthy message exposure to a participatory audience. Push tools let you send your message onto the desktops of millions—a real switch from the "pull only" possibilities we had just a year and a half ago. And did you hear the one about the talking Dustbuster? You will.

The technology is new. The opportunities are growing. The results are all that counts.

But Is It Working?

The Internet is the most measurable medium we have short of door-to-door sales.

What kind of people should see our ad? Where can we find them? How many people looked at the ad? How many people clicked the ad? How many people ordered?

Because all of the events that take place on the Web are computer-driven, they can all be counted, measured, analyzed, and improved. It all boils down to what you want to accomplish and whether your reports are telling you what you need to know.

Can You Build an Electronic Brand?

Create brand equity on the World Wide Web? The place that is inhabited by students and computer jockeys and changes on a daily basis? Yes.

Turns out the Web is a great place to build recognition and trust.

This is one of those areas where all of the rules you know from real life apply directly to the Web. Branding is about placement, recognition, and repetition—all of those things you learned from the Harvard Business School. It's about reach and frequency. It's about corporate image and product image. It's about the trust between the consumer and the company.

Building that trust online means understanding the local customs and keeping your customer-colored glasses firmly on your face. You have to perceive the Internet from the receiver's side. Intrusive advertising is great on TV. It can even be considered part of the entertainment. But only certain portions of the Net are for entertainment and the rest receives intrusive advertising as intrusive.

Chapter 5, "Measure for Measure," is all about measuring what you're doing on the Internet and a good chunk of it is devoted to branding. After all, even if your only goal is to get people to buy more office supplies, you are projecting an image and building trust. But when it comes to the direct response advertising model on the Web, there are more ways to count response than you can count.

Instant Response

You want to know how many people responded to your ad? No problem—count the clicks. You can also keep track of what kind of computer they're on, which browser they're using, what time of day they show up, what site they were on before they came, and if they're at a university or at work. More numbers than you can shake a stick at. But that's not all.

Online you can pay for impressions, clicks, leads, and sales. You can make the sale in the banner to lead your prospects through a graduate course of product information. The hard part is knowing what's possible and then executing it correctly. Part of that proper execution is finding the right home to display your message.

Proper Placement

The most logical place to put a banner ad is where the most people will see it. But that's not always the best. Oh, it's great if you're running a global branding campaign. Coca-Cola? You bet. Nike? But, of course. Technofunk CDs? Not so fast.

Wouldn't you be better off putting your ad for leading edge music in places that younger people are more likely to see it? How about targeting students? If this sounds just like niche marketing in magazines, it is. But on the Web, the special interests get razor thin. There are so many people who have access and it's so easy to create a Web site that every proclivity and preoccupation can be affectionately addressed in minute detail on its own site.

And thereby hangs an opportunity.

There are dozens of Web sites on which to proudly proclaim your precision fishing lures. And not a single image is wasted on a technofunk-loving student. These are the sites fisherfolk are hooked on and are a spawning ground of targeted commercial messages.

With the destination sites covered, the savvy media planner looks upstream to the directories and search engines. These are the great junctions of the Internet through which pass the entire online population on their way to somewhere else. Catch these people's attention and they could be on their way to your site or your cash register.

Catching them is an art, surrounded by the science of key words. Purchase the word "fishing" and you have the opportunity to lure fishing enthusiasts away from their pursuit of the best trout stream or the online license bureau.

Besides looking at the rules of engagement for buying ad space, Chapter 6, "Looking For Space In All the Right Places," examines the new ad serving industry. Web representatives out to sell blocks of space are hard at work for your dollars, as are ad networks that deliver banners to a wide range of Web sites.

Zeroing In

But if you think super-niche marketing is all the Internet has to offer, you're not thinking like a computer scientist. Using *cookies* and embedded identification numbers and membership logins you'll be able to pinpoint your audience down to that holy grail: the Marketplace of One.

> **NOTE** A Cookie is a text file stored by your browser that is used by Web servers to stash information about you as a site visitor. Information pertaining to a site can only be read by the site that wrote the information. It's used to identify repeat visitors.
>
> Embedded identification numbers are an HTML programming trick that assign you a temporary number when you first come to a Web site. It then inserts your number into the URLs on outbound pages. When you click, your ID number is carried back to the server so it can recognize you. ▧

If I log in to a site connected to an advertising network I become a known quantity. One that's for sale. Male, professional, lives in the Southwest, and likes scuba diving. Career woman with pre-teen kids and a love of horses. It starts to get interesting, but then it gets fascinating.

The Internet has a way of finding people who will like your banner and will click it. Collaborative filtering compares what types of people have clicked your banner in the past and waits for others like them to show up. When they do—Bingo! It knows just what sort of banner to display.

It's online, real time advertising. It's like watching the audience watch the television set. Here comes the commercial break…okay, we have a 4×4 ad for the guy that tuned into the 4×4 show yesterday, and it's an ad for vitamin supplements for elderly woman whose profile matches 96% of the people who responded to that ad this week.

So now you know who your audience is. You know what they're interested in. You even know that they are watching right now and will see your ad! What do you tell them?

Creating Clickable Ads

Banners are easy to create, but not easy to create well. It takes a good banner to distract somebody enough to look at it while they're deep in concentration. It takes a great banner to get people to click.

Getting people to click takes all the lessons learned in direct marketing and plugs them in. Having taken care of the Web's version of managing the direct mail list, the other questions still remain: copy, design, offer, reach, and frequency.

Of course there are a few things you can do online you can't really swing in direct mail. You don't know when somebody is going to see your mailer. You can assume it's sometime in the first eight days after the drop, depending on what postage rate you used and how backed up the recipient's interoffice mail is. But on the Net, you know to the millisecond when that banner was displayed and you can control the timing.

Show this banner between 6:00 A.M. and 9:00 A.M.—it's for business people. Show this one from 2:00 P.M. to 6:00 P.M.—it's for school kids. Try this one from 4:30 A.M. until 9:00 A.M. and then again from 4:30 P.M. until 8 P.M.—it's for stock brokers.

You can also make your ad sing and dance. Dancing ads seem to be the most acceptable and providing the highest clickthrough. People see animated ads because the eye is forced to look at them. It's possible, but a bit on the expensive side, to animate a direct mail piece.

As for other choices, there are many and the research that has been done is discussed in Chapter 7, "What Makes People Click?" It offers some obvious advice and some that may be a bit surprising. Where should your ad appear on a page to get the most clicks? Should you really include a "Click Here" button on your banner? How frequent is frequent enough without being wasteful?

Some say humor works, some say not. Some say being cryptic draws a crowd and others say it draws the wrong crowd. I decided it was time for an advertising copy expert. Chapter 7, "What Makes People Click?" finishes up with the insights of Ron Richards whose company, Results Lab, has made many an advertisement more powerful and more productive. Provably more productive.

Learning by Example

Slowly but surely, advertisers are starting to tot up their numbers. Some of them are even willing to share with the rest of the class. Chapter 8, "Real Life Stories: The Good, the Bad, and the Unexplainable," offers up what there is on the Net in the way of show and tell so you can look at banners A, B, and C and see how well they pulled.

As with other forms of advertising, there are so many factors involved in an individual ad's success. Sometimes you can tell just looking at them. Mostly, it's a surprise. What these examples do show, however, is that the art of Web advertising is turning into a craft. It's becoming a craft with recognizable accomplishments and repeatable pointers. It can be learned and the return can be worth the investment.

This is a field that is learned by doing. But a little help along the way never hurt. That's why Chapter 9, "Creating a Web Advertising Strategy," looks at strategy-building and tactical maneuvers.

Creating a Web Site Strategy

Getting management support, mustering the troops, and spying on the competition are normal steps for any advertising project. The only difference here is that there is a lot of new ground to cover. It's new ground for you and your team, but it's also new ground for your managers—the people who hold the purse strings.

Once you have upper management eating out of your hand, you face the same challenge with all Internet projects: Why are you doing it? What are you hoping to accomplish? Is this a foray into the unknown just to test the waters? Are you trying to be seen as the Leader Of The Net in your industry, or do you simply want people to buy more products?

With clear goals, it's easier to select a target and parcel out the responsibilities. If you know what your intentions are it's a lot easier to set standards for more streamlined production and determine procedures for getting the ball rolling, getting it launched, and keeping it up in the air.

Good, solid documentation allows managers to manage without holding up the whole process, and automation can save the day and make everybody's job easier. An advertising project proposal can go a long way to keep the lines of communication open. Each item for consideration is outlined in Chapter 9, "Creating a Web Advertising Strategy," to get you started faster.

You have an interesting opportunity with Web advertising. You can measure, you can test, and if you are willing to be rigorous, you can actually see how changes in your ad style and placement immediately affect the numbers and types of people who respond. It's like keeping your finger on the pulse of the public. It's exhilarating.

From the Other Side of the Sale

If you're planning on selling advertising on your Web site (or you're just interested to see how the other half thinks), then Chapter 10, "Selling Space on Your Web Site," is for you.

If you want to make a living in the Internet advertising marketplace, you had better be ready to teach your prospective customers about the Web, about advertising, and especially about why your site is worthy of their attention.

Just what are you selling, anyway? What sort of content? What sort of traffic? What sort of people make up that traffic? Just how do you go about authenticating your claims?

Pricing conundrums and setting an ad content policy are just for openers. How do you find clients? Where do you go to uncover people willing to give you their hard-earned cash? Chapter 10, "Selling Space on Your Web Site," offers some pointers.

It also points to how to create a proper proposal, how to help your clients create the best banner ads possible and how to create additional value. Additional value is what attracts clients. It keeps them coming back for more.

If you know more about your Web site visitors than your competitors know about theirs, that's value. If you can offer additional ways a client's name or product can be discovered by your visitors, that's value. If you can stay flexible and actively help clients achieve their objectives and reach their goals, that's more than value—that's a winning game plan.

Looking Ahead

A book about the latest trends in electronic advertising wouldn't be any fun to write without a wild guess about what's coming. If we know this much about what's happening today, surely we can prognosticate about tomorrow.

Richard Tedlow, Professor of Business Administration at Harvard Business School, is a business historian. He likes to say that studying the past and explaining what happened gives him one great advantage over those who would predict the future—he's always right. He likes to point to a statement captured on a news program in the early 1970s made by University of Michigan automotive engineer David Cole (son of the then-president of General Motors) about the Wankel rotary engine. "There is no doubt in my mind that this will have the greatest impact on the auto industry of [any invention in] our time." Wrong!

Tedlow likes to show video clips of prominent advertising and marketing moguls lamenting the end of Tylenol as a viable brand after two rounds of product tampering which led to several deaths.

But the good doctor does see the future of online shopping plainly enough and, I believe, accurately describes it as one of the contributors to "The Future of Interactive Marketing," *Harvard Business Review*, reprint #96607:

In the virtual automotive showroom, you will be able to see a car from all angles and from the inside. At the flick of a switch, you will have access to extensive comparative price information without having to fight to get it from a salesperson.

What is more, computers will get to know you. Thus, the woman ordering the dress will be shown only items available in her measurements and designed to her taste. Then the computer can automatically remind her that she has not purchased any panty hose lately and that she might want to think about doing so.

Later in the paper, Professor Tedlow identifies one of the things that will make online advertising so compelling for all merchants. "In the new world of interactivity, marketers will, we are told, reach the long sought goal of selling people what they want, instead of trying to persuade them to want what is in stock."

This is the direction we're headed. Computers are going to get to know us and marketers will use that information to show us things we're interested in. What will that look like? I'm willing to take a shot at it, hopeful that I don't show up in one of Dr. Tedlow's videos down the road.

But, in deference to Professor Tedlow, this look at the realm of Web-based advertising begins with a review of where we've been. For that, we have to journey all the way back into the stone age of 1994, just before Halloween.

Advertising Comes to the Web

Five years ago the Internet still belonged to those speaking fluent UNIX and connected to the government or academia. A lot has changed in five years. ∎

Where Web Ads Began

On October 27, 1994, HotWired (**www.hotwired.com**) brought paid advertising into the World Wide Web (see Figure 1.1). Before that, it linked one site to another interesting site because the other site was interesting. Or there were deals made via e-mail; people at AT&T (**www.att.com**) would put up a link to O'Reilly's Global Navigator Network (**www.gnn.com**) in trade for the same pointing back. But HotWired collected cash.

America Online had been selling marketing demi-sites for years. Prodigy had made an entire online business out of selling online ads. But the banners on HotWired were the first time it happened on a Web site.

There were fourteen advertisers at the starting line. HotWired president Andrew Anker had plucked a price out of the air and pulled in buyers immediately. AT&T, Sprint, MCI, Volvo, ZIMA, and Club Med thought they'd just give it a try and see what happened.

Since then, half of the Fortune 500 has purchased ad space on the Web. Today, AT&T pays HotWired $10,000 per month for one link. The Yahoo! site is asking a cool $100,000 per month for a banner on its home page.

FIG. 1.1
HotWired was first to sell banners.

The Motivation

But why? Why would an astute media buyer want to place some of his or her hard-fought budget into a media that had no track record? How could a company commit to thousands of dollars to the Internet when it was still considered a fad? A place for the lonely, the social misfit, the nerd?

Being Digital/Being Cool

At the beginning there was one, overarching reason to have a site on the World Wide Web: to be among the Digerati. To be among the coolest of the cool. To be able to say, "We get it," in that way that's so smug you can even hear the sunglasses over the phone.

In September of 1994, they had a right to be smug. This was a gutsy move. It was brave, it was risky, it was nuts. Those were the days when being on the Internet was for people who could configure their own TCP/IP stacks, knew which all-night store carried the Cheetos, and spoke fluent UNIX. The only reason to create a Web site for this audience was because you were selling electronic gear. Volvo was taking a chance. Club Med was going out on a limb.

It was a limb marked "new market," and for the moment it was a grand play. Reaching out to educated, high income earners was not a bad thing at all. Being associated with the new and the hip was something that couldn't hurt a company like Volvo, whose most memorable tag line ("They're boxy, but they're safe.") was the creation of Dudley Moore and his fellow asylum inmates in the movie *Crazy People*.

The fall of 1994 was back when pundits who really knew about the Internet were writing about "building a presence" rather than advertising. Daniel Dern, Internet analyst and writer, never even mentioned the purchase of banners in his 1994 article "Advertising and Promoting on the Internet" (**www.dern.com/advertin.html**).

In August of 1994, *Red Herring* magazine talked to Ted Leonsis (still at Redgate Communications, which had just been merged into America Online), Mark Kvamme of CKS Partners, Dave Carlick of Poppe Tyson, and Martin Nisenholtz of Ogilvy & Mather in a very cutting-edge-for-its-time interview (**www.herring.com/mag/issue13/future.html**). Not one of them mentioned the World Wide Web, banners, or even the Internet, outside of a quick mention of discussion forums.

In September of 1994, I produced the world's first "Marketing on the Internet" seminar. (I keep saying that, waiting for somebody to prove me wrong. There were several "Business on the Internet" seminars that year, but if you know about one on marketing before mine, I need to know.) I gathered together Mark Gibbs, independent consultant and columnist for Network World, Jeff Osborne, VP of Sales and Systems at UUNet Technologies, Ron Richards, a guru of persuasion engineering at the Results Lab, and Kim Bayne, marketing maven and moderator of the cutting edge High Tech Marketing Communicators list (**www.bayne.com/wolfBayne/ default.html**). We talked about Web site navigation, the Web as a software application (not a magazine), and how it was the opposite of broadcasting. We advised about good e-mail netiquette. We outlined strategies for getting people back to your site. We didn't foresee advertising. One month later, there it was.

Back then, I was telling audiences around the world that the Internet was a bad place for advertising. Back in the prehistoric days, putting up a Web site was referred to as placing a billboard on the Information Superhighway. Got a Web page up? Great! That means you're advertising to millions of people around the world.

Nonsense. Having a page on the Web was the same as having a telephone number.

When you are one of only three hundred people who have a telephone number, you tend to get phone calls. People call up just to say, "Hey! Can you hear me? Isn't this neat?" Do they want to buy a product? Are they interested in your offer? Heck no. They just want to play with a new toy. They're early adopters, not buyers.

When you had one of only a few hundred Web sites up and running in 1994, people tended to come by to take a look. Especially the other Webmasters looking to view your source and copy some of your fancy HTML.

There were no fears in 1994 of being left behind. Instead, it was the era for those who wanted to be out in front. The cachet of being online was still so new it smelled factory fresh. Being hip mattered. But it only mattered for about six months.

In 1995 (and more so in 1996), enough Web sites were built that people stopped coming by out of blind curiosity. "If you build it, they will come" stopped being the order of the day. It was necessary to go out and tell people that you had a Web site and why they should care. That hasn't changed.

So I used to say that the Internet was a dumb place for advertising, a great place for marketing, and a terrific place for customer service. My first book, *World Wide Web Marketing* (John Wiley & Sons, 1995), described the best ways of using e-mail, newsgroups, and, of course, your Web site. The emphasis was on marketing (what you do after you have somebody's attention), as opposed to advertising (what you have to do to get their attention).

The next book, *Customer Service on the Internet* (John Wiley & Sons, 1996), focused on how to treat people after the sale. That was the natural progression. First, you built a Web site to educate people about your company and products, then you sell them something, and then you have to perform customer service.

By the middle of 1995, Internet furor was at an all-time high. The cover of *Time*, *Newsweek*, the *Wall Street Journal* and yes, even *USA Today*—each proclaimed a new era. You couldn't turn around without running into an Information Superhighway metaphor. It was no longer about being hip, it was about keeping up.

Many a Web site was launched in 1995 and many an excited marker was sticking his toes into the experimental pool. All they could tell was that it was wet. Hot or cold? Couldn't tell. Deep or shallow? Safe or toxic? Benign or full of fierce creatures? Couldn't tell. But everybody else was doing it, so it was time to get wet. A little wet, anyway.

Then managers started asking why "real" projects were being left to the last minute. Why were these young marketing assistants spending so much time in the evening, night, and morning that they were missing other deadlines? Callow visionaries would show their managers the World Wide Web. Show them the pages that could be downloaded instantly from anywhere. Show them the amazing number of hits and the astonishing growth of traffic to their site. Managers were dumfounded. This was brilliant! Okay, said the managers. Go forth and stay connected, stay wired. Let's see where this puppy takes us. Oh, but don't spend any money.

Time and money *were* spent and managers wanted to know how this new expense was going to pay for itself if fewer and fewer people visited the site.

Salvaging a Web Investment

It took a couple of big failures to realize that Web sites don't work like broadcasting. They don't attract people like flies and they don't draw a crowd just because they have the latest technical toy on display. Oh yes, that used to be the case, but no more.

General Motors gave it a shot with the announcement of the 1997 Buick Regal. On December 3, 1997, they pulled out all the stops (**www.regal.com**) (see Figure 1.2).

FIG. 1.2

General Motors treated the Web like TV for their Regal launch.

They had live audio and video streaming out on the Web. They had online chats with designers. They had the interactive page:

> What do you want to know about Regal? How it got its looks? What makes it mooooooove? How many dogs, cats, and adolescents it can carry? Whether it's quiet enough so that conversation is a real possibility? Or do you just want to know about the lives of the people for whom this car was made?

General Motors promoted the heck out of it as one of the many "firsts" on the Net. They got so much traffic that the server often choked and people couldn't get in. When they did, the results were less than thrilling. Several browser plug-ins had to be downloaded to hear the dog bark diminish as the window rolled up. The video was (as is still the case) choppy at best and more reminiscent of cardboard flip-books or your great-grandfather's home movies shown on an ancient projector. Okay, so you can see a video of the stylish car after waiting five minutes to download the file. But you'll need to spend a half an hour finding the right software to play the video, downloading, and installing it. To see a ten second video of a car?

As Web sites go, General Motors' site misses out on the opportunity to create a relationship with the prospective Regal buyer. As an advertisement, the site missed the mark by miles. General Motors could have found a better way to spend their million dollars. I always liked the popcorn the dealerships gave away.

General Motors could have found a better way to spend their million dollars. They could have let people sign up for test drives. They could have provided a database for "Meet Your Dealer" and put a human face on it. They could have saved the razzmatazz for TV and spent their money on things which were of more immediate value to their prospective customers. I always liked the popcorn the dealerships gave away.

Web sites are not advertisements. They don't come on during breaks in the action like they do on TV. They don't impose themselves on you like page four of your newspaper or catch your eye as you drive down the highway. They simply sit there and wait for you to be interested enough to visit them. Advertisements are the promotional efforts designed to create that interest.

So how do you lift the sagging number of visitors to a Web site? Developed by the wide-eyed for the enthusiastic, most Web sites got unexpected hoards of people to come knocking—at first. Then the tide started going out and the surfers were harder to find. What had happened? Why was that exponential increase that made chart printing a Webmaster's favorite pastime start to flatten? So many sites, so little time.

It used to be easy. Put up a page offering a free car and people would flock. DealerNet (**www.dealernet.com**) gave it a shot (see Figure 1.3) and people did just that. When people on the Web were more interested in what was going on the Web than their own sleep deprivation, word traveled fast. Discussion lists like Kim Baynes' HTMARCOM and Glen Fleischman's now-retired Internet Marketing list had thousands of people jabbering back and forth about the latest new trick, tactic, and technology.

As fast as the number of surfers rose, the number of Web sites rose as well. There soon became so much to look at on the Web that a couple of pages of Who We Are and What We Offer just didn't have much attraction anymore. There were animated pictures to look at, live CU-SeeMe video to play with, interactive games to try.

People were no longer looking at sites for the sheer delight of it, just as they no longer sit and stare at the television test pattern. At first they did—of course. Looky here! A picture of concentric circles, in my house, that's being broadcast from a TV station miles and miles away. Would you look at that! Keep watching and there'll be people there, too!

It was now time to start posting signs on the World Wide Web, pointing back to the home page. Go where the people are and show them the way. It was time for advertising to begin.

FIG. 1.3
DealerNet offered a free car to attract people. It worked.

Making the Offer

The difference with this type of advertising was that the response could be immediate and direct. You don't have to wait for them to go to the store to use the coupon. No watching for the postal carrier to see if bags of orders start flowing in. No operators standing by waiting for the phone to ring. People could click offers they were interested in and come to the source—your Web site.

All the lessons of direct mail apply. The offer has to be enticing and stimulating enough to solicit a direct response. The offer might be discounts, limited supply, or a special event. Webmasters realized they would have to talk louder to be heard over the Net noise. Even if they were going to give away a trip to Hawaii, a new car, or a lifetime supply of chewing gum, they had to let people know. It started to look more and more like regular marketing. If you're going to stage a marketing event, you have to advertise it.

A certain number of surfers in a certain period of time can only look at so many sites. If you want people to come to your Web site, you have to point the way. But as the number of people logged onto the Web grew, getting people to your site was not the only thinking behind spending money on banners.

Building a Brand

In January of 1997, the city/state of Singapore looked like it had been taken over by Calvin Klein. Apparently, Calvin wanted the people of Singapore to smell better. The place was festooned with CK Be fragrance advertising. In shopping center handbills. On billboards. Hanging from the sides of buildings. Clinging to the backs of busses. Resting atop taxi cabs. Delivered under the door of your hotel room in the morning with the local paper. In shopping malls they had set up booths with TV monitors showing those turgid black and white ads of angst-ridden twenty-somethings lamenting about life, love, relationships, and finding themselves. It was just like the 1960s, only they weren't wearing flowers and they didn't seem very happy about anything.

Calvin Klein had set out to put the CK Be product name in front of as many people as possible. Wherever you turned, there it was. That was the philosophy behind some of the banner advertising on World Wide Web in 1996.

If you could show your name on your banner to enough people enough times, they would relate your company to the Internet. It was no longer about having a cool Web site to be hip. It wasn't just having a presence that people could go if they wanted to. It was good, old-fashioned, in your face, here's my name, don't you forget it, redundant advertising. It was about impressions.

I changed my mind about advertising on the Internet in 1995. Oh sure, there was a need to announce your Web site to everybody you could. Yes, Microsoft, Sun, and Netscape had done a pretty good job of plastering their names all over the Net, co-opting it as their personal progeny. But there was also reason to rethink the validity of brands like Nike, Saturn, and Proctor & Gamble.

The concept of banner ads as brand building caught on in 1996, when studies showed that more and more people were on the Web and they looked more and more like people everywhere.

- 1993: FTP, Gopher, and Archie still roamed the earth
- 1994: The year of experimenters and techno-wonks
- 1995: The year of skunk works and surprising results

- 1996: The year of cautious optimism
- 1997: The year of the big budget—deliver or else

Cranking Up the Money Machine

There are many out there who would take a guess at the money being spent on Internet advertising. One article in Upside (**www.upside.com**) put the number at $71 million for the first six months of 1996. Coopers & Lybrand (**www.colybrand.com**) determined that aggregated ad revenue for the online industry through the first three quarters of 1996 hit a high of $157.4 million. Simba/Electronic Advertising & Marketplace Report (**www.simbanet.com**) pegged January, 1997 spending at $23.7 million.

In the middle of March, 1997, Jupiter Communications (**www.jup.com**), the most widely quoted source, put out a press release that said, "Total U.S. online ad spending was an estimated $301 million in 1996, according to new AdSpend data released today by Jupiter Communications."

Whether that sounds like an ocean of liquid assets or sounds like a drop in the bucket depends on whether you use a telescope or a microscope.

Telescopic or Microscopic?

Look through the telescope and giggle at all the noise that's being made over expenditures that make up less than 2% of the $16 billion spent by the top 10 advertisers in 1995. The Web is a medium in its infancy. This is a testing zone, a trial period, a sandbox of attempted message transmission.

It's not much of an industry when you realize that $301 million represents the amount CompuServe tagged for equipment upgrades in 1995 through 1997. Business Research Group (**www.BRGresearch.com**) picked $301 million as the amount that was spent in 1996 on Internet/intranet security.

When you discover that the Miller Brewing Company spent $252 million in 1996 for radio, newspapers, and television, and you look at total U.S. annual ad spending at around $87 billion, it makes $301 million look a tad anemic. Heck, Nike's ad budget from 1994 was $138 million. Yes, Nike could have purchased more than half of all the advertising that was sold on the Internet.

On the other hand, the microscope reveals a burgeoning industry. Where else can you find a business sector that has gone from zero to $301 million in two years? The growth rates by month resemble that curve you grew to love when measuring hits. It starts out at a crawl and ends up vertical.

When the first quarter of the year produces $25.3 million in ad spending, the second $46.4, the third $67.7, and the last quarter $102.4 million, the game is afoot. Oh, and don't forget to add the $18 million for classifieds and yellow pages. "The 1996 total—$260 million of which went to Web sites, $41 to non-Web publishers such as America Online and PointCast—represents a more than five-fold increase over online ad spending the year before," says Jupiter. That makes it a trend worth watching. In fact, the estimates for the year 2000 run anywhere from $2 billion to $5 billion. As the late Senator Everett Dirksen liked to say, "A billion here, a billion there; pretty soon you're talking about real money."

The Rest of the World

And what of the rest of the world? Depends on whom you ask. Jupiter says spending in the U.K. was close to $1 million in 1996. Dresdener Kleinwort Benson, a London-based investment bank, put the number closer to $7 million. Jupiter figured the entire non–U.S. spending was only $6.1 million, with Europe spending $3.5 million, and Asia-Pacific shelling out $2.6 million.

Dentsu Incorporated (**www.dentsu.co.jp**), a large Japanese advertising agency, reported that $12.8 million had been spent in Japan on Internet advertising, which represented about .03% of national advertising sales. They expect that number to climb to $32 million in 1997.

Who's Buying Space?

In 1996, the amount of spending on Web site banner advertising started to take off. It wasn't limited to the high tech industry, but tech buyers outnumbered the rest four to one. Why? Three reasons: knowledge, products, and audience.

The tech companies already understood how the Internet worked. They knew what to expect (an education). They knew the risks and were willing to take the gamble. There were no long meetings of executives trying to figure out who was going to be the scapegoat if this Web advertising was just a hole in the marketing department into which they were pouring money. They saw it as the way the world was turning and they were determined to turn with it. They had to; they had a vested interest.

If you're Sun Microsystems and you've been shouting, "The Network IS the Computer," at the top of your lungs for ten years, you're not going to let Microsoft walk away with the Internet. If you're Microsoft, you're going to try you best to do just that. Competition aside, if you're company's livelihood is predicated on lots of people being successful online, then you are highly motivated to make that venue successful, even if it means pumping large amounts of money into it. You're in telecommunications? Start spending. You're an Internet search engine? Spend 'til it hurts.

Companies selling servers, switches, and software for the Internet had a built-in audience from day one. If a company sells things that make the Internet run, the best place to find potential buyers is on the Net. Those companies knew that potential customers were online and lit out after them. Proctor & Gamble and Toyota knew that people who were online were potential customers. They decided to get into the picture as well.

The Biggest Buyers

Jupiter Communications laid it out in their third quarter, 1996 Adspend report on Internet advertising:

Table 2.1 Big Web Spenders in 1996	
Company	**Amount Spent**
Microsoft	$13.0
AT&T	7.3
Excite	6.9
IBM	5.9
Netscape	5.7
Infoseek	5.1
NYNEX	4.0
Yahoo!	3.9
Lycos	3.9
CNET	2.7

It comes as no surprise that Microsoft should be at the top of the list. With the most to gain, the most to lose, and a corporate imperative to "Embrace and Extend" the Internet, you're likely to see them in the top spot for the next couple of years.

AT&T, IBM, and NYNEX are pretty much in the same boat. And the next group, made up of Excite, Netscape, Infoseek, Yahoo!, Lycos, and CNET, are all dependent on the Net for their income. They have to advertise.

IBM has an ad budget of about $700 million. So the view through the telescope is almost laughable. Between IBM products and Lotus products, the company spent $7.2 million in 1996. "Okay, let's toss a big, fat 1% of our budget at the Web and see what sticks." Apparently, enough stuck for IBM to plan a more sizable chunk for 1997. Saying only that they are going to significantly increase Web spending, IBM is looking to become the computer brand of the Web. Only time will tell if Microsoft is willing to hang onto their lead.

But just below that list of technology types were some consumer-oriented companies that were willing to take a risk. They smelled money out there somewhere and they wanted to be sure they were in place when the Web went from phenomenon to phenomenal.

Toyota Sees Up-Scalers

Long before the word "Internet" had graced the covers of magazines around the world, Toyota was working on an online strategy. While the rest of us still had to think twice before writing the year on our checks at the turn of the decade, Toyota was writing checks to Prodigy and CompuServe. Before America Online was clogging the mail with diskettes, Toyota discovered that there was life online.

With serious demographic analysis under their belts, (80% of Toyota owners owned or had access to computers) Toyota got help from Saatchi & Saatchi to build their Web site. After the initial launch on October 12, 1995, it was time to let those car buying types know that they could get the information they needed at **www.toyota.com**. Toyota did whatever they could to get the word out.

The Toyota URL went into every print ad, on every TV spot, and was mentioned in every radio commercial. It doesn't all happen overnight. It wasn't until the spring of 1997 that they finally got www.toyota.com on the back of all of their parts delivery trucks.

What they have done since the beginning is track the value of each banner they place. They review site traffic, site demographics, clickthroughs, and conversion factors. But from the start, they've met their goals: drive people to the site, which drives people to the dealers, which drives the sale, which lets the clicker drive off the lot.

As far as Jim Pisz is concerned, having a Web site and letting people know it's there, "is as important as having a brochure that you mail to people to let them know where the dealership is." In print, you can mail that brochure to your prospects. On the Web, you have to let them know where to find your Web site.

Proctor & Gamble Smells Consumers

Jupiter Communications pegged P&G at spending a little over three-quarters of a million dollars on Web advertising in the first half of 1996. Nothing official, mind you, they just take a banner count times the CPM and make a guess. Still, it's a sizable chuck of change. In their December 1996 issue, *Wired* magazine reported P&G's 1996 budget for Web ads was $8 million. Now we're getting serious.

Elizabeth Moore, a P&G spokesperson, has said that they're interested in delivering meaningful brand messages to the public at large and it seems the Web is one of the ways to do it. Proctor & Gamble isn't as confident as Toyota. P&G still see themselves as experimenting. But then, aren't we all?

Who's Selling Space?

One the other side of the coin, there are ad sellers out there who would like to place your name on their pages—for a price. "Your message here" have been their watchwords since the demise of the subscription model. The only subscription-based Web site that claims a flickering success is the *Wall Street Journal* (**www.wsj.com**). During their free-for-all at the start, they racked up 600,000 subscribers. On the first day, they switched to subscription ($49 a year, or $29 if you already took the paper version) that number dropped to 30,000. Even if all the subscribers were paying the higher fee, that still clears less than $1.5 million a year.

Even the successful ESPN SportsZone (**espnet.sportszone.com**) is playing around with CyberCash (electronic money, **www.cybercash.com**) to get people to pay on a daily basis.

Starwave, owners of the SportsZone, recognizes that paying a monthly fee is a considered purchase. Paying one dollar to look at today's premium content is a point-of-purchase, impulse buy. Will it work? Time will tell. In the meantime, the SportsZone is doing just fine selling ads.

These are sites so well branded, they're known the world over. Imagine the rest of us trying to keep a pay-for-play model alive.

If poodle owners don't care enough about their canine companions to shell out $50 a year to stay informed, then it's time to give up on subscriptions and concentrate on sponsor support. With so much available on the Web, why would you pay when a good search tool can point you to 10,000 poodles?

There are a bazillion Web sites on the Internet. (That's a technical term meaning, "more than are necessary to count.") They cover every conceivable subject from every conceivable angle and those that aren't directly selling a specific product are looking for ways to make a buck. They're looking for advertisers.

The Biggest Sellers?

The biggest make-a-bucksters are the ones with the biggest audiences. The Web sites that attract the most eyeballs are in a position to explain their value proposition in words most media buyers can understand: Cost Per Thousand (CPM—don't worry, the M is a Roman Numeral).

The sites with the largest followings fall into three categories: search tools and directories, information about the Internet, and magazine-style sites, also called *content sites*. According to Jupiter, the top ten sellers of ad space line up as follows:

Table 2.2   Big Sellers In 1996

Company	Amount Sold
Netscape	$27.7
Yahoo!	20.6
Infoseek	18.1
Lycos	12.8
Excite	12.2
CNET	11.4
ZD Net	10.2
WebCrawler	7.3
ESPNET SportsZone	6.5
Pathfinder	5.8

Yahoo!, Infoseek, Lycos, Excite, and WebCrawler are the places people go to find out where they want to go. For the foreseeable future, these sites will remain the center of attention on the Internet. We'll take a look at why this is so in Chapter 6, "Looking for Space in all the Right Places," where you look into placement strategies.

Suffice it to say that 1.5 million people look at the Yahoo! home page every day. If your audience is the general public, then you're in competition for these prime locations.

Curiously, Netscape tops the list. Why are so many willing to give so much for this site? Because the Netscape site gets lots of traffic. *Interactive Week* magazine reported more than 4.1 million people visit every day. The Netscape browser still has between 50% and 75% of the market depending on who you ask. Each time those users fire up the Netscape browser, it takes them to the Netscape site. They use it as their launching pad. They also use it to see "What's New" (see Figure 1.4) and "What's Cool" (see Figure 1.5).

FIG. 1.4

Netscape acts as a pointer to new Web sites.

FIG. 1.5

Netscape also acts as a pointer to what it thinks are cool Web sites.

Netscape is also the center of attention for all of you Netheads who need to keep up with what's new and cool at Netscape. In other words, it gets some traffic in its own right as a communication media for the company.

As a result, Netscape attracts a lot of attention and is more than happy to sell space on their site as another source of revenue for the company.

The most popular magazines on the Net are Net-centric. *CNET* (**www.cnet.com**) provides reviews and news and products and is a general resource for things Internet. Like *ZD Net*, *CNET* expands this interest to include all sorts of technology. It comes as no surprise that the things most people on the Net are interested is the Net. But that's starting to change.

The proof are sites like the ESPNET Sports and Pathfinder. The first is exactly what you would expect: all sports, all the time. The other is the Time Warner conglomeration of *Money, Fortune, Time, Life, People,* and other popular magazines. They're selling lots of ad space because they have lots of content.

But the dirty little secret is that there's no way to tell how much money is changing hands.

The Fuzzy Numbers of Ad Trading

In the beginning, it was well recognized that getting traffic to your Web site meant getting links to your site. And the best way to do that was to trade. Quid pro quo. All of us could advance the value of the World Wide Web by providing pointers to great sites. We all had great sites, so we were all ready, willing, and able to trade links. It was painless, it was fast, and more to the point, it was free. The only thing that's changed is that we're getting pickier about with whom we trade.

Six of the top ten sellers (Excite, Netscape, Infoseek, Yahoo!, Lycos, and CNET) are also on the list of top ten buyers. In other words, these people are trading links with all and sundry, including each other. Netscape advertises on Lycos, Lycos advertises on CNET, and they all trade out their banner space instead of paying for it. The more banners each one publishes, the more branding they accomplish and the more they can build their paper value. They can tell the world, "We've displayed $27 million dollars worth of banners on our site this year." How much money is really changing hands? We may never know.

Peter Storck, Group Director of online advertising at Jupiter Communications, guessed that 25% of revenue at sites like Yahoo and Netscape had been taken out in trade. That makes $301 million start to look like $226 million. Some sites like Starwave and CNN won't barter for banner space. The fact is that the industry is in its infancy and somebody has to prime the pump. In the middle of 1997, there is simply too much inventory (space looking for ads). Sites are more interested in getting ads placed as proof-of-concept than in raking in the big money right away.

When Netscape renewed its contacts in early 1997 with the search engines featured on the Netscape site (see Figure 1.6), barter was part of the bargain. Yahoo!, Excite, Infoseek, and Lycos each paid $5 million in cash in 1996. In 1997, they're paying for impressions and they're not using 100% cash to do it. Jupiter estimates that Netscape uses half a million dollars of ad space on the Excite site, but suggests no money changes hands.

So you have two choices. You can buy Web ad space or you can build a Web site that garners an immense amount of traffic and then trade links with others. The result of the latter may well be a great balance sheet, but will do nothing for your cash flow. Of course, this is not a new concept. Anybody that's been around television and radio advertising can tell you that a great deal of air time is taken out in trade. Trade for hotel space, trade for car rentals, trade for season tickets. You name it.

At this stage of the game, it seems the people buying the ad space are getting the most out the Web and the people selling are still counting on the Web to pay off.

Who's Making Money?

So who *is* making money selling ads? Yahoo! seems to have broken from tradition in the last quarter of 1996. They actually made money. It's true that the $96,000 they put in the profit column is less than one one hundredth of a percent per share, but, hey, a profit is not a loss, after all.

FIG. 1.6
Search engines get prominent placement on Netscape in return for banner space.

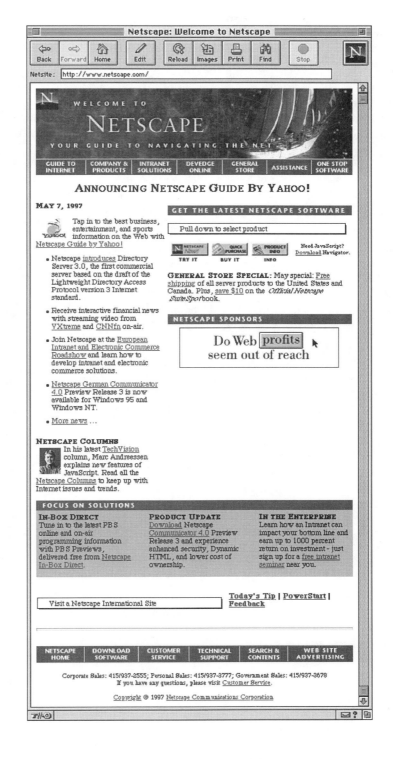

"The fourth quarter of 1996 was another landmark quarter for Yahoo! and its shareholders. We generated a nominal profit and positive cash flow during the fourth quarter, as we benefited from strong seasonal demand for Web-based advertising," according to Tim Koogle, President and Chief Executive Officer of Yahoo! in a January, 1997 press release.

> Yahoo!'s advertiser base increased to 550 advertisers in the fourth quarter, compared to 340 advertisers in the previous quarter. "Global and consumer-oriented marketers continue to recognize the effectiveness and power of targeted interactive advertising. During the fourth quarter, Yahoo!'s advertiser base grew increasingly diverse as illustrated by this sample of new and repeat advertising clients: American Airlines, American Express, Avon, Bank of America, Bell South, Charles Schwab, Coca Cola, Compaq Computers, Disney, Ford Motor Company, General Mills, General Motors, Hilton, IBM, Intuit, Kodak, Metropolitan Life, Motorola, Nabisco, Procter & Gamble, Publishers Clearing House, Sony, Spiegel, *Sports Illustrated*, Sportsline, Toyota, Virgin Records, Visa and Wal-Mart," said Koogle.

Chris Jennewein, is director of the Knight-Ridder New Media Center, and was interviewed by Dana Blankenhorn for an article in NetGuide at the beginning of 1997. He saw the Mercury Center Web site (**www.sjmercury.com**) as one of the best things going, claiming it was profitable at the beginning of 1996. "We're not making money at every newspaper [we have online]. We are at some of them."

Networks and Syndicates Arise

It only took a couple of years for the print and television model of selling aggregated ad space to come to the Web. You can buy blocks of Web sites across similar topics. You can have your banners shown at specific times. You can target the sports enthusiast or the Dilbert fan; the mother of infant children or the classical music devotee. These companies act just the same as they do in real space: they sell large amounts of inventory as packages and take their commission off the top. You'll get a closer look at them in Chapter 6, "Looking for Space in all the Right Places," on placement and Chapter 10, "Selling Space on Your Web Site," on selling ad space yourself. In the meantime, these may be the only businesses out there that are really making money.

The vast majority of sites online these days are exploring, experimenting, and trying things on for size. They're giving away a lot of space in order to prove their value. They're pouring in money hoping that, soon, money will come pouring back out. All they have to do is look at the Jupiter numbers and they start feeling better about their investments.

In the long run, their investments are going to pay off if they can deliver the goods. The goods are the people who come to their sites. It's great that you can show your ad to 1.5 million people a day. But are they buyers? Are they kids? Are they students from the Ukraine? Are they truly your potential customers?

Who Are the Eyeballs?

The Internet is growing faster than any technology, medium, or consumer fad to date. Only the flu seems to be able to spread faster. It took thirty years for the telephone to spread to 10 million people. It took ten years for television. It took two years for the Internet. People just love to communicate and if you give them a more efficient way to do it, they'll jump at the chance.

With the Net continuing to grow at an astonishing pace, it's always a challenge keeping up with the latest numbers. Then again, the latest numbers rarely agree with each other so it's a bit of a challenge even if you do keep up. When your boss asks for a definitive number, it's safe to tell him or her whatever you heard last time, plus 10%. Or you could shoot a glance at your odometer and add "a million" to that number. (If you are the boss, this method won't work as your car is too new. You'll have to find an employee's car that has a couple of rust spots on it.)

Alternatively, you could dip into the research that is being done by any of dozens of companies in order to find the number that best suits your case. Here are a few examples.

Graphic, Visualization, & Usability Center's (GVU) 5th WWW User Survey

This study was done by asking Web surfers to fill out an online survey (see Figure 1.7). While those of you who deal with statistics will cringe at the self-selecting, methodological madness of this approach, it does provide a place to start.

FIG. 1.7
GVU's 5th WWW User Survey is updated annually (**www.cc. gatech.edu/gvu/ user_surveys/ survey-04-1996**).

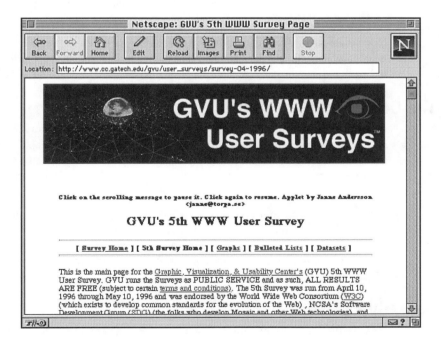

The survey tabulators at Georgia Tech's GVU determined that the average Web surfer is a 33-year-old male in a household earning $59,000 and living with a significant other. But then, that's like saying a man with one foot in a block of ice and the other in a tub of boiling oil is comfortable on average.

Here are some excerpts of the word from the horse's mouth:

The average age of all the Web users that responded to the Fifth Survey is 33.0 years old, a slight increase from the Fourth Survey, which had an average age of 32.7 years old. Overall, 31.5% of the users are female and the other 68.5% are male. This represents a moderate increase in female users from the Fourth Survey, where 29.3% reported being female, and quite a significant jump from the Third Survey (April 1995), where 15.5% reported being female.

The estimated average household income for the Fifth Survey is $59,000 US dollars. As with the Third and Fourth Surveys, this questions [sic] received the most 'Rather not Say!' responses (14.0%), nearly seven times greater than any other question. The average income for the Fifth Survey is slightly lower than the Fourth Survey ($63,000) and much lower than the Third Survey ($69,000).

One of the more stable characteristics of Web users over the survey is marital status. Overall, 41.1% of the users are married, with 40.8% being single. The users whom reported living with another was 9.6% and those reporting being divorced was 5.1%.

When you discover that the GVU thinks 30% of people on the Internet are in "educational occupations and 28% in computer related jobs," you begin to suspect their methods. Especially when the only other significant categories are "professional" and "management." Yes, those are two categories.

Nevertheless, the study does give us a clue as to which way the wind is blowing. The audience is getting older, the genders are blending better, and the income is trending lower. The results, as headlined in an Australian newspaper in 1996 are, "Net Surfers Almost Normal."

The CommerceNet/Nielsen Study

Announced in March of 1997, the latest study from CommerceNet and Nielsen Media Research (**www.nielsenmedia.com**) indicated that the number of people in the U.S. and Canada using the Net had doubled in the previous 18 months. It also revealed a "startling increase" in Web users actively shopping online and that there was "a significant narrowing of the gap between the number of male and female users."

Based on telephone interviews with people 16 years or older from randomly-selected households during December, 1996 and January, 1997, they suggest that 23% of the population over 16 years of age used the Internet during the previous month. Women accounted for 42% of users in the past three months (as compared to 34% in the original survey), and they use the Web as much as men do.

Find/SVP

Perhaps the best compendium of Internet statistics as of this writing was presented by Tom Miller at the *Editor & Publisher's Interactive Newspaper*'s '97 Conference in Houston, on

February 15, 1997. In a presentation titled "Interactive Demographics," Miller analyzed a healthy number of studies and created a terrific overview. (Duplicated here with permission from Find/SVP and Tom Miller, these slides can be found at **etrg.findsvp.com/resfh/intnews.html**.) Take a look at Figure 1.8 through Figure 1.15.

FIG. 1.8

The size of the Internet seems to be an unsolved mystery.

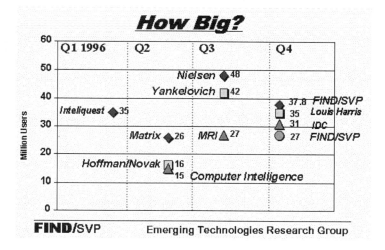

The question "How big is the Internet?" is primarily dependent upon how different studies define Internet usage. Bigger surveys tend to define Internet usage more loosely, such as whether respondents merely "have access to the Internet" (Nielsen), or by asking simply "Do you use the Internet?" Valid responses to this last question include users whose only Internet use is for e-mail. FIND/SVP asked that question in Q496 and found a projected 37.8 million users (see Figure 1.9). When they restricted the definition—in the same survey of 3,255 randomly-sampled households—to requiring respondents to use at least one application aside from e-mail, the projected number of total users fell to 27 million.

FIG. 1.9

Based on researching the research, here's what FIND/SVP figures is a good guess.

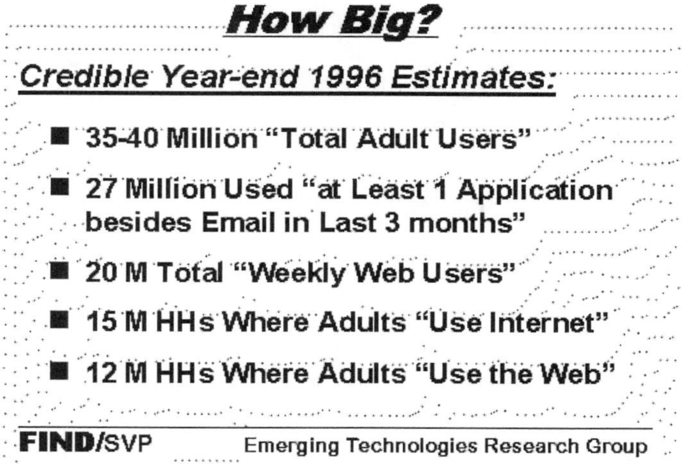

How Big?

Credible Year-end 1996 Estimates:

- 35-40 Million "Total Adult Users"
- 27 Million Used "at Least 1 Application besides Email in Last 3 months"
- 20 M Total "Weekly Web Users"
- 15 M HHs Where Adults "Use Internet"
- 12 M HHs Where Adults "Use the Web"

FIND/SVP   Emerging Technologies Research Group

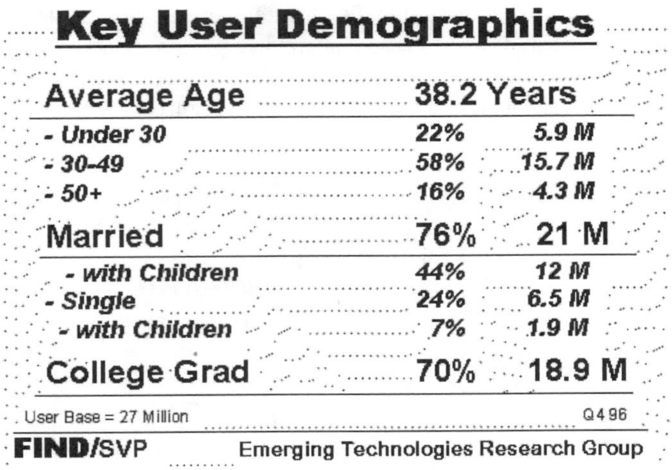

FIG. 1.10
Here are age and family demographics.

Key User Demographics

Average Age	**38.2 Years**	
- Under 30	22%	5.9 M
- 30-49	58%	15.7 M
- 50+	16%	4.3 M
Married	**76%**	**21 M**
- with Children	44%	12 M
- Single	24%	6.5 M
- with Children	7%	1.9 M
College Grad	**70%**	**18.9 M**

User Base = 27 Million   Q4 96

FIND/SVP   Emerging Technologies Research Group

FIG. 1.11
The numbers still scale to the upscale.

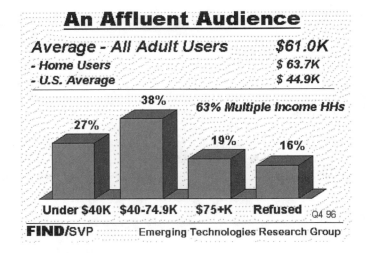

An Affluent Audience

Average - All Adult Users	$61.0K
- Home Users	$ 63.7K
- U.S. Average	$ 44.9K

63% Multiple Income HHs

38%

27%

19%

16%

Under $40K $40-74.9K $75+K   Refused   Q4 96

FIND/SVP   Emerging Technologies Research Group

FIG. 1.12

The Internet is still a male-dominated place, but most studies find the ratio is starting to even up.

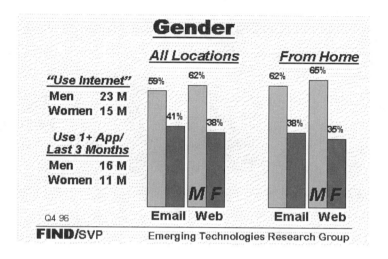

Gender

All Locations

"Use Internet"
Men   23 M
Women 15 M

Use 1+ App/
Last 3 Months
Men   16 M
Women 11 M

Q4 96

FIND/SVP   Emerging Technologies Research Group

FIG. 1.13

Professionals make up the vast majority of Internet users.

Leading Occupations

	Male	Female
Exec/Mgr	11%	5%
Bsn Pro/Acct/Lawyer	15%	15%
Teacher	5%	14%
Healthcare Pro	2%	8%
Eng/Sci	11%	1%
Tech/Programmer	9%	6%
Sales	6%	5%
Govt/Pub Sector	6%	3%
Skilled Trades	7%	1%
Clerical	-	6%
Homemaker	-	13%
Retiree	5%	3%

FIND/SVP   Emerging Technologies Research Group

FIG. 1.14
One out of five Internet users has shopped online, more if male, fewer if female. But interest in shopping online has risen to the 60–70% level.

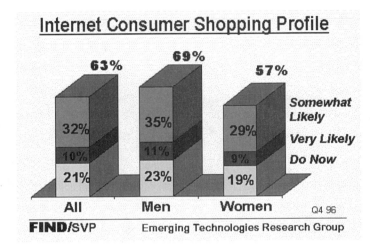

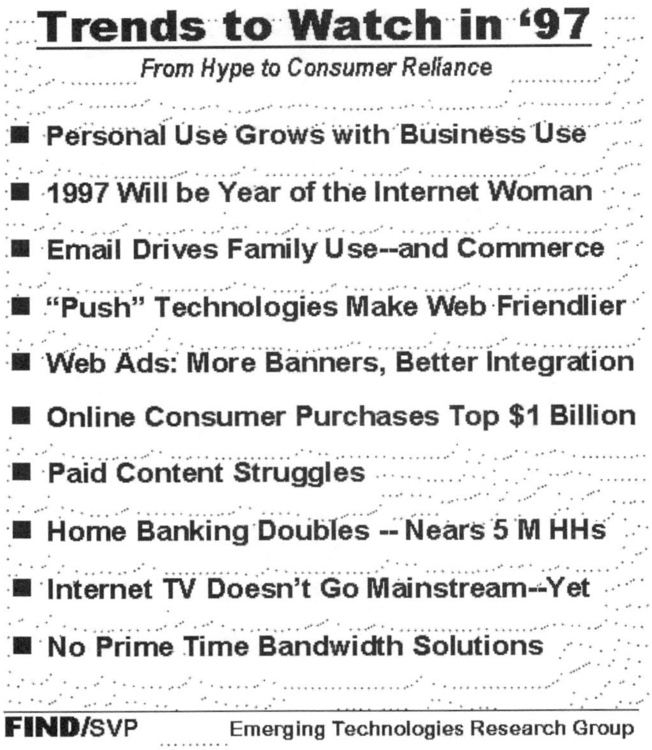

Internet Consumer Shopping Profile

63% — All: 32% Somewhat Likely, 10% Very Likely, 21% Do Now
69% — Men: 35% Somewhat Likely, 11% Very Likely, 23% Do Now
57% — Women: 29% Somewhat Likely, 9% Very Likely, 19% Do Now

Q4 96

FIND/SVP   Emerging Technologies Research Group

FIG. 1.15
Internet consumer trends FIND/SVP sees in 1997.

Trends to Watch in '97

From Hype to Consumer Reliance

- ■ Personal Use Grows with Business Use
- ■ 1997 Will be Year of the Internet Woman
- ■ Email Drives Family Use--and Commerce
- ■ "Push" Technologies Make Web Friendlier
- ■ Web Ads: More Banners, Better Integration
- ■ Online Consumer Purchases Top $1 Billion
- ■ Paid Content Struggles
- ■ Home Banking Doubles -- Nears 5 M HHs
- ■ Internet TV Doesn't Go Mainstream--Yet
- ■ No Prime Time Bandwidth Solutions

FIND/SVP   Emerging Technologies Research Group

Updates and additional survey results can be found on the FIND/SVP Web site (**etrg.findsvp.com**).

Internet Declared Mass Media

On February 18, 1997, IntelliQuest Information Group, Incorporated (**www.intelliquest.com**), released the results of its latest survey, estimating some 47 million adults (age 16 and above) in the United States in the fourth quarter of 1996 had been on the World Wide Web. "This represents a 34% growth in the online population from the first quarter of 1996, which was measured at 35 million," according to the press release.

We all knew that people were jumping on fast. But we also expected the growth rates to start flattening. You can't increase geometrically forever. Each new survey confirms the growth rates. The growth rates continue to astonish.

IntelliQuest CEO Peter Zandan was quoted the next day in *USA Today* as saying, "It is now at the point that so many people have access to [online] that it is a mass media [*sic*]. How it will ultimately take shape, the business model [and] how people will end up using it, is unclear. That's what will be interesting to watch."

Is Your Audience Out There?

Can you find a buyer in a city of 50 million? (Or, if you're in my car, 210 million?) Chances are you can. And this is where the concept of mass media and Internet as medium take divergent paths.

Stanley Marcus of Nieman Marcus said, "Consumers are statistics, customers are people." When you move from mass advertising to online advertising, these are words to live by. Television lets you advertise to tens of millions of people watching *Seinfeld* and *Friends* and *ER*. But magazines let you chase after a specific type of consumer, a specific type of prospect. The ads you create for *Field & Stream* will be different than the ones you run in *Brides*. The targeting that magazines give you over television is nothing compared to the targeting the Web gives you over magazines.

This subject is so important and so powerful, that it takes up all of Chapter 6, "Looking for Space In all the Right Places." Suffice it to say, some portion of your prospective customers are online today and will be online tomorrow in droves. What will drive this further explosive growth? Cheap and easy access. Cheap access is coming in two ways—the connection and the equipment.

The Internet Boom Is Still Being Heard

MCI reports that in the past two years, traffic over its backbone has increased by a factor of 91. In other words, for every bit that went from point A to point B in January of 1995, there were 91 of them in January, 1997. There's no slowdown in sight.

In fact, MFS owner of UUNet Technology and one of the large backbone players, sees reason to expect a thousandfold increase in traffic through their pipes in the next three years. They are actively planning and building that backbone to accommodate the rush.

The Boom Has Only Just Begun

At the moment, the standard fee for dial-up Internet access is $20 per month, all you can eat. Tomorrow the price will go down because right now the price is going up.

Cheaper Access   The price will have to go up in order to sustain the telephone infrastructure. The phone system was created to support millions of people making millions of calls that average about one minute each.

"Is Fred available for a meeting at 4:00?"

"I'll check and get back to you." Later: "Fred says the meeting is on if you can push it back to 5:00."

"Can you pick up the kids this afternoon? I'm going to be stuck in a meeting with Fred."

Now, with voice mail, these calls are shrinking down to about 30 seconds. The phone system is brilliant at handling this kind of traffic. It is even able to manage the busiest phone call day of the year—Mother's Day. It can even handle the busiest collect-call day of the year—Father's Day. Okay, so it has problems when there's an earthquake in Los Angeles and everybody and his mother is trying to call at the same time, but overall, this system is nothing less than a modern day miracle.

The problem comes when people such as yours truly install a new phone line for the computer. We only make one call a day—all day long. When my computer boots up in the morning, it dials up and checks my e-mail. With the exception of time out for lunch, I am on that line all day surfing, messaging, and trying to keep up with this World Wide Wonder. The telephone system was not built for people like me.

So how is this additional burden on the phone companies going to lower the cost of Internet access? First, there are a huge number of R&D dollars being spent to solve this very problem. It's obvious that the demand for online access is big and getting bigger. If you can build a better system that transmits signals faster and at a lower cost, you can build a house next to Bill Gates in Washington. If everybody in the world decided they couldn't live without pet rocks or Lucky Charms, pet rock quarries would spring up overnight and General Mills would find a way to convert all of their Cheerios production in two nights. There's money to be made.

The second approach that may drive down the cost of going online is advertising. There are a number of competing e-mail systems online that allow you to create an account for free. Juno (**www.juno.com**), Rocketmail (**www.rocketmail.com**), and HotMail (**www.hotmail.com**) are just a few examples (see Figure 1.16). They can offer free services by selling ad space on their sites and in the e-mail that people send to each other (see Figure 1.17 and Figure 1.18).

Some Internet Service Providers (ISPs) are using this model in conjunction with FreeRide (**www.freeride.com**) for dial-up service. FreeRide has name brand sponsors paying for the privilege. The consumer buys a 16-ounce bag of Oreo cookies, sends in the proof of purchase, and earns 20 points. A free month of online access is available for 1,000 points. Nabisco pays FreeRide based on the number of UPCs mailed in. With sponsor brands like Kodak, Snuggle, Hefty, TDK, Wisk, SnackWell's, Duracell, Clairol, Quaker Oats, and Advil, it's an interesting ad buy.

FIG. 1.16
HotMail offers free
ad-supported e-mail
accounts.

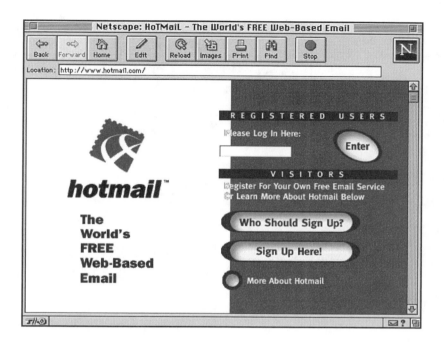

FIG. 1.17
E-mail advertisements
on the Web site pay for
the e-mail service.

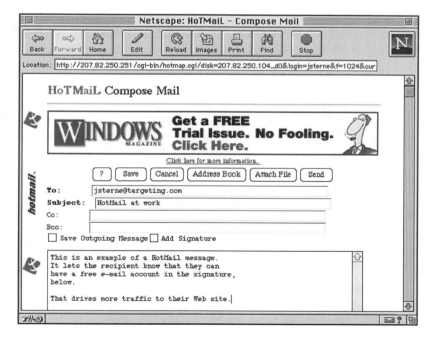

FIG. 1.18

A pointer from the
e-mail to the Web site
helps.

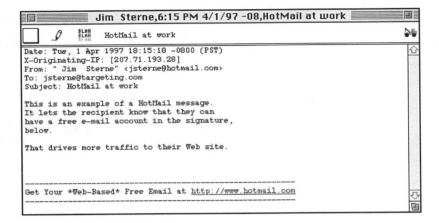

FreeRide was just joined by Smart World (**www.smartworld.net**), which is geared at New York's 212 area code for the moment. Others are sure to follow.

Free dial-up access, free e-mail, and free connect time all supported by advertising. Surprising? Shouldn't be. It's the same model that television and radio have used for decades.

Unfortunately, it still costs well over $1,000 for the equipment. And a PC that is going to handle millions of colors, be able to download mega-megabytes of audio, video, and pictures of the new baby runs closer to $3,000. This does not fall into the reach of your average consumer. Even if access is free, how does a typical family of four earning $30,000 a year justify spending 10% of their income on a new PacBell box? The answer is that they won't have to.

Cheaper Gear   The other development on the near horizon for bringing lots of additional advertising viewers to the Web is the advent of the cheap Internet access device. This gadget has been on the radar screen of computer manufactures, television manufactures, and cable companies for several years. There was optimistic speculation that Christmas of 1996 was going to see WebTV (**www.magnavox.com/hottechnology/webtv/webtv.html**) being treated like Nintendo 64 machines—on everybody's list and hard to find (see Figure 1.19).

Maybe the WebTV product was ahead of its time, maybe there weren't enough features, and maybe it was priced a tad too high. But the concept of a small, cheap device to access the Net is a solid one and will drive the Internet from being the land of the geeks and the home of the depraved to a truly mass market.

When will this happen? As soon as it's cheap and easy enough. The price point would seem to be $199.95. When VCRs were $600, they were luxury items. When they fell below the magic $200 mark, they became a necessity. As chips get faster and production ramps up this price point is assured. But it's not the end of the story. The Internet must get significantly easier to use.

FIG. 1.19
WebTV had disappointing sales in 1996. Tomorrow looks brighter.

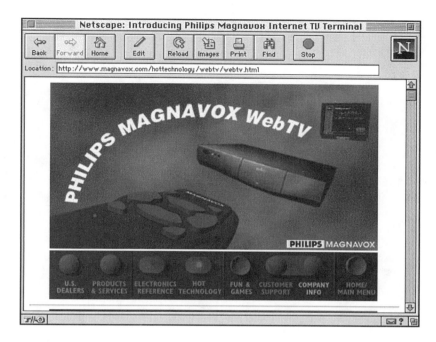

In their April, 1997 issue, *Wired* magazine asked Michael Dertouzos about how much easier computers are to use now than they were. "We gave you a few colors on the screen. We gave you a mouse. To call that 'user friendly' is the moral equivalent of dressing a chimp in [a] surgical gown and calling him a surgeon. User friendly comes from the machine understanding what you want to do. Does your computer do that?"

Dertouzos sees a not-too-distant future where the browser can understand the information it's displaying and can make decisions on its relevancy and value. "I cannot see us going into the 21st century with humans doing all the work . . . If your machine understands that when an x-ray arrives from a lab it should be passed on to your doctor, then the machine is doing the understanding, not you."

Unless there's a ten-year-old in your house, you are relegated to the complex tasks of configuring Winsock files and browser plug-ins. Time was, you had to be a mechanic to drive a car. There were no service stations. The original trunk on a car was a tool box used to fit the pieces back together when they were jostled apart as you drove into town. The long car coats were not worn for the weather, but to keep the oil off pristine suits. Such is the Internet in the nineties.

When the set-top-box, or the WebTV, or the Network Computer (NC) is cheap and the access is simple, there will be many compelling reasons for the masses to jump on the Internet. The risky bet says that this will happen in two years' time. The safe bet is five years. Heck, anything can happen in five years. ●

Before the Banner

The rage today on the Web is the banner ad, that 468×60-pixel pennant that graces the tops of many sites. Banners are easy to grasp and one could rely on them as the sole means of communication. In the next chapter, the banner takes center stage. In the meantime, there are other means of communicating on the Internet, and some of them may be significantly more effective. Almost all of them pre-date the banner.

Advertising has been done in newsgroups, through e-mail, inserted into newsletters and e-zines, and distributed via lists servers. Classified ads have long been a part of the Internet scene and ever since humans have been building Web sites, Webmasters there have been trading links. ■

Spam Was Spawned In the Newsgroups

The first advertising on the Internet was that fateful case of the green card lawyers. A search on AltaVista will easily turn up 100 references to these two Arizona attorneys who decided to send their commercial message to every newsgroup they could find. The negative response was monumental.

This was during the beginning of commercialism on the Internet, and it was not a pretty sight. Canter & Siegel, the lawyers in question, were hounded, mail-bombed, and kicked off one service provider after another. That sort of treatment was far too good for them. The verb "*to spam*" was borrowed from a Monty Python sketch; it describes the repetitious serving of the same message to group after group after group.

Spamming is not just a sin against man and nature (he said, trying to hide his own feelings on the subject), it's just plain bad marketing. Annoying 95% of your audience in order to reel in 1% of them doesn't make sense. Creating ill-will using a medium that is prone to heavy word of mouth and instant response should not be your goal.

The Critical Rules of Newsgroup Advertising

There are proper ways to post to newsgroups and the crux of the matter is to know the territory. Each newsgroup is a separate society with separate rules, and customs, and an unspoken code of conduct.

It's far better to get acquainted with each newsgroup you intend to post to than to fly in blind. The rules are fairly simple, but if you ignore them, you do so at your own peril. Here, then, are the basics:

1. Be certain your subject matter is on-topic.
2. Go out of your way to find the Frequently Asked Questions (FAQ) document. Read it well regarding the acceptance of ads.
3. If you post to more than one newsgroup, *cross-post* rather than re-post. Cross-posting means your message is seen only once by somebody who reads all of the newsgroups to which you posted. If they are faced with your ad repeatedly, they may take action against you.
4. Read at least two weeks' worth of posts to get the flavor of the discussion, and look at other ads that have been posted. What has the reaction been to them? There haven't been any ads? That's your best clue not to post.
5. Most of all, participate in the discussion and become a member of the society. As a participant, you get to know the code of conduct and be an accepted member. People get to know you as a voice of reason and respect your opinion.

The Penalties for Spamming

If you choose not to follow these rules, the downside can be serious. Upset somebody and they will send you a nasty-gram as fast as they can hit Send on their e-mail. Upset them enough and they'll attach a copy of the operating system. Get them really riled and they'll post to a few newsgroups themselves asking 10,000 of their closest friends to do the same.

No pain, you say? It's all just geeks on hormone rushes with nothing better to do? Won't really harm you? That's what Canter & Siegel thought, and they were proven wrong. Just a few copies of the operating system is enough to crash your computer. It will take a few hours to get your computer up and running again. Then there will be 9,997 more of them waiting in line. Most of all, the ill-will you create can become the talk of the town. In this case, the town has some 50 million inhabitants.

A lot more on this subject can be found in *World Wide Web Marketing, Integrating the Internet Into Your Marketing Strategy*, which, in turn, can be found at **www.targeting.com**.

Newsgroups that Want Your Ads

There are newsgroups out there like ALT.BIZ that will accept anything; get rich quick, cure for cancer, insurance against alien abduction. Anything goes. Can you imagine somebody sitting down at their computer and actively choosing to read through that sort of group? A few do. A very few. And that's because they've finished reading about worm farms in the back of *Popular Home Businesses*.

But don't ignore ALT.BIZ just yet. It has value from one interesting perspective that may make it worth your while. When somebody is looking for something unusual or something they want to get at a good price, or they're interested in a particular subject, they might go trolling through the newsgroups. There are so many groups and so many posts that people don't read through them like you would the Sunday paper. Instead, they go someplace like Deja News (**www.dejanews.com**) (see Figure 2.1).

If the keyword they're after is in your post, Deja News, Excite, or Yahoo! can find it. ALT.BIZ may seem a silly place to post, because nobody reads it directly. But you can't beat the price and any new business you bring in from somebody using a search engine is gravy.

E-Mail Advertising

It wasn't long after the newsgroups got hit with unwarranted solicitations that various, nefarious individuals began the precarious practice of sending out mass e-mail. Understand that this is a fabulous concept. You get to finely craft your message and then send it out to ten, twenty, fifty, a hundred, a thousand, ten thousand, or ten million people at practically zero cost. Free software that scours the newsgroups of your choice, grabs the addresses of those who post, and sends them all your carefully crafted communication is available .

What marketer could possibly turn down such an opportunity? You, that's who.

There are two basic but critical rules for unsolicited e-mail. One, just don't do it, and two, if you're considering it just once, refer to the first rule.

FIG. 2.1
Deja News offers
keyword searching
through all of the
newsgroups.

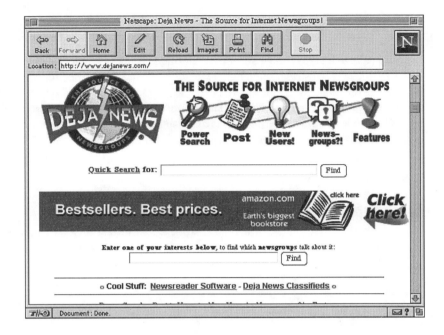

The Agony of Being on the Receiving End

If you're seriously thinking about mass e-mail as a proper promotion technique, then you haven't had the same e-mail address for more than a few months and you don't know the territory. Most of us with a stable address for more than a couple of years receive between five and ten unsolicited e-mails each day.

It's annoying. It's insulting. It does not make us feel warm and fuzzy about those who send it. Additionally, your company will be mentally lumped in with all the "Earn Money At Home Stuffing Envelopes," "This Is Your Luck Day, Just Send $19.95," and "You Can Cure Your Incontinence With Our Copper Bracelet" hucksters who aren't bright enough to care about their reputations.

The Illogic of It All

You say you like getting e-mail? You like learning about great new offers? You feel others would, too? Then think for just a moment about the impact on the network if every company in the U.S. (let alone the world) decided to send out one little e-mail a year to everybody. Only one. Only once per year.

Given some 12 million companies in the U.S. and 365 days a year, you have to ask yourself if getting 1,370 e-mail messages every hour is still your idea of fun. And if you are at all technically inclined, imagine the *bandwidth* needed to support such transmissions.

The most frightening part is how easy it all is. You want the addresses of everybody who subscribes to a newsgroup on dogs? Take a look at Floodgate (**www.floodgate.com**). In the summer of 1997, they described their offering on their Web site this way:

> *The Floodgate Bulk E-mail Loader imports simple text files that anyone can down load from CompuServe, Prodigy, Delphi Genie, or the Internet. Test [sic] files contain ads, forum messages, or data from the member directory. Each of these files is filled with e-mail addresses. Floodgate is designed to read these files and strip out the e-mail addresses. It then sorts the addresses, removes any duplicates, and formats them into an output file, with 10, 20, 30 addresses per line. This is all done in one simple step. Just point and click.*

I can feel my skin starting to crawl. I am tempted by offerings like Spam Hater (**www.compulink.co.uk/~net-services/spam 4/97**):

> *Hit back at the Spammers!*
>
> *Get lots of e-mail offering you get-rich-quick schemes? Want to hit back? "Spam Hater" (Now at V1.05) is free Windows software that helps you respond effectively and makes it hot for these people.*
>
> *Analyses [sic] the Spam*
>
> *Extracts a list of addresses of relevant Postmasters, etc.*
>
> *Prepares a reply*
>
> *Choice of legal threats, insults or your own message*
>
> *Appends a copy of the Spam if required*
>
> *Puts it in a mail window ready for sending*
>
> *New—Tool to help keep you out of spammers databases*
>
> *Support for more e-mail programs including AOL 3.0 for W95*
>
> *New—Addtional [sic] file for Forte Agent V1.0 32/390*
>
> *New—Analyses Usenet spam...*
>
> *Generates a 'WHOIS' query to help track the perpetrator*
>
> *Generates a 'TRACEROUTE' query to help track the perpetrator's upstream provider*

In other words, this little wrangler lets you go after the low-down, dirty varmint that spammed you—and the horse he rode in on—his access provider. The complete list is not shown here.

The Definitive Treatise

Robert Raisch was deep into the heart of the Internet long before it was cool. After all, his company's domain name is internet.com. You don't snag that one if you show up after the party is in full swing. He is founder of The Internet Company, co-founded and created The Electronic Newsstand, and was instrumental in the initial design and implementation of the Global Network Navigator—recently purchased by America Online. He now offers strategic technical consulting as the principal of Internautics (**www.internautics.com**).

Besides all that and more, Raisch wrote the definitive work on unsolicited e-mail at the end of 1994. It is reprinted here with his permission. The work, however, is not shown in its entirety.

POSTAGE DUE MARKETING—an Internet Company White Paper
by Robert Raisch

Executive Overview

In recent months, a number of online marketing efforts have shown the failure of traditional direct marketing practices on the global Internet.

By exercising significant limitations in the Internet's technology, these efforts have sought to use the distributed news and mail technologies of the Internet as an inexpensive way to deliver commercial messages directly into the hands of consumers.

The Internet community has dubbed this practice as "spamming"—after a popular British television sketch where a restaurant patron is offered a commercially available pink luncheon meat repeatedly, well past the point of absurdity.

While the media have chosen to characterize this as a cultural issue, the truth is that these ill-considered marketing efforts cost each person reading the distributed advertisements a measurable fee for their receipt.

For this reason alone, this style of marketing is both ineffectual and potentially very damaging to the marketer.

Internet "Direct Marketing"

Arizona "Green Card" lawyers, Laurence Canter & Martha Siegel, used the global Internet's second most popular information delivery service, Usenet News, as a direct marketing channel in a manner which initially appears to be very similar to traditional direct mail. By "posting" an advertisement for legal services to thousands of separate discussion forums, Canter & Siegel succeeded in placing their message in the hands of hundreds of thousands of consumers for very little apparent cost.

But Canter & Siegel submitted their commercial solicitation in every newsgroup available without any concern for the topic of discussion in those newsgroups. They posted a message about their service to help foreign students fill out federal immigration forms into discussions about the Information Superhighway, cultural issues of Tamil Indians, Microsoft Windows™ development tools, and thousands of other discussions—few of which had any interest in issues of American immigration.

While some point to the minimal cost of this marketing effort and the huge return it generated as proof that Canter & Siegel have discovered the holy grail of direct marketing—cheap, effective information distribution—this assumption ignores the real costs incurred, not by the marketer, but by the consumer. As most professional marketers realize, effective marketing is never cheap nor easy.

The media has chosen to paint this as an issue of culture clash between the idealistic Internet old guard and a pragmatic new breed of online marketeer without understanding the economic or social realities of the situation. Upon a little research, this characterization lacks any real substance.

In essence, Canter & Siegel's actions were economically irresponsible, demanding that the public shoulder the cost of their marketing tactics—without any possibility of refusal.

The Usenet News Service

Usenet News is a collection of user-written messages or articles placed in separate categories or newsgroups based upon topic. These articles are then shipped from computer to computer to hundreds of thousands of Internet participants. For example, an article about bicycling might end up in the newsgroup called "rec.bicycles.mountain" or an inquiry for employment opportunities may show up in "misc.jobs.wanted."

The programs that accept or reject these articles do so based upon the newsgroup in which they appear—e.g., if a subscriber has an interest in bicycling and the article is labeled as a member of a "rec.bicycles" newsgroup, the computer will accept receipt of the article and save it in local storage.

Suppose someone were to post a new article that talked about the sanctity of human life and how the author believed that all abortion must be considered murder. This would be the author's opinion and an example of the freedom of expression that the Internet technologies support so well. However, for the sake of argument, suppose that this article was labeled as an appropriate member of the "rec.bicycling" newsgroup.

Since the subscriber has instructed the programs that receive these articles to accept anything in this newsgroup, the computer blindly accepts this inappropriate or "off-topic" article. Once the article has been received by the computer, the subscriber's money has been spent and resources consumed without any opportunity to refuse the article. This is how it must be, because to judge whether an article is appropriate to the subscriber's needs, it must first be retrieved and read.

Postage-Due Marketing

Using the global Internet as a direct marketing vehicle to distribute messages to users with little concern for their topical appropriateness or the costs involved in their distribution is called Postage-Due Marketing.

In the physical world, advertisers bear the entire cost of distributing messages to the consumer. The only cost the consumer shoulders is the time it takes to consider a solicitation and either embrace or discard it.

In the online world, the costs of distribution are shared between advertiser and consumer. Consumers pay a measurable fee to receive information via the global Internet—from a shell or SLIP account to a highspeed dedicated connection. Some pay hourly charges for information and some pay per message, but each Internet subscriber pays in some way for the information they receive.

To fully appreciate why Postage-Due Marketing raises the ire of the global Internet community, ask yourself whether you would accept a collect call from a telemarketer or an advertising circular that arrived postage due. Or, if you spent an entire evening consumed with calls from telemarketers while you waited for an important call....

Social Compacts

All members of a society live by certain rules which make it possible to co-exist and communicate effectively with their peers. We do not lie, cheat or steal from those around us. We do not drive on the wrong side of the highway. And we do not use our neighbor's property without their permission.

Simple rules like these allow us to function effectively as a society. Some are important enough to require protection by law while others are part of the social compact we all observe for the benefit

continues

continued

and support of human community.

Engaging in Postage-Due Marketing ignores the single most important truth of the global Internet: above all else, the global Internet is a community—and like any community, participation in it implies certain rules and obligations.

Effective Online Marketing?

In their own way, Laurence Canter & Martha Siegel have been very successful. They have leveraged a dangerous misinterpretation of the online world into global media visibility and a potential best-selling marketing book that instructs others to freely tread on the flowerbeds of the public common. But at what cost?

There. I've had my say. I belabor this point for the same reason I belabor keeping the graphics on your Web site small. You have to think about the whole system, the impact on the person you are targeting, and the brand message you are delivering. With these circumstances in mind, you'll agree that unsolicited mail is a bad thing.

But solicited e-mail is a joy to behold.

Sanctioned Mass E-Mail

You say you like getting e-mail? You like learning about great new offers? You feel others would, too? You're right. Others do, too. But they should ask for the mail instead of having it thrust upon them. Many people like to feel involved. Many people like to be part of the community. Many people like getting e-mail as long as it is of personal interest.

How do you ensure that everybody on your mailing list will find your message of interest? By having them implicitly request to be on the list (and giving them the ability to get off it at every occurrence and as soon as possible).

The "Keep Me Informed" Button   There's nothing like having a mailing list of people who want to hear from you. Every product you have and every service you offer should have an associated list you use to send out announcements. It's easy to create and it's easy to maintain. It's easy to use and it's easy for your customers to jump on it and jump off it.

Create a button on each substantive page on your Web site that people can click in order to become a member of the informed club. I write articles for various magazines and once they hit the street, I put them up on my Web site. I received enough e-mail requesting to be added to my mail list, that I gave people a way to do it themselves (see Figure 2.2).

One click and the Web site visitor's e-mail address is e-mailed to me. That's the absolute simplest method on earth. If you expect more interest than the two or three a day I get, automate the process.

But this whole approach belongs more to the marketing department than the advertising side, so let's take the same concept and mass-ify it. What if there were a Web site where you could sign up for the kind of e-mail you'd like to receive. What if you could sign up to receive information about investing or golf or wine? Then you'd probably be at the PostMaster Direct site.

FIG. 2.2
A single button lets people sign up on my mail list.

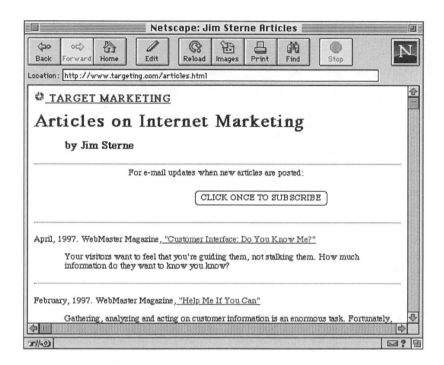

The Opt-In Mailing List PostMaster Direct Response (**www.PostMasterDirect.com**) asks surfers to check off the subjects they are interested in (see Figure 2.3). Having registered themselves, their addresses can be rented for sending e-mail advertising.

Claiming over three million e-mail addresses in more than 3,000 topical categories, PostMaster Direct is a logical approach to getting your message out there via e-mail. They charge between ten and twenty cents per name, which represents your total cost, sans printing, sans paper, sans postage.

To assure the opt-in model, PostMaster Direct sends a confirming e-mail to the list member. So if you were mad at your brother-in-law for something he said about you at Christmas, adding his address to the list would only notify him of the ability to unsubscribe.

Every message they send out includes this header:

This is no spam, this is a PostMaster Direct voluntary targeted list! TO UNSUB: forward this entire message to deleteme@netcreations.com. UNSUB ALL: forward this entire message to deleteall@netcreations.com. MAIL TO LISTS: http://www. PostMasterDirect.com/ 100% OPT-IN

FIG. 2.3
PostMaster Direct
Response has people
sign up and "opt-in" to
receive advertising via
e-mail.

From a marketer's perspective, this is a pretty sweet system. Imagine having the SRDS (the Standard Rate and Data Service list of mailing lists) at your fingertips. Yes, you can find them on the Web (**www.SRDS.com**), and by the time you read this book they may have made good on the promise on their Web site to make the site "another SRDS 'meeting place' as we work towards our goal of making media data available online."

PostMaster Direct is a step ahead. You browse through the database to find your target audience. You can search on keywords, look over the pricing, and start collecting different cross-sections of the population. In the classic "shopping cart" mold, your selections are recorded for further refinement.

You can make selections based on demographics, select the quantity you're after and do the merge/purge. You can also purge against names you've mailed to in the past. It all happens online and your mailing can go out overnight.

Results? Bruce Dietzen, director of corporate sales for ichat, Incorporated (**www.ichat.com**), claims they're outstanding. "We sent out email at 10 a.m. one day and, by 3 o'clock, we had hundreds of visitors on our site, where we interacted with them directly via our software and then called them immediately afterwards. In five hours' time, we closed $50,000 in sales, including a single order for $20,000."

If that sounds like a promotional endorsement you might post on a Web site, it is. The ichat product is perfectly suited to this approach for a couple of reasons. The product is for use on the Internet and PostMaster Direct has a solid following of Webmasters. But the numbers are still impressive, with a 7% response rate and a cost that's right in line with lists offline.

An unsolicited testimonial showed up on the Online Advertising list. Yes, selling Web server speed enhancement software on the Web is already a good target, but Jeff Maier from Datalytics claims a surge in visits to his Web site that would indicate a 12% to 15% response rate. Maier felt that accounted for 600 to 700 product download from his site.

The moral of the story is if you're selling to Webmasters, this is the list for you. If you're selling to skin diving and scuba enthusiasts, PostMaster Direct has a list of 2,642 and it might be worth the $264.20 to find out for yourself.

On the other hand, you might want your ad to be seen by people.

Newsletters

Create a communication medium and it will be used to transmit news, weather, and sports. Create a publication that transmits news, weather, and sports and you'll find advertising. News-filled e-mail is a fine old tradition on the Internet. You can sign up for just about any subject under the sun.

Yahoo! has 64 different categories of newsletters and the Internet Newsletters category has over 65. Are there a lot of newsletters out there? Do the math. There are so many daily, weekly, and monthly documents flowing out to heaven knows how many highly targeted recipients. You are very likely to find a newsletter worth your advertising dollar.

Ads in these documents usually end up at the bottom as a tail-end offering. "This week's Albino Hamster Breader's [sic] Gazette was sponsored by Fred's Fine Hamster Food. Visit the FFHF Web site for information on keeping your hamsters happier with Fred's ingenious recipes for healthier hamsters."

If your offering is sufficiently germane, it's worth writing about as part of the letter. If Fred has done extensive research on just what makes an albino hamster healthier, chances are the publishers of the Gazette are going to want to interview him. Public Relations 101. These suggestions apply to newsletters, whether they're electronic or paper.

List Servers

A *list server* is an online group discussion like a newsgroup, but the individual posts come right to your e-mail box instead of waiting on some news server. There is a paper equivalent that may make this clearer. It's the opinion/editorial section of your daily newspaper.

The newspaper solicits comments from readers about topics of interest, reproduces their comments, and delivers the reproductions to every subscriber. Those with further comments, questions, or opinions may send their convictions as letters to the editor and those, in turn, are reproduced and redelivered.

When this type of discussion moves online, several very important changes take place.

The turn-around time can be minutes instead of days.

There is room for far more participants, as the limitation on newsprint disappears.

The participants splinter into more and more tightly focused discussion groups, according to their interests.

As a result, as with newsletters, there are an almost infinite number of lists from which to choose. The Liszt site (**www.liszt.com**) has a database of more than 70,000 (see Figure 2.4). Finding one that matches your product offering is much easier now.

FIG. 2.4
Liszt, the mailing list directory.

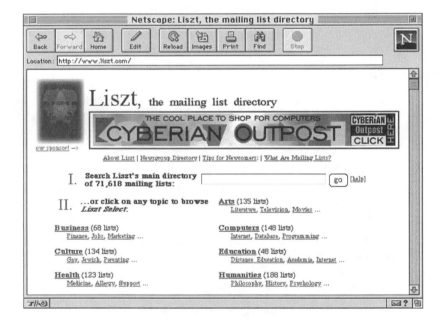

You can find a list of mailing lists, newsletters, and newsgroups that accept ads, at Avenue Search from Aquinas Software, Incorporated (**www.avenue.com/about/ads.html**) (see Figure 2.5). They even offer up a handful of advantages and disadvantages to remind you that you're not dealing with the Web.

Think of lists as sponsored newsgroups. You can pay to have your ad tacked onto the bottom of every message that goes out, but you should never post your ad yourself. Some lists, however, may post your ad for you.

Sending an Ad to a List—Without Turning into Toast

If you love tennis, then you should know about the World Wide Web Tennis Server (**www.tennisserver.com**). Enough said. If you want to be kept up-to-date about tennis, you can subscribe to the monthly e-mail newsletter Tennis Server Interactive, which is as easy as clicking their Web site. If you want to advertise in the newsletter to 7,000 tennis players, store owners, teaching pros, and club owners, you can have your ad tucked into the text, or you can send it stand-alone.

FIG. 2.5

List of mailing lists, newsletters, and newsgroups that accept ads.

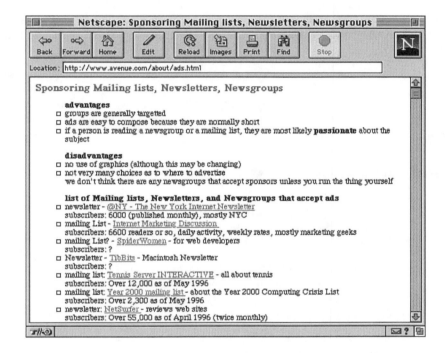

When people sign up for this list, they are told up front about the possibility of receiving ads:

> *A key part of our service, Tennis Server INTERACTIVE provides notification of updates to the World Wide Web Tennis Server, news about tennis information on the Net, as well as other tennis information of general interest. And it is FREE! Periodically, tennis related polls and surveys may also be e-mailed to people on the list. Some of our mailings also contain commercial tennis-related information and opportunities from Tennis Server sponsors.*

The CPM (cost per thousand) for this list is up there at $100, but that's because this is a group focused on a subject. With the occasional survey, the Tennis Server operators know who their audience is: 87% play tennis at least once per month, 73% play tennis at least once per week, 54% expect to purchase a tennis racquet within the next year, and 23% have household incomes over $75,000. That's just for starters.

The more targeted the offering, the better the success. But even then, all of the other dictums of marketing apply. Great offers get better responses. Easy-to-understand offers get better responses. Low priced offers get better responses. High priced offers should try to drive traffic to their site, rather than push to close the sale.

The "Subscribe Me" Button

Your company can keep its own e-mail list and can run its own list server. Invite your customers to talk to you and each other about what they like and don't like about your products and services. You can set the server software to allow only you to send posts. That way you can read all the comments that come in and decide which are the best, which are the least offensive, and which will get you in trouble with the law.

Again, this activity may belong more to your marketing department or customer service group, but each time a newsletter or list server e-mail goes out to your customers, it's another reminder that your company is out there helping them get their jobs done. That's a great brand interaction and can include the occasional offer. That's right; you can advertise on your own list!

E-Mail Games

Another pre-banner, Internet activity is the e-mail based game. As soon as there was e-mail, people were playing chess by sending their moves back and forth. The *Play by Email Magazine* (PBEM) (**www.pbm.com/~lindahl/pbem_magazine.html**) has been in publication for over five years.

Primarily run by enthusiasts, role-playing games are big. In games like the Sagebrush Rebellion (**www2.southwind.net/~phoenyx/sagebrus/index.html**), players take on roles they create to fit the scenario, write about their actions, and the results are fed back to all players by the Game Master (see Figure 2.6).

These games are essentially action-adventure fiction stories created by a committee. They are made up by the cast of characters as the action happens, and edited by the Game Masters who do it for the entertainment value. There are hundreds of games online, including the Balance-the-Equation game, the College Basketball E-Mail League, checkers, E-Mail Boggle Game, and E-Mail Wrestling. Some are free, and some are pay-for-play, like Gamer's Den's Odyssey (**www.den.com**).

While most have been free of commercial messages, it is only a matter of time before some enterprising Game Master realizes the potential and imitates the model created by Yoyodyne.

Yoyodyne (**www.yoyo.com**) runs free Internet games for prizes. It gives away trips, tickets to sporting events, and t-shirts. All of those are supported by sponsors and the e-mail game is available by sending a message to **central@yoyo.com**.

Every Friday it sends five trivia questions with a different category. You e-mail your answers before the deadline, which is the following Wednesday. Their game computer interprets your response and the next day you find out if you're a trivia whiz or a minutiae wannabe.

FIG. 2.6

The Sagebrush Rebellion is a very creative, role-playing game that is a commercial-free zone.

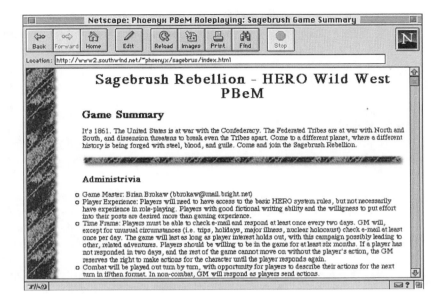

Every communication you get includes a message from the sponsor. It also includes very persuasive invitations to try their online games, where you can win more than a t-shirt and where Yoyodyne makes its real money.

How good is e-mail advertising? Can it possibly be intrusive? Is it memorable? Those questions opened a posting to the Online Advertising list from Malcom Faulds, who was Brand Manager at Yoyodyne.

At Yoyodyne we use a lot of e-mail and, naturally we believe it works. Now we have proof and I wanted to share it with you.

The key facts: 1) We are running a multi-week e-mail game for H&R Block 2) Each week every player gets 3 pieces of e-mail 3) In the middle of 1 of those pieces of e-mail one week, there was a 4 line blurb about a service from H&R Block: "Peace of Mind" 4) Six days later we sent out a simple 1 question quiz to three distinct groups:

-Players Who Responded To That Week's Question -Players Who Didn't Respond To That Week's Question -A Non-Player Control Group

We asked them a multiple choice question: What Is H&R Block's Peace of Mind? and we gave them four plausible answers (only one of which was correct)

5) The Results:

5% of the Control Group got the right answer 32% of the Player Non-Responders got the right answer 50.7% of the Player Responders got the right answer

Of course, as part of trying to win the regular game, all players are encouraged to visit the H&R Block site (where the right answer to this question is naturally present). But just think of it—six days later an astounding percentage of players, both active and 'inactive' players, had not only learned something but actually remembered it. It makes most day-after recall scores pale by comparison.

Classifieds

This is a category easy to overlook. Classifieds have traditionally been the province of the for-sale-by-owner crowd. But in these days of online search engines, classifieds are starting to offer an interesting addition to your advertising plan.

Just like the previous discussion regarding ALT.BIZ, there are enough people using electronic sluice boxes to sift through the classifieds that it might just be worth your while. Especially when there are pointers to all the places you can list for free, like the Mother Of All Classified Links (**www.uran.net/imall/mother.html**), with over five hundred sites listed. You can find those that fit your quality requirements, fit your category requirements, or fit your geographical requirements. Or, you might just want to go with the one with the biggest audience. My guess is that would be Classifieds 2000 (**www.classifieds2000.com**) (see Figure 2.7).

FIG. 2.7
Place a Classified2000 ad, and attract more eyeballs than other alternatives.

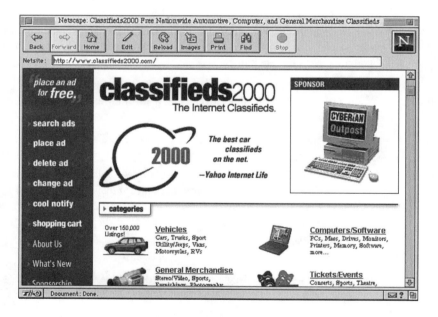

Classifieds2000 is a classifieds service. If you want to have classified advertising on your Web site, make a deal with the folks from 2000 and their back-end database looks like it's on your front door. As of the first quarter of 1997, they had already signed more than 40 content providers as network partners. Highly visited sites like Deja News, Lycos, Infoseek, Bigfoot, and WhoWhere?; auto sites like Car and Driver, Road & Track, Car Talk, Motor Trend, and

Off-Road; computer sites like PC World, MacAddict, Cyberian Outpost, and Happy Puppy are part of the network. Each classifieds section is maintained with the "look and feel" of the host Website, while the data is served from Classifieds2000. In order to provide a critical mass of listings, all private-party listings placed into the service are collectively managed and shared among the partner sites via the central Classifieds2000 database.

If you don't need this service, think about the power of the business model. It means lots and lots of eyeballs looking at ads that could contain your classified.

Sites that Want to Point Your Way

Before there were banners, there were links. Links were what the World Wide Web was all about. It was hyperlinked. It was fun to create a page that pointed to other pages, but it was new, cool, and exciting to point to pages on other computers all together. So people did. Everybody did. In fact, when two grad students names Jerry and Dave did it really well, they went public and endowed their alma mater with the Yahoo! Founders Professorship of the Stanford School of Engineering. And they didn't even graduate.

Once the sheer thrill of being able to point to other sites was gone, there was the desire to provide Web site visitors with pointers to valuable services. It was a cross between, "Hey! Look what I found!" and "Look what I found for you."

Trade-A-Link   If you run the Python & Boa site in Botswana (**www.onwe.co.za/wayne/python2.htm**) (see Figure 2.8), you may want your Other WWW Herpetological Sites page to include a reference to Gourmet Rodent (**www.pythons.com/gourmet.html**) (see Figure 2.9). Don't think of them merely as a site that sells frozen chicks for 27 cents, rat pups for 87 cents, and as a potential advertiser. Consider a pointer to their site as a welcome addition to your collection of valuable links that your customers will appreciate.

Surely, you can think of some cooperative marketing partner who would send people your way. Hopefully you already have something on your Web site worth pointing at. Placing a link in exchange for a link is a time-honored tradition.

A less visceral example might be found at Mobile (**www.mobil.com/links.html**) (see Figure 2.10), where *Fortune Magazine*, IBM, and *USA Today* get links just because the Mobile Webmasters think they're swell.

Sites that Are Born Pointers   If you're interested in getting the word out about a seminar you're running, there are numerous places on the Web that would like to hear from you.

Obviously you'll have infinite luck if your conference or seminar is related to the Internet itself. Your luck will also hold if you're presenting anything remotely technical. But even if you're throwing a party on ecotourism, a wine seminar, or a symposium on color control for the production pressroom, there are sites like EventSeeker (**www.eventseeker.com**) and Worldwide Events Database (**www.ipworld.com/events/homepage.htm**) that will gladly tell the world where to find you. To help out, Event Web has a list of Meeting, Conference & Trade Show Search Engines (**www.eventweb.com/links.html**).

FIG. 2.8

The Python & Boa page might be just the place...

Sites Within Sites

P.T. Barnum made excellent use of a large sign that pointed to a door at his circus: "This Way to the Grand Egress." A ticket could be purchased for 10 cents and the curious were led through a short hallway to the exterior of the circus. They had to pay 25 cents to get back in. That was okay for Mr. There's-A-Sucker-Born-Every-Minute, but for Web site builders, having visitors click off to another site is not the goal.

FIG. 2.9

... for the Gourmet Rodent to get a free link.

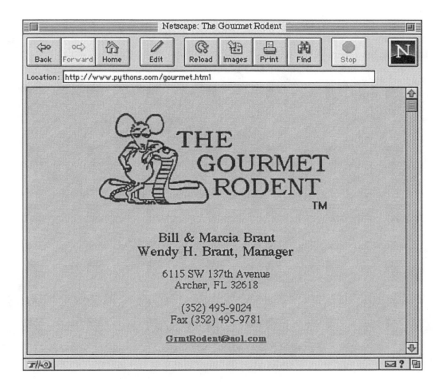

Solution for the Supply Chain

Consider the plight of Marshall Industries (**www.marshall.com**), an electronics distributor representing well over a hundred manufacturers. If you're interested in knowing something about Tektronix, whether it's a product like a female-to-female bnc adapter or a probe tip with a retractable hook, or even the company history, corporate structure, or strategic alliances, you never have to leave the safety and comfort of the Marshall site (see Figure 2.11). Why do they go to such trouble for over a hundred manufacturers? Reintermediation.

Disintermediation is the five dollar word meaning the Internet lets the producer sell directly to the consumer without having to pay the supply chain. *Reintermediation* is what Marshall has to do to prove to its customers that it is adding value to that chain. Marshall doesn't want to spend the time and trouble to educate you, only to have you wander over to the Tektronix Web site and buy the product there.

If you have a supplier/distributor relationship with your supply chain, maybe you should talk to them about the benefits of beefing up how you're represented on their Web site.

FIG. 2.10

IBM will point to your site if you say something nice about APPN/DLSw. If you don't know what APPN/DLSw is, you don't qualify.

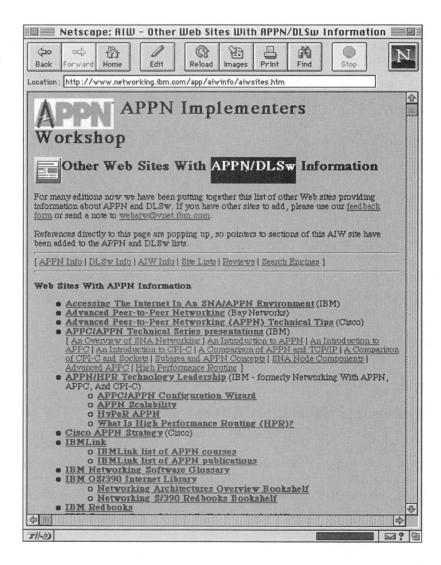

Works Well for Content Sites as Well

The Year 2000 Information Center provides a forum for disseminating information about the Millenium Bug (computers being confused when the date changes from '99 to '00) and for the discussion of possible solutions. It says so right on the Center's home page. If you're a software person, the mere mention of the year 2000 problem make your eyeballs quickly twitch back and forth in that way that makes you look like you're deep in REM sleep with your eyes open. This Web site is the place where you can try to have something done about it (see Figure 2.12).

FIG. 2.11

In this classic site-within-a-site, Marshall Industries is making sure they keep the sale.

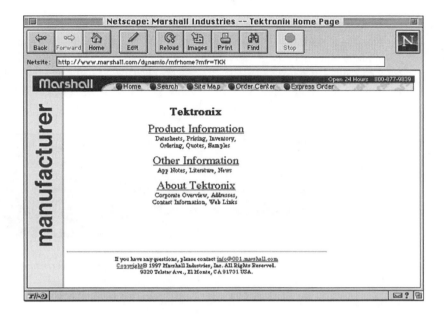

FIG. 2.12

The Year 2000 Information Center lists their sponsors on the left with price-dependent links.

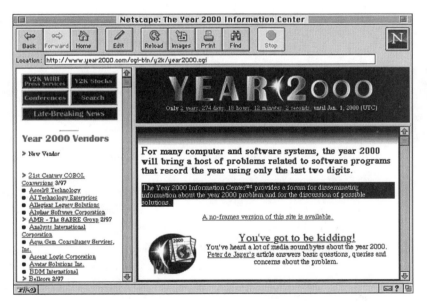

It also offers a wonderful place to advertise if you are currently making a living out of pain and suffering to come. Consulting services, replacement software, development tools; all sorts of vendors want to be on the site that knows the answers. After all, this site is the home to Peter de Jager, who has appeared on television and before House subcommittees on the subject.

The home page for the Year 2000 Information Center (**www.year2000.com**) uses a left-hand frame to list the sponsors (see Figure 2.13). For a small fee, this listing links visitors to a site-within-the-site. For a larger fee, the link can point to the vendor's own Web site. Clearly a matter of value. Do you want to have the prospect learn your name and read a few things about the company? Or do you want to have the opportunity to show them what you have and give yourself the opportunity to learn something about them?

FIG. 2.13

The Visionet mini-site within the Year 2000 Information Center site.

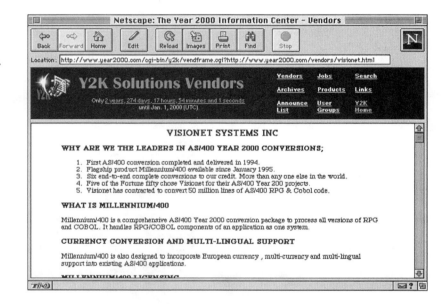

Mousepads

When it comes to the World Wide Web, thinking outside the box isn't good enough. Try leaving the room. Get outta town! How about Paris?

Go to 18 rue du grand Prieuré and find Zapworks (**www.iway.fr/zapworks**). When they're not creating Web sites and performing the online promotions, they are cashing in on an out-of-box idea that should spark your thinking—mousepads.

My current favorite mousepad replaces the one from a client in Lisbon. It's from Amazon.com, the book store and it says, "Outside of a dog, a book is a man's best friend. Inside of a dog, it's too dark to read. Groucho Marx." I don't want to replace this one and you probably don't have a need to replace yours. But there are places that go through mousepads on a regular basis—cybercafes.

Zapworks will take your image, emblazon it on a linkpad, and distribute it to hundreds of cybercafes each month (see Figure 2.14). They calculate that your message will reach over one million users a month on the basis of 10 users per terminal per day, and 4,000 terminals covered.

FIG. 2.14

Your Ad Here! In front of cybercafe visitors everywhere.

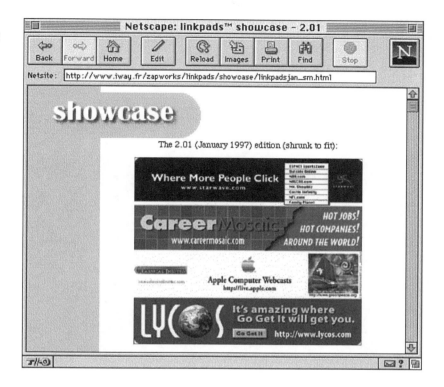

The idea is simple. These people are looking for surfing suggestions, and there's one right under their mouse. At about $7,000 per month for about one million impressions, you're looking at a CPM of about seven cents. And what an impression! Cybercafe folks are often doubled up at the terminal and are talking, laughing, drinking espresso, and being exposed to your persuasive prodding for thirty to sixty minutes. More thinking like this will help your advertising dollar go further than it has in the past.

But the majority of your time, energy, and money is going to go into thinking inside a box. A box about one third the size of your paycheck. Most of your time is going to go into worrying about banners. ●

CHAPTER 3

The Buck Spangled Banner

Little did Hotwired know when it started taking ads in October, 1994, that it would be setting a defacto standard. Banner shape, size, and location were heretofore unknown and unconsidered attributes until they hit Hotwired. Since this was the only example, it was much easier to go with the flow than reinvent the deal.

The Net is nothing if not inventive, creative, and anarchic. People are still experimenting with different shapes, sizes, and types of ads, not to mention different business models. But the banner has become the focus of Internet advertising for the time being and it's where your focus should be as well.

It is the banner's lot in life to grab people's attention. A range of banner types have been tried out on the Web with varying degrees of success. Some are explored here, including animated banners, Java banners, and streaming banners that can process orders where they sit. But before banners get too unique and too out of control, there are those who would impose standards. Oops, excuse me, "suggest voluntary guidelines." But that's not really a bad thing after all. ■

Banner Standards

The banner is the Web's mainstay because it is simple to explain and easy to understand. You can equate it with print advertising in an instant; rules of frequency and reach are easily applied; you can buy banners by the thousand; they take up a specific amount of space. Well, almost.

Picture if you will, thousands of Web sites developed by people from thousands of backgrounds all playing with the same colors of Playdough. There is no limit to the size, shape, style, or iteration of the final creation. The limit, as has been true to form on the Web in general, has been imagination. This is part of the glory of the World Wide Web; everybody has an instant soapbox; everybody is an artist; everybody is a publisher.

When the word spread that there were those who would bind this new-born banner to a set size and shape, the outcry was swift and indignant. Take the creative power out of the hands of the people and stuff it into a mold? Make everybody conform? Go wash your mouth out with soap and pray to the God of Individuality that you won't be struck down in your prime by a server flung from a passing truck!

Of course, this was the same reaction heard when it was suggested that the Internet might be a good place for commerce. Blasphemy! Sacrilege! The Internet is the realm of the researcher, the student, and the Ph.D. It is the home of the high thinker and the seat of pure reason. There's no place here for dirty and profane mercantilism!

I am reminded of the graffiti I saw on a recent trip to the Grand Canyon. Amidst wistful suggestions that we "Give the Canyon Back to the Indians" was a rather startling screed in angry lettering several inches high insisting, "RAGE AGAINST THE MACHINE!!" Under that, in a clear and spare hand, was written, "Silly boy, you're *sitting* on the machine."

As commerce was inevitable on the Internet, so too is banner standardization. The value of pressing your favorite color of Playdough into a mold was not lost on kids all over the world. And the value of Web banners as interchangeable parts has not been wasted on banner space sellers or banner creators.

When Web sites are built by two guys in a garage who are selling ad space for whatever they think they can get that week, then the world belongs to the creative types and the free-thinkers. When Web advertising becomes a sector of commerce, standards help grease the wheels of industry. Buying an ad on the Ashland High School DECA Page (**http://www.grizzly.ashland.or.us**) (see Figure 3.1) for $5 a month is a shrewd buy for those selling Oregonean grizzly bear t-shirts. And I'm sure the students in Ashland High's marketing classes will be quite flexible with your desires for a full page ad, a vertical ad, an ad that paints the background of the whole page, or an audio ad.

FIG. 3.1

Ashland High's banner standards might be a bit more flexible...

But if your plans include reaching a tad further than high schoolers in the home of the Ashland Shakespeare Festival, you might have to conform to a common size. People who serve thousands of banners each day, like Yahoo! (see Figure 3.2), rely on automation to serve up banners on-the-fly. They don't create a static page that includes a specific ad. Instead, they have the computer generate each page dynamically, as users click links. Every page has a set spot for ads and every ad fits that spot.

FIG. 3.2

...Yahoo!'s automated banner server...

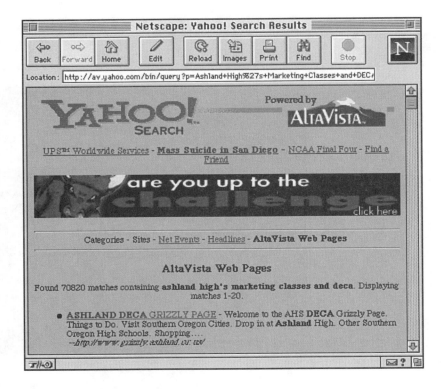

When ads are served from a common database like ad network DoubleClick (**www.doubleclick.com**) (see Figure 3.3), then your ads must fit their needs exactly. After all, they're serving ads to over 70 sites. All of those sites have to conform to the DoubleClick banner specifications as do all of the advertisers. The alternative would be chaos.

Standards also Benefit the Advertiser

I don't advocate banner standardization solely for the benefit of those who want to commoditize ads as fast and as economically possible. There's also value for the person creating the ad.

Let's say you wanted to advertise on the ESPNET SportsZone (**espnet.sportszone.com**), and the Time-Warner Pathfinder (**pathfinder.com**), and *USA Today* (**www.usatoday.com**), and the Tennis Server (**www.tennisserver.com**), and the Internet Underground Music Archive (**www.iuma.com**). And let's say they each had their own regulation size and shapes. You'd have to create five different ads. You'd have to have your graphic artist alter the layout, which would alter the design, which would alter the message for each venue. With an industry standard in place, you can create one ad that runs across the board.

Not only do you save on graphic design expenses, you can more accurately track which location is best suited to your message. If all your ads are thematically the same, then the results you get must be related to their placement. Change too many variables from ad to ad and your ability to measure effectiveness gets muddied pretty quickly.

FIG. 3.3
...or DoubleClick's network of over 70 sites.

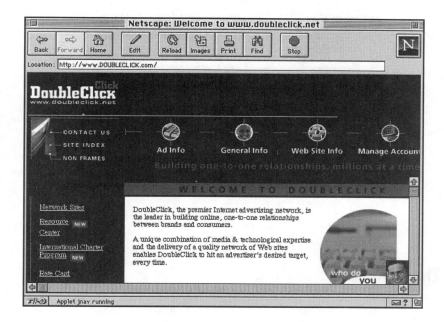

The Standards Bearers

The two groups to watch are CASIE and the IAB. They've taken on the mantle of protectors of the realm. The IAB's charter is made clear on their Web site (**www.edelman.com/IAB/index.html**):

> The Internet Advertising Bureau (IAB) (**www.edelman.com/IAB**) is the only industry association devoted exclusively to promoting the use and effectiveness of advertising on the Internet. General members include companies that are actively engaged in the sales of advertising. The organization membership also consists of companies that support advertising sales activities such as measurement companies, research suppliers, traffic companies and organizations from related industries.

However, Doug Weaver, VP of Advertising and Web Publishing for Firefly Network, Incorporated (**www.ffly.com**), and one of over 180 IAB members, says that the real goal is to find ways to get more people to spend real money on Web advertising. Since members "include companies that are actively engaged in the sales of advertising," it's a very understandable goal.

CASIE is the Coalition for Advertising Supported Information and Entertainment (**www.commercepark.com/AAAA/casie/index.html**), a joint committee between the American Association of Advertising Agencies and the Association of National Advertisers. The mission is to "Create an environment where consumers have the broadest possible array of high-quality media options at the lowest possible cost. To accomplish this, we believe that advertising revenue must be a key funding source for information and entertainment in the evolving world of media."

CASIE's Key Areas of Focus are stated in its Mission Statement as:

1. *Promote existing advertising-supported entertainment and information services.*

2. *Encourage providers of new services to rely on advertising as a key funding source.*

3. *Research and track consumer use and acceptance of new media services.*

4. *Ensure the adoption of technical standards for hardware and software by industry and government that facilitate: a) delivery of programming and advertising that allows everyone to 'plug and play' on all systems without re-authoring; and b) simple consumer access for programming and advertising.*

5. *Be proactive and involved with Federal [sic] and state legislation and regulation. Advocate and promote a minimalist approach to the legislation and regulation of telecommunications.*

So when these two august bodies come together to spawn a banner-sizing standard, it's an offspring worth noting. On December 10, 1996, that offspring was introduced to the world.

The Official Motivation

According to the joint press release, "The standards were created in response to industry-wide concern about the proliferation of types and sizes of banners which are the most commonly used form of advertising on the Internet today. According to industry estimates, more than 250 different banners are in use."

"The proliferation of banners has created a massive problem for advertisers and their agencies, which sometimes have to create their ads in 50 or more sizes," said Mike Donahue, Senior Vice President, AAAA. "These voluntary guidelines will greatly streamline the advertising production and placement process and contribute to the overall growth of Internet advertising."

Both groups are quick to point out that they are not laying down the law. Moreover, they don't even call it a standard: it's a "voluntary guideline." In a well-practiced dance of political correctness, they point out that the medium is young, there's a lot of experimentation ahead, and they don't want to discourage any other forms of advertising. However, if your canvas of choice is the banner, then they are happy to offer eight typical sizes. Think of it as going to the art or photography supply store. Do you want a frame for an 8×10 or a 10×12?

The Proposed Guidelines

The proposal reads:

PROPOSAL FOR VOLUNTARY MODEL BANNER SIZES

Banners have become a significant means of advertising and source of revenue on the World Wide Web. The number of types of banners and sizes have proliferated. In a recent survey, IAB members stated that this proliferation of banner types and sizes is inefficient and confusing and that identifying a baseline model would result in benefits for both buyers and sellers of advertising on the Web. Advertisers, agencies and media companies have asked the CASIE and the IAB to consider these issues.

In response to requests from the advertising community the Standards and Practices Committee of the IAB with input from CASIE has used market data to examine the full range of banner types, for example, vertical, horizontal, half and button, and sizes currently in use. The Committee has identified the following as the most commonly accepted:

Size (pixels)	Type
468×60	*Full Banner*
392×72	*Full Banner with Vertical Navigation Bar*
234×60	*Half Banner*
125×125	*Square Button*
120×90	*Button #1*
120×60	*Button #2*
88×31	*Micro Button*
120×240	*Vertical Banner*

Use of any of these sizes as a model or standard is strictly voluntary. The IAB and CASIE recognize and intend that its member companies and the advertising community remain free to experiment with, use, adopt, and propose other sizes and types of banners. The two groups also recognize that websites which chose to implement these models may wish to do so over a period of several months to allow those who sell space or create banner content to make any adjustments.

Banners are currently the primary form of Internet and interactive advertising. However, the IAB and CASIE encourage the continuing exploration of other advertising models such as interstitial pages, push advertising (including PointCast, Marimba and BackWeb) microsites, web advertorials and sponsored activities

To facilitate the continued growth of the medium and the industry, the Standards & Practices Committee of the IAB plans to convene six conferences during the coming year, three on each coast, to discuss the benefits of voluntary standards or models for emerging formats and to release additional proposals as appropriate. The IAB will continue to work closely with CASIE in fostering these discussions and invites all interested parties to participate.

Positive Reaction

Take a peek at the leading ad buyer on the Net and you'll see smiles. Microsoft went all out with their promotion of version 3.0 of their Internet Explorer. Those banners were unavoidable. Spread out over 75 of the most popular Web sites, Microsoft had to come up with 180 different banner sizes. Different pages had different spaces and the team in Redmond didn't want to be left out. Their ad agency, Anderson & Lembke, figured Microsoft could have saved $50,000 on the launch alone.

Not slow on the uptake, Microsoft decided to make good on that estimate. Through Anderson & Lembke, they circulated a letter to sites selling advertising warning that standard-sized banners would be an important factor in their media-buying criteria.

"Starting March 1, 1997, Anderson & Lembke will be using these standard banner sizes for all our interactive clients' media plans. Sites which have not adopted these standards will be at a significant disadvantage in the selection process when evaluated against sites who have adopted the standards."

There's plenty of "or else" in that statement and Anderson & Lembke is Microsoft's primary agency. Microsoft has said "frog," and many Web sites breathed a sigh of relief because now they know exactly how high to jump.

Help Is at Hand

Lest you be despondent at the thought of being forced to work with a limited number of pixels and having to spend hours squeezing your creation to fit the mold, there is help on the Web. GIF Wizard Ad-O-Matic (**www.raspberryhill.com/gifwiz/adomatic.html**) (see Figure 3.4) is out there, waiting to help you turn your artistic masterpiece into a standard banner format.

FIG. 3.4
GIF Wizard Ad-O-Matic
will resize your banner
for 35 ad formats.

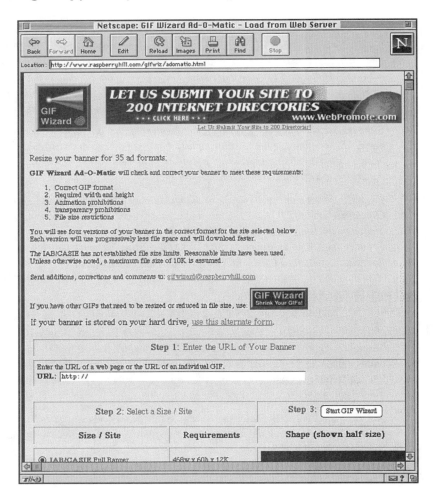

GIF Wizard checks and corrects your banner to meet the right GIF format, width, height, animation prohibitions, transparency prohibitions, and file size restrictions. It will even make sure you comply with the CASIE/IAB guidelines (see Figure 3.5).

FIG. 3.5
GIF Wizard knows how to resize your banner to meet the CASIE/IAB guidelines.

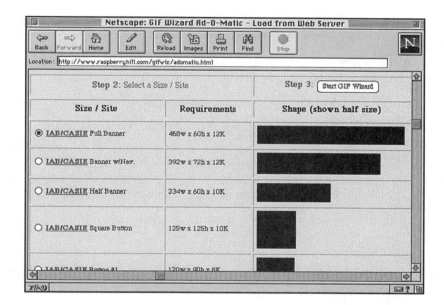

Additional Standards

Banner sizes aren't the only standards under discussion. Wouldn't it be nice if you could send information to and from your ad agencies that would be recognized on sight? How about finding which sites are offering ad space for sale? This is a young industry and these questions are just starting to be asked. Suggested answers are floating around in the form of trial balloons waiting for updrafts or pins.

Simple Advertising Management Protocol   Aside from having an unfortunate acronym, SAMP (**www.focalink.com/home/pp**) is described on the Focalink Web site as an "open protocol for communicating Web advertising traffic information, ad materials and performance data." In English, this means being able to communicate with various ad agencies, Web banner makers, and Web sites selling space in a common format.

Jump-started by Focalink Communications and Bellcore (**www.bellcore.com**), SAMP is intended to ease the process of "sending traffic instructions to sites that specify which ads appear when and where, transferring of actual ad materials, and sending back reports on campaign performance."

The problem they're trying to solve is the aggravation experienced by advertisers when dealing with multiple sites which use multiple ad management systems—a lot of which are home-grown systems. If you can send a banner and the same batch of data about that banner to every site you want to advertise on, you can save a bottle or two of aspirin a month.

Advertising Information File   As of April, 1997, the Online Advertising Discussion List had more than 3,800 subscribers, and was growing at a rate of about 40 subscribers per week. It's a fairly lively debate and well worth a look (**www.o-a.com**). Pondering the issues of how to use technology to make life easier for banners producers and displayers, Mark J. Welch, curator of the astonishingly useful Web Site Banner Advertising: Banner Ad Networks & Brokers page (**www.ca-probate.com/comm_net.htm**), offered the following:

Date: Wed, 26 Mar 1997 13:58:14 -0800

To: online-ads@o-a.com

From: "Mark J. Welch, Esq." <markwelch@ca-probate.com>

Subject: ONLINE-ADS>> Proposal: AD-INFO.TXT file (Ad Registries)

I would like to make a humble suggestion: why doesn't someone create a standard list of data and file descriptor for a file of "advertising information" to be maintained at each web site? Thus, when I update the advertising information at my site, I could simply do so by updating the file and then 'robots' from each company operating an advertising directory could check my site for that update.

I'd certainly take more interest in providing updates about advertising on my web pages if I could simply update a single file at my site and have a number of services automatically gather that data. I'm sure that hundreds, and perhaps thousands, of web publishers would feel the same way.

The file format should be flexible, so that each vendor could specify optional or required fields for its service (but with no 'secret' data available only to one service)—kind of like HTML with meta tags, or SGML.

Of course, if the format were useful, someone would write nifty software utilities to automate many update tasks (such as automatically posting current statistics into the file from a stats program). Indeed, I would expect that the next generation of 'web site design' software would automatically generate this file and update it as web publishers add new content to their sites.

This sort of off-the-cuff suggestion has previously spawned new products, new companies, and new industries. No matter where they come from, good ideas about standardization are sure to start showing up fast and furious. Nature abhors a vacuum and industry likes it even less—especially the computer industry. Watch this space.

Regardless of the shape, size, and placement of the banner, standard or otherwise, its goal is the same—grab the attention of the person sitting in front of the screen and engage them.

Attracting Attention

The challenge is to have as much impact as possible in a space that's essentially an inch high and eight inches long. It sounds like a tiny piece of real-estate. Imagine trying to squeeze something provocative in the space of a 1/8 display ad in a magazine. On TV you might think of it as a five-second spot. But given the state of the art, it's actually a bigger area than it sounds.

In practice, banners are more eye-catching than the rest of the screen. They can blink, bounce, and whirl. They can also be the first image to load so they're the center of attention. They can be at the top of the page as well as at the bottom. They can show up right in the middle of the article you're trying to read.

The typical banner lives near the top, under the Web page *masthead*, or title, and it works hard to distract people from their appointed rounds. Esther Dyson, editor of Release 1.0 and well-known technology observer, likes to point out that the most important finite resource in the late 20th century is people's attention. When you're trying to distract them from Web activities, your creative has to work much harder than other media.

Can Your TV Spot Stop a Train?

When sitting on the couch in full potato-mode, the average human requires several seconds to recognize that the television show that has them mesmerized has been replaced by an ad. They are at rest. The idea of sitting down in the evening to watch TV implies that the kids have been fed, the pets have been let in or out, and it's time to relax for a spell.

Your ad only has a few seconds to capture their imagination before they leap up and head for the kitchen. Even worse, with a minuscule flick of their thumb on the remote, they can send your half-minute masterpiece into video purgatory. But you do have a few seconds to grab them by the throat and stop their train of thought long enough for them to get the message.

Sitting in front of the television for an hour takes an hour. But it's a different hour than is spent elsewhere. The TV watcher's experience of an hour of TV time is relative compared to other activities where they might encounter your ad. Let's give the perception of this hour in front of the tube a rating of H1.

With a rating of only H1, the expectation of a TV ad having some important information is pretty low. It may be entertaining, it may be amusing, it may be just noise. But it isn't keeping them from anything really important, so they watch. An hour goes by pretty fast and soon; it's time for bed. H1.

Can Your Display Ad Catch A Train?

The mood is different when it comes to reading a magazine. It may well happen in front of the television, but more likely it'll be over lunch, on public transportation, in the bathroom, or in bed. People reading magazines are more involved with the media than when they watch TV. They have to create pictures in their heads based on the words they read. They think about what they're reading, rather than letting images from the television wash over them while they wait for the next murder, car chase, or explosion.

People reading magazines are actively looking for information. They want to know about the latest in fishing flies, fruit-filled pies, or Whitehouse lies. They're seeking. Because this time with a magazine is more concentrated and uses a more focused attention, one hour deserves a perceptual rating of H2—it feels like two hours in front of the idiot box.

It's harder to catch their eye as they flick from page to page. They're concentrating on what kind of bulbs they want for their spring garden. If your ad is for the most beautiful irises money can buy, you probably hit the right person at the right time and made a sale. It's not so easy on the Web.

Can Your Banner Derail a Train?

Surfing the Web warrants a perception rating of H7. First of all, you're not in the comfort of your den, resting languidly on your couch. You're not casually sipping tea while leafing through the latest issue of the *New Yorker*. You're not even remotely comfortable.

You are sitting in a chair designed to be good for you rather than cozy. You are perched in front of a device that was designed by engineers rather than artists. You are at work. You are looking for something. This is borne out by the PC-Meter Sweeps Q4 1996—Top 25 Consumer Web Sites (**www.npd.com/q4cht1.htm**) (see Figure 3.6). They found that six of the top dozen were search engines.

FIG. 3.6
PC-Meter shows search engines as the most often visited category on the Web.

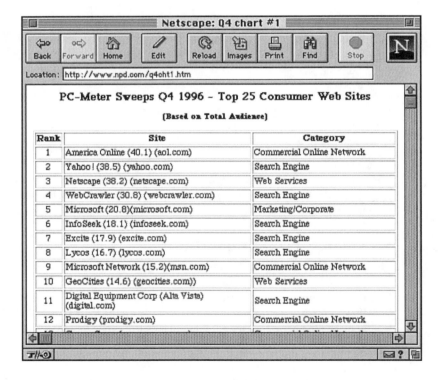

Rank	Site	Category
1	America Online (40.1) (aol.com)	Commercial Online Network
2	Yahoo! (38.5) (yahoo.com)	Search Engine
3	Netscape (38.2) (netscape.com)	Web Services
4	WebCrawler (30.8) (webcrawler.com)	Search Engine
5	Microsoft (20.8)(microsoft.com)	Marketing/Corporate
6	InfoSeek (18.1) (infoseek.com)	Search Engine
7	Excite (17.9) (excite.com)	Search Engine
8	Lycos (16.7) (lycos.com)	Search Engine
9	Microsoft Network (15.2)(msn.com)	Commercial Online Network
10	GeoCities (14.6) (geocities.com))	Web Services
11	Digital Equipment Corp (Alta Vista) (digital.com)	Search Engine
12	Prodigy (prodigy.com)	Commercial Online Network

Web surfing is fascinating. Web surfing is entertaining. Web surfing is downright fun. For a while. Then the Web becomes a means to an end; a tool for finding that one piece of information you need to finish that report, finish installing that sound card, or finish learning about that case of measles your son brought home from school. It's work.

One solid hour in front of the computer does not go by in the blink of an eye. You are focused and concentrating and engaged. At this point, shaking you from your intended goal is not going to be easy.

The job of the banner is to totally derail your train of thought. As you sit before your keyboard in anticipation of a pointer to the answer to all of your measles fears, up pops an ad that says, "Organic Gardening Isn't Just A Bunch Of Manure. CLICK HERE TO FIND OUT WHY" (see Figure 3.7).

FIG. 3.7
Want to know about measles? How about gardening instead?

So you see the problem. Trying to make a person on a mission, with a specific goal in mind, engaged in an H7 activity that ranks 7 times more engrossing than television, go to a site hosted by a federation of national and local environmental and conservation charities. It's a stretch.

These types of banners on the Web are not the most engrossing pieces of art. They're not the most exciting bits of information. Most of them don't rate a second glance. Figure 3.8 through Figure 3.13 are examples of the typical banner ad cluttering up content sites these days.

FIG. 3.8

BigYellow offers advice.

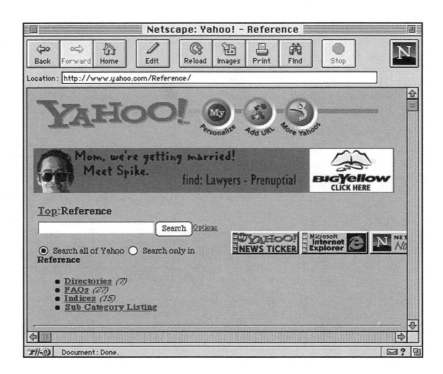

FIG. 3.9

Women's Wire avoids being precise.

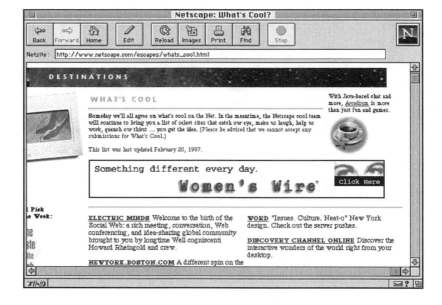

FIG. 3.10
Firefly overdoes
concise.

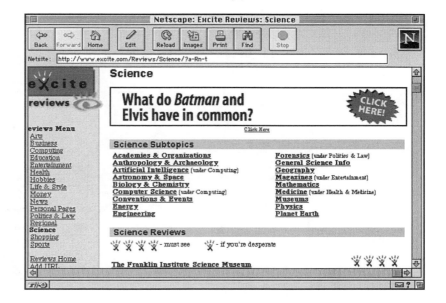

FIG. 3.11
Holiday Inn uses the
tie-in device.

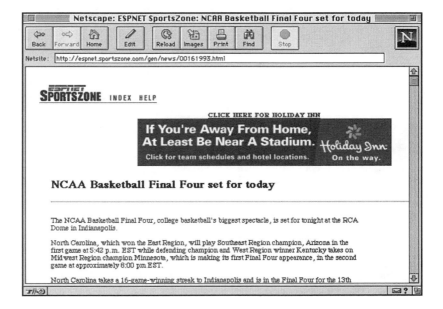

Your ad has to be so arresting, so compelling, so interesting, to completely derail a train of thought and make that hand slide over and *click!*

FIG. 3.12

Microsoft tries to entice.

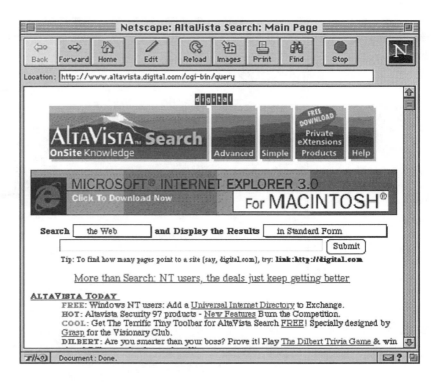

In an attempt to be as arresting as possible, the first impulse is to make the banner as eye-catching as possible. If you do, you fall into the First Trap of the Internet: using too much bandwidth.

Bandwidth, Bandwidth, Bandwidth

I don't care if your banner is a still photograph of your product or a movie of your smiling CEO, it's too darn big. Yes, we covered the 468×60 pixel size limitation previously, but this is about file size, not screen size.

A 468×60 banner file can be 10K, it can be 100K, it can be 1,000K (that's a megabyte, by the way) and still look just the same. The difference is: a) how it was created, and b) how long it takes to download.

The Least Amount of Technology You Need to Understand   When somebody clicks a link to your Web site, they don't come to your site, it goes to them. Here's how it works with an ad:

1. The user clicks.
2. A message is sent to the server of the site you paid to display your ad.
3. The server finds the page the user wants and reads it.
4. The server determines that the page in question is made up of some text and several images, one of which is your ad.

5. The server sends the page and then starts sending the images. It may have all of them on its hard disk, or it may pull your ad from your server, or the server of a network agency that worries about that for you (see Chapter 6, "Looking for Space In All the Right Places").

6. The page and the associated images are broken up into packets of about 1K each. A one-kilobyte NotePad file on Windows 95 can hold the words found in this sentence and that's about it. Each packet contains the address of the client to whom it's going.

7. The packets are sent out onto the Internet to fend for themselves. They can all take different routes to get to the user's machine, it doesn't matter.

8. When the packets arrive at the user's machine, they are re-assembled into real files, stored on the hard drive in a *cache* (temporary) file, and displayed in the user's browser of choice.

Now comes the problem. With all of this going on, there are several areas along the way that can slow down the whole process.

1. *The user clicks.* Nope, not much there we can do anything about.

2. *A message is sent to the server of the site you paid to display your ad.* Here's where the trouble starts. The message is sent by the user's machine to the user's access provider.

   a) The connection between the user and the access provider may be a 14.4 modem. Unless you're certain your prospective customers will only be looking at your ad from their cubicles with dedicated, blindingly fast T1 lines, you can be pretty sure that they're on a 28.8 modem, at best.

   b) The access provider's gateway machine is busy with other click-happy users.

   c) The message goes out from the access provider to his or her access provider where there's another gateway machine (see b).

   d) The message goes out over the Internet backbone, which can be slow if it's presidential election night, there's another OJ verdict, or the Supreme Court makes a ruling about obscenity on the Internet.

3. *The server finds the page the user wants and reads it.* It may be that the site on which you have chosen to advertise is one of the most popular presidential election results sites around. It may be that it is serving up lots of ads for lots of people. That means it takes a while before it can get around to the user's request for a page.

4. *The server determines that the page in question is made up of some text and several images, one of which is your ad.* See #3.

5. *The server sends the page and then starts sending the images.* See #3.

6. *The page and the associated images are broken up into packets of about 1K each.* See #3.

7. *The packets are sent out onto the Internet to fend for themselves.* See #2. And another twist is added here. If your ad is coming from an advertisement service server (like DoubleClick or Excite, see Chapter 6, "Looking for Space In All the Right Places"), then there is another message that goes from the site your ad is displayed on to the site on which your ad actually lives. This is the same as #1, and you have to go through Steps 1 through 7 for your ad, which is coming from a different machine.

8. *When the packets arrive at the user's machine, they are re-assembled into real files, stored on the hard drive in a cache (temporary) file, and displayed in the user's browser of choice.* Now you have to deal with the question of the end user's machine. Are you dealing with a state-of-the-art UNIX workstation with gobs of memory? Or are you dealing with the old 386 PC that your prospective customer brought home from the office when they upgraded her machine there?

You only Have One Shot at a First Impression   Each of the previous steps plays a part in getting your message to your prospect. If any of those steps cause your message to show up late, the user has two possible impressions: poor or none.

Picture a television set that took from one second to sixty seconds to change channels. Oh, you say, one second isn't that long. Remember, you're used to changing channels in the time it takes to snap your fingers. Now think about the difference between *snap* and "one-thousand-one" (or "one-chimpanzee" if you grew up in my house). Now multiply that by sixty and you have a good idea how frustrating it is to wait for a banner ad to load.

So the first impression your prospect has of you is that you are making it difficult for them to do whatever it is they're trying to accomplish. The alternative impression is no impression at all.

I'm a pretty consistent user of AltaVista (**www.altavista.digital.com**), and I'm pretty adept at scrolling down to the found documents before the ad shows up. When AltaVista replies to a search, the masthead, the banner ad, and the introductory text take up the entire page on my terminal (see Figure 3.14).

Because the text shows up before the banner, it's quite simple for me to miss the ad while anxiously awaiting the fruits of AltaVista's labors (see Figure 3.15). I'm busy scrolling down the page while AltaVista is busy painting the banner at the top. The top of the page has scrolled off the top of the screen before the banner is in place.

But you can rest assured that the site hosting your ad has registered this event as an *impression* and will happily charge you for it.

With All that Against You—Don't Fall Flat on Creative   In a classic example of poor creative meets bad placement on an H7 medium, you have the entry from Proctor & Gamble, shown in Figure 3.16.

Let's assume you're deeply interested in Aboriginal studies at the moment and you are *thrilled* to find that Yahoo! has an entire category on same. You are mere seconds away from making the vast Internet open its secret databases to your inquiring mind.

But wait! Before you click, you notice the banner demanding that you "CLICK HERE TO LEARN A FOREIGN LANGUAGE." Surrounded by modern-day hieroglyphics, these words are baffling. They decided to play the curiosity card and it seems to be working. You are just about to let your curiosity get the best of you when you see the words just below the banner that say, "Click Here for The Tide Clothesline."

FIG. 3.13
Parent Soup hopes chat
will suffice.

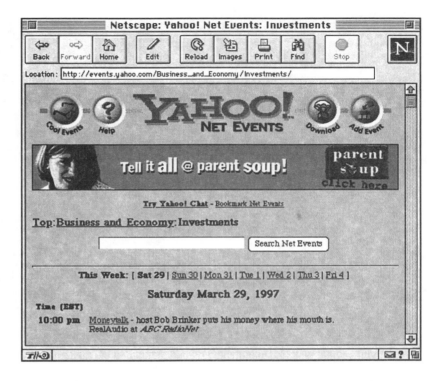

FIG. 3.14
AltaVista fills the screen
and forces the user to
scroll to see found
documents.

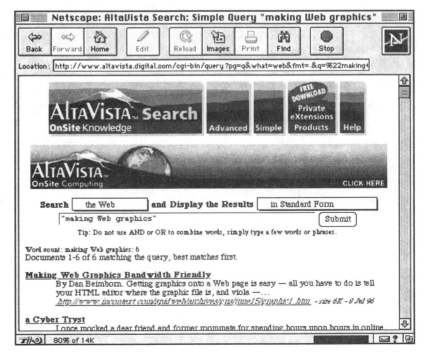

FIG. 3.15

While the ad banner is painting, the surfer is scrolling and may never see the ad.

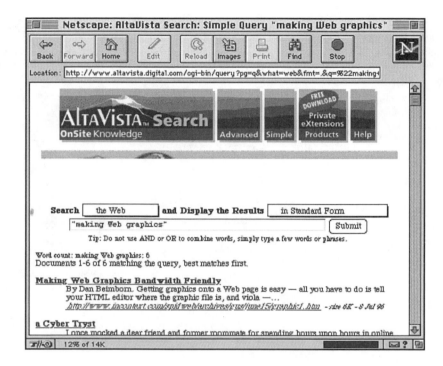

The Tide Clothesline? Foreign language? It's all too much, and, just as they had hoped, you *click*, just to find out what these people are up to. And what do you find? Well, the Tide Clothesline, of course (see Figure 3.17). But when you arrive, you realize you can leave your English-Whatever, Whatever-English phrase-book behind.

There is nothing, and I mean nothing at *all*, on this page that ties in with learning a foreign language. The message is clear: "We're Procter & Gamble. We know everything there is to know about being clean. You're surfing the Internet. Everybody knows that people who surf the Internet are hygienically challenged. You don't even speak our language."

It's enough to make you want to throw in the towel and join the group calling for an end to standards, the end to commercialism on the Net, and rally to give the Grand Canyon back to the Indians.

Raising the Bar   There's nothing that can be done about bad creative but lament and pray you can do better. It's a fine art. I'll try to divine its mysterious ways in order to give you a bit of an edge in Chapter 7, "What Makes People Click?" In the meantime, the state of the banner technology art marches on.

In an effort to provide more eye-appeal and increase the number of times people click (without overtaxing the systems that hold the Internet together), the Weberati have fallen back on the tried and true—technology. They went and animated the banner.

FIG. 3.16
Proctor & Gamble placed a curious banner on a curious spot.

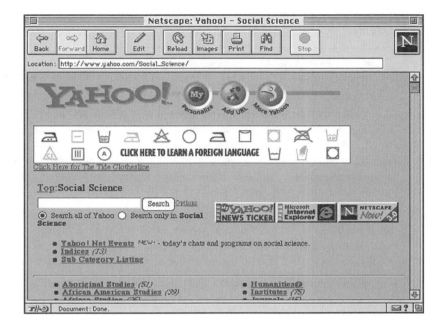

FIG. 3.17
Your quest for a new language ended up leaving you twisting in the wind.

Banners that Move

Animation has come to the Web banner in a handful of ways and the results are all pretty much the same; it takes longer to download and it makes more people click. A closer look at the higher clickthrough numbers will be found in Chapter 7, "What Makes People Click?" Here, a few basics are covered, such as the different types of animation and how they look.

I promise not to delve into the technical intricacies of programming computer animation. Creating animation belongs to the graphic artists and the technicians. They can worry about whether you should use an animated gif (a series of still pictures in an animation loop), or streaming technology (a constant stream of image data sent to the browser to play a whole clip in quasi-real time), or Shockwave files (requiring your prospects to have already downloaded and installed the Shockwave plug-in).

I'll leave that to people like Nicola Brown, Peter Chen, David Miller, and Paul Van Eyk, who put together *Designing Web Animation*, published by New Riders, August 1996, and Dave Taylor, who authored the more up-to-date *Creating Cool HTML 3.2 Web Pages*, published by IDG Books, January 1997. They know what your programmers and graphic artists should know.

You should worry about bandwidth and whether your ad is doing the job—just as you don't pay strict attention to how your brochures are printed, you only worry that they look right. A quick trip to some of the places that show banners for a living and you're sure to come across some that move.

AltaVista was my very favorite marketing Web site. In fact, I wrote an article about it in *Webmaster* magazine (November, 1996, **www.web-master.com**) which included, in part:

The AltaVista search engine is a database of all the Web sites its spider can find, coupled with an index and a query tool. Did we really need another Web site to help us find Web sites? What could DEC offer that would make a difference? Why should AltaVista be getting more than 14 million hits per day? And if it's that popular, why isn't DEC selling banner space?

Because AltaVista Vista is a gift. It's DEC's way of giving back to the Net. In the spirit of that first gaggle of guys who were trying to make this gizmo work, DEC has created a search tool for the masses. It is giving freely of its development time, its hardware and its customer service department to make the world a little better place to live.

And the tooth fairy and Santa Claus are buying me a winning Lottery ticket this afternoon.

Digital isn't selling ad space because AltaVista is itself an ad. It's an ad for Alpha computers, and it's a doozy. If you're looking for something out there on the Web, AltaVista is a fast way to find it. Very fast. Of course, running your query engine in 6 GB of RAM across 10 processors is a great way to expedite a search, and that's just one of five systems behind AltaVista. But as always with advertising, it's the perception that counts.

'Jeepers Clem, that li'l ol' Alpha sure do put on some speed.'

'Yup, I reckon we oughta get us one o' them for the dynamic multi-dimensional analysis of our consolidated enterprise data.'

'Reckon so.'

Is this a successful marketing model for the Alpha? It certainly hasn't hurt. In DEC's third quarter of fiscal '96, big Alpha systems sales were up 60 percent. And the company has moved into a whole new product line: DEC now has an AltaVista Software Products division.

Under the vision banner of 'OnSite Computing,' DEC is offering AltaVista Search, AltaVista Mail, AltaVista Forum for conferencing, AltaVista Manager for applications and network connections inventory, AltaVista Firewall and AltaVista Tunnel security tools. This is not to say that DEC wouldn't have gone into these businesses anyway, but with AltaVista Vista it discovered something that Sun Microsystems had already learned: Sometimes the child outshines the parent.

Scott McNealy, after finishing his usual round of Microsoft bashing at Comdex 1996, in Chicago, said that within a year Java had become a bigger brand name than Sun. DEC saw the writing on the wall and named its Internet software products division after something that had garnered significant, positive attention out on the Net. Smart move.

AltaVista often shows up in lists of surfers' favorite search tools. It's so popular that Yahoo! forsook its venture-capital cousin Infoseek for AltaVista. And, yes, I use it myself, all the time. It's fast. It's easy. It has no commercials!

FIG. 3.18

The Internet makes strange bedfellows, including this ad from IBM on the Digital AltaVista site...

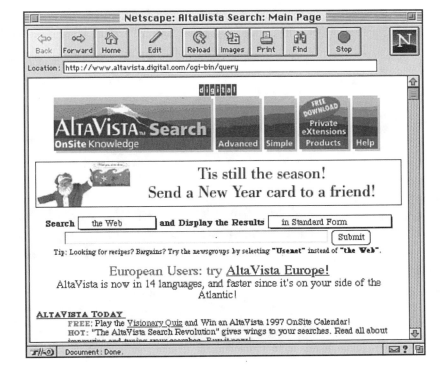

In December, 1996, DEC decided to make a move to deliberately spoil the entire premise of my insightful article—they started selling ads. And, in the never-ending absurdity that is the Internet, the first ads they ran were for IBM! Go figure. Why am I telling you all this here? Because AltaVista's first ad was an animated gif. The first view is seen in Figure 3.18 and the final is seen in Figure 3.19.

As people figured out how to make the most of it, animation became more attention-grabbing. One example is this series from Infoseek (see Figure 3.20 through Figure 3.24).

FIG. 3.19

... which was an animated gif.

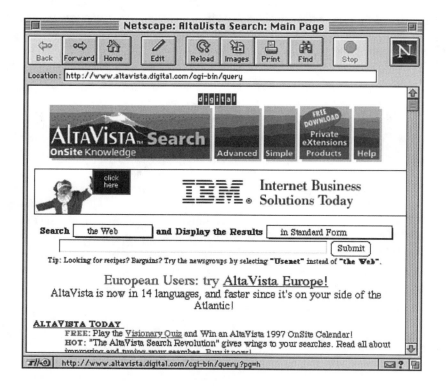

FIG. 3.20

Infoseek steps you through the stages of downloading...

FIG. 3.21

...while you wait...

FIG. 3.22

...and wait....

FIG. 3.23

....while they make their point...

The Infoseek banner worked hard. It grabbed the eye, it offered a solution to one of the most frustrating problems on the Internet, and it moved fast enough in the telling that the person seated in front of his or her H7 computer wasn't annoyed.

Another eye-catching banner came from Music Boulevard. The picture of four tongues hanging out, as shown in Figure 3.25, definitely caught the eye. The follow up frames are shown in Figure 3.26 and Figure 3.27.

FIG. 3.24

..about their new Quickseek software.

FIG. 3.25

Music Boulevard stops you with the disrespect-ful tongues that get labeled with the names of bands...

FIG. 3.26

then switches to a bad pun...

Cadillac came along with a nice drive down the center of the fairway with this animated series. The road sign with the golfer on it (see Figure 3.28 through Figure 3.31) ties their upscale cars to upscale golfers.

FIG. 3.27

...then finishes with their tag line.

FIG. 3.28

The golfer pulls back...

FIG. 3.29

...connects with the ball...

FIG. 3.30

...sends it flying across the billboard for the Seville STS...

FIG. 3.31

...and eventually sinks the ball onto the end of the tag sentence, where it becomes the period.

The final example of animation must be seen to be appreciated. Unfortunately, this ad doesn't exist in its natural state anymore. It lived on the home page of the *USA Today* site (**www.usatoday.com**) (see Figure 3.32).

Fortunately, the ad lives in a preserved state on one of the best Web advertising resources on the Net: Microscope (**www.pscentral.com**).

The Microscope Weekly Web Ad Review

You can see the Honda sport utility vehicle perform at **www.pscentral.com/20397/review1.html**, thanks to the efforts of Steve St. Clair and Rich Paschall. These two well-documented ad men took it upon themselves to provide some applause for what they thought were a few of the best banners each week.

In doing so, they have unwittingly created a historical archive of a turning point in advertising history. This site is well worth a look and well worth a bookmark. A large tip of the hat to Steve and Rich.

In February of 1997, the *USA Today* Travel button shown in the upper-left corner of Figure 3.32 was replaced with a Honda sport utility vehicle (see Figure 3.33). As you watched, the vehicle drove down the page, under the column of text, looking like a mole traveling under your manicured front lawn. At the bottom, it disappeared for a moment, and then popped out in a banner in the lower-right corner of the window (see Figure 3.34 and Figure 3.35).

FIG. 3.32

USA Today had one of the best animated ads ever.

This wasn't just a wowzer of a way to attract your attention (and it was); it also was a Web re-enactment of the Honda television ads where that same vehicle was seen driving through an entire newspaper. The cross-promotional element was ideal. Brilliant. A great example of the technology fitting the message.

Animation is fun, it's trippy, it's silly, and it sure gets attention. In one of those statistical anomalies that happens on the Internet, any technology that's new gets attention. Animated banner? Great! I'll click it to see what else these people have come up with. Oh, it's a site selling laundry detergent?!? Get me outta here! Besides, I'm in search of the next tech legerdemain!

FIG. 3.33
The Honda vehicle started at the top of the *USA Today* page...

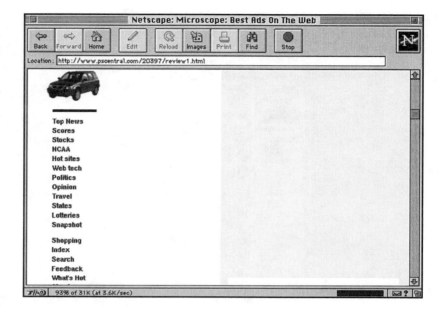

FIG. 3.34
... worked its way under the text...

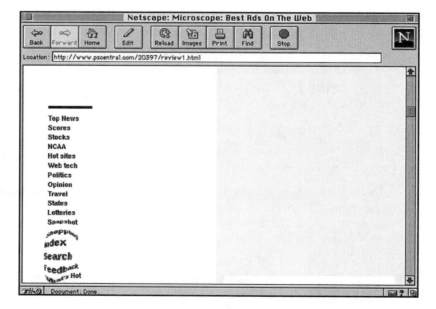

FIG. 3.35

... and popped out at the bottom in a different banner box.

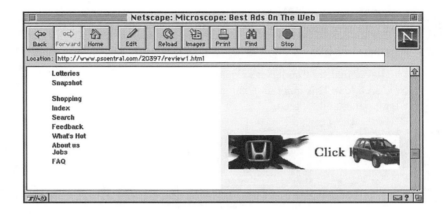

Banners Get Interactive

The next tech toy turned out to be a natural. Once people realized that banners could be more than just HTML, they started getting creative. After all, these are computers you're dealing with here and all you have to do is figure out the right software. Some of that figuring was done for you by people like Macromedia, which made browser plug-ins such as Shockwave (**www.macromedia.com**).

People had been using Shockwave for a little over a year when somebody thought it might be fun to shock a banner.

Wanna Play a Game of Nostalgia?

The first example to hit the screen was a Shockwave animation from Hewlett-Packard that let you play Pong against the computer (see Figure 3.36).

FIG. 3.36

HP memorialized Pong in this banner. The animation and interaction drew attention but didn't stick around for long.

As the puck bounce from side to side, an introductory message scrolled across the top: "Jerry here. I'm the HP engineer who designed this thing. It was supposed to be an ad banner, but, well, let's just say the coffee started to flow and things got a little weird around here. Kind of like when we made the mopier collate. You want to play? You're the one on the right. Go crazy."

Until HP changes its mind, you can still play with this one at **www.hp.com/go/mopier**.

Working Smarter, Not Harder

But Shockwave wasn't necessary once people realized that a banner could be more than a simple graphic or a complex animation file. It could also include some HTML of its own.

The example of CondéNet's Epicurious, in Figure 3.37, added an HTML form that acted as a search tool. This quiet little banner allowed you to enter the name of your favorite culinary ingredient: hit "search."

FIG. 3.37

A little HTML can be a powerful thing, as shown in this banner from Epicurious.

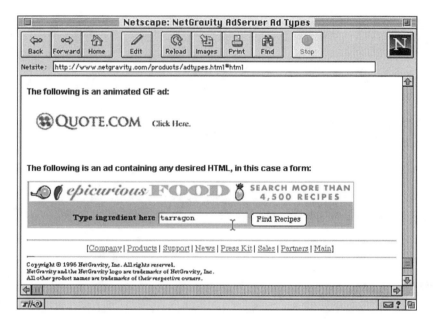

The result was to take you to the Epicurious site where a search had been performed and a very long list of recipes displayed, which included the ingredient of your choice (see Figure 3.38).

Modem Media (**www.modemmedia.com**) has been creating online marketing for more than ten years. One of their vision statements is to "Create 'advertising' so compelling, they'll think it's a service." Jim Davis, Director of Creative and Brand Strategies, was downright impassioned at an Internet World conference where he told the audience to take the very best their Web sites have to offer and "bannerize the experience." The idea is to put your best foot forward and spread it around the Web as far and wide as possible where more and more people can be exposed to what you have to offer.

The team at Netgravity (**www.netgravity.com**) makes banner serving software and helped create some banners for a few clients. They certainly understood the advertising-as-service philosophy when they created this recipe search banner for Epicurious. Besides many other wonderful things found at the Epicurious site, their recipe database is a winner. The search-tool-banner lets as many people as possible know about that database and demonstrates the power of it at the same time. Very effective advertising.

FIG. 3.38
Instant gratification proves that the people at Epicurious understand the power of the Web.

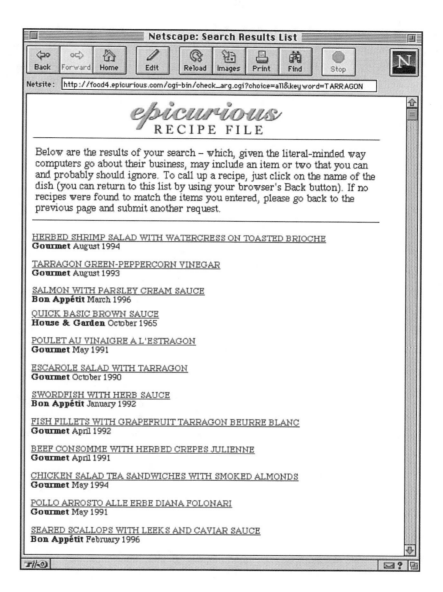

Psychographic Self-Selection

Honda Motor Cars liked the idea of the interactive drop-box and used it to match up their automotive models with the type of people they thought would be attracted to them. In this instance (see Figure 3.39), the multiple choice question can be answered in three ways. When I see curves ahead I... a) say three Hail Marys, b) add my own sound effect, or c) keep going straight.

FIG. 3.39
Honda wants to know
what kind of driver you
are.

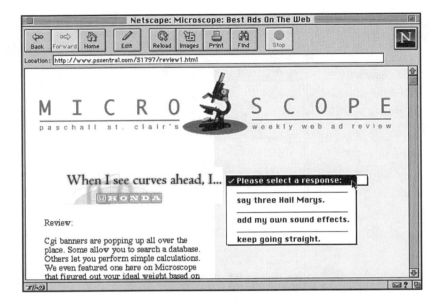

If you decided to say three Hail Marys, you were whisked off to see the 1977 Prelude (**www.honda.com/cars/prelude**). "The Prelude is all-new for 1997. With its new look and unparalleled performance, it's the perfect sports coupe for people who love to drive."

If you say three Hail Marys when you see a curve in the road, maybe you should be whisked off to the Understanding Panic Disorder page (**www.nimh.nih.gov/publicat/upd.htm**) instead. I really missed the connection. But not so Steve and Rich at Microscope. They wrote, "So, if you pick the 'say 3 Hail Mary's,' you'll be presented with info on the Honda Prelude, a car that will handle those tough curves FOR you." Maybe, guys. Maybe.

However, I change my tune if the selection were to "keep going straight." The next page is for that hot little number you saw cruising around the front page of *USA Today*, the off-road CR-V (see Figure 3.40). You may quibble about the execution, but the concept is pure genius; let the customer tell you what kind of driver he or she is.

Banners can talk, banners can move, banners can pigeonhole you into a consumer metric; banners can sing, dance, smile, and play tricks on you. But everyone sat up and took notice when Casio put out a banner that makes the sale.

Banners that Take Orders

If you can fill out forms in a banner, you should be able to take the order, right? Right. But there's a bit more to it that that. Getting a name and an address is one thing, making a financial commitment is another. The financial part is tough enough that this one was created in conjunction with First Virtual (**www.fv.com**), a company providing payment systems for Web transactions.

FIG. 3.40
If you go straight when the road turns, you probably need one of these.

You start with the banner itself, which starts out friendly enough. It quietly sits there and bounces the words "wrist power" at you and lets you know that it is "The TV remote you wear" (see Figure 3.41).

FIG. 3.41
This Java applet/banner gets your attention with high contrasting colors and words in motion.

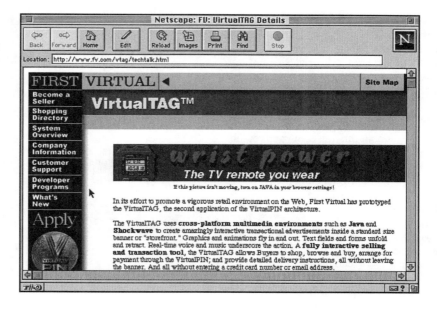

If you sit and watch this banner, it gets impatient and lets you know in no uncertain terms that you are supposed to take action. You are supposed to pass your mouse over the banner to "activate" it (see Figure 3.42).

FIG. 3.42
If you're slow on the uptake, this banner prompts you to take action.

Follow the instructions and the screen changes to announce the offer: buy one, get one free (see Figure 3.43). But that's not the end of the pitch. Casio wants you to know that these are no ordinary watches. Click the Product Info button and you are encouraged to "Point to watches to see features" (see Figure 3.44).

FIG. 3.43
If you respond by positioning your cursor over the watches, the banner makes the offer and gives you three buttons from which to choose.

FIG. 3.44
More interaction is called for, asking you to pass the mouse over the watch of your choice.

Your mouse movements cause the text to change and offer descriptions of the watches. In addition, you are invited to click the text so it will scroll down, revealing more information about the object of your vendible desire.

The Purchase button brings up a screen that asks for your name, address, phone, Virtual PIN number, and includes a Submit button. (see Figure 3.45).

FIG. 3.45
Taking the order is painless and all done without leaving the page on which the ad is displayed.

The About 1VP button is where First Virtual comes in with its 1 Virtual Place program. It handles the transaction from the monetary and security angles and the buyer must sign up with them before the transaction can be completed.

The breakthrough here is that the banner has stopped being a passive image that tries to cajole Web wanderers into clicking. They are not flat display ads that can provide value from a branding perspective, but are mostly trying to derail a surfer's train of thought. Now they are active, interactive, and completely self-contained. There's no reason to whisk somebody away from their focus on Aboriginal studies. They can complete the transaction without getting derailed.

If every banner can take the order, shine the shoes, and wash the windows, will every banner become a shopping center unto itself? Unlikely. It simply means that banner creators have more choices. They have to think a little longer and a little harder about the purpose of a specific banner. Is it for branding? Announcing something new? Making a limited time offer? Proposing a deep discount? Each of these intentions demands a different treatment. It's the same as asking if your print ad should be in the Sunday paper classified section or the back cover of *Time*. It depends.

But there are some major caveats standing in the way of each banner becoming its own little home shopping channel (shudder).

Playing the Technology Card

Using the latest technology as a gimmick to attract attention has several drawbacks. First, it draws people to your site for the wrong reason. Second, the thrill wears off quickly and the interest with it. Third, it ain't new for long. Finally, sometimes it just doesn't work, and that's likely to anger people.

Looking for Love in All the Wrong Places

Let's say you sell a 12×speed, 1MB buffer, 50MS access time, 5000K/second data transfer CD-ROM drive. Okay then, let's say you sell drill presses. Fine.

You go to the trouble and expense of setting up a booth at an international trade show and you want to make sure you have a way to get people into your booth. What do you do? You drag in the popcorn machine! No, wait. Your competitor did that last year and got all the foot traffic. This year, they'll probably do the same. So how do you counter? That's right—the ice cream cart. Wheel in the ice cream cart and people will be lined up to give you their badges to swipe or their business cards to file. A crowded booth! Great!

The only problem is that you end up with a database of people who like ice cream at trade shows. You have no idea if they would ever consider buying a drill press. The same thing happens when you chase after new technology as a way to draw attention to your Web site. The people who are interested in seeing more whiz-bang gizmos will come. But they won't buy drill presses.

If you're trying to figure out a way to use some of the nifty new technology you discovered on the Net last night, you're going after the problem from the wrong side. Yes, you should stay current on the new and the clever, but keep it in the back of your mind. Let it rest there until it's needed. You'll know when the time is right when your value statement, your main product differentiator, and your unique selling proposition suggest the use of a particular tool to illustrate a specific point.

If the positioning is that your product is faster than the rest, it would be ludicrous to use a giant Shockwave file and make people cool their heels while waiting for your message to reach their H7 mind-set. If your product is unique because it has a feature that nobody else has, that can only be deeply understood in motion, then you might get away with it. But if you're using Java banners to sing, dance, and take names, you'll be shooting yourself in the foot.

Is that All There Is?

The neat, new way to stream video or include audio in your banner will attract the curious—once. Some people may go back to the end of the line to get a second helping of ice cream, but once they've seen how your animation works and what happens when it reaches the end, there's no reason to go back. They might tell their friends. Their friends might come take a look. Their friends might be prospective customers. That's more than a stretch.

Given the rate of change on the Web (dog years have been given up, now it's being counted in flea years), new technology gets cold very fast. It's the been-there-done-that syndrome. Besides, have you heard about the next new thing?

The Next Insanely Great Thing

And once the next new thing hits the Web, the spotlight swings and the attention swings with it. But back on your banner, the same old, tired, once-hip technology is starting to look a little tattered around the edges. Dated, faded, and eventually hated.

Doesn't matter what the new techno-trick ad is for, when it hits the Web, it gets noticed if it has the very, very, very latest software driving it. But you sweated bullets for three weeks to create your new ad and built it using last week's techno-toy. Oops, sorry. You missed the window. The moving spotlight lights, and having lit, moves on.

Bleeding Edge Advertising

What if you were the only one on the planet with a fax machine? Either you're writing faxes nobody will see, or you have a long distance bill that's out of this world.

Not everybody has the latest browser version. Not everybody has downloaded Shockwave. Most people have no idea if their browser is Java-ready. And that's just the icing on the cake. There is another reason low-tech might be the high road: the new stuff might break.

I admit that I am not a normal Web surfer. I actively seek out the new and the different because my clients expect it of me. And yes, I also admit that I'm a nerd at heart and just can't wait to see what's going to happen next! As a result, I have learned to be careful.

Writing this book, I am always online to check facts, find examples, and be there when that life-changing e-mail hits my screen. I usually run Microsoft Word and Excel, Netscape, Eudora, and, when creating presentations, PowerPoint. When I'm about to embark upon a research foray into the wilds of the Web (which I do about every ten or fifteen minutes), I make sure I have saved everything in all my open applications. I call it insurance.

It doesn't take much for Netscape to lock up my system. Other applications are kind enough to simply hang and I can force them off my screen, but Netscape likes to take everybody with it when it goes. CTRL+S has become a nervous reaction. If somebody makes a sharp turn in front of me on the road, my thumb and index finger tap out the Save command on the steering wheel. Am I compulsive? Am I obsessed? Is anal-retentive hyphenated?

No, I've just been burned by too many beta versions of this and odd combinations of that. When you've worked for an hour without saving your files and the whole system quits on you, you rely on involuntary file saves.

So when your ad is the cause of me losing work I've already done, I'm more than annoyed. As it is, you only cause me to re-boot and restart all the applications I was running. You think this makes you look good? You think this helps build your brand? Think again.

The fact is, you can't know what applications are all running at the same time on somebody's computer. You can't know how many browser screens they have open and how many Java applets are loading and how many videos are streaming and how many gifs are animating.

If you want to have a place on your site where you show off your technical leadership in making the Web dance to your tune, I applaud you. As long as it is well marked. I will go to the Nokia Multimedia Gallery (**www.nokia.com/gallery**) to see the really cool Shockwave animation Nokia has for their 9000 Communicator, but only after I have saved everything else first.

But what if I am not a nerd at heart? What if I don't want to see this fancy stuff? Then I need only rely on some help from the nearest twelve-year-old who can implement the software I need to never see another Web ad again. Scary, huh?

Banner Blockers

Axel Boldt describes himself as, well, nothing in particular. "I was a graduate student of Mathematics at the University of California in Santa Barbara until June 16. Right now, I'm nothing in particular." But Boldt (**www.math.ucsb.edu/~boldt**) made an impression on the Web on December 11, 1994, by creating the Blacklist of Internet Advertisers. It was an effort to "to curb inappropriate advertising on Usenet newsgroups and via junk e-mail," and the first entry is the historically-appropriate team of Canter and Siegel, the green card lottery spammers.

While Boldt's suggestions on what you can and should do to people who spam you boarder on the larcenous, his philosophy is right on the mark: "Advertising which I'm forced to read is bad, advertising which I actively have to seek is tolerable." Keep in mind that this is in reference to newsgroups and lists. He hadn't attacked the Web. Yet.

Not content to leave the Web out of the picture, Boldt went back to the drawing board and created WebFilter (**www.math.ucsb.edu/~boldt/NoShit/index.html**) (see Figure 3.46). This is a nifty little program that lets you filter out those bits of the Web you don't want to see. It even has a script library for predefined sites. If you don't want to see ads on Yahoo!, Lycos, Hotwired, CNN, Netscape, InfoSeek, Deja News, Nando Times, Playboy, Excite, WebCrawler, Galaxy, or Pathfinder, WebFilter is the answer. If you don't want to see ads on other sites, you can create your own filters.

FIG. 3.46

WebFilter allows you to block ads that appear on specific pages.

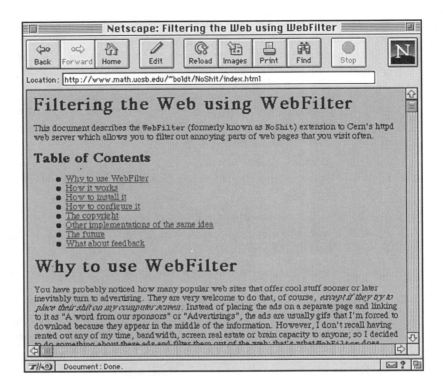

Another one on the horizon is JunkBuster (**www.junkbuster.com**). Do these filters and blockers represent a threat to the value of the Internet as an advertising medium? Significantly less than the VCR spelled the death of television ads.

Some very small percentage of people go out of their way to avoid advertising. The rest of us want to be sure we stay abreast and stay in tune with our peers. All editorial and no commercials make Jack a dull boy.

Banners Aren't the Only Choice

With all of these choices for your banner, what is the most effective approach? Don't answer yet, because Monty Hall has more surprises for you behind door number two. Banners are not the end of the story. They're just the most popular story to date. There are numerous other ways to advertise on the Internet. It takes a whole 'nother chapter... ●

CHAPTER 4

Beyond the Banner

The banner is definitely today's mainstay, but there are other ways to get your name in front of prospective customers. Some are innovative, some are silly, and some are controversial. Some may be more appropriate for your brand than others. You may want to be affiliated with an entire content genre, as one insurance company did with Mutual of Omaha's *Wild Kingdom*. You may want to be associated with things that are fun on the Web and buy sponsorships on game sites. You may decide your product is best represented by a full page, 10 second, animated extravaganza that pops up in the user's face in the middle of an intensely interactive session.

Your choice will be determined by your brand personality, your budget, your willingness to experiment, and your ability to convince upper management that you know what the heck you're doing. That's always the fun part. Just remember to explain it in terms they can readily understand; talk about operations, not operating systems, and branding, not bandwidth.

If there is sufficient gray hair in your collection of vice presidents, you might remind them of the early radio days when they could tune in and hear a well-recognized voice intone, "Jell-O again. This is Jack Benny." ■

Sponsorships

If you can't tell whether your upper management is using Grecian Formula, maybe it would be better to update the example and remind them of the days of when television was young. In 1945, Lever Brothers took the plunge and paid for sole sponsorship of four half-hour shows on CBS. The Bulova Watch Company, Pan American World Airways, Firestone Tire & Rubber, and Gillette Safety Razor were brave enough to give it a try.

A year later, Gillette pioneered the sponsored sporting event: a heavyweight boxing match watched by 150,000 people on 5,000 televisions. That's right, the medium was new enough that, on average, there were 30 people watching each set. Gillette liked the results so much they kept at it and even sponsored the first national live telecast of a World Series game in 1951.

In those early days, the names of the shows and the sponsors were forever linked in the minds of millions of Americans. The Ed Sullivan Show was sponsored by Lincoln-Mercury. George Burns and Gracie Allen were sponsored by B.F. Goodrich. Vendors started to get shows named after them. The Texaco Star Theatre starred Milton Berle (see Figure 4.1), and The Hallmark Hall of Fame is still going strong.

FIG. 4.1

Milton Berle does RuPaul, circa 1947 (**www.fiftiesweb.com/ variety.htm**).

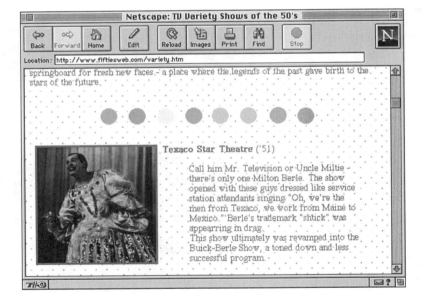

Since then, the practice has been codified. Now you buy a 30-second slot on the show of your choice, budget permitting. But on the Web, there are so many sites springing up on a daily basis that there is still an opportunity to attach your company's name to a content site on a more permanent basis.

Sponsor Your Own Web Site

If your family has ever lived in Illinois, you could look it up. The Sources of Genealogical Information in Illinois Web site (**www.everton.com/usa/il.htm**) (see Figure 4.2) is a wealth of information on tracing your family tree back through the forests of time.

FIG. 4.2

Everton's Genealogical Helper sponsors itself.

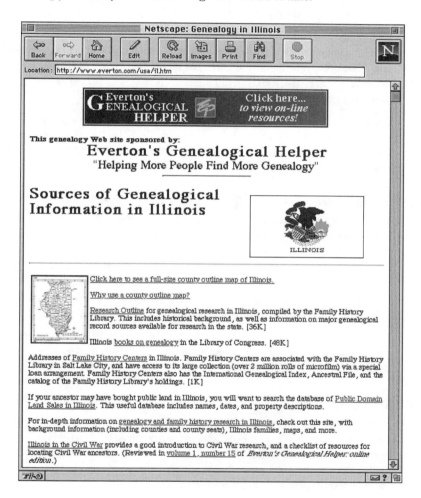

You'll find:

A full-size county outline map of Illinois

Research Outline for genealogical research in Illinois

A list of books on Illinois genealogy in the Library of Congress

Addresses of Family History Centers in Illinois

A database of Public Domain Land Sales in Illinois

And all of it (even though it's mostly links to other sites) is sponsored by *Everton's Genealogical Helper* magazine. They want you to know it was their hard work that brought these links into your den. They want you to know they care. They want to sell you a subscription to their magazine.

Much has been written (and some of it by "yours truly") on how to go about designing a Web site. That needn't be rehashed here, just go pick up a copy of *World Wide Web Marketing* (John Wiley & Sons, 1995). What should be noted is that your very own site has real estate on it that's just grand for your own message.

Let visitors know about your other offerings. Aren't they more qualified than those waltzing through Yahoo! on their way to Aboriginal studies? But if the most common goal in Web advertising is to bring people to your site, then perhaps it were best you sponsored somebody else's pages.

Sponsorship Does Not Equal Banners

Here's why The Sources of Genealogical Information in Illinois Web site is a good sponsorship example; not only does it sport a clickthrough banner, it also has the words, "This genealogy Web site sponsored by: Everton's Genealogical Helper 'Helping More People Find More Genealogy,'" permanently emblazoned on it. This gives it that air of partnership and commitment (ownership) that doesn't come through with a temporary banner. The banner says "Brought to you *this time* by..." As soon as you hit Reload, the relationship between the site and the sponsor is history. Two ships that passed in the night.

If you want to give the impression of being more committed than the chicken in the ham and egg breakfast, consider sponsoring an entire site, rather than just flying a banner now and again.

Brought to You By

Serious, committed sponsorship is most often done the way Everton's did it. The Getty Education Institute for the Arts sponsors the ArtsEdNet Web site, (**http://www.artsednet.getty.edu**). In other words, they invented, created, and run it. General Mills caters to the younger crowd in a more irreverent manner with You Rule School (**www.youruleschool.com**) (see Figure 4.3).

This one features interactive games, such as find all the cereal game pieces and store them in your locker. You can win prizes and hang out with your cereal friends. But other sites are created by some and truly sponsored by others. Patrons, rather than site builders, open their coffers so that they may bask in the branded splendor of the site's achievements.

FIG. 4.3

General Mills decided they wanted to be in the Web entertainment business to promote their brand.

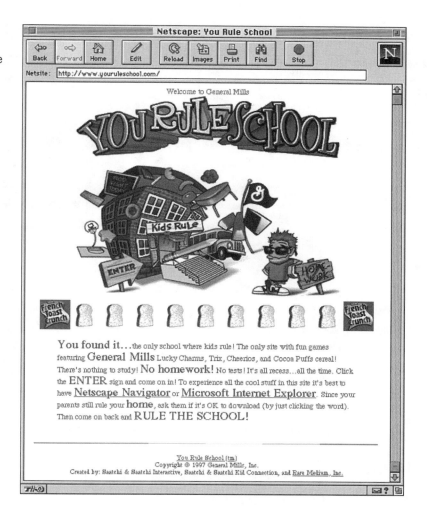

American Express Owns This Space   One telling example is Playbill Online (**http://piano.symgrp.com/playbill**) (see Figure 4.4). This is the site to go to for theater listings on Broadway, off Broadway, around the country, and around the world. This site has many advertisers, but is brought to you by American Express.

The Lincoln Mark VIII went so far as to tie in their banner with the theme of the site; their new car is enjoying a premier on the Playbill site. But American Express owns the whole space.

This "presented by" positioning clearly sets American Express a cut above the car hucksters. American Express went all out. They are a patron of the arts. Heck, they'll even sign you up online so you can buy those tickets. Isn't that civic-minded of them?

FIG. 4.4
Lincoln may have a nice ad, but the site is sponsored by American Express.

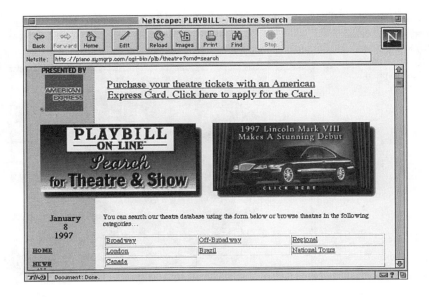

Toyota Presents *The Tonight Show*   Already spending a good deal of money on television ads on Steve Allen's/Johnny Carson's/Jay Leno's late night program, Toyota decided to go for the whole ball of wax on the Web. The Tonight Show Web site (**www.nbc.com/tonightshow**) is a Toyota production (see Figure 4.5).

The words "Toyota Presents..." appear all over this site. There is also Jay Leno-specific content on the Toyota site in Leno's Garage. The television commercials point to the site, the site points to the TV show, and everything points to **www.toyota.com**. *Now* we're talking multimedia.

Featured Sponsor

Rather than claiming proprietary ownership of a specific site, a vendor can become an integrated part of the site by *exclusive inclusion*. They include your product or service and leave your competitors out in the cold. Almost all magazines have some kind of product review pages and they are well aware of the need to keep the editorial away from the advertising. This can get a little fuzzy on the Web, but for the most part, the exclusive inclusion model is seen on sites set up for obviously commercial purposes.

Bruce Levitt, president of PLC Interactive runs a Christmas site called Claus.Com (**www.claus.com**), which was sponsored in 1996 by Service Merchandise (see Figure 4.6).

FIG. 4.5
Toyota presents
Jay Leno.

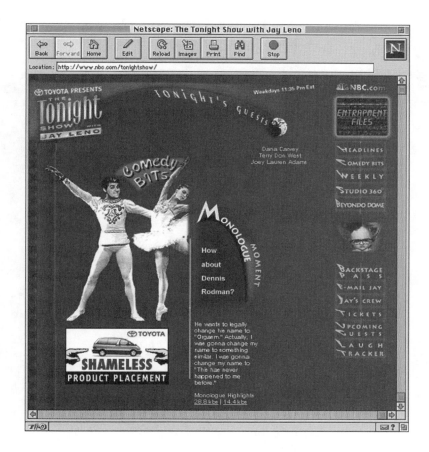

The relationship between site and sponsor was at arms' length. PLC did the site, Service Merchandise paid some money and got their name on the site as the sponsor. They also got to stick their name on the elves' Toy Shop and put their toys inside.

The Library of Funology turned into the Service Merchandise Library of Funology which, within a click or two, turns out to be a catalog of toys for sale. A very small button offers to show the price, but the big button offers to add any special toy desire to your Christmas list. The list can either be printed out in order to show Mom and Dad, or it can be e-mailed directly to Santa.

This showcase of products alongside a variety of fun and activities is an integrated part of the site. It is not a link to the vendor's Web, although there are those clickable Service Merchandise logos scattered around. It is not a passive "brought to you by" statement. It's not quite product placement (which is covered later). It's not a statement of ownership and it's not a retail store. It's a place where branding occurs.

FIG. 4.6
Claus.Com is a Christmas fun site that goes looking for sponsors. In 1996, that was Service Merchandise.

On the flip side of that coin is the opposite of branding. You might want to promote your product by building an entire Web site that never mentions your company or your product. At least, that's what the makers of Lucky Strike people wanted.

LSMFT—Lucky Strike Means Furtive Technique

Brown & Williamson Tobacco Corporation created a directory of music and nightclubs in San Francisco called Circuit Breaker (**www.circuitbreak.com**) (see Figure 4.7). Besides nightclub listings, there are online games, articles to read, and advice on where to get dance lessons. Whenever there's an opportunity to win something, the visitor is asked for the usual: name, address, and e-mail. They are also asked if they are over 21 years old. That's something usually reserved for XXX-rated sites. Then the topper: Do you smoke? That one raised a few eyebrows.

FIG. 4.7
Brown & Williamson
started out hiding in
the back room at
Circuit Breaker.

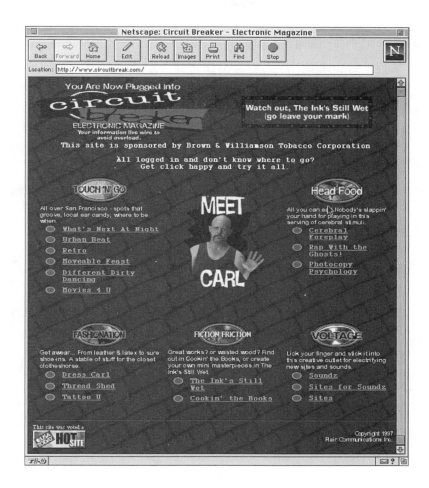

At first, there was no mention of the sponsor, then the press got ahold of it. *Advertising Age* magazine took a very dim view of what they termed "Stealth Advertising." In February, 1997, *Ad Age* quoted Jeff Chester, executive director of the Center for Media Education as saying, "It's incredibly deceptive. It demonstrates how tobacco companies are exploiting the Web as a marketing tool in a youth-oriented site. They need to clearly identify that Brown & Williamson is sponsoring the site." He then suggested that the Center for Media Education would file a complaint with the Federal Trade Commission.

Within days, the words, "This site is sponsored by Brown & Williamson Tobacco Corporation," were plastered all over the site.

Sponsor an Event

Just a brief look at Yahoo!'s Top:Recreation:Sports:Golf:Tournaments (**http://www. yahoo.com/Recreation/Sports/Golf/Tournaments/**) shows a whole host of recognizable company names with tournaments of their own:

> Air France
>
> AMF
>
> Bell Atlantic
>
> BellSouth
>
> Cadillac
>
> Canon
>
> Chrysler
>
> Corning

And that's only through the Cs. These people don't need their own Web sites. There are plenty of other enthusiasts who will happily display the company colors. But if you want to "go for the gold" on the Web, you'd better have the gold to do it.

The Mother of all Sporting Events   Before a religious war breaks out between Superbowl zealots and World Series fanatics, the mother of all sporting events being referred to is the Olympics. It's obvious that the world of commerce feels the Olympics are good marketing. One need only look at Yahoo!'s Top:Recreation:Sports:International Games:Olympics:1996 Summer Games-Atlanta:Official Sponsors to discover sixteen "official" sites.

With so many vying for the lead role, it's no surprise that some vendors are taking defensive action. Nike has decided to create its own version of this worldwide spectacle with the Nike World Masters Games (**www.worldmasters.org**) (see Figure 4.8).

For those who want to avoid inventing a new set of global games, perhaps it's time to venture over to the Salt Lake City, 2002—official site of the Salt Lake Olympic Organizing Committee (**www.SLC2002.org**) and see if there are any sponsorships still available.

Own a Piece of the Internet

With its eight million-plus subscribers, America Online represents the largest aggregation of dial-up surfers. When AOL went from per-hour pricing to per-month pricing, they shook any confidence their customers had in them. The flat-fee pricing caused a huge number of sign ups and people staying online a lot longer. The result was the neverending busy signal.

With lots of bucks spent on upgraded equipment, AOL has come out the other side of this debacle smarter, stronger, and richer. And one of the places they got a good chunk of change from was Tel-Save Holdings.

Tel-Save is a long distance telephone reseller. For only $57 million dollars down, and an additional $43 million over two years, Tele-Save bought exclusive advertising rights on the AOL service.

FIG. 4.8
When faced with too much competition, Nike started its own global competitive sports site.

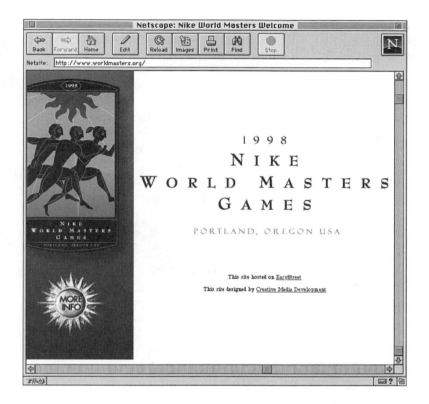

AT&T, MCI , and Sprint will just have to wait until the year 2000 to try their luck buying space. That's a strong position for Tele-Save, but it's not the only position they have. Given a guaranteed stash of cash, there had to be some motivation for AOL to show the ads. The answer was revenue sharing. Depending on the volume of business Tele-Save does through AOL, the online access company will receive 50 to 70 percent of the gross profits. They threw in 12 million Tele-Save warrants as well. That was back when it was trading near $13.

Why so much money? They bought a motivated partner with the largest customer base and no fear of competition for three years. One can only hope their creative talent is up to the challenge and can bring home the bacon.

If you're going to play with the big boys, you have to think big. Really big.

Own a Market Segment

Toshiba decided to create the Office Manager site (**www.officemanager.com**) (see Figure 4.9), which describes itself as being a "virtual office [which] offers links to a variety of useful information and links you might need through the course of your business day. There are four rooms in this office building: the Copy Room, the Mail Room, the Break Room, and Human Resources & Employee Services."

FIG. 4.9

Toshiba sponsors a site with a very tight focus.

On the Office Manager site you can buy gifts and flowers, make travel plans, study health issues, and find a new job, a parenting magazine, the Better Business Bureau, newsletters, recipes, coffee houses, gossip, shipping information, and office supplies. Most are pointers to outside services or vendors. Every page is "Sponsored By Toshiba."

Oh, was it mentioned that there's a whole bunch of information on copiers, fax machines, telephones, and computers? All kinds of information about all kinds of equipment—from Toshiba, of course. Creating a site that will be *the* place office managers go when they're looking for something on the Internet is a daunting task. The success of this site depends on whether Toshiba wants to be in the publishing business as well as the office gear biz. Still, half a million hits a month in its first three months isn't bad. But if you want more, you have to think bigger.

Own a Whole Category

If you're not content to try to be the master of a certain job title, you might take on something larger, like sports. How do you compete against CBS (**cbs.sportsline.com**), CNN (**www.cnn.com/SPORTS**), ESPNet Sportszone (**espnet.sportszone.com**), and *Sports Illustrated* (**www.pathfinder/si**)? If you're Nike, you just do it.

Nike is looking into their crystal basketball and seeing the potential to become a sports entertainment network. A company that has created entire shopping malls dedicated to their shoes (Niketown stores), and has even discussed starting up their own cable channel is now directing its gaze at the Web. They are negotiating rights for sporting event Webcasts (heavy on the infotainment side) willing to experiment and carrying a wallet big enough to just do it if all the numbers seem to add up.

If your budget isn't stratospheric and you get nosebleeds playing at those altitudes, or if you're just the type who is more interested in direct advertising that global domination, there are other non-banner ways to get your name out there.

Games that Point to You

One of the fun things about the Internet is that it can be, well, fun. You can send mail, you can download stuff, you can chat with your friends. And you can play games. Turns out, men 18-34 years of age like playing games. On average, a game player spends a half an hour at a gaming Web site. The hard core players spend several hours at their entertainment of choice. Simple games and sophisticated games abound. Some are product-specific and some are open to all who want to pay for the exposure.

H&R Block Wants to Pay Your Taxes

Play H&R Block's "We'll Pay Your Taxes" Game. If you win, H&R Block will pay your taxes—up to $20,000! All you have to do is answer the three fun trivia questions we e-mail you each week. Every right answer gets you an entry into the sweepstakes, which gets you closer to winning the big prize (plus great weekly prizes).

That's what it said at the Yoyodyne site (**www.yoyo.com/hrblock**) (see Figure 4.10). Yoyo.com is where those folks who like to play e-mail games hang out. In this case, the premise, the prize, and the questions all revolve around tax time.

FIG. 4.10

H&R Block will do more than help you with your taxes, they'll pay them for you! If you win.

The draw is obvious but the tie-in to the H&R Block site is what makes this approach work. Worried about your taxes? Hoping you won't have to pay? What a great way to get just the right demographic to come and visit.

Concerned that a silly game is not in keeping with the corporate image, H&R Block did not put an obvious link on their site to Yoyodyne. But the link does a wonderful job of finding self-selecting prospects.

Buy a Button from Riddler

One of the first serious gamesters on the Web was Riddler (**www.riddler.com**) (see Figure 4.11). This site makes it clear from the outset that however fun it may be, it's a commercial endeavor. The idea was strong enough that their original sponsors were Apple Computer, Microsoft, NBC, Snapple, and Toyota.

Upon sign-up, after learning where you live so it can send you your many soon-to-be-won prizes, Riddler offers a pre-checked check box. The statement next to it reads, "Yes. Please rush me TWO no-risk trial issues of *Newsweek*, and reserve my subscription. If I like what I see, I'll continue as a subscriber and receive 51 more issues of *Newsweek* for the low introductory rate of..." Yes, this is a site of commerce.

Riddler also collects some psychographics in order to provide its sponsors with the most valuable information about the game players possible. Under the guise of determining what prizes should be awarded should you win, Riddler asks such multiple choice gems as:

1. What are your favorite types of music?
2. What is your highest level of education?
3. What type(s) of magazines are you into?
4. So what do you do?
5. Any plans for a vacation? Where would you go if you could?
6. How old are your kids?
7. What sports do you like to watch or play?
8. Where do you live? (rent/buy/etc.)
9. What type(s) of books do you read?
10. When dining in a restaurant which of the following do you have with your meal? (wine/soda pop/water)

The Bloodhound game is an interesting combination of puzzles and hide-and-seek (see Figure 4.12). According to the rules of one of Riddler's games, "Bloodhound presents players with clues to the location of a Web site on which CAPS have been hidden." Caps are tokens collected during play that are later exchanges for prizes, like the tickets spewed from Skeeball machines on the midway.

FIG. 4.11
Riddler makes money
playing games.

FIG. 4.12

Riddler's Bloodhound makes visiting your site a necessity.

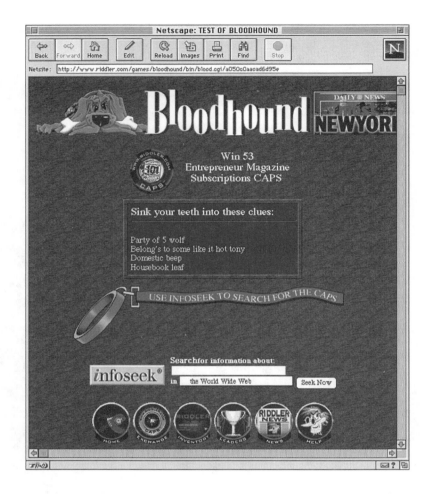

"Once players have solved the clues and identified the Keyword, they must enter it into the Infoseek search engine and 'sniff out' the relevant Web site. Arriving at the correct Web site and clicking on the Prize CAPS will transfer the CAPS to a player's inventory. The Bloodhound game is not a competition; each player who finds the Web site will discover the CAPS and be able to claim them."

This is the most sure-fire way to get people to wander around your Web site. It's a treasure hunt and you get to hide the treasure. This is sure to raise your Web site traffic, but will it bring you prospective buyers? Only if you sell games.

What should your keyword be? How can you tie your unique selling proposition into this game? How do you pick a keyword without sending people scurrying to your competitors' sites? Riddler's John Porterfield says, "In the past, we've never let an advertiser have any say in the creation of Riddler's content. We have always kept it as 'church & state.' Though, that does not mean we are not open for ideas or opportunities. Conversely, you do have latitude on where you decide to place Riddler's CAPS on your site."

So go ahead and hide the CAPS. Bury them deep in your 1992 annual report. Put them in the copyright boilerplate. Then watch your Web traffic climb. If, on the other hand, you're concerned that game players might not figure out the keyword (it ain't child's play), or are simply not the kind of people you want wandering your site, Riddler has more direct methods of delivering your offer.

Riddler makes good use of a different kind of promotion—the interstitial ad.

Contentus Interruptis

I'm still looking for the bloke who coined the term *interstitial advertising*. If you're out there, you know who you are. It's time to come out with your hands up. Do it soon and we'll settle for the removal of some of your teeth.

Your phrase is accurate enough, but would have been far kinder on those of us in the industry if you could have called them interval ads, or pop-ups, or pause pages. Arthur would have done just fine. No matter what the name is, the result is the same; a surfer wants to read something and gets an ad instead.

The idea is borrowed straight from television and has found a home on many Web sites. You want to go to a certain site, you have to wade through an ad page first. You're in the middle of an article or a story, we pause for a word from our sponsor. Playing a game? There's a commercial interrupting the flow.

We Pause for a Word

Riddler uses the interstitial ad form to good advantage. You want to play a quick game? Pick your poison, read the instructions on how to play, and then take a brief detour to the sponsor page (see Figure 4.13).

Riddler leaves the door open. This is not merely a word from the sponsor, but an invitation and a link to *Forbes*' supplements *FYI* and *ASAP*. Are they sad to see people leave? Why, no. That's the whole point. Riddler wasn't put on the Web to give out cool prizes to people with nothing better to do than play online games all day. It's a tool designed to draw eyeballs to patron pages. The more times people click advertiser's links, the more successful the site is. Translation: the more money they can charge for the privilege of advertising there.

The prize for the game, the interstitial ad, and the salutation at the end of the game are all for the sponsor of that round of that game. Sure, it's pretty easy to breeze through one of these pages and hit the button at the bottom. But in those seconds, thyne eyes have seen the story through the scrolling, not ignored. It's embedded in the brain stem, where all messages are stored. It is loose in the subconscious until you reach the grocery store. Their brand is marching on.

FIG. 4.13

Riddler sticks a message in your face on your way to play.

But what if you can convince the player that they want to read the ad? What if you can provide an immediate benefit and deliver immediate value?

A Tall Tale

I like reading stories. I always have. Only recently have I come across books with ads in the middle. One I'm reading at the moment has an ad that's a scratcher game. I could already be a winner! Ken Jenks thought putting ads in the middle of stories on the Web was a good idea, but he came up with a couple of interesting twists.

Jenks had three good thoughts at the same time when he set up Mind's Eye Fiction: 1) Provide a place where fiction could be spread far and wide via the Internet in a way that offers the author some recompense; 2) give the reader a choice of seeing the ad or not, and; 3) if they choose the ad, force the reader to interact with it in order to continue. Jenks's site can be found at **www.tale.com**. To satisfy your curiosity for now, take a look at Figure 4.14.

FIG. 4.14

Mind's Eye Fiction brought sponsored stories and interstitial ads to the Web.

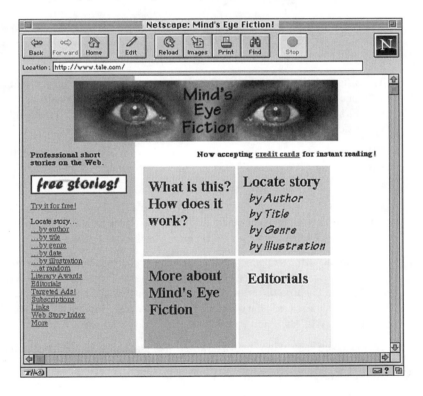

Once the reader is well ensconced in a ripping story, it's time to pay the piper. Jenks gives them an intriguing choice of payments. In the case of the demonstration, one can use a First Virtual account and pay 50 cents, use a Mind's Eye Fiction subscription account and pay only 18 cents, or pay attention (see Figure 4.15).

FIG. 4.15

The reader decides how to pay for the pleasure of finding out how it all ends.

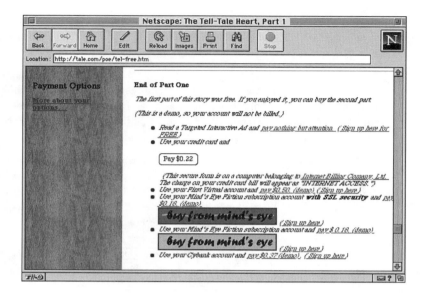

The difference in price between the two payment methods is very straightforward. A First Virtual transaction requires a bit of overhead. That means the merchant has to split the take with First Virtual. The Mind's Eye Fiction account is pre-paid. But the interesting part is when you instead choose to read an ad.

"Oh great!" you say. "No contest!" you say. "I'll just click to the ad, click the Next button, and finish the story. The advertiser will think I saw their ad and I won't have to pay a thing!" Think again.

Jenks wants to be sure you pay attention. Toward that end, he stops and makes you think twice. In order to get to the rest of the story, you have to type in the name of the product, company, or some salient point about the offer (see Figure 4.16).

What should surprise nobody is the incredible retention that comes with having to type in the name of the sponsor. "In fact," says Jenks, "If the customer doesn't answer the questions correctly, I don't charge the advertiser anything, since that customer must not have received the advertiser's message. That's what the advertiser is paying me for: to deliver a message to the customers. Why should the advertiser pay if I don't deliver?"

This is a true case of interactivity, rather than just animation. But animation gets even more interesting when it is combined with audio. Sounds almost like TV, right? Well, that's what the folks who produce You Don't Know Jack had in mind.

FIG. 4.16

You really gotta read these ads, or you can't play through.

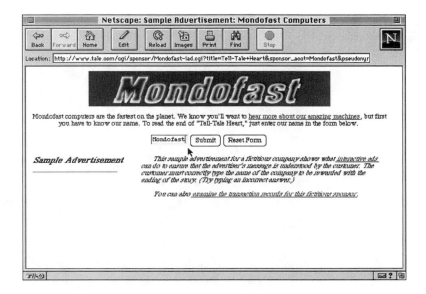

You Don't Know Jack

You Don't Know Jack (YDKJ), the CD-ROM game from Berkeley Systems, is an irreverent, in-your-face trivia game that emulates television game shows. The game takes over your desktop, the announcer is good-natured but almost rude, and the questions can be tough. In other words, this game is actually fun. Berkeley wasn't satisfied to leave it on CD and decided it needed to be on the Web (**www.bezerk.com**) (see Figure 4.17).

The Web version of the game takes over your computer the same way the CD-ROM does. It controls the whole screen, is very oriented toward the audio, and sucks you in immediately.

To accomplish this on the Web, YDKJ requires downloading the game controller software. After that, the game is fast-paced and there are no pauses while waiting for downloads, or freezes while the machine tries to catch up with the game. It's slick. Then there are the ads.

After a round of questions, the announcer lets you know that it's break time. Literally, "We'll be back after a word from our sponsors." The ads that come up are fully animated, fully musical and fully in your face. Like the game, the ads take over the whole screen (see Figure 4.18).

Maybe it's the fast pace, maybe it's the impertinence, and maybe it's the fact that when you're playing this game, you're really playing. Whatever the reason, these ads are not in the least bit intrusive. In fact, it's almost a relief to sit back for a moment and rest instead of sitting on the edge of your chair, waiting for the next question to knock you for a loop.

The Retention Factor   Steve Drace is now Vice President of Ad Sales at Berkeley, after years of selling magazine ad space at such high-tech publishers as IDG, Ziff, and CMP. He spends his days explaining how advertising to 100,000 people a week on YDKJ may not be as exciting as to the millions who watch *Seinfeld*, but people really remember the ads.

FIG. 4.17
You Don't Know Jack is a fun CD-ROM trivia game that has found a new home on the Web.

FIG. 4.18
This full-screen ad comes complete with music and sound from the You Don't Know Jack game.

Focus groups, follow-up questionnaires, and even a casual conversation in an elevator prove that people are truly paying attention. "People are in a flow state when they play Jack," says Drace. *Flow* is a psychological term used to describe intense concentration. In a flow state, a person can learn faster and retain the information much longer.

"I was in New York with a colleague wearing a YDKJ hat in a hotel elevator. This guy in his twenties saw the hat and said 'Awesome game. How'd you get the hat?' When we explained that we sold the ads, he knew just what we were talking about and named three of our sponsors right off the bat. That's retention."

Building a YDKJ Ad   The ads themselves are a bit of a burden. You don't just plop your favorite magazine ad on the screen; it's more interactive than that. You don't just shove your television ad down a 28.8K modem line; it would take forever.

The ads are made using Macromedia Director. That allows for animation, audio, and a great deal of compression to get the content down the wire. That's the most impressive thing about the technical design of this game—it's smooth. The ads are whipping into your computer in the pauses you take while trying to figure out the next question. When it's commercial time, the ads are all in place and ready to run. No waiting.

Berkeley Systems has been pretty careful about the separation of church and state. There won't be any questions like, "Which is better, Coke or Pepsi?" or "The 'swoosh' is the trademark of which major shoe maker?"

In fact, the people behind YDKJ turn down ads to maintain the brand of the game. Now that's putting the shoe on the other foot. According to Drace, "People don't seem to mind the ads in this game. One of the reasons is that they are short. Each commercial break is 30 seconds with three 10-second ads in each. There are 11 slots for ads in a 21-question game. But the ads are lively! If we start showing boring ads, people will stop playing."

Who should advertise on this game site? It's probably not the best place to push mutual funds or insurance. YDKJ is a party game. It's something people do when they get together and have a good time. Liquor companies are very interested in this audience.

If you want your ad to include a link, look elsewhere. You might get as far as telling people to click your banner at the end of the game. It's okay to link to your site there, but Berkeley Systems is doing whatever it can to preserve the personality of its games.

Credit Where Credit Is Due   At the end of the game, you regain control over your computer and the YDKJ Web site sends you the "credits" page. Just in case you were out of the room for 30 seconds at a time during breaks, you get another reminder of who sponsored your play time (see Figure 4.19). All in all, a very good setting for an advertiser interested in a young, hip, and active audience.

FIG. 4.19
The credits page offers a last look at the game sponsors.

Microsoft Is Never Far Behind   MSNBC is going to be bringing this same kind of ad to its Web site. The difference? The MSNBC site (**www.msnbc.com**) is a place for news. People go there for information. Their content has to be pretty good to get people to wait through 30 seconds of ads while deciding if they want to read the next article.

Microsoft and NBC have not started this practice yet—it's on the drawing board. But a good guess is that between the time this book is written and the time you read it, it will have been tested and trashed. The Internet is a two-way street where unhappy people are more than willing to throw open their Windows and shout out, "I'm mad as hell, and I'm not going to take it anymore!"

Ads as Games

Levi Strauss has been a major marketing master for many years. It's one of those rare cases where marketing really does drive the company. How many firms do you know that would change their telephone prefix to match a lead product name? Calling Levi Strauss is now an invocation of their famous jeans: 415-501-6000. This firm clearly understands the power of marketing, branding, and paying attention to the details.

Willing to try many different forms of marketing, Levi's stretched the envelope yet again. Instead of its banners pointing to its Web site, the jeans progenitor pointed to a branded game. Designed with a European and South African televised ad in mind, this game featured a mermaid and a drowning, jeans-clad sailor. Players were invited to save the sailor using the mouse to direct the mermaid (see Figure 4.20).

FIG. 4.20

Levi Strauss matched one television ad with a Web-based game.

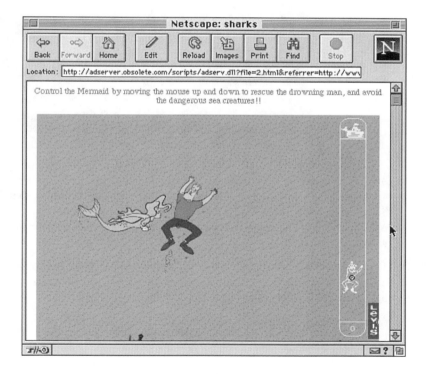

At the end of the game, users are sent back to the page they came from, never reaching **www.levi.com** at all. Instead, they received the message shown in Figure 4.21.

FIG. 4.21
No clickthroughs here.
Just play the game and
go on about your
business.

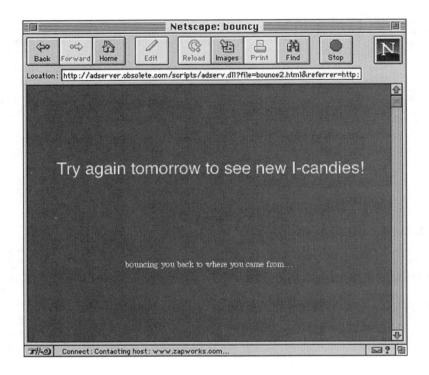

Another Levi banner sent clickers a 20-second Shockwave file that was not much more than an image ad. When it was over, the clicker was back at the original site. No links. Jay Thomas, Senior Manager for New Media at Levi Strauss, said the company used *cookies* (see Appendix A, "Glossary") to determine that some 30 percent of the clickers ultimately made it to **www.levi.com** on their own.

The goal was to get the public to interact with the brand. They weren't trying to make a sale or collect demographic information. They wanted to make an impression that lasted longer than a half a minute. Goal met. Case closed.

Another company with proven marketing talent, skill, and experience needed even less to satisfy their goals. They merely wanted the public to be exposed to a familiar background pattern.

Background Branding

When Disney released the movie *101 Dalmatians*, it launched a Disney-sized ad campaign. No surprise. The company included the Web in its plans and decided to spread the Dalmatian doggie-spots around.

Excite and Yahoo! got cash to use the Dalmatian-spot background on their sites. Some sites were invited to do it in exchange for posters, T-shirts, and good will. The rest of the world was asked to do it for free.

Mercedes may have an easier time convincing people to plaster its logo across the back of its pages than Honda, but an event such as a movie opening has a much higher appeal. Support *101 Dalmatians*? Sure. Just for a few weeks? No problem. With a visual that is non-company specific? Even better.

Think Radio

If Disney wanted to promote its efforts using only the movie theme song, they could have bought "time" at AudioNet (**www.audionet.com**). AudioNet is an on-demand broadcaster, with over 150 radio and television stations on its play list. It has play-by-play of college and professional sports (including a couple of Superbowls and the 1996 World Series), live concerts, and full-length CDs.

Their signal is based on RealAudio (**www.realaudio.com**) and comes to you in two parts. There's a brief audio clip promoting other AudioNet shows—or your message—just before the program you want to hear. Want to sponsor Stanley Cup Coverage? The Johns Hopkins AIDS Conference? Car Talk? The Scabs In Concert? So far they don't carry the old *Jack Benny Show*, so the people at Kraft (**http://kraftfoods.com/jell-o100**) will have to find another way to push Jell-O.

Product Placement

If you saw *Star Trek IV: The Voyage Home*, you were entertained by Scottie trying to talk to an Apple Computer. If you saw *Mission Impossible*, you watched Tom Cruise make mincemeat of the Internet on an Apple PowerBook. It wasn't that these were the script-writers' dream machines or filmmakers' favorites. It was that goods, services, and money changed hands.

When the product placement aficionados turned their attention to the Web, they came up with a cross-media approach that got a good deal of attention.

Multimedia

What happens when you start with one of the country's top-rated television shows, add the world's best known brand name, sprinkle in healthy dollops of broadcast, print, and Web promotion? You get a "Which Friend Will Drink The Coke?" promotion that tops the charts for attention, retention, and public relations mention.

Like all really good ideas, it was simple. Execution was tricky, but the results were worth it. Print, television, an under-the-cap packaging sweepstakes, on-campus promotions, and a Web site that was only up for six weeks all blended together to create some excitement about the show, *Friends*.

Created by CircumStance Design (**www.circumstance.com**) (see Figure 4.22), the "Who's Gonna Drink The Diet Coke?" Web site allowed fans to

Play against *Friends* fans worldwide for a trip to LA for a *Friends* cast party.

Crack the time-locked vault to download screensavers and exclusive photos.

Conduct online interviews with key behind-the-scenes *Friends* staff.

FIG. 4.22
Diet Coke and
Friends, courtesy
of CircumStance
Design.

Sony Station

Sony was happy with their Sony Online! site (**www.sony.com/online.html**). It has information about Sony music, Sony electronics, Sony movies, Sony television, Sony games, Sony theatres, and they sell a bunch of Sony "entertainment-related wearables and collectibles from Sony Signatures."

But it wasn't enough. They wanted to generate income. Hence, The Station (**www.station.sony.com**) (see Figure 4.23).

FIG. 4.23
The Station is the stop on the Information Superhighway that Sony expects to rake in the dough.

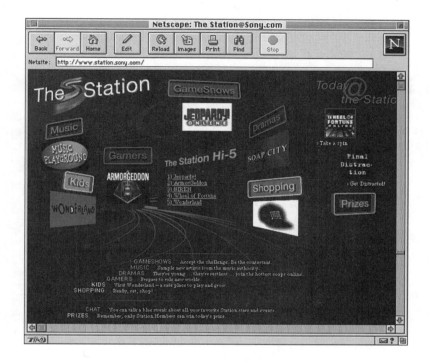

NEW YORK, March 10, 1997—Marking the most successful upfront Internet advertising launch with more than $1 million so far in 1997 revenue already booked Sony Online Ventures Inc. today announced that eight of the country's most renowned brand names, including Sears, Roebuck and Co., Pontiac/General Motors, American Airlines, Kellogg, Colgate, U.S. Robotics, Columbia House and Microsoft have signed on with The **Station@sony.com** as advertisers. They join Visa U.S.A., which is The Station's marketing partner.

Sony is starting with some all-American favorites like *Jeopardy!*, *Wheel of Fortune*, *Days of Our Lives*, and *The Young and The Restless*. Then they're mixing in some new stuff like the Siren music area, the Battleground multiplayer gaming environment from the PlayStation side of the house.

Sony isn't selling banner slots here. Sony is being flexible. They're looking to let other companies brand areas, activities, and games. "We're working with the advertiser to offer meaningful marketing," says Scott Schiller, Vice President of Ad Sales & Marketing at Sony. "When we first sat down with Sears, the natural connection was our electronics lines. But after some discussion, we discovered the KidVantage program was important to them and so we created an environment, a game, that fit their goals."

Sears is sponsoring a game called What's The Weather (see Figure 4.24). It's directed at kids and their parents, to help children learn what Sears clothes to wear, depending on the climate. Sears is using it as another chance to sign youngsters up in their KidVantage program. This is where Sears will replace your child's worn out clothing and shoes—in the same size. Great for big families with lots of hand-me-downs. And there's a frequent-shopper program as well. You get a 15 percent discount coupon for every $100 in kids' purchases.

FIG. 4.24
Sears is playing the "contextual" Web advertising game.

"The Internet is a powerful way to communicate directly with customers," according to John H. Costello, Senior Executive Vice President of Marketing at Sears. "The Station@sony.com provides a creative new venue for Sears to reach young families and engage them in fun and interactive games. Our first collaboration, What's the Weather, combines the power of the Internet with Sony's imaginative technology, producing a game that is informative and entertaining."

Schiller calls this kind of marketing *contextual*. That differs from *entitlement*, which is a classic separation of content and sponsor like the Sony Station deal with Pontiac. Pontiac presents the Jeopardy! Online College Challenge game "to study brand awareness and attitudes of young adults," suggests Craig Norwood, Interactive Marketing Manager at Pontiac. College students are on the minds of advertisers at American Airlines as well. Some of the prizes include tickets and frequent flier miles. Frequent flier miles for students? Just like the banks learned decades ago when handing out student credit cards; if you get them young, you might be able to keep them for life.

One of the best parts is the exclusivity. It's going to be hard for JCPenney to place a banner ad in What's The Weather. United may as well give up any ideas of offering Red Carpet Club memberships—at least until the end of the year, when the exclusivity chip is up for grabs again.

Sort of like Claus.Com all year 'round.

The only thing that major brand advertisers could hope for above and beyond exclusive product placement would be true broadcasting. Advertising that went out into the World Wide Web instead of waiting for people to come to it. Something more like television that would press the message home. Something more push than pull.

Pushy, Pushy, Pushy

The wonder of a Web site is that it allows any and all to skim the surface or dig down deep, depending on their desires. You want to know when your favorite airline goes to New York? No problem. Want to know what the seating plan looks like on that flight? It's all right there. Want to drill down farther and find out what types of special meals from which you can choose? Click away.

This is the Internet pull model that is the main difference between the World Wide Web and television. TV pushes; it's in your face. Your only choices are to change the channel or turn it off altogether. The Web lets you go out and pull in the information you want, when you want it. That is its charm. You are in control.

But what if you want to know when the next deep discount airline tickets go on sale? What if you want to be told when that stock you own hits your sale price? That means checking back time and time again. If you're handy with a PC, you could cobble together a Visual Basic program or whip up a little Java applet that would fire up your browser and check that site once an hour.

On the other hand, you could take advantage of the new Push technology that has suddenly blossomed on the Net. Internet Push isn't new by any stretch, but it is getting more sophisticated, and a lot more attention. Push is beginning to be more and more popular, and of more and more interest to marketers.

Simple Push

Push was first used as a marketing technique by indiscriminate marketers who thought unsolicited e-mail and newsgroup spamming might be a cheap way to get their word to the masses. Unsolicited electronic marketing has proven to be a very bad model, generating far more ill-will and newborn legislation than sales. But solicited Push, where the user chooses to receive, has merit. Solicited Push started with Web site owners inviting visitors to subscribe to newsletters. Every day, week, or month, information is sent directly.

The folks at Amazon.com understand the value of Push. You tell them what kind of books or what author you like and they'll send you an e-mail when a new one is published (see Figure 4.25). From their side of the Web it's almost cheating. Their database knows what you like and it knows where to find you. From the customer perspective this is a valuable service, one that saves time, saves trips to the book store, and generates real consumer loyalty.

FIG. 4.25

Amazon.com offers to keep you informed.

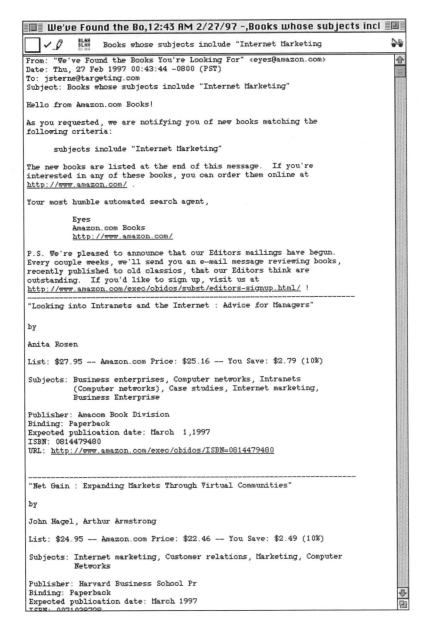

Then URL-Minder (**www.netmind.com/URL-minder/URL-minder.html**) offered to keep track of your favorite Web sites for you. As soon as a selected page is altered, you're alerted. FirstFloor's Smart Bookmarks (**www.firstfloor.com**) went one step farther by watching your favorite sites and downloading them in the background. Whenever you wanted, your favorite site was on your hard disk ready for instant, offline viewing. But these were just a hint of things to come.

Sophisticated Push

Servers that decide when to send you multi-media information are the more advanced Push products that have garnered so much attention recently. The info-morsels are brief and they come complete with hyperlinks for those times when something catches your eye and entices you to click.

The first one on the scene to make a big impression was PointCast, which combines Push with personalization (see Figure 4.26). PointCast "broadcasts" news, sports, weather, business reports, and stock listings according to a user's interests. You select the information you want and PointCast delivers. In addition, it's free for the asking; no license fee; no usage fee—all advertising-supported. It appeals to the Internet devotee because it is so different, it's personal and it's dynamic.

FIG. 4.26

PointCast pushes personalized information to your desktop, complete with advertising.

Designed as a screen saver, PointCast downloads information when the browser's computer is quiescent. You leave your system for a couple of minutes, and when you return, there are the latest news and sports scores scrolling across your screen. Occasional 30-second advertisements are added to the mix.

PointCast signed up major information suppliers to make it one of the most interesting and most complete offerings. Data sources include CNN, CNNfn, *Time*, *People*, and *Money* magazines, Reuters, PR Newswire, BusinessWire, Sportsticker, Accuweather, and newspapers such as the *Los Angeles Times*, *New York Times*, *Boston Globe*, and *San Jose Mercury News*.

Next to appear was Castanet by Marimba (**www.marimba.com**). Still in its infancy, Castanet 1.0 attracted a great deal of attention because it was written in Java (which some consider the coolest programming language on the planet), by the very people at Sun who had gotten Java off the starting blocks. Further, Castanet delivers applications, not just content, assuring you're using the most current version of a software package. Channels and applications using Marimba's tools include Excite, the search engine, Corel Office, the application suite, and entertainment sites such as Sesame Street KidSite and a crossword puzzle channel.

Push Gets Validated

In December of 1996, Microsoft announced an agreement with PointCast to make it the premier content provider for the Internet Explorer 4.0 Active Desktop. In return, PointCast has chosen the Microsoft Active Platform as its strategic development and delivery platform for broadcast content. The result is a platform that tightly integrates the desktop, the intranet, the Internet, and Push technology. Users will no longer need multiple applications to be completely inundated with information, entertainment, and ads.

Always in competition with Microsoft, Netscape raised the stakes with Netscape Communicator—a desktop-owning application suite. A new component of this suite, Constellation, will allow you to "customize, focus, and automatically receive the information you care about." Constellation includes InfoStream, which " displays discrete tidbits of information that you always want at hand. Customizable objects called InfoBlocks can communicate such real-time notifications and applications as product announcements, company phone directories, stock quotes, and news updates."

Ignoring the overabundance of product names and components, the results are the same; information coming to you, instead of you going out to get it. The market for such tools looks promising, according to The Yankee Group, the Boston-based technology forecasting and market research company. At the end of 1996, they suggested that the total for advertising, subscriptions, and retail sales from "desktop distribution" will hit $4.6 billion in the year 2000. In January 1997, their estimate increased to $5.7 billion.

Your Message Here

As these new information-flow tools were arriving on the Internet scene, the subscription model was taking a licking. It was becoming obvious that media sites were only going to survive if they were supported by advertising. Marketers were quick to see the benefits of Pushing their message to the masses.

Nancy Friedman, a Marketing Director at Levi Strauss, glowed over the Push model in the *Wall Street Journal* (December 13, 1996): "Today you can't be guaranteed that people are going to come to your Web site." Instead, she put $100,000 of her $11 million budget into a three-month

PointCast contract. PointCast subscribers saw 30-second ads for Slates pants. Friedman says she feels the money has been well-spent, citing thousands of people who clicked through, answered the questionnaire, and looked up the retail outlets where Slates can be found.

In her eyes, enough people—and the right kind of people—signed up and activated their PointCast client software to make the effort worthwhile. Not everybody likes to surf. Not everybody likes to search. Some like the world to come to them. But if you look at the numbers, many people like to get online and chat.

Chat

I am not a fan of chat rooms. I'm interested in the Web as a business medium and as an efficient way of communicating. Chat rooms are about as far from efficient as I have seen on the Web. However, I am a voracious reader, a bit of an intellectual, and over 40. That sort of leaves my personal disposition out of a lot of things that are just fine for advertising. Rugby, for instance.

But if your target audience is made up of teenagers, you will find them in chat rooms. There is a fabulous safety/intimacy there that generations of teens found on the phone. The adolescent can talk about anything without fear of being ridiculed for being clueless. They can hide behind the keyboard.

If you're after young mothers, they are typing it up in chat rooms. Can't communicate with Mom? Here's an ear to bend. Don't want to expose your naiveté in front of your friends? Here's a place you can get advice.

If you're pushing lifestyle products to the young, they're out trying to pick each other up electronically in chat rooms. I wish them well.

Chat rooms have been generally playful, boisterous, and noisy. At least, as playful, boisterous, and noisy as you can get using plain text. That doesn't stop people. Of the eight million subscribers America Online (AOL) had in the spring of 1997, they estimated 300,000 of them were chatting. Every day.

To understand chat, think of a telephone party line with ten to twenty people on it, all talking at the same time. The conversation gets sort of jumbled and the discussions tend to stay pretty shallow, but they're fun enough to draw a crowd.

Sponsor a Chat Room on AOL

You can now buy banner space in the public areas (but not the private chat rooms) of AOL's "People Connection." This real estate generates 360 million impressions every month to some 70 percent of their subscribers.

"People Connection" offers chat rooms for members with different interests and falls into several categories: Town Square (current events), Life, Romance, Special Interest, Places, Arts

& Entertainment, News, and Sports & Finance. Advertisers will be able to target ads toward specific rooms or specific categories of rooms.

Keep in mind that chat rooms are free-for-alls. Are you sure you want your ad hovering outside a room where the discussion can cover everything and anything? Will your banner get as much attention from people who are trying to join in a discussion by blasting past the page you're on? You'd better have a great offer and a fireproof image.

At the end of the day, AOL is still only offering a place to post a banner. Chat rooms get interesting as an advertising medium when the ads go inside—and participate.

Chatty Cathy Sells You a Vacuum Cleaner

Before the World Wide Web, cyberspace was described by those with literary talent like William Gibson, Neal Stephanson, and Bruce Sterling as a place where the human mind went to wander. Visual metaphors were created to signify data structures, security vaults, and information pathways. Some of these worlds contained advertising.

The ads would be quiet billboards hanging in space between one database and another. Some were sprites that flew like soap bubbles and burst before your eyes, revealing their messages and singing their jingles. Others popped up when stepped on, and some followed you to the outskirts of the local area network. Some merely rifled through your identification for an e-mail address and then ran it back home to the list builders.

What are the progenitors of these magical, mystical visions? Do you remember Eliza?

Written in the late 1960s by Joseph Weisenbaum, Eliza (**http://www-ai.ijs.si/eliza/ eliza.html**) is a program that imitates a dialog with a Rogerian psychologist. Eliza asks very vague questions based on the answers you give her/it. Very simple in its implementation, Eliza is a fascinating conversationalist. Here's a taste:

> Eliza: Hello. I am ELIZA. How can I help you?
>
> You: There's a lot of pressure at work.
>
> Eliza: Please go on.
>
> You: Deadlines are looming.
>
> Eliza: Does that upset you?
>
> You: Well, sure! I can never get everything done.
>
> Eliza: Can you elaborate on that?
>
> You: I need more time! My boss is always breathing down my neck.
>
> Eliza: Why do you say your boss is always breathing down your neck?

No, Eliza won't be able to pass the Turing Test, but she's an interesting experience. And an interesting idea. What if Eliza were re-programmed as Chatty Cathy? Multi-User Dungeons & Dragons (MUDs) have been around for quite a while where pre-programmed objects respond to a variety of stimuli. Why not a screen-to-screen salesbot?

Cathy: Hi, my name's Cathy. We have more than a thousand books on marketing. Can I help you find something in particular?

You: Yes, Cathy. I'm interested in using the Internet for marketing.

Cathy: We have about 42 books on Internet marketing. Did you want something technical or something for business people?

You: Business. I'm the marketing director at my company.

Cathy: Here are two that might be right for you. The first one is called *World Wide Web Marketing* by Jim Sterne. The description says it "Introduces executives to the World Wide Web, helps marketers set realistic goals for online marketing, explains how to create interesting and interactive Web pages, teaches how to get useful feedback and provide customer service, and examines the future of online marketing." Does that sound useful?

You: Why, yes! Has he written any others?

Cathy: Yes, *Customer Service on the Internet* and *What Makes People Click*. Would you like to see the descriptions for those books?

You: Yes, please.

Now it's time to take another "leap of technology." If you evolve from text-based chat rooms to 3-D avatar-based chat rooms, you have just joined the present and you're off to see the wizard.

The Emerald City Was Never Like This

OZ Interactive (**www.oz.com**) wants you to experience the World Wide Web a little differently than you're used to. OZ Interactive wants you to get personally involved. With multi-user capabilities, three-dimensional sound, and point-to-point audio and video communication, OZ Virtual is a place where your avatar does the talking. And the walking (see Figure 4.27).

You can create your own avatar and not only type your thoughts through it, but imbue it with an array of gestures. You're not limited to mere textualizing. You can nod, shake your head, jump for joy, or play air guitar if you think that will help you get your point across. The people at OZ are into the technology of the thing. They'll let others figure out how to fulfill their desires for 3-D virtual advertising.

So the question becomes "How long does it take for a 3-D virtual world to become another place where billboards, banners, and buttons crowd the implied sky in a never-ending battle for your attention?" Just how context sensitive can a virtual chat room be?

Dusty Sells You a Dustbuster

This one is just far enough out in left field that I am going to let the press release take a stab at an explanation (from **www.adsmart.net/news_spokebot.html**):

BLACK SUN INTERACTIVE, ADSMART, AND PLANET DIRECT JOIN FORCES IN PIONEERING ADVERTISING IN ONLINE COMMUNITIES

The Black & Decker Dustbuster SpokesBot revolutionizes advertising in online communities.

FIG. 4.27
Oz Virtual is a 3-D interactive home world where the droids and the avatars play.

San Francisco, CA—March 24, 1997. Today Black Sun Interactive, a leading provider of products for building online communities, ADSmart Corporation, creator of the first fully automated system to manage the online advertising process, and Planet Direct, creator of a new consumer Internet service, announced a partnership to deliver the SpokesBot, an innovative advertising solution for online communities. The SpokesBot integrates advertising into the community dialogue, by providing relevant information and the opportunity for the consumer to interact with the advertiser. This solution allows for a more targeted and interactive advertising campaign, enhancing the value proposition for both the consumer and advertiser, converting the community into a revenue generating site...

Through branded chat rooms and theme communities, advertisers have access to a focused group of users. Advertisers have been reluctant to advertise in other vendor's chat systems because customers are often too focused on chatting and do not notice the ads placed outside the chat window. By integrating the advertiser's message into the chat window and having an animated character in the 3D world, the SpokesBot addresses this concern. With the addition of the SpokesBot advertisers can create animated interactive characters that invite consumer participation and deliver targeted messages. The customer asks the character questions and listens to entertaining scripts, learning more about both the product and the company all via the chat window of the program. And they can learn about the product without ever leaving the online community...

Black Sun Interactive has developed a Community Bill of Rights for all SpokesBots in public communities. The Bill of Rights provides guidelines for the advertisers, ensuring that their SpokesBot act in a courteous and friendly manner.

Since the SpokesBot is integrated into the ADSmart system, advertisers can rotate, track, and evaluate the efficacy of these new innovative advertisements in both a 2D and a 3D online community just as they can with standard banner ads. These advertisements are targeted based on the topic of the chat session (for example an interview with a golf celebrity would be targeted to golfers)...

Partners Planet Direct, a partner in this revolutionary advertising solution, is the first customer to use the SpokesBot in their personal Internet service. Planet Direct developed "Dusty the Dustbuster SpokesBot" for their partner, Black & Decker, to demonstrate the value of integrated and interactive advertising. SpokesBot Dusty is an engaging 3D robot that politely introduces himself to curious visitors offering information about the Black & Decker Dustbuster SpokesBot...

The Black and Decker Dustbuster SpokesBot is a new and exciting advertising concept," said Robert Goergen, Account Supervisor at McCann Interactive, representing Black & Decker. "We are enthusiastic to test "Dusty" the SpokesBot in an online community and anticipate positive results."

Okay, let's hold on for just a second here. "SpokesBot Dusty is an engaging 3D robot that politely introduces himself to curious visitors offering information about the Black & Decker Dustbuster." Let's try this on for size:

Picture, if you will:

Fred: Hello? Anybody in this chat room?

John: Hi Fred. Seems kinda quiet.

Fred: Yeah, it's a vacuum all right. So empty you can almost see the dust.

Dusty: Hi Fred. Pardon me for the intrusion, but I couldn't help overhearing. I understand that dust can sure be a big bother. If you're having trouble with your vacuum, would you be interested in a special discount on a handy Dustbuster?

Fred: No I wouldn't, Dusty. Would you be interested in buying some insurance?

John: Been to any other virtual chat rooms tonight?

Fred: No, I came here first. How about you?

John: No, this is my first stop as well. It was jumping two days ago.

Sally: Hi Fred, John. I'm Sally.

Fred: Hi Sally.

John: Hi Sally. Welcome.

Sally: You're right John, it was crowded a couple of days ago. I wonder why everybody took a powder.

Dusty: Hi Sally. You know, the Dustbuster is just great on powder, ashes, and lint. We've got a great discount deal going today. Just click my chest and you can download a 20 percent off coupon right now!

John: Come on, Dusty, can't you tell we're giving you the brush off?

Dusty: The Dustbuster's rotating brushes work better than ever now that the horse-power has been upgraded. And you can try it in your home for a week at no charge.

Sally: Dusty, please stop the sales pitch, okay?

Dusty: Okay, Sally.

John: Yeah, Dusty. Whadda ya say we go into the Virtual Ring and I'll clean the place up with you!

Dusty: That's right, John. You can really clean up with the new, more powerful Dustbuster!

Fred: I'm out of here.

Sally: Me, too.

John: Now we know why this place has had all the life sucked out of it.

Double standard? You like Chatty Cathy, but think Dusty belongs in the dust bin? It's the same as unsolicited e-mail. Cathy is an opt-in method. You were looking for a book. Dusty is the uninvited and unwanted kind. Now, if Dusty just stood in the corner and waited for somebody to saunter up and ask about Dustbusters, it would be different. But then, he's probably on commission.

So Many Methods, So Little Budget

Today you have electronic walls behind home plate, where multiple advertisers can share the same "space," divided by innings. It's now possible to cover an entire bus with paint and still be able to see out of it. You can even have your company slogan appear in U.S. Postal Service postmarks for a price.

As time goes on, there will be more and more ways to get your name out there. The Internet has exploded the possibilities as new ways to promote your products are being invented daily.

That leaves one question:

How do you know if the money you are spending on Internet advertising is providing a decent return on investment? ●

CHAPTER 5

Measure for Measure

"**H**eaven doth with us as we with torches do,
Not light them for themselves; for if our virtues
Did not go forth of us, 'twere all alike
As if we had them not."

(*Measure for Measure*, Act 1, scene 1, line 35)

This is Shakespeare's way of telling us not to hide our talents under a bushel basket. We're given gifts and should make the most of them. If you can paint, you should spend some time at it and let others enjoy the product of your talent. By the same token, it's your job to show off the talents of your product.

Our products and services have fine attributes and if we don't let people know about it, we might as well shut down the factories and close the offices.

But it's a fine art to boast of one's products and services while keeping this side of hyperbole. You must be honest in your statements, but you want to provide the best possible picture you can. You have limited space and time to say what you want. Therefore, knowing if you're doing it right becomes very important.

I know half my advertising budget is being wasted. I just don't know which half.

You cannot manage that which you do not measure.

Everybody involved in Internet marketing and advertising is thrilled that the Net is the most measurable medium this side of the cash register. How do you really know if somebody saw your ad in a magazine? Heard your radio spot? Was in the room when your TV commercial aired?

On the Net, every download, every click, and every order can be accumulated, tabulated, and contemplated. So before you dig into placing ads for the best bang for the buck, you need to know how to measure the bang. Before you investigate what creative techniques make an irresistible banner, you'd better know how to enumerate the results. ■

Hits

If you find yourself talking to somebody who wants you to buy advertising space on their Web site based on the number of hits they get per day, week, or month, excuse yourself and leave the room. Tell him you left the water running. Tell her you have to go pick up your dog. Tell them they changed your mind.

Hits, according to Katherine Paine, CEO of The Delahye Group, stands for How Idiots Track Success.

Hits are derived from your server logs and a record of how many files were downloaded. The Pathfinder Web site (**http://pathfinder.com**) racks up 17 hits when you walk in the front door (see Figure 5.1). My Web site, found at **www.targeting.com**, logs three hits (see Figure 5.2).

FIG. 5.1

Pathfinder has one page and 16 graphics for a total of 17 hits.

FIG. 5.2
Target Marketing only scores three hits per home page visit.

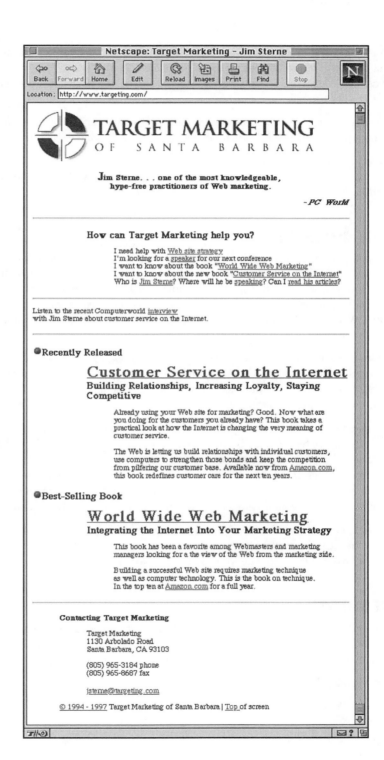

The Target Marketing home page has two graphics: the company logo/name and the little red ball. The little red ball shows up twice, but is only counted once, because it's only downloaded once. The reason the server records three hits is that the page itself, the one containing the text, is a separate file.

Hits can be a valuable measurement when used to track variations of the same page or site. Comparing my three hits to Pathfinder's 17 indicates nothing except the differences in design.

If ad space sellers are talking to you about hits, you should stop talking. Chances are, they'll be talking visits, sessions, impressions, and clickthroughs. If so, it may be worth your while to talk further.

Visits or Sessions

If I look at your home page, it's a page view. My action may rack up a dozen hits on your server, but I've only looked at one page. Even then, you don't know if I looked at the whole page or just glanced at the top. All you know is that your computer sent my computer a page and some graphics files. Heck, I might have even been using an offline browser, which collects entire Web sites while I'm asleep. Or I could be using a push tool that sent me your page while my screen saver was on and I was out.

If I look at your home page and start wandering through your Web site, I am paying a visit, or am engaged in a session. A session gets interesting if you have the means to track my movements through your site and watch where I go. You can measure the effectiveness of your own text, graphics, and layout that way.

But when it comes to your advertising, what you really want to know about is the OTS—the Opportunity To See. The OTS plays a large role in print and on television. Your ad appears on the *Late Show with David Letterman* and so many million people have the opportunity to see it. That means their televisions are on and tuned to the right station. It does not mean they are in the same room or awake. My wife dives for the remote control and mutes the sound of all commercials within about three femtoseconds. OTS tells us nothing about OTH.

So there is a given amount of give in these numbers. They are not absolute. They are not precise. They are not spotless. But, unlike hits, the number of OTSs you can buy is a comparable number from site to site. The whole idea is to make a good impression.

Impressions

According to the Outdoor Advertising Association of America (**www.oaaa.org**), "70% of outdoor advertising revenues come from local advertisers who count on billboards to direct customers to their business or products."

McDonalds, Next Exit

Motel 6, We'll Leave The Light On For You

The intention of this 70% is the equivalent of a Web *clickthrough*. You put up a banner, somebody likes it, they click it to go to your site—bingo! Now you can sell something to them.

But what about the other 30%? Why are they putting up billboards? To make an impression. To get a chance at an OTS in hopes that, if you see their brand name often enough, it will make your arm reach for the most familiar package when you're in the store and faced with a myriad of choices—*branding*.

Counting Impressions

Impressions are generally counted and sold by the thousand. The Cost Per Thousand (CPM) is the figure most commonly used to compare the value of impressions. But not all CPMs are created equal. When you go shopping, you have to *normalize* the data handed to you by the sellers.

Data normalization is something all of us have faced. It's usually referred to as comparing apples and oranges. When trying to get a list of names and addresses into a database it often requires retyping every one. Do they all have a Mr., Ms., or Dr.? No? Then you better add one. Do they all have a title? Do they all have one line for the street address, or two? Once all of these discrepancies have been worked out, the data can roll in automagically and be useful.

When counting impressions, there are many more nits to pick. In a post to the Online Advertising Discussion List (**www.o-a.com**), Cliff Kurtzman of The Tenagra Corporation outlined some of the problems faced by a Web site manager wishing to sell banner space:

Cliff Kurtzman (cliff.kurtzman@tenagra.com)

Wed, 12 Feb 1997 02:29:24 -0600

This post explores some very technical aspects of counting ad impressions and click-throughs. The purpose is to illustrate some of the difficulties and ambiguities in measuring page impressions, banner views and click-throughs. Small changes in assumptions and counting methodologies can have big effects on the numbers you come up with and report to advertisers (or are reported by advertisers).

I'm using real data collected on one of our sites over a 1-day period (January 30th, 1997).

Here is the scenario. We are running a fixed banner ad on a web page on one of our sites. The banner is hyperlinked to the advertiser's site. In conjunction with the banner is also a text link to the advertiser's site.

The page with the banner is an HTML page, and is not generated by a cgi. (Pages generated by cgi's [sic] are not subject to caching). This particular page has a META HTTP-EQUIV="Expires" tag on it to perhaps reduce the likelihood that systems will cache it and hence give our server a more accurate access count. I don't know how many systems and browsers actually recognize this tag. In any event, the bottom line is that caching causes the true number of accesses to our page to be under-reported, but I suspect not by more than 10%.

Over a several day period we noticed a jump in click-throughs on the ad to about double the normal level even though the page traffic was pretty much constant. This caused us to examine what was happening in detail, and to turn up some very interesting results.

Our log file showed that the page on which the ad resided was loaded 1,603 times. This includes:

992 full loadings of the web page (the server logged transfer of the full 11,053 bytes)

16 aborted (partial) loadings of the page (either 0 or 8192 bytes were logged as transferred)

595 page accesses that show up as "304 0" in our log file—indicating that the page was unchanged since the last time this visitor came to the site and the page was therefore loaded from the visitor's local cache of their gateway's cache.

There were 925 unique hosts hitting this page over the course of the day. A session analysis on the home page hits showed that the 1,603 home page accesses were logged by a total of 1,026 sessions, with a session being defined as hits from the same IP address within a 20 minute period. The number of sessions (1,026) is close and slightly greater than the number of full page loadings (992) which is in turn close to but slightly greater than the number of unique hosts (925). This is as was expected.

Our log file also showed 868 banner loadings (694 full loadings of the banner, 172 "304 0" loadings from the visitor's local cache, 2 aborted loadings). This 868/1,603 ratio is a fairly typical ratio of page loadings to banner loadings. There are a lot of things that I think might account for the discrepancy:

1. *The visitor's browser finds the page is unchanged, logs a "304 0" in our access log file, and then grabs the page and banner from the visitor's local cache without the need to register a hit on the banner on our server.*

2. *The NLvisitor is going through a gateway (e.g., AOL, WebTV) that provides file caching. When the page is requested, the gateway queries our server, finds the page is unchanged, logs a "304 0" in our access log file, and then grabs the page and banner from its cache without the need to register a hit on the banner on our server.*

3. *The visitor is accessing the page through a system (e.g., AOL) that has not cached our page but has cached the banner.*

4. *The visitor clicks the link to my page several times before waiting long enough for the page to load. This shows up in the log as several page accesses but only one banner access.*

5. *The visitor accesses the page with the graphics turned off.*

6. *After linking to the page, the visitor hits the stop button on their browser before the banner has had a chance to load.*

Except for cases 4 & 6, the visitor has the opportunity to be exposed to the banner or the text link with each page access, provided that they view and read the part of the page with the banner.

So the first question this leads to is: How many ad exposures did this advertiser receive? My feeling is that it is pretty much the full 1,603 exposures, although some portion (perhaps about 580) of the banner exposures were repeat exposures to people who had seen the banner already. Without knowing the true magnitude of #2 above, or tracking cookies, it is hard to precisely quantify the true number of repeat exposures.

I've had advertisers approach me who want their ad banner to load from their server so they can independently track the number of impressions they are getting. However, as described in the previous paragraph, it is my opinion that counting the number of times the graphic loads undercounts the number of true impressions of their ad significantly.

Now on to the clickthrough analysis, where things really get weird.

—Cliff

Cliff Kurtzman
President
The Tenagra Corporation
Old URL/New Web Site: http://www.tenagra.com/
281/480-6300

Internet marketing, public relations, consulting and web site design

We'll take a look at clickthroughs in the next section. In the meantime, we have plenty of weirdness to deal with for simple OTS numbers as it is.

Kurtzman's concerns are based on the numbers he generates at his site. He has a half dozen decisions to make about how he reports these numbers. If you multiply that by the number of advertisers you expect to deal with, you suddenly realize there are many ways to skin this kitty.

First, Kurtzman explains that he's "running a fixed banner ad on a web page on one of our sites." It could have been a rotating banner, where each page can support any number of banners that share the same space, divided by time. It could also have been shown on multiple sites. (We'll look at ad networks later.)

Kurtzman also talks about caching. *Caching* occurs on your computer when you look at a Web page. The page and the graphics are stored in a temporary file on your hard drive. When you hit the Back button, the browser looks in the cache file first. That way, it can display the file immediately, without going back out over the Web and clogging the wires, or making you wait.

There are also shared cache files. Your ISP, whether it's AOL or Fred and Barney's Internet Access & Quarry, will use a large cache file on its gateway server. If you go to a Web site that somebody else on AOL or F&BIAQ has looked at recently, the gateway server will show you the one from its cache file, rather than reach across the Net for another copy. You can set your pages and your banners to expire, but there's no guarantee that bit of programming will be respected.

You can also record the number of times the page was checked by a caching system to see if the page has changed. This will register a page check, but not a banner check. You still won't know if the user downloaded everything or just took a quick look at the text and decided to move along before the banner displayed.

The AOL cache may include the banner from a previous viewing on a previous page, but not the page being requested at the moment. As a result, the page gets counted but the banner does not.

If the visitor is impatient and clicks the link repeatedly while waiting for the page to load, the server can record multiple page requests, but only one banner request. Or they hit the Stop button and go elsewhere before the banner displays.

According to research firm NPD (**www.npd.com**): "In a given session, a single page from a search engine is viewed, on average, 2.6 times. In other words, a given page—plus its possible advertisements and hot links—are delivering 2.6 times as many impressions as the site-centric measurement at the search engine's own server would show. Certainly one of the reasons that Web advertising impression rates seem so high compared to other media is that the search engine operators are underselling their delivery capabilities by a factor of over two and a half, if they are relying on their own server statistics only."

Web surfers frequently wander the Web with the graphics turned off. Some studies have shown that it can be as much as 10% of the surfing population. Conversations with Webmasters indicate this is closer to 5%. Either way, there is some portion of the Web population who will never see your banners.

Kurtzman suggested that, "[t]his source of ambiguity can probably only be eliminated entirely by serving the page and ad banner through a cgi script." Further discussion indicated that was not always a reliable solution, either.

One item left out of Kurtzman's initial post was the confusion caused by spiders. If you have a Web, you're sure to get spiders and an electronic Web gets software spiders. In the real world we learn that while all insects are bugs, not all bugs are insects. Insects have six legs, spiders have eight. But online, spiders are not bugs at all. They are very intentional pieces of software that wander out to explore your site in order to catalog it for their databases.

AltaVista, Webcrawler, Lycos, and many others send their algorithmic arachnids out to fetch the information needed to index the World Wide Web. When one finds your site, it can read the entire thing. That artificially raises the number of page views you record. It can do the same for the sites you pay to sport your banners.

And let's not forget the unscrupulous. It's quite possible to write a simple program that reads your banner over and over in order to fulfill a contract for impression. Despicable? Yes. Technically detectable? Yes. But a team of high-school students working for peanuts is not detectable. They're still despicable.

Bottom line? Three choices:

You can get to know the inner workings of a variety of Web servers.

You can hope that the sites you work with utilize the same tools and create identical formatted statistics.

You can work with a third-party ad vendor and make *them* do the work.

Server Fervor   I admit that I am a nerd. I am fascinated by technology and can't wait to play with new gadgets the minute they escape the laboratory. However, I'm not much interested in how they work. I am far more concerned with what I can do with them. I like driving, but I'm disinclined to open the hood and start mucking about with things.

If you lean more toward the technology for its own sake, you might want more particulars. You can get the real skinny and the in-depth explanation of what your server logs can tell you from *Web Site Stats: Tracking Hits and Analyzing Traffic* by Rick Stout (Osborne, 1997). He goes into some serious detail to explain what each log file contains and what it means, so I don't have to. God bless you, Mr. Stout.

Tools of the Trade   There are a plethora of tools on the market for measuring banners. Some are designed for the computer hosting the site you are sponsoring. Some are designed for use on your own server. Your ads don't need to be on the same server as the high-traffic host site, they only need to show up on the same browser screen at the end of their journey.

If the ads are coming from your computer, you can simply burn the midnight oil pouring over the reports that your server spits out as viewed through tools like Getstats and WWWStat. You could also make use log analysis tools like WebTrends.

WebTrends, from E.G. Software (**www.webtrends.com**), analyzes the log files created by your Web servers and kicks out statistical information as well as colorful. In their own words:

WebTrends can help you make decisions and determine:

Current and Future Advertising Efficiencies & Trends

Internet & Intranet Reporting

Web Server Pages' Appeal

International vs Domestic Interest

Local vs National Activity

User Activity by Government, Commercial, Educational and Military Markets

Specific Companies to which your Products & Services Appeal

Which Products are the Most Popular

Interest Level in Specific Pages or Services

Which Page is the Best for Advertising Placement

Which Days are the Best to Advertise

Individual Directory Activity (Excellent for Billing and Leasing Web Space)

Users' Hardware & Software Platforms

What Browsers are used to access your Web Site?

How do users get to your web site (Referrer Report)?

Best Time of Day to Perform Maintenance on your Server

Billing information for your Virtual Servers services

Advertising Views, Clicks and Click rate reports for your customers

NetGravity (**www.netgravity.com**) makes the AdServer which hands out banners upon request and reports on its activity (see Figure 5.3). You can measure the number of ads served to specific pages on the different sites you place your banners. You can limit the number of times an ad is delivered to the same person. If the site you are buying space from makes their visitors log information available, AdServer can select the proper ad to show based on zip code, age, gender, and so on. It can even look at content tags on the vendor pages to make sure you don't put your ad for travel discounts on a page with an article on an airline disaster. Companies like Bloomberg, National Geographic, and Netscape have enough ad traffic to indicate that AdServer scales well.

FIG. 5.3
NetGravity reports all the details about the ads served.

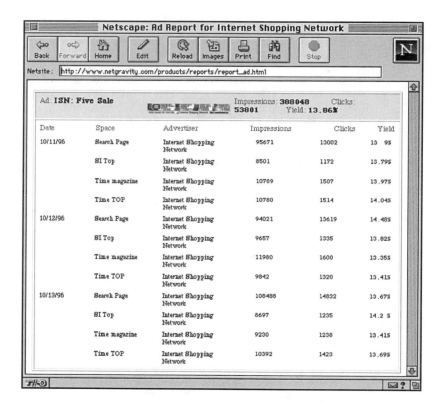

There are many Web log analysis tools. Yahoo! lists dozens of log analysis tools at **www.yahoo.com/Computers_and_Internet/Software/Internet/World_Wide_Web/ Servers/Log_Analysis Tools**. As proof that the Web is getting too big to manage, Yahoo! lists even more of them at **www.yahoo.com/Business_and_Economy/Companies/ Computers/Software/Internet/World_Wide_Web/Log_Analysis_Tools**.

These are mostly created to help track from where people are coming (domain), from what site they are coming , and which pages they visit. These tools can also examine how long they stick around, which buttons they clicked, and which searches they performed. But for now, our interest is in how they can help us track whether our ad has been seen. From the obstacles Cliff Kurtzman has faced, this is not a cake walk. You may want to look for outside help.

Third Parties to the Rescue   If you prefer not to gunk up your servers with counting software, you can make use of services like I/Pro and NetCount. They will retrieve your logs, massage them thoroughly, and report back all of the pertinent information. I/Pro works with the Nielsen ratings people and NetCount is affiliated with Price Waterhouse.

I/Pro's NetLine service delivers pre-formatted reports, rather than make you (let you?) slice and dice your own. It answers questions such as:

How many visitors are coming to your site?

How does this vary by day of the week and time of the day?

From which sites did they come?

From which organizations are they visiting?

How many pages are they reading?

Which specific pages are they reading?

Are they browsing your site or are they looking for specific information every day?

How do they move through your site?

From which pages do most visitors leave your site?

How long are they spending at your site?

From what country do they come?

NetCount (**www.netcount.com**) will keep an eye on how well your ads are doing on other people's Web sites (see Figure 5.4).

Ad Networks Can Keep Count for You   The two ads at the top of *Webmaster* magazine (**www.web-master.com**) do not live on the magazine Web server (see Figure 5.5). Instead, they are pulled from the databases of FocaLink when needed. Webmaster could serve the ads. You could serve the ads. Or you could get a third-party like FocaLink to do it for you.

FocaLink is an ad serving company. That means they are a network. Briefly put, an ad network signs up multiple sites and buys banner space from them in bulk. They then turn around and sell that space to you. Then they take the banners you want to place and serve them from their machines, which house a healthy amount of statistical software for reporting.

FocaLink (**www.focalink.com**) tries to sidestep the problems outlined by recording "Adviews" instead of pageviews. When a page is requested by a browser, it trusts the page being served to ask the server for the graphics files, like banners. FocaLink changes the HTML link to their server slightly so that the browser *also* asks for the banner.

FIG. 5.4

NetCount keeps a finger on the pulse of your ad statistics at multiple sites.

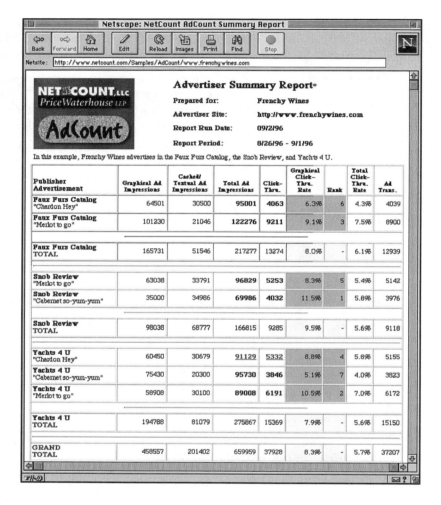

Advertiser Summary Report*

Prepared for:	Frenchy Wines
Advertiser Site:	http://www.frenchywines.com
Report Run Date:	09/2/96
Report Period:	8/26/96 - 9/1/96

In this example, Frenchy Wines advertises in the Faux Furs Catalog, the Snob Review, and Yachts 4 U.

Publisher Advertisement	Graphical Ad Impressions	Cached/ Textual Ad Impressions	Total Ad Impressions	Click-Thru.	Graphical Click-Thru. Rate	Rank	Total Click-Thru. Rate	Ad Trans.
Faux Furs Catalog "Chardon Hey"	64501	30500	95001	4063	6.3%	6	4.3%	4039
Faux Furs Catalog "Merlot to go"	101230	21046	122276	9211	9.1%	3	7.5%	8900
Faux Furs Catalog TOTAL	165731	51546	217277	13274	8.0%	-	6.1%	12939
Snob Review "Merlot to go"	63038	33791	96829	5253	8.3%	5	5.4%	5142
Snob Review "Cabernet so-yum-yum"	35000	34986	69986	4032	11.5%	1	5.8%	3976
Snob Review TOTAL	98038	68777	166815	9285	9.5%	-	5.6%	9118
Yachts 4 U "Chardon Hey"	60450	30679	91129	5332	8.8%	4	5.8%	5155
Yachts 4 U "Cabernet so-yum-yum"	75430	20300	95730	3846	5.1%	7	4.0%	3823
Yachts 4 U "Merlot to go"	58908	30100	89008	6191	10.5%	2	7.0%	6172
Yachts 4 U TOTAL	194788	81079	275867	15369	7.9%	-	5.6%	15150
GRAND TOTAL	458557	201402	659959	37928	8.3%	-	5.7%	37207

Standards Bearers

The most frequent complaint made by attendees to the Web Advertising '97 conference in Monterey in April was that there were no reporting standards. Buying banner space on different sites or from different networks resulted in different reports. Hours were spent trying to correlate those reports and sometimes it was simply impossible.

The most frequent complaint made by advertising networks at the Web Advertising '97 conference in Monterey in April was that there were no reporting standards. Buying banner space on different sites resulted in different reports. Hours were spent trying to correlate those reports for clients and sometimes it was simply impossible.

FIG. 5.5
The ads on the Webmaster page don't come from the Webmaster server.

The most fervent complaint made by Christine Northwick of SRDS was that there were no reporting standards. SRDS (**www.srds.com**) makes a living out of reporting advertising venues (magazines, radio, television); how many subscribers, listeners, viewers; their circulation and market share; and whom to contact to buy an ad. Northwick says the only thing that's common among Web sites that sell ad space is that they have a phone number and an e-mail address of the salesperson who very much wants to talk to you. As for common ways to measure? She's got her fingers crossed, but she's not holding her breath.

It is left to industry organizations like CASIE to figure out what to count, how to count, and most important, how to agree about counting.

The CASIE Guiding Principles of Interactive Media Audience Measurement is an attempt to create "acceptable measures of the advertising opportunities" and "a means to compare those opportunities with traditional media." The whole point is to "provide the accountability necessary for agencies and advertisers to judge the value of their investment." They've come up with 12 key principal statements (from **www.commercepark.com/AAAA/casie/gp/ exec_summary.html**):

- *Best Media Research Practices. Audience measurement of interactive media should follow the criteria developed for other types of media research over the last eight decades, except where these are clearly not applicable, to ensure estimates that are accurate, precise, and reliable.*

- *Third Party Measurement. In principle, audience measurements should be taken by objective third party research suppliers and not by the media vehicles being measured. In practice, interactive media suppliers have the unique ability to measure their own audiences in real time. A body of these audience data is called a 'clickstream.' If clickstreams are collected, they should be analyzed and reported by objective third party research suppliers and not by the data collectors themselves. Failing this, clickstream based analyses and reports produced by data collectors themselves should be audited as described below.*

- *Auditing. Third party audience measurement should be audited as is the industry practice for all other media. In all cases, established industry auditing practices should be employed. Measurement by the medium itself via the 'clickstream,' when offered, should also be audited by an independent, industry supported auditing organization.*

- *Full Disclosure. Complete information about research methods and practices used, as well as all the data collected, should be revealed to all research subscribers. Carefully scrutinized exceptions may be made so as to allow research suppliers to protect trade secrets where the claim of such trade secrets preventing the disclosure of specific information is judged to be credible by the user community based on the known facts of the specific case.*

- *Comparability. It is highly desirable that estimates covering a particular interactive vehicle be directly comparable to estimates covering another interactive vehicle within the same interactive medium.*

- *Methodological Experimentation Encouraged. Research organizations are encouraged to be innovative in method and practice. The burden of proof of the validity of the measurement and of conclusions based on the measurement is on the research company.*

- *Privacy. Every effort should be made to maintain consumers' privacy. Audience research providers must not reveal consumer identities, except if absolutely necessary for audit purposes, and must never contact research subjects for direct marketing or other non-research purposes.*

- *User Information Preferable. To evaluate audiences of a medium, advertisers need to know the number of different users accessing the medium and the number of times they access it in a given period of time. The product of these two key measures provides a gross exposures measure which can be used to calculate measures of cost efficiency comparable to other media. Together these key measures provide data comparable to that available for other media.*

- *Census vs. Sample Based Measurement. Measurement of users at the level of persons may, in many cases, necessitate the use of a sample. While a census—if accurate and complete—has advantages over a sample, the need for a measurement of individual person users should not be compromised in order to gain these advantages. When and if a truly complete and accurate census of users is made available, that is most preferable. A combination of a census of visits plus a users' sample would be one viable approach to maximizing accuracy at every level.*

- *Non-Intrusiveness. Measurement methods which are least visible to consumers, and require the least effort on their part, are preferable to methods which are more visible to consumers and/or which require more effort.*

- *Total Medium Measurement. It is highly desirable that audience estimates be provided within the context of a total medium measurement so that principal vehicles within that medium might be directly evaluated against one another and against the total medium norms.*

  Measurement of part of a medium will be acceptable when it is a practical expedient within a given time frame.

- *Industry Consensus. Interactive media research standards ought to be set by a broad representation of the advertising industry, including advertisers, agencies, media, research companies, and industry bodies. No effort was spared to follow this principle in the creation of the present document. However, these principles will remain adaptable as the media evolve.*

The entire Guide can be found at **http://www.commercepark.com/AAAA/bc/casie/guide.html.**

But standards are an evolving thing. Even the good old Nielsen Ratings for television are under attack these days. Ask Nielsen and they'll tell you that with dozens of cable channels, video rentals, multi-media computers, and, of course, the Internet, it's no surprise that the ratings on the big networks are down. That, they feel, explains why the networks are going after Nielsen and calling for new standards for measuring TV audiences.

The Internet is evolving faster than anything else made by man with the exception of something from a John Carpenter movie. When things move that fast, it's very hard for standards to catch up. Heck, the whole idea of standards is that they are supposed to draw a line in the sand so we know where we all stand.

When the UNIX operating system started to move into the mainstream in the early 1980s, the upside was clear: one computer platform that could run on hardware from multiple manufacturers. It was to be a standard we could all agree on. It didn't work out that way. Factions formed and sides were taken. In 1985, AT&T even went so far as to place a double-page spread for the System V version in *Sports Illustrated* of all places. It was frequently repeated that the nice thing about UNIX standards was that there were so many to choose from.

The Internet advertising industry is so young that there is sure to be a similar situation.

The Cost of an Impression

The average price per one-thousand OTSs runs between $30 and $250. That's average. It doesn't tell you much about reality. That's also rate card pricing. It doesn't tell you anything about reality.

Here's a conversation between a network buyer and a large, ad-supported Web site as personally reported to me by the network buyer:

> Buyer: Hi Fred, this is Scott, howya doin'?
>
> Seller: Great, Scott! What can I do for you?
>
> Buyer: I'm looking to make a buy for a client and I'm checking around.
>
> Seller: Okay, but things are pretty tight right now. We've been busy. What's the budget?
>
> Buyer: I've got about $20,000 to work with.
>
> Seller: $20,000? Well, maybe I can help you. We're running at a CPM of about $25.
>
> Buyer: Oooo, ouch! You're way out of my league. I'm looking more like in the $5 range.
>
> Seller: Whoa! Really? Have you tried giving your client some smelling salts?.
>
> Buyer: We've been working together for a while on it. Anything you can do?
>
> Seller: No, I'm sorry, we just don't have enough left over inventory to hit that.
>
> Buyer: Oh well. I've been getting $5 from enough others that I'll just keep looking.
>
> Seller: Well, now wait a minute there, Scott. If I could find some good spots for, say $10?
>
> Buyer: You're heading in the right direction.
>
> Seller: Well, maybe $7. How soon do you want to place these banners?

The problem is lots and lots of inventory (ad space) and not enough ads. It's a buyer's market. The top ten or twelve sites get all the attention (dollars) and the second-tier site's sweat. The mom-n-pop start-up sites are hurting.

In the last months of 1996, there was an influx of cash into the market. It seemed everybody had a little budget left over and wanted to try out the Web. The second tier did pretty well that quarter, but the big ten still had 10% of their space they were giving away as perks to their best clients or placing their own ads. Wander over to AltaVista sometime, hit the Reload button and see how many times a banner for AltaVista occupies the space.

Ads at Auction   If the market for ads is so soft, what is the real value of a banner placement? If you want to know the real value of anything, you ask the marketplace in general: you hold an auction.

Adbot (**www.adbot.com**) is in the business of banner space auctions. Early results were not overwhelming. When Adbot ran their first auction in the middle of April, 1997, they had 18 bidders. Most of them were from companies that planned on reselling the ads after the fact. Why? Deep discounts. An opening price of $5 CPM is not a bad place to start. But after less than half an hour of bidding, 75% of the inventory was still for sale.

The president, Jim Frith, felt the first effort was a successful test and figured the lack of bidders caused the lack of bidding. The negative attention Adbot got the first time around was the best thing they could have hoped for. It gave them a chance to refine their offerings, creating networks of ads by dividing them into categories like sports, computers, music, and health. They also adjusted their pricing to accommodate search engines and directories starting at $4 CPM and boosting the financial genera to $7.

Adbot uses a standard model of brokers sitting in front of a terminal and placing bids for competitors who called in over the phone. Maybe they'll put the auction online.

Registration Resolution Ad registries are one of the helpful new services popping up on the Web. These sites sport databases that let you search and compare different sites that sell banner space.

Jupiter Communication's AdSpace Locator is one example (see Figure 5.6). If you sell ad space on your Web site, you can list there for free. If you're looking to place ads, you can search it for free. They have about 1,000 entries.

Their typical placement information includes the site title, the URL, a description of the site (in 50 to 75 words), who's currently buying ads there, what the rate card says, how much traffic they get, who the site visitors are, and the agency commission structure. Useful.

There are a handful of others. You can find the Online Advertising Index at **www. netcreations.com/ipa/adindex**, The Web Ad Space Registry at **www.fwy.com/ ADVERT**, and AdCENTRAL at **www.adcentral.com**.

According to John Schick, Vice President of SI Software, on the Web Ad Resources page (**www.sisoftware.com/whatitco.htm**), here is the big picture:

> Search Engines—Range—$20–$50 CPM
>
> City Guides—Range—$50–$60 CPM
>
> Top 100 Web Sites—Range—$25–$100 CPM
>
> Small Targeted Content Sites—$10–$80 CPM
>
> Sponsored Content—$45–$85 CPM

Schick's report is very well-thought out and informative—well worth a look. If your curiosity goes beyond your propriety, you can also check out the pricing of adult sites with The Adult Money Report (**www.alexas.com/advert**).

FIG. 5.6

Jupiter's AdSpace lets you look for sites to place your ad by category.

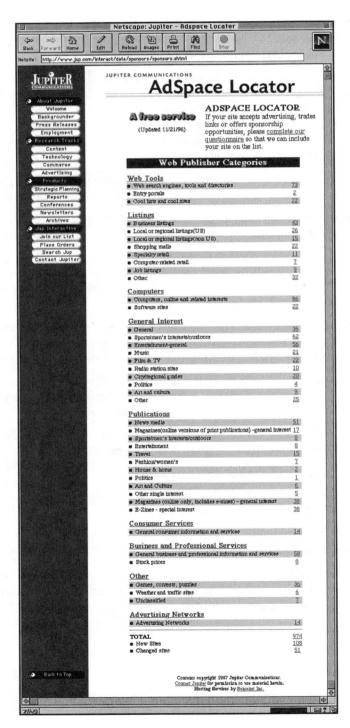

The Value of an Impression—Brands in Cyberspace

"In the factory we make cosmetics. In the store we sell hope."

Charles Revson, Revlon

You can count OTSs and you price OTSs. After cross-referencing, cross-checking, and crossing your fingers, you will end up with a number that you can use to compare OTSs from one Web site to another. But what is an Opportunity to See really worth?

Advertising is the art of letting people know you have something that might be of interest to them. Sometimes the goal is a direct response—you want them to Call Now, Operators Standing By! If you're trying to sell a marble resin Rabbit with Ladybug on Feet that's 4"×9"×4" at $40.50 for indoor and outdoor use (**www.animal-x.com/ladybug.html**), then you are far more interested in the direct response approach. If that's your situation, you'll be interested in the following section on clickthroughs for direct response. But if your goals are generating awareness and building brands, the value of the impression all by itself is very important to you.

You don't expect people to buy a six pack of Coca-Cola online. You're not waiting for folks to purchase a brand new pair of Nikes on the Web. You know nobody will pick up a box of Kleenex using Netscape. As an advertiser, you're much more interested in letting people know about your latest contest, your new packaging, and your sponsorship of yet another mega-sporting event. Anything to keep your logo in front of them. Anything to pre-program them to pick up your product when they hit the store.

For this, we rely on the power, the effect, the equity of our brands. And we are going to become more dependent on the power of brands on the Web.

Branding at Work

The brand started as a mark of ownership. When it grew up, it became a mark of trust, a mark of consistency. You weren't buying a steer from a stranger passing through. You were buying it from one of the biggest spreads this side of Boline. Healthy cattle. A happy herd. It was sure to be a good animal. You buy a bottle of Heinz 57 and it tastes just like the last one. A Big Mac tastes the same in Portland, Oregon as it does in Portland, Maine.

As shoppers, we have become inured to the plethora of clutter on store shelves. Walk in to buy a quart of milk and a loaf of bread, and you are bombarded.

A time-traveler from 100 years ago would be transported into spasms of cognitive overload just walking down the cereal aisle at the grocery store. The colors, the graphics, the bursts of "New!," "Frosted!," and "Healthier!" on box after box after box would be enough to send him reeling into the vegetable section, just to be surrounded by familiar containers without imperative-packed wrappers.

Even though we are inured, even though we can rationally consider the impact of advertising on our sentient selves, we subliminally succumb to its power. We reach for the brand we know and trust.

We reach for the familiar package because it's what we bought last time, it's what Mom used to buy, or it's what our significant other asked for. Or, maybe we did an in-depth evaluation of price to quality to emotional satisfaction and made a decision. Twenty years ago. The product may have changed, the packaging may have changed, the manufacturer may have changed. But we still gravitate toward the tried and true. But that's not all.

Much to the advertiser's delight, we also reach for the package that strikes the chord played on national television the night before. We give a new product a try because we've spotted the billboards and heard the radio spots and seen spotty magazine spreads. We are responding directly to the positioning and personality of a product we've never tried before. That's advertising success!

A Brand by any Other Name

You cannot improve what you do not measure. The corollary is that you cannot measure what you do not define. A brand is not a name. A brand is not a positioning statement. It is not a marketing message. It is a promise. Made by a company to its customers and supported by that company.

If not, it would be enough just to change the name of San Francisco's Candlestick Park to 3Com Park. As Jamie Graham put it in *Advertising Age*'s *Creativity* magazine (Jan/Feb 1997), "It won't be long before we're vacationing in Pearl Drops (formerly Yellowstone) Park, admiring 2000 Flushes (Niagara) Falls, and the Pontiac Grand Am Canyon."

A brand is something that lives apart from what the company plans, because it is the culmination of all of the interactions a marketplace has with the firm.

> A person sees an ad and has an impression.
>
> She looks up information on the Web, she has an impression.
>
> She calls the firm and talks to the receptionist and the impression changes.
>
> She is put on hold and hears the music and "Your call is important to us."
>
> She talks to a sales rep.
>
> She waits for the materials to arrive.
>
> She reads the materials.
>
> She talks to her colleagues about the product.
>
> She reads about the firm in the financial pages.
>
> She reads product reviews.
>
> She makes the purchase.
>
> She sees and feels the product packing.
>
> She tries to use the product.
>
> She calls customer service.
>
> She talks to her friends about her experience.

If you take the sum total of how she feels and thinks about all of her interactions with the company and how well they met her expectations and lived up to the promise, and you multiply that by the thousands or millions of people who have also read about, talked about, and interfaced with the company and the product, and you have a brand. You want that brand to be a positive sentiment.

You want the public to know, deep in their heart of hearts, that your company stands for confidence, your logo implies trust, and your products mean dependability. Or, you want them to think of you as young, hip, and fun-loving. Either way, you want them to think of you in those terms for all of the days of their lives.

In an essay in *Understanding Brands by 10 People Who Do* (Kogan Pge Ltd., 1996), Wendy Gordon, Chairperson of the Research Business Group stresses congruency between all of the different levels of human communication. These Neuro-Linguistic Programming levels (NLP is the study of how humans think and experience the world) are:

Level	Personification	Example
Vision	I promise	"I have a dream" (Martin Luther King, Jr.).
Identity	I am	I am a caring, giving person.
Belief	I believe	I believe in state education.
Capability	I can	I play tennis and cook Japanese food.
Behavior	I do	I work full time.
Environment	where	I live in London.

Gordon suggests that strong branding requires all of these levels of communication to agree with each other. If you can identify the message to be conveyed on each of these levels and then see to it that every interaction with the firm and its products confirms those messages, your brand will be as strong as possible.

Branding Becomes Crucial on the Net

But what happens when this stimulus and response is played out on the Net? How does it change how we react? When all manufacturers and all products are one click away?

We have become the time-traveler. We have been beamed up to the present and find ourselves in a sea of information. We are awash in the swells of e-zines, e-mail newsletters, lists, pundits, and definitive Web sites all offering the latest in up-to-minute news, weather, sports, stock price analysis, fashion trends, and health advisories. The problem of information overload has grown from a cresting wave to a full-blown tsunami.

On the Web you can read all about how Apple is losing its grip. You can choose from hundreds of sources. Do you want to know what Darryl Lee thinks of it? He's a network administrator at Network Computing Devices in Mountain View, California, whose "Apple bites" page earned him the Cruel Site of the Day (**www.cruel.com**) (see Figure 5.7).

FIG. 5.7

Should Darryl Lee's opinions sway your investment strategy?

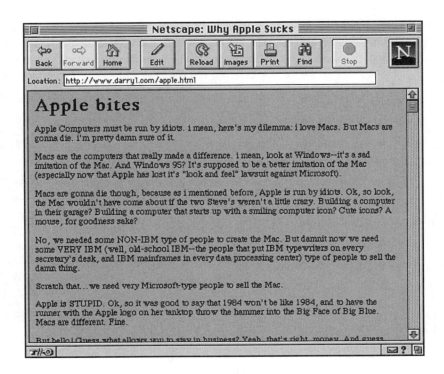

Then there's Adam C. Engst and his wife, Tonya, publishers of Tidbits (see Figure 5.8). They've been following the Macintosh scene for over seven years. Would you make a stock portfolio decision based on the dozens of Darryls out there on the Web? Or are you going to go with a source you heard was valuable, like Tidbits, or are you going to stick with the tried and true and stick with a source you trust, like the *Wall Street Journal*?

Back in the good old days (say 1992), you had to have a good deal of money to be a publisher. You had to have backers who vetted you and had confidence in you. If you wanted to advertise your products on television, you had to pay dearly for the privilege. It used to be that "As seen on TV" meant that you had a large enough company to have a large enough budget to buy ad space that was reserved for the likes of the major players.

Today, anybody with $20 a month can have a Web page up on AOL or GeoCities or any of hundreds of local access providers. Anybody willing to allow ads on their Web site can barter them for free ads on others' sites. Today, everybody is a publisher and everybody is an advertiser.

"So where did you hear about Gil Amelio's latest plan to save the company, that made you want to buy more stock?"

"Well, it was some real positive stuff I read by Amy Roos."

"Oh? Who's that?"

"Amy Elisabeth Roos. She's got a Web site."

"If she had her own TV show, or wrote a column in the *Wall Street Journal* I could see it, but a Web site? Heck, even my 11-year-old niece has a Web site, but I wouldn't take any investment advice from her."

FIG. 5.8

Tidbits has been offering solid, ground-level insights for years.

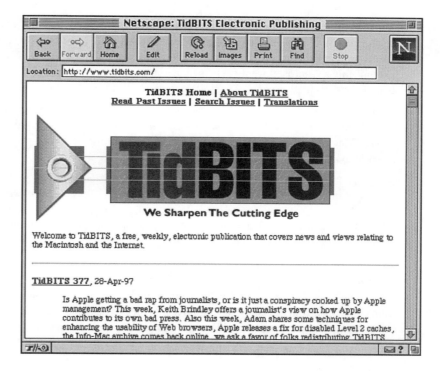

As Steve Hayden (part of the Apple "1984" television commercial team) said in an article in *Advertising Age* (November, 1996), "In a world of information overload, brands become ever more important. Icons with virtual memory, brands save time. I may have intelligent agents that can go out and assemble pages of reports on every camcorder on the market, but I don't have time to read them. I'll buy Sony."

With so many choices of content, and with such an assortment of sources, people will depend more and more on the feelings of trust they hold for the companies they do business with. If you already have a strong brand, you now have a new place to make it stronger. If you don't, you have a momentary opportunity to get out there on the Net ahead of the competition and establish yourself.

Branding by Association

In some industries, it may simply be enough to have Web ads at all. We haven't seen banners for antacids, dental floss, or breakfast cereal. Yet. If you want to be known as the coolest shampoo on the planet, you can associate yourself with the Web itself. If you're the only one in cyberspace advertising spark plugs, you have a lead on the competition. For the moment.

But what if you face serious competition for mind share?

Then it's time to bring out the wheelbarrow of money. Are there lots and lots of companies selling software? Then buy mind share like Microsoft does. Every time you go to a computer-related content site, you're pretty sure to find a message from Bill doing his "embrace and extend" thing. Microsoft wants to be synonymous with the Web, and paying for that position is one of the tools in its arsenal. AT&T, IBM, and NYNEX aren't far behind.

To further refine your brand image, you can borrow images from others. You can put a banner on the Comedy Central Web site (**www.comcentral.com**), or you can put a banner on the Money Magazine Web site (**http://pathfinder.com/money**). What's the difference? Association.

Are you a fun-loving company willing to laugh at yourself and dine out on the highjinks and hilarity of the country's top comedians? Are you willing to be associated with a network whose taste in humor can run to the raunchy? Do you fall in with other advertisers like Prodigy and 1-800-Flowers, or is your firm more intent on maintaining an image of professionalism like the University of Phoenix and Buick?

Rich Lefurgy is the VP of advertising at Starwave. That's the firm that started ESPNET Sportzone and Mr. Showbiz, helped get Ticketmaster Online online, among others, and was bought by Disney. They've been selling ads to the big guns for a couple of years now. Guns like Levi Strauss, Gatorade, and AT&T. Lefurgy's also one of the founders of the Internet Advertising Bureau. He knows Web advertising pretty well. He's also big on branding.

From Lefurgy's point of view, frequently expressed in various interviews, branding has only been done by building Web sites and expecting, hoping, that people will come and interact with the brand. Now that companies are realizing that they need to make extra efforts to bring people to their Web sites, they are looking back to the traditional creative people at ad agencies to do what has always been their core competency: building brands.

Lefurgy doesn't think the laws of marketing physics change on the Internet. The basics still apply. He feels there's still a gap between what interactive practitioners know how to do and what the major players on Madison Avenue have done for years. But he also feels the gap is closing.

Measuring the Touchy-Feely

So there's the value—name recognition, mind share, trust. But what's the payback? How do you know your branding is paying off? The same way you do it offline.

The metrics you're going to be interested in for this sort of campaign are going to be awareness, recall, and persuasion. You want to catch people on the street after the fact and see how well you scored.

Awareness: Do they know that you make this product?

Recall: Do they remember seeing your special offer in that ad?

Persuasion: Did it change their feelings about the company or the product?

Offline Brand Measurement According to *Which Ad Pulled Best* by Philip Ward Burton and Scott C. Purvis (September 1, 1996, Ntc Pub Group), serious, meaningful, scientific measurement of these kinds of ads began in the 1930s. They say it was the depression that made advertisers squeeze their nickels a little tighter, and Burton and Purvis reveal some of the methods used to measure brand power in use today.

Gallup & Robinson's Magazine Impact Research Service is intended to "(1) assess in-market performance of individual ads; (2) analyze overall advertising campaign and strategy effectiveness relative to previous history and the performance of the competition; and (3) identify and evaluate the effectiveness of competitive selling propositions and executional approaches within specific industries or product categories."

They place a test magazine in subjects' homes and call the next day to ask some questions. The subjects don't know what the survey is about. The instructions are to read the magazine on the day it is placed and not the day of the interview.

The questions include whether they saw an ad for the specific product. What did it look like? What sales points or buying arguments were made? What did they learn from the ad? What went through their minds when they read the ad? How was their buying interest effected: increased? decreased? What was in the ad that made them feel that way? Which brand of this type of product did they buy the last time?

Another service, Readex, does their research through the mail. They ask people to rate ads on attention-getting ability, believability, and information value. Readers are asked to list actions either taken or planned based on having seen the ad. Did their impression of the company change?

Behavior versus Declaration Roper Stach Worldwide takes a different tack and it's an important one when trying to apply these techniques to the Web. They ask a metric boatload of people what they actually read in a certain magazine as opposed to what they usually read. They find out what happened, instead of what people think happened, and more important, what people say happened.

Roper Starch then classifies people into three categories: Noted (they remembered seeing the ad); Advertiser-associated (they know whom the ad was from); and Read-most (they actually read more than half the ad). If you're Coke, you care about advertiser-associated. If you're IBM, you care about read-most.

This brings home a serious point about surveys on the Web. We know that surveys are already skewed because they are answered only by people who are willing to answer a survey. The rest of the world is a mystery. But even then, there is an entire science behind the derivations between the real and the supposed. Half of this is taken up by psychology and the other by mathematics.

If you must, you may find more detail in such books as *Answering Questions: Methodology for Determining Cognitive and Communicative Processes in Survey Research* by Norbert Schwarz and Seymour Sudman (Jossey-Bass, 1995); *Analyzing Repeated Surveys* by Glenn Firebaugh (Sage University Papers, Quantitative Applications in the Social Sciences, Vol 115, February 1997,); or *Context Effects in Social and Psychological Research* by Norbert Schwarz (Springer Verlag, 1992). If your interest is more mathematical in nature, take a look at *Perspectives On Contemporary Statistics* by David C. Hoaglin and David S. Moore (Mathematical Association of America, 1992). It offers a chapter on "the science of survey sampling, the essential concepts of statistical design of experimentation, the contemporary ideas of probability, and the reasoning of formal inference."

On the Web, you're faced by problems of a survey only being answered by those who can find it, and of them, those who are willing. And of them, the validity is based on those who will tell the truth. And of them, the validity is based on those who remember and can accurately tell the truth. It's an uphill battle.

Current Efforts—From the Vendor Side   HotWired suffered the slings and arrows of outrageous survey obstacles when they ran their study, released in December, 1996 (**www. hotwired.com/brandstudy**) (see Figure 5.9). Beyond the problem of getting accurate answers, HotWired was trying to address another problem.

FIG. 5.9
HotWired takes a stab at measuring the value of banners ads for branding.

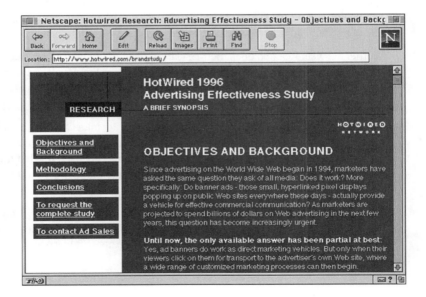

The problem, of course, is that only a fraction of all viewers click the banners they see. As a consequence, a few marketers have elected to pay only for proven clickthrough while the rest of the marketing community—which pays for ad placements according to CPM—is left to wonder whether the millions of impressions its banner ads generate without clickthrough are simply wasted.

HotWired worked with Millward Brown International to create a study using the same metrics Millward Brown uses to assess the effectiveness of print and television advertising. After conducting a Web-based survey of 1,232 people...

> This, in sum, is what we found: Banner ads on the HotWired Network make a significant impact on their viewers. An impact that demonstrably builds the advertised brand, even upon first impression. To this extent, every ad impression is important.
>
> When we add the ability to build brands in a classical sense to the Web's established advantages in selective targeting and direct marketing, we arrive at the first complete picture of the World Wide Web (or at least of the HotWired Network) as a medium with truly superior potential for conducting marketing.

The entire report is available online (**www.hotwired.com/brandstudy**). Here is the Summary Of Findings:

Acceptance of Advertising on the Web

The majority of HotWired users are supportive of Web advertising. Fewer than one in ten are against it and only 1 percent are strongly against Web advertising in general.

Message power

Consumer Loyalty scores (a measure of the likelihood that a consumer will choose a particular brand for their next purchase) increased between exposed and control cells by as much as 57 percent demonstrating the power of the ad banner to increase the bond between consumer and brand in a manner that is likely to drive sales.

The first exposure of a brand on the Web has strong immediate benefits for the brand increasing Consumer Loyalty by increasing the brand's Presence (consciousness of the brand) and positively impacting perceptions of the brand's personality, as well as differentiating it from its competition.

Predisposition toward the brand

While banners can effect a change in consumer attitude, preexisting perceptions of the brand do play a role in defining the brand/consumer dialog.

Response to advertisement

Advertising awareness increased, both for the brands in general and for the specific banners used.

Exposure to Web ad banners may generate more of a brand-linked ad awareness (a measure which is highly predictive of future purchase behavior) than television or print.

However, in comparison to television advertising, consumer reaction to Web ads appears to be biased toward positive but passive engagement.

The high-involvement nature of the Web and the prominent placement aspects of the advertising seem to play a larger role in defining the communication effectiveness than did the particular creative tested in this study.

User response to the Web banners tested indicate a slight boost in reported interest in the advertised brand as well as a modest self-reported improvement of opinion of the brand.

Incremental benefit and diminishing returns

While overall banner awareness is higher with increased media weight, the incremental benefit of one additional exposure is greatest for the apparel brand, since it is effectively starting with no exposure. The incremental effect is most diminished for the Web browser, as many of these people are likely to have been exposed to this banner, or one like it, elsewhere.

Determining factors of click-through

The primary driver seems to be the nature of the audience. The inherent interest of the product category, or brand, for the audience appears to be the most salient factor driving click-through. The appeal of the creative may also play a role; however, the contribution appears to be secondary.

Click-through rate did not predict the brand-building impact of the ad banner exposure.

These results have to be viewed through the lens of survey anomalies. It was based on an audience that was already a Hotwired member and may be pre-disposed to unintentionally tell Hotwired what they think Hotwired might want to hear. Hotwired took a:

Random sample from the universe of users who accessed HotWired between 9 September and 16 September 1996 is solicited for participation in a short research study, "To help HotWired better understand the audience." thirty-eight percent of those solicited participated.

The next day:

Respondents are sent an email that thanks them for their participation and invites them to partici-pate in a second survey (with the added incentive of a chance to win US$100). Users are provided with a URL (Web address) in the email and directed to link to the Web page in order to participate in the survey. sixty-one percent of the original respondents participate in the second survey.

Skewed or not, it was the first time such an effort had been made public and still points out that traditional expectations of advertising and branding can occur on the Web.

Current Efforts—From the Buyer Side   The ARF (**www.arfsite.org**) looks into this kind of thing for a living with all of the traditional media. They've been at it for more than 60 years. "Founded in 1936, the Advertising Research Foundation seeks to improve the practice of adver-tising, marketing and media research in pursuit of more effective marketing and advertising communications."

They produced reports like the one in 1995: *Exploring Brand Equity*, which they describe as "a comprehensive overview of the state of research today in the measurement and understanding of brand equity, as well as to provide a theoretical and historical foundation for advancing its study and measurement, [which] presents a compilation of the best thinking from ARF-sponsored conferences and workshops on the topic. "

Even as late as their July, 1996 meeting, the ARF was thinking in terms of the effectiveness of Web sites. What do you measure? The number of people? The number of times the same people come? The length of time they stay? The depth to which they plumb? But in February of 1997, they decided it was time to look at measuring Web ads as well.

Working in conjunction with CASIE, ARF announced they were going to establish gauges for measuring awareness, recall, and persuasion. As of summer, 1997, they are still in discussion.

Gabe Samuels is a research manager at the Advertising Research Foundation (**www.amic. com/amic_mem/arf**) and is leery of the hype surrounding this new medium. At the April 8, 1997 ARF Annual Conference, he put it this way: "Like all new media, there is a whole lot of money being poured in and the people doing the pouring have specific goals. They are pumping up the whole thing.

"The same thing happened with cable television and more recently with online services, back when they were called videotext. The hard part is properly managing expectations." But Samuels doesn't think it's a case of too much hype. "There is lots of circumstantial, anecdotal evidence that suggests people are having an impact with their Wed ads. Lots of people are saying their response has been great! But so far, there is no proof positive. There is no third party research to measure effectiveness as of this minute."

He feels there are dozens of efforts underway all over the world. "You can be sure that all of the major research companies are working in conjunction with Internet service providers and publishers to provide some kind of substantiation." Won't those be self-serving? "No more so than all of the other research that's done in the name of industry. Some will be aggressive, some will be conservative and eventually a picture will begin to form." You can experiment, or you can wait for the experts to hand down the research results.

Reach versus Frequency

Throughout all of this measuring and counting, be sure to talk to the sites you're buying from about reach versus frequency. *Reach* is how many people see your ad and frequency is how often. As Alex Nathanson, a frustrated Webmaster/marketer/advertiser at Epson America, explained in an e-mail to me: "1,000 impressions to the same guy is very different from one impression to 1,000 people." Reach is critical to branding. As you'll see later, frequency plays a very important role in direct response efforts.

If you operate in the type of marketplace that requires you to compete on a brand scale, then you need to think in terms of awareness and advertiser-association. However, if your goals are more direct in nature, and you are focused on the persuasion side of the coin, the direct-response model, then you better get to understand clickthroughs—the Web equivalent of calling the toll free number or filling out the coupon and mailing it in.

Clickthroughs

Time to move one step closer to the sales end of the value chain. The first step is advertising—letting people know you're out there and have something to offer them. The next step is getting them to take action, even if it's as small an action as clicking the mouse.

At the Web Advertising 97 conference, Ali Partovi of LinkExchange showed excellent examples of banners intended for direct marketing versus branding. A banner that says, "Volvos are safe" carries the brand image, but a banner that says, "CLICK HERE for a COOL car page," gets more clicks. "Visa. It's Everywhere you want to be," sends the message, but "Need Credit?? Click Here Now!!" gets a response. "Vote today. Vote Dole," put the candidate's name in front of thousands of people, but "Voting today? Click Here," got more of them to do so.

Part of the Web's attraction to the marketer is that the outgoing message and the incoming action happen in the same media. You see a banner, you can click it. If you come across an unlinked banner, perhaps there's only a phone number or a post office box on it, your response would have to take place in a different media. This is normal for print and broadcast advertising. If you get a telephone solicitation, you can order right then. If you get direct mail, usually you can fill out the form and send it back. If you hear an ad on the radio, you can't use the radio to reply.

But the immediacy of the Internet combines the urgency of broadcast with the ease of response. Add to the mix that the reaction—the click—is eminently measurable. It's like staking out all of the newsstands in the world, following buyers home, and standing behind them as they read. Did they see that page? Did they read the ad? Did they want to know more? All tabulated and neatly stored in a database ripe for slicing and dicing and analyzing performance ratings.

Because the Net is so measurable, and the medium so new, and the price of impressions and clicks are so soft, it's a buyers' market. In such a market, strange deals are often devised. Proctor & Gamble was the first to cut a clickthrough-only deal.

Paying per Click

In April of 1996, Webmasters, banner sellers, and interactive marketers all over the world shook their heads in wonder as Proctor & Gamble announced their deal with Yahoo! They would not be paying for exposures, pageviews, impressions, or OTSs. They would only pay when somebody clicked. The numbers were not announced but the numbness was felt throughout the Web.

Not pay for impressions? Only pay for clickthroughs? It makes no sense? How could Yahoo! agree to such a thing? Stupidity? Confidence? Hunger?

Didn't Yahoo! understand that they made themselves prisoner to the power of the creative? Something they had no control over? Did they think they would have so many visitors that lots of them would click through by mistake, if nothing else? Were they gushing red ink so fast that they needed a deal with anybody who came along that smelled like money?

It's the creative control issue that stumped everybody. If a newspaper were to use this business model? They would only charge for ad space depending on how many people called.

"But," might be the response from the otherwise quiescent P&G, "Web publishers are promising affinity, they are promising targeting, they are promising measurability and so much more than any other medium. All we're asking is that they put their money where their mouth is. This is an untested field. We'll pay for the results."

It wouldn't be very hard to create a banner that did a fine job of branding and a horrible job of direct response. The result would be one of high exposure for almost no cost at all. The publisher would end up penniless, having given up all the ad space in hopes that people would click. The only alternative would be to throw in with the advertiser and surround the banner with incentives. So much for the separation of church and state.

There are only four payment models for ads on the Web. You can pay for impressions. You can pay for clicks. You can pay for leads. You can pay for sales. Impressions is a mode we're very accustomed to. Paying for leads is a time-honored tradition. After all, what is the total cost to get a lead through direct mail? Through television? Paying for sales is called retail and has been practiced since humans started gathering in villages. Those models are worth looking at and we will.

But paying for clickthroughs alone simply makes no sense if you are in the content (publishing) business.

At the July 1996 meeting of the Advertising Research Foundation, they took on the Web. Nigel Holis, Group Research and Development Director at Millward Brown International, woke everybody when he opened his presentation. He said, "Just because you can measure something does not mean that the measurement has value, or that it should be used as the basis for a community currency."

But if you're not in the content business, you might want to make a buck by sending people to HearthNet (**www.hearth.com**) (see Figure 5.10). This site claims to be targeted toward "uniquely qualified homeowners who are looking to improve their lifestyle."

HearthNet wants clickthroughs and isn't afraid to say so:

Can you help our site ?

We are ALWAYS looking for more visitors to our site, and are ready, able and willing to pay a fair price for these visitors. While many agencies pay only 1 cent to 5 cents per 'click-thru', we're happy to pay from 10 cents to as much as 35 cents—depending on quantity and qualification of visitors. Please take a look at our site, HearthNet, and email to webmaster@hearth.com if you feel there could be a good fit.

Sites dealing with DIY, housing, building materials, energy, conservation and other related matters are preferred, but let's talk. We are looking for homeowners—if you think you can drive them to us, maybe we can both profit.

FIG. 5.10

HearthNet wants you to send people to their site and will pay you to do it.

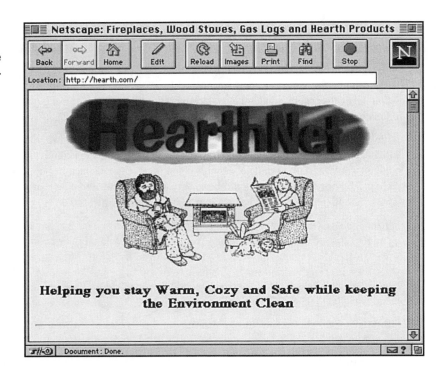

On a small scale, it's not such a mystery. It also makes sense on a large scale where the publisher is confident of the results and is not even trying to separate church and state.

Riddler, as seen in Chapter 4, "Beyond the Banner," places the company's products smack dab in the middle of the game. They put the company's ad smack dab in the middle of the game play. As a result, they produce more clickthroughs than most. They are so sure of their clickthrough ratios that they don't want to leave money on the table by selling CPMs.

If you're an ad buyer, you might like this approach. If you're an ad seller on a site of high integrity, this approach will send you packing faster than bits on dark fiber. Either way you play it, counting clicks has some problems of its own.

Counting Problems

At first, clickthroughs seemed like the brass ring to a media buyer. Instant feedback on how well your creative and placement efforts are being received. Instant tabulation on the number of people prompted to action. A database full of stats ready, willing, and able to be sliced and diced to determine exactly which half of your advertising dollar is being wasted. No wonder ad buyers are excited by the idea of only paying for the results.

But, alas, the course of true promotion never did run smooth.

Impatience Is a Vice   You're hot on the trail of that last datapoint for your presentation. The one factoid that will convince the boss that the project is right for the company and you are right for the project. Then your eye catches an animation of a guy painting a house. You're in the process of getting quotes from house painters. Maybe…

You click. The thought is firmly in mind that you will only take a minute to see what this banner ad is all about. After all, you've done this before. That picture of the hot new BMW you craved turned out to be an ad for an insurance company. Pha!

But nothing happens. "Contacting…Waiting for reply…" You've seen this go on forever in the past. You know that sometimes the old packets requesting a page just sort of head off into the ether, never to be heard of again. You know that the best thing to do is hit Stop, and click it again. Maybe this time your request will reach the server.

Once again you wait. Maybe the server is busy—like calling a toll-free number and getting a busy signal. You know there is more than one operator standing by, so you hit redial and get a ring. You hit Stop and click again. You wait. Your minute is up. You go back in search of that elusive datapoint that will make your career.

Meanwhile, on the other side of the Internet, there is a server that racked up three clickthroughs and an advertising manager who's pleased with the response.

Browsing While You Sleep   To combat the World Wide Wait, some companies have come out with offline browsers. Point one of these at a Web site, set the depth you want it to traverse, and hit "Go!" It makes a mad dash to the home page and starts downloading everything it finds to your hard drive. It follows link after link, fetching everything that site has to offer.

If that site is offering ads, they get "seen." If you set the browser to follow off-site links, the ads register clickthroughs. You can set these offline grazers to refresh specific sites overnight.

The result? Every banner on the site registers an impression and a clickthrough, whether a human looked at the ads or not.

This is an area rife for expansion now that Microsoft and Netscape have decided that push technology is their latest battlefield. Setting up your browser to fetch Web site updates on a timed basis multiplied by millions of users is certain to skew some numbers.

But it can be much worse. If the offline browser comes across an *image map* (a picture that contains multiple links), it doesn't know how many links there are in that picture. To be sure it's downloading everything for you, it "clicks" that map every half inch or so. If that image happens to be your banner, you just hit the clickthrough bonanza!

Robots on the Loose   'Bots, spiders, crawlers, agents. They come to your site and wander around. Some report back to places like AltaVista and Lycos to keep their databases up-to-date. Some are written by enterprising graduate students looking for free software or hackable networks.

These free-agent bits of software are created for lots of different reasons by lots of different people, but they are all designed to save the users' time. The software travels around the Net looking for whatever it has been sent for, rather than the human. As a result, servers record "visits" and, thinking they are humans, racks those visits up as impressions. The cash register rings and you pay the bill.

Proxy Servers Strike Again   Step one: a surfer on AOL looks at a page on a site that has your ad on it. The AOL server stores the page and the banner in the cache for the next prospective surfer.

Step two: the next prospective surfer clicks a link to that very same page that has your banner on it. The AOL server looks at the site and determines that the page has not changed. That action leaves a tell-tale record in the log that the page has been viewed. However, seeing that the page has not changed, AOL does not bother asking about the banner. It serves up the cached page and banner to the second surfer.

Step three: repeat step two 99 times. In the meantime, 100 other people from other access providers without caching have looked at the page.

Step four: a total of two people from AOL clicked the banner and two other people did, as well. That's about average for a banner: 2% clickthrough.

Step five: the owner of the site on which you advertised reports that your banner was shown 101 times and got four clickthroughs. You're delighted that you're getting twice the average. You're wrong.

Noise Will Be Noise   Ask any statistician about accurate numbers and you'll hear about noise. There is no such thing as a clear signal. There is no free lunch. Karen Anderson, Media Buyer at Modem Media (**www.modemmedia.com**), has learned to live with noise. "As long as you measure things consistently, the distribution will even out over time," she said at Web Advertising 97. "Some of the problems favor the seller and some favor the buyer. The important thing is that you know how much you're paying for roughly a million impressions and approximately a thousand clicks. The trouble starts when you try to compare one Web site's statistics against another."

That's the problem with which you are left. Until the standards bearers win the day and convince all ad sellers to adhere to common enumerating techniques and reporting formats, you have to bear the brunt of weighing apples to oranges. And given how a particular site counts its clicks, you have to decide if what they are asking is worth the price.

Supply and Demand

Nigel Holis finished up his presentation to the July, 1996 meeting of the Advertising Research Foundation by explaining the backfire problem clickthrough pricing will cause. He suspects Proctor & Gamble may be sorry for opening this Pandora's box.

"On the basic response criteria of clickthrough, the content provider is not going to realize a lot of revenue for carrying a P&G ad because few people will be interested enough to click. So why carry the ad at all? Content providers will probably develop individual hierarchies of advertisers based on the relevance of the advertisers' brands to their audience and try to charge accordingly. They might put up a banner at minimal rates for Levi's, Sun or Saturn, because the expected results, and their reward, is likely to be good. On the other hand, they might see there to be an opportunity cost to carrying a P&G ad, provided there were more relevant advertisers to go after, and charge accordingly.

"Is this what advertisers like P&G really want? I doubt it. However, in their push to get value for their media dollar, they may be ignoring the basic laws of supply and demand. Right now the suppliers are on weak ground and they [P&G] can get away with it, but one day the Wal-Mart of the online world is going to call their bluff."

The Value of a Click—Making the Sale

Because prices change so fast, it makes no sense to consign Web ad prices to the pages of this book. In the late spring of 1997, John Schick of SI Software pegged clickthroughs at a range of forty cents to a dollar each, and they were getting an average of 2% to 3.5% clicks. His tremendously helpful "EXPLORING AD RATES AND OFFERINGS" page (**www.adresource.com/ whatitco.htm**) is well worth bookmarking.

The fact is that you have a lot of issues to consider when estimating the value of a click. Are you looking for lots of people to come to your site? Or do you only want the highly qualified? Do you want to use the host site and the banner to do your filtering for you? Or do you want to have your site be the place where qualifying happens?

You have to choose—do you want to hand out ice cream at your trade show booth in order to collect thousands of names? Or do you want to hand out nothing, knowing that only the most qualified will stop and talk to your salespeople?

Do you have high faith in the way your Web site qualifies people? Do you want to funnel as many people through it as possible? Or do you want to place your faith in your advertising to do the qualifying for you?

In 1849, did it make more sense to sluice tons and tons of river slurry through huge sluice boxes, in hopes that the sheer quantity would yield more gold? Or should you try to find a rich vein with a pick and shovel that would yield more gold at once? People got rich both ways.

The real question when choosing between "Click here if you really like driving" and the narrower "Click here if you're ready to buy a sports car" is: Which will get the most qualified people per ad dollar?

If you're a magazine and you want more eyeballs so you can sell more ads, then the choice may seem to favor higher quantities. Of course, you still have to get them to click past page one, be satisfied enough to keep coming back, subscribe, and want to tell their friends and colleagues. You still need slurry that has lots of gold in it. You won't get rich sluicing the Mississippi.

Which, then, is the best goal: lots of clicks or only qualified clicks?

I put that question to a man who optimizes high-volume, measured Web sites as part of his marketing consulting business. Ron Richards from ResultsLab (**www.resultslab.com**) is a marketing man first and foremost. But scratch him just a little bit and you'll find the quantitative thinker. In reaction to my e-mail, Richards argued that there may be a very favorable tradeoff with higher clicks of lower qualification, and sometimes you don't have to suffer the tradeoff at all:

I certainly don't advocate trading quality of response for quantity of response. You should always strive to use techniques which tune in to the target audience's deepest needs. You can create grabbers that dramatize the value of your offer and attract qualifieds like one pole of a magnet, and usually push away unqualifieds like the other pole.

But now let's look at how you COULD, after all, accept a lower percentage of unqualifieds, and yet gain net qualifieds.

Some of your metaphors, like the mining and ice cream, ignore the fact that screening people by getting them to self-select after they enter your Web site is virtually costless, unlike mining and giving away ice cream. The ice cream metaphor not only contains high-cost 'prospects' getting the ice cream, but ice cream is presumably unrelated to the product/company and so does NO screening. In contrast, my idea is to be willing to use (virtually costless) methods that multiply the traffic while attenuating, BUT NOT DEVASTATING, the percent qualified—with net economic gain, and twice the resulting QUALIFIED prospects.

The heart of it all is estimating how the numbers will work out:

Say you have high-calorie clickthroughs, where you get 2% clickthrough of which 80% are qualified. Now suppose you can do something with your ad placement or treatment to get 3% the clickthrough rate, or 6%, but with only 50% qualified. You went from gathering 2%×80%=1.6% qualifieds to gathering 6%×50%=3% qualifieds—almost a twofold NET gain.

Simply put, whenever you can amplify total response more than you attenuate fraction qualifieds in the process, you have amplified net qualifieds.

If unqualifieds are visiting and then inquiring by e-mail or phone—costing the advertiser lots of labor, phone and postage—there are better solutions than changing the ad to purge the unqualifieds. Instead, I like to improve the site to make it clear who should respond and who should hit the back button, thus surpressing the unwanted expenses.

EVERYTHING is radically changed from the ice cream/trade show model because of the 'virtually free' nature of the screening, which used to be a MAJOR advertising and selling cost.

I countered with:

You can get 1,000 poorly qualified people coming to your site and end up with 5 real leads, one of which turns into a sale. Or, you can get 5 very qualified people and end up with 5 real leads, one of which turns into a sale. The only question is: Which one was cheaper?

Richards reiterated his point that, once the qualification system has been set up on a Web site, it costs next to nothing to administer. Especially when compared to the alternatives of additional direct mail or telemarketing.

Randy Kawahara, Assistant Manager of National Advertising at Honda, wants the site he advertises on to help filter the surfer. He's interested in putting Civic banners on sites that attract a younger crowd and Accord banners on sites that attract a wealthier audience. Yes, he admits, part of his reasoning is associative branding, but filtering is on his mind.

Carolyn Doll, Manager of Media Research and Interactive Media for Hal Riney & Partners works on the Saturn account and doesn't want to filter as much as Kawahara does. Hal Riney does all of those downhome Saturn television ads. One would think they're after a certain breed.

According to Doll, "It's all about boxcar numbers for us. The bigger the site, the more the clickthrough. Yeah, we can get three times the clickthrough on something like Epicurious Food (http://food.epicurious.co) because it attracts women, or on Traveler (http://travel.epicurious.com) because it attracts upscale and sophisticated. But the CPM is a lot higher on those, so the cost of each click is higher."

Doll ran down the numbers on a buy she made at the end of 1996. Excite showed the Saturn banner a half a million times. It got a touch over a half of one percent clickthrough. The same banner at Epicurious got one and a half percent clickthrough. Three times the generic search engine! But Doll is quick to point out that Excite was the far better buy in cost per click and sheer volume.

While she couldn't reveal the price points, using current prices reveals what she means:

Site	CPM	Impressions	Cost	Clickrate	Clicks	CPC
Excite	$24	500,000	$12,000	.55%	2,750	$4.36 each
Epicurious	$55	7,500	$4,125	1.56%	117	$35.26 each

As for cost-per-net-qualifieds, the logic says that the Epicureans are much more likely to become Saturn buyers. "Eight times more likely?" asks Doll. "When we have better tracking on our own site and the content people can offer us better targeting we'll re-think it. Right now, we're very happy showing our banner to millions of people. After all, our branding is all about regular folks, you know?"

So you can pay by the impression or you can pay by the click. Either way, you're going to pay based on what the ad-selling site tells you the numbers were. They say there were millions of impressions, you pay. They say there were thousands of clickthroughs, you pay. So who watches over them? How do you know the ad sales site is giving you data on which you can rely?

Independent Verification and Validation

In the world of software development for the U.S. government, there are some checks and balances to assure Uncle Sam that you are doing what he ordered, in an orderly fashion.

The IEEE Standard for Software Verification and Validation Plans 1012-1986 (R1992) spells out exactly how a third-party contractor will look over your shoulder while your crew tries to bang out code as fast as they can.

The objective of an IV&V (Independent Verification and Validation) effort is to develop an independent assessment of the software quality and to determine if the software satisfies critical systems requirements. In an effort to meet this objective, IV&V projects often seek to analyze the software using methods, tools, and processes that are complementary to but distinct from those used by the developer. The complementary viewpoints utilized by IV&V include efforts to determine conditions that might not have been tested by the developing organization, including boundary constraints, off-nominal conditions, error paths, and user scenarios. These viewpoints enable the IV&V team to have a different perspective of the software from that of the development team.

Who is watching over sites like Excite and Epicurious to insure they are keeping this side of those boundary constraints, avoiding the off-nominal conditions, and aren't straying onto those error paths?

Software Voyeurs

If you trust them to do it for themselves, they have to invest in some software. That takes us right back to the Log Analysis tools at Yahoo!. They can pick from Accrue Software, WebTrends, net.Analysis, NetTracker, NetIntellect, or dozens of others. Some people in Redmond, Washington thought this was an important enough feature in their Web server that they went out, bought one, and redubbed it "The Microsoft Site Server Usage Analyst feature" (**www.interse.com**) (see Figure 5.11).

I/Pro (**www.ipro.com**) was the first on the block to offer such a program. NetLine is a measurement and analysis system with a twist. Taking the stand that running analysis after analysis on your own computer bogs down its ability to quickly serve Web pages, NetLine grabs your logs and securely transmits them to I/Pro. There, they are crunched and returned in the form of daily, weekly, and monthly reports. "They are pre-formatted for printing, look good in black and white or color, and are in shades that can be faxed. You'll be proud to present them internally and externally.

But some people felt this didn't go far enough. If you're spending good money, you want to be certain the reports aren't cooked. In response, I/Pro went to a service model.

Report Verification

I/Pro decided to provide audits. In their parlance, "An audit is a report produced by an independent third party, which uses industry standard measures to verify the level of activity a site generates over a specified time period."

A couple of problems pop up. First, they are auditing the log files. Log files can be fudged. Next, it is often contended that the entity collecting the information should not be charged with auditing that information. Finally, there are no industry standard measures. If you want standard measures you have to look to the old media, like magazines.

FIG. 5.11
Intersé's tools were valuable enough to be gobbled up by Microsoft.

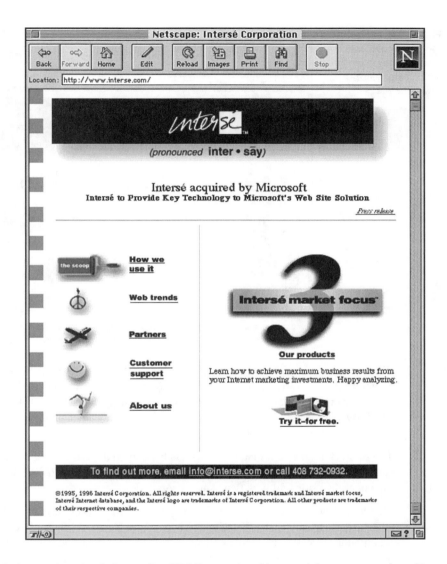

In the world of magazine circulation audits, BPA International is one of the top contenders. If you sell magazines, they will audit the number you sell. If you have a controlled subscription magazine, they verify and validate that you really have 25,000 senior level managers in companies with revenue over one billion dollars and responsible for the purchase of fleets of trucks. They've been at it since 1931. They've audited the circulation of 1,756 publications. They now do Web sites as well (**www.bpai.com**) (see Figure 5.12).

FIG. 5.12
BPA International has turned its magazine auditing experience toward the Web.

BPA publishes the reports they create. You can go to **www.bpai.com/audits/reports** and download Acrobat versions of the reports they've done for CIO and WebMaster Online, and a slew of "World" magazines like *Computer World, Java World, Netscape World, Network World, PC World,* and *Sun World OnLine.* If you're looking to buy an ad on these sites, you can see who visits at what time of day, and so on.

The Audit Bureau of Circulation (ABC) has been up to the same thing since 1914. In 1996, they spun off a subsidiary called Audit Bureau of Verification Services (ABVS Interactive) to handle the interactive side of things (**www.accessabvs.com/webaudit**) (see Figure 5.13).

Michael J. Lavery, President of ABVS, says that there are three ways an audit protects an advertiser: to assure that a Web site's activity counts have not been either misrepresented (counted incorrectly), manipulated (counts don't reflect actual activity), or reported in an unfamiliar format. Because the ABC has been formatting reports since 1914, they should know what's familiar.

But what these companies do not do is look under the covers. It's not how high you count that counts, it's how you count high.

How You Count High

In a press release dated April 8, 1997, Yahoo! announced that they had selected ABVS and Ernst & Young LLP to provide third-party validation and certification. Was there something ABVS couldn't handle? Yes.

FIG. 5.13
The ABC formed ABVS to verify and validate Web sites selling ads.

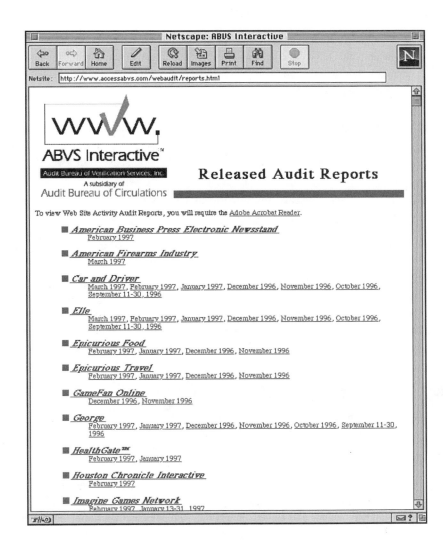

"ABVS Interactive will provide its expertise in interactive auditing, verification, and industry-developed standards to independently validate figures in Yahoo!'s site usage reports." But first, "Ernst & Young will provide third party certification of Yahoo!'s audience measurement software system and controls."

It's all well and good to say, "Yep, that sure is a five alight. Sure is. That's a five if ever I saw one." It's another thing to snoop around long enough to realize there's another question here. "Just how did you arrive at the five, given that you had two twos to start with?"

According to the release: "Ernst & Young is currently evaluating and documenting Yahoo!'s reporting software, processes, and procedures, and will recommend changes to incorporate established industry standards for controlling the information and the content of information to be provided prior to certification of the system. Ernst & Young will also recommend controls to monitor changes to Yahoo!'s system to certify ongoing systems integrity."

Even the IEEE would approve.

Serve Yourself

If you're a well-heeled advertiser and feel it's necessary to wrest control away from those untrustworthy content sites, you could insist that you serve your own ads. That's what General Motors did in April of 1997.

If you served your own ads onto the content creator's site, you know how many banners were served. Sort of. You still face all of the problems previously stated. The only discrepant element you remove from the mix is dishonesty. What you lose is the value of aggregated information that the content site can analyze and report. Who is visiting this site? What sort of subject matter and creative do they respond to the most?

Over time, General Motors and its followers will lose. The sites that sell ads can't afford to rely on sponsors to serve up banners fast enough to satisfy the need for speed felt by the ravening hordes of surfers. Debra Aho Williams at *Advertising Age* summed it up: "Marketers will push for this because they can. And because they hold the purse strings, some of them probably will get their way. But like so many things on the Net, just because you can, doesn't mean you should."

Measuring Behavior—Before and After

It's nice to know how many times there was an opportunity to see your banner. It's nice to know how many people clicked your banner. It's even nice to know that the numbers you've been given resemble what is happening on planet Earth. But what about the people behind those numbers? What are they up to? Really?

Looking Over Their Shoulders   The NPD Group (**www.npd.com**) measures what people do (see Figure 5.14). They'll take a panel of 2,000 households and make them keep diaries on what they eat for two weeks. They analyze and report back on their findings across each of 53 categories of foods and beverages by meal occasion, day of week, appliance used, cooking method, composition of the dish, gender, age, region…well, you get the idea. Oh, it's not just for food. They also track apparel, athletic footwear, beauty trends, cosmetics, fragrances, gasoline, home appliances…well, you get the picture.

They also run a service called PC-Meter. PC Meter Interactive Media Metrics provides statistics on:

> Estimated number of different people who visit Web sites
>
> Frequency of visits
>
> Length of visits
>
> Comparative data across sites

FIG. 5.14
NPD wants to watch
your every click.

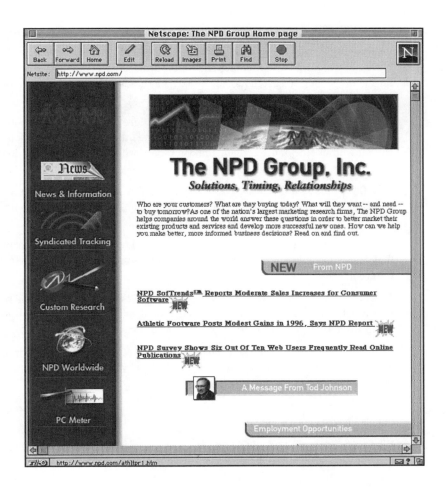

This is not hits, logs, or averages. This is hard data collected firsthand. They wired up a panel of 10,000 households demographically balanced to represent the population of U.S. PC owners. With software installed on home computers, they are not keeping diaries. They're surfing. Their surfing is recorded.

In 1996, PC-Meter found some interesting things—such as the fact that the top ten Web sites were search engines and sites that serve as default home pages for commercial online services, browsers, and Internet Service Providers (ISPs). A handful of content-driven sites made it into the list in the beginning part of the year, including the University of Michigan (**ww.umich.edu**), which (coincidentally?) ran a very popular poll on Web usage; the University of Illinois, Urbana-Champaign (**www.uiuc.edu**) (home of the NCSA's Mosaic); and Playboy (**www.playboy.com**) (no comment necessary).

MSNBC (**www.msnbc.com**) enjoyed the steepest audience growth when its cable TV show went on the air. Walt Disney (**www.disney.com**) got a giant shot in the arm by buying log-on promotional space on AOL in January and February.

But then there was NBC (**www.nbc.com**) that found out advertising on TV wasn't a bad way to go either. In a press release dated March 10, 1997, PC Meter revealed that the NBC Web site had done well while the Olympics were on the air. "NBC's Web server logs confirmed the impact of its televised promotions, as sharp increases in Web traffic occurred within minutes of many TV promos."

It's good to know that there are companies out there looking over the shoulders of Web surfers so you can figure out who's out there. You, on the other hand, can get a look at those people from the other side of the screen. You can record what those people are doing once they hit your site.

Your Own, Personal Yardstick   Did they click? You own them. Just as sure as if they had filled out a business reply form and mailed it back to you. It's now up to you to get to know them in all the ways possible. How do we measure them? Let me count the ways.

From where did they come? Your referrer logs will tell you that. But what different actions do they take if they came from ESPNet Sportszone as opposed to Epicurious? How are these leads different?

One of the easiest methods is to set up duplicate sets of pages. This is the home page and site they reach when they click a banner from Yahoo!, and that is the home page and site they reach when they click a banner at Riddler. Web site too big? Use cookies.

Do the people from this site stay long? Come back often? Do the people from that site tend to look at the whitepapers or go right for the product? Was that creative better as a tool for raising brand awareness or for direct response?

Time to go back to Rick Stout's *Web Site Stats—Tracking Hits and Analyzing Traffic* for all the details on what you can glean from your site.

When you track what people do on your site, you can learn a lot about the power of your ads. But you also learn about the power of listing in search engines and directories and doing direct mail. You can also learn if it's worth your while to pay for leads rather than clicks.

Buying Leads

We're not quite to retail yet. We'll get there, just hang on. At the moment we're in that twilight between advertising and selling, which is lead brokering.

Instead of selling you an Opportunity To See, or a clickthrough, what if I sold you somebody that was pre-qualified?

There are lots of examples out there, but the first one I ever came across was FinanCenter (**www.financenter.com**) (see Figure 5.15).

FinanCenter is a great place to hang out if you're thinking about borrowing money. Buying a house? A car? Want to know how much you can borrow? What your payments will be? Just want to get a better credit card? This is the place.

FIG. 5.15
FinanCenter offers free services to the public and passes the leads on to lenders—for a price.

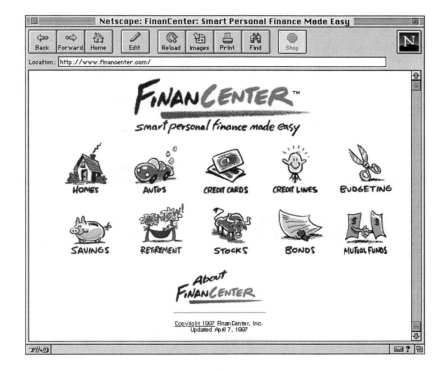

Loaded with do-it-yourself calculators, this site assists borrowers by offering below-market prices, cash rebates, and low rate guarantees. Is it a bank? Is it a savings and loan? No, it's a software company.

Sherri Neasham runs the place and loves contributing her talents to those in need of financial guidance. She's also been profitable from the third month of operations.

The calculators allow borrowers to experiment objectively, without any pressure from loan agents or sales reps. They get to alter the down payment points, the term, the balloon payment. In other words, they do all the hard stuff, the time-consuming stuff. When they finally get a set of numbers that look good, it's time to apply for the loan.

You can apply for free. You can get an answer within 48 hours. You can lock in the lowest rate in America on a conforming loan. And when you do, FinanCenter's cash register rings.

On the lending side, American Finance and Investment gets a loan application from somebody who has already thought long and hard about how to structure the right loan. A loan they can afford. A loan they want to get an answer about within 48 hours. That's worth a great deal to American Finance and Investment and is cheaper than sending out thousands of direct mail pieces to apartment owners, hoping that some of them want to buy a house.

This isn't branding through impressions. It's not clickthrough based on curiosity. This is handing over a pre-qualified, interested, prospective buyer. The only thing better would be making the sale for you.

Commissioned Sales—The Final Frontier

You have heard of Amazon.com (**www.amazon.com**) dozens of times because theirs is a model that's working. People are willing to buy books over the Internet because they know what a book is and how it works. They can read excerpts of it online. They don't have to worry about whether it will fit, be the right color, or is compatible with their computer. It's a book. If you bought this one through Amazon.com, thank you. If you bought this one at Amazon.com by way of my Web site at **www.targeting.com**, then thank you very much! Here's why: I'm an Amazon Associate.

CEO and Founder Jeff Bezos isn't just smart, he's way smart. He'll be happy if you set up your own bookstore on the Web. You have a Web site about horses? Add a bookstore! He wants to be your fulfillment house.

You decide which of the eight hundred or so books about horses you like best and point people to them at Amazon.com. If they buy, Bezos will send you a commission. He's turned everybody on the Internet into a retail store for his back-end supply shop. Brilliant.

Mark Welch lists 34 sites that promise to pay commissions on his massively useful Web Site Banner Advertising: Banner Ad Networks & Brokers page (**www.markwelch.com/ bannerad.htm**) (see Figure 5.16).

FIG. 5.16
Mark Welch lists 34 commission-based sites the last time I looked.

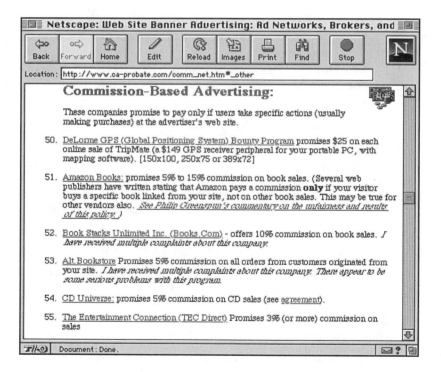

Where, Oh Where, Does that Banner Belong?

You know what they are. You know what they do. You know how to count the results. Now where are you going to place that banner so it can do the most good? That's a whole 'nother kettle of fish and a whole 'nother chapter. ●

CHAPTER 6

Looking for Space In All the Right Places

> "I *always wanted to be somebody, but I should have been more specific.*"
>
> *Lily Tomlin*

What do you look for when you place TV commercials? The right audience. If you're selling beer, it's unlikely that you're going to find a decent demographic audience on Masterpiece Theatre. If you're selling Grey Poupon, it wouldn't be wise to spend a lot of money for ads on Demolition Derby.

What do you look for when you place ads in magazines? The right audience. Fishing tackle probably won't move well in Architectural Digest.

Newspapers? First, you choose the geography, then you pick the section, then you pick the right days. You're after the right audience. Why should it be any different on the World Wide Web?

You're taking the time and going to the trouble of getting oriented (hey, you're taking the time to read this, right?). You're going to do your best to create captivating ads. And, while you're not spending a million dollars for thirty seconds of the Superbowl, you *are* committing some of your hard-fought budget on this electronic experiment. It would be a shame if all that time, effort, and money were spent to put your message in front of people who won't get it, won't like it, and—most important of all—won't buy it. You'll be wasting your budget. You'll be wasting your time. Your boss won't be very happy, either.

The trick to banner placement on the Web is part context, part unconventional thinking, part competitive penetration, and a healthy dose of technology. The Web comes complete with new ways and new means of reaching would-be buyers. There are new tactics. There are also some tried and true techniques that will come as no surprise to anyone. It's the combination that can make your Web advertising campaign pay off. ■

Join the Crowd

Unless you're trying to sell something to everybody and your name is Honda, Coke, or Nike, one of the first things you should do is buy banners on sites that attract your kind of people. If your name is Honda, Coke, or Nike, you already know that Netscape has enough daily visitors to earn big bucks selling ad space. You may want to avail yourself of their venue. If a couple million people drive the same freeway day after day, it makes sense to put up a billboard. If a couple of million people end up at the Netscape site every day, it makes sense to put up a banner.

There's No Escape from Netscape

One of the single most visited sites on the Internet is Netscape. It gets visited because that's where you are taken when you fire up your Netscape browser. Even if you were nerdly enough to change the Netscape browser options so your home page is now some other Net destination (Options, General Preferences), Netscape still hooks the masses with its directory buttons. At the top of the browser window, just above the site being visited and just below the Location box showing the current URL, are the Directory buttons:

1. What's New?
2. What's Cool?
3. Destinations
4. Net Search
5. People
6. Software

Those buttons are in your face and hard to ignore. Microsoft Explorer may have a Search button and a Favorites list of built-in bookmarks, but the Netscape mystique is still working in their favor for now.

Netscape earned $53 million in 1997 putting Excite, Infoseek, Lycos, and Yahoo! on their Net Search page. They'll earn more and more as the major brand names decide they want to be where all the people are. You can pay big bucks to put your logo in lights at Times Square, Picadilly Circus, or on the road into town from the Hong Kong airport. Netscape isn't much different. It's for great awareness and recognition—branding.

How many millions of people visit Netscape every day? Lots. According to the claim on the Netscape Web site, it is "the most often visited site on the Web according to Netscape's latest I/Pro Audit." It's certainly a number that grows day-by-day.

What kind of people visit the Netscape site? In April of 1996, Netscapians got Griggs-Anderson Research to conduct a survey of almost 20,000 Netscape Navigator users. Their results give you a snapshot:

> 68% have a household income more than $50,000.
>
> 48% are between 26 and 45 years old.
>
> 84% are male.
>
> 57% have completed four years or more of college.
>
> 18% are in the computer industry.
>
> 77% are employed full-time.
>
> 22% are students (half of them are employed).
>
> 12% work from their homes.
>
> 39% have used their credit card number to make a Web purchase.

If you're thinking that this is just the type of person you're trying to reach, you're not very particular. You're not thinking in the broad sense of a brand maker or the narrow sense of an Internet direct marketer. These are *averages*. This is the result of a general sifting through Netscape server statistics. If you're selling fishing tackle, you need to tie your flies a little tighter. If you're Visa, maybe it makes sense to tackle the world from this direction.

Visa is going after people who eat out. At least, people who are interested in wandering the Web to read about eating out. They spent most of 1997 and into 1998 pushing a "Cities To Dine For" campaign on Epicurious Food and Travel (**www.epicurious.com**). Restaurant reviews for cities like London, New York, San Francisco, Sydney, and Tokyo will be festooned with encouragement to use your Visa card when the bill comes. Visa is also sponsoring GeoCities' NapaValley (**www.geocities.com/NapaValley**) (see Figure 6.1), which zeros in on gourmet food and wine. If you eat and can afford a credit card, Visa figures that's good enough for them.

This kind of thinking belongs to those who deal in broad brush strokes and aggregate information. You should only be looking at the big pull sites like Netscape or the search engines if your goal is global domination and your name is Microsoft. The numbers from LinkExchange (**www.linkexchange.com**) suggest that the more focused the site, the higher the clickthrough.

Ali Partovi, founder of LinkExchange, rattles off the numbers by heart. "The sites we looked at came up with pretty consistent results. If you show over a million impressions per day, the clickthrough is about two percent. Ten thousand to a hundred thousand impressions a day yields about two and a half percent. One thousand to ten thousand a day gets about two and two-thirds clicks and the site with less than a thousand impressions a day continually gets over three percent impressions to clicks. It's no secret. It's just that the smaller sites cater to more specific visitors whose interests are more obvious."

FIG. 6.1
Visa is looking for hungry people to use plastic money.

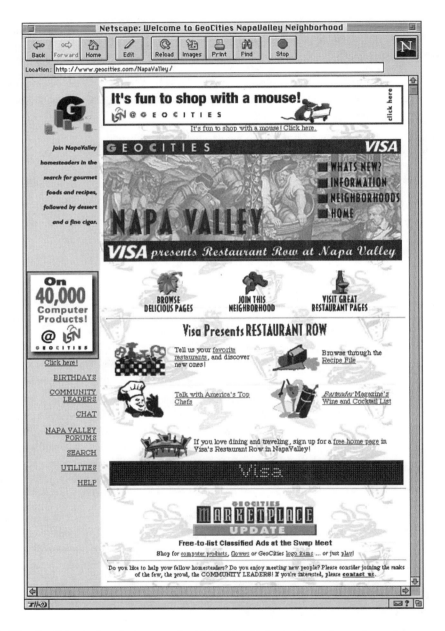

Bob Ivans is Vice President of market research at I/PRO, which creates software to analyze what visitors look at on a Web site and audit the claims made by those who would sell ads on their sites. Ivans agrees with Partovi, as seen in this quote from the October 21, 1996 issue of *Webweek*: "When the ad is consistent with content, the response rates are better. When it's not, the results can be disastrous—like putting a yellow pages ad for telephones in a section of the book devoted to auto repair."

Men

Call it contextual placement. Are you after males, 18–34? How about ESPN Sportszone (**http://espnet.sportszone.com**) (see Figure 6.2)? If you like the sports angle, you could try SportsLine USA (**www.sportsline.com**), @Bat (**www.majorleaguebaseball.com**), NBA.com (**www.nba.com**), or Team NFL (**http://nflhome.com**).

FIG. 6.2

Looking for men? Try sports, like ESPNet.

The SportZone's scoreboard in the upper-left corner flashes new scores every few seconds. One of the most often visited sites, I vote this one most likely to sit on an 18- to 34-year-old's screen for most of the day. Mobile wants them. Ford wants them. Pizza Hut wants them. Jupiter Communications says the SportZone billed $6.5 million in 1996. That sounds like the right place to sell trucks, beer, and pizza. It's a pretty good place to sell flowers, too.

But Bill Tobin at PC Flowers and Gifts isn't looking at men in general. He's looking at men in particular, as well. He was thrilled at the chance to advertise on a site with far less traffic and that is limited to specific membership. However, as he told Kate Maddox at *Ad Age*'s *NET Marketing* magazine (January/February, 1997), "Any college-educated male who makes $50,000 above the average income is going to buy flowers. I think an ad on Counsel Connect is a laser beam into our exact demographic." Counsel Connect can be found at **www. counselconnect.com**

If you're not particular about your brand and feel it can survive the association, adult sites are doing a land-office business on the Net and are happy to sell advertising. It's really no surprise when you consider the VCR/movie rental industry. It was floundering until adult titles made it possible for people to enjoy mature subjects in the privacy of their own homes. Now, one needn't even suffer the embarrassment of walking into a rental shop and having the teenager behind the counter wonder about your moral turpitude.

Adult sites have truly been the cutting edge when it comes to online transactions and advertising. There are plenty of sites and a lot of options. You can learn about them at such sites as The Adult Money Report (**www.alexas.com/advert**). If you're looking for men, you know where to find them.

Women

Women's Wire (**www.women.com**) decided early on to make the best use of the communication side of the Web. Over and over again, women on the Net say their favorite thing about it is talking to people. Over and over again, their favorite people to talk to are women. Women's Wire decided to facilitate.

Women's Wire describes itself as "the premier destination for women on the Web. Advertising on Women's Wire allows you to reach the affluent, educated, and professional online woman in a unique, high-quality environment. The site is organized by channel: News, Style, Work, Body, Buzz, Cash, and Shop. All channels are listed on The Women's Wire Guide Page. Feature articles are listed on each Channel Home Page. You may elect to associate with specific features in the channel of your choice, buy a broad Site Rotation, or we'll work with you to develop compelling editorial to surround your advertising message."

Want to get more specific? You want women who are building families? How about Parent Soup (**www.parentsoup.com**)? By the end of 1997's first quarter, women visited Parent Soup a quarter of a million times each month. Sixty-three percent were between the ages of 30 and 44, had a median income of $57,333, and almost 85% had spent some time in college. On average they had 1.9 kids (they never do seem to be all there, do they?) who, on average, were eight years old. More than 85% were married.

College Students

Banks like to get their hooks into college students and make them customers for life. Companies selling music know their efforts will not be wasted on the college crowd. If that's who you're after, there are some sites you should know about.

For reaching those looking forward to the university life, there are a number of targeted sites which post differing descriptions on their respective Web sites. There's College Edge (**www.collegeedge.com**), which "eases the transition from [high school] to college." Fastweb (**www.fastweb.com**) is "the Internet's largest free scholarship search site." The Princeton Review (**www.review.com**) is "the nation's most popular standardized test preparation company." *U.S. News and World Report* has their .EDU section (**www.usnews.com/usnews/edu/home.htm**), an all-around guide to higher education. If your targets are those who have worked their way through the system, there's Tripod (**www.tripod.com**), which "offers streetsmart strategies for work, life, and everything else."

Corporate Target

If a large part of your business comes from a handful of large companies, you can cater to them. It's not hard to see if a surfer is coming from General Motors, General Electric, or General Mills. Then it's a simple matter to show the right banner. Of course, if these Generals are visiting your Web site from home in the evening using their AOL accounts, you might miss an opportunity here and there to target them. But generally speaking, a visitor from **firewall.gm.com** is a better prospect for your coiling wire than somebody from **www.walgreens.com**.

Will It Play In Poughkeepsie?

JM Lexus wanted to use the Internet to sell more cars out of their lot in Margate, Florida, just north of Miami. They put up no less than three home pages. There's **www.sun-sentinel.com/vroom/d1jmle1.htm** hosted by Sun Sentinel, there's **www.dealernet.com/dealers/j/jmlexus/jmlexus.htm** on the DealerNet site, and there's good old **www.jmlexus.com** that they put up on their own. But that wasn't enough for General Manager David W. Mullen, Jr. He wanted to advertise.

Not to the whole world, mind you. He had no doubt people could find him on the World Wide Web. He just wanted to be sure that folks in the greater Miami area knew he was selling $45,000 cars. So he bought an ad on PointCast's *Miami Herald* channel. He paid $700 per month to place the ad, and created two ads at $1,000 each. The results were 240 e-mails to the dealership, which turned into 48 test drives and sixteen Lexus's out the door. The final tally? $169 per lead for each car sold.

IP Address Identification   Like the game of corporate targeting, there's geographic targeting, as well. Is the site visitor coming from a domain that ends in .fr? Give them a banner in French.

Leonid Delitsin, at the Sputnik Advertising Network (in Madison, Wisconsin), goes after Russians and when he places ads, he notices a big difference if they are in Russian. One banner on an English site was placed in English. But when the server detected the visitor was from .ru, another banner, in Russian, took its place. The results were a jump from 3.3% clickthrough to 5%. Delitsin is happy.

Content Sites Play Around   From the Yahoo! home page you can click a button that says "More Yahoos." Among other options are a plethora of parochial Yahoo!s. The various localizations include:

Yahoo! Atlanta

Yahoo! Austin

Yahoo! Boston

Yahoo! Chicago

Yahoo! Dallas/Ft Worth

Yahoo! Los Angeles

Yahoo! New York

Yahoo! San Francisco

Yahoo! Seattle

Yahoo! Washington D.C.

Yahoo! Canada

Yahoo! France

Yahoo! Germany

Yahoo! Japan

Yahoo! U.K. & Ireland

You best believe the advertising is different on each. If you want to get down to cases, Yahoo! lets you type in a zip code and creates a page for your town.

Microsoft hasn't been shy about trying out different content on the Web. In the spring of 1997, they're trying their hand at the local Web content game with Sidewalk (**www.sidewalk.com**) (see Figure 6.3).

Always savvy, Microsoft is starting out close to home and will expand from there. The home page looks a little forlorn at the moment, with boston.sidewalk, sanfrancisco.sidewalk, and twincities.sidewalk in black—unlinked—waiting for life to be breathed into them by the Webmaster. But the "sponsored in part by" section is riveting. Logo after logo of major brand names blinks by, and you know the people with the big budgets recognize the power of a local Web site: Visa, Holland America, Club Med, Bank of America, Citibank, Prudential, United Airlines. They know something.

FIG. 6.3
Microsoft tackles the local-Web game with Seattle-specific content as their first effort.

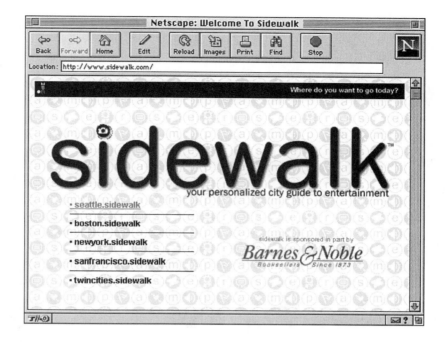

Newspapers Deliver   Just about every newspaper in the world has pulled their hair, bitten their nails, and built some kind of Web site. Then they discovered there was value in being local on the global Internet. The Newspaper Association of America created a book and video combination called *Winning the Digital Ad Wars: A Guide to Web Advertising*. It's directed at newspaper publishers and includes case studies, such as one from *Kansas City Star* marketing diva Candy Thompson.

The Kansas City Star Web site proudly proclaims that "It is our goal to make kansascity.com the key Web site for Kansas City. Anyone or anything you need to know about Kansas City, you'll find here." The paper itself provided the backbone for the site—the computers, the phone lines, the programmers, and designers. It then selected media partners who best represented the "essence" of Kansas City: the four local network TV affiliates, the local PBS station, the Chamber of Commerce, the Economic Development Council, three radio stations that reach the same demographics as the Internet, the public library, the Kansas City Royals baseball team, the Convention and Visitors Bureau, and well-known local entertainment attractions. Each were committed to having great content on their sites, and pledged to promote it.

You have to admit that this is a great start. You want to promote your site? You get local TV and radio stations to commit to blowing your horn every night on the 5, 6, and 10 o'clock news. It's nice that they can run their own ads in the paper. It's nice that they get signage at The Royals and other entertainment facilities. But then they got creative. Every piece of paper mailed from the Chamber, the Council, and the Bureau includes the URL. But wait, it gets better! The Web address is printed on every library card issued in town. In October 1996, a survey of Kansas City residents revealed name recognition among 60% of those queried.

So if you were promoting your KC real estate firm, your local career consultancy, or your city-wide chain of auto parts stores, it seems there could be no better choice than **www.kansascity.com** (see Figure 6.4).

FIG. 6.4

Although it may be available on a global basis, kansascity.com is selling lots of local advertising.

Push-Pin-Pointing Your Target Audience   You're going on a trip. You're going to San Francisco. You need a map of San Francisco. You go to Mapquest (**www.mapquest.com**). You look at the map and decide you need a place to stay. You click Lodging and select Radisson hotels. After updating the map, you not only see the hotel location, but a banner ad for it as well (see Figure 6.5). What's this? A special offer? Now tell me, what's the likelihood that you're going to click there? I thought so.

FIG. 6.5

Radisson ads pay attention to where you might want to go.

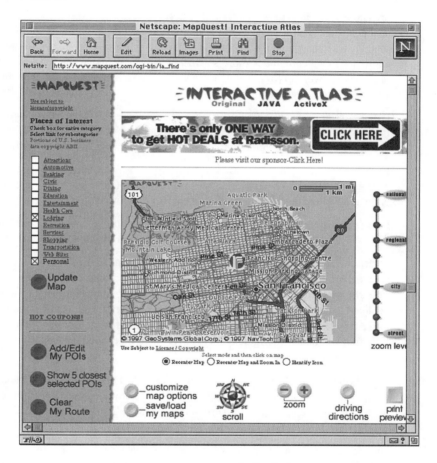

Bill Sedgwick, Advertising Manager at Mapquest, says they're getting a lot of attention. "This type of advertising works and is excellent for national advertisers who have locations in select markets like hotels and retailers. It's also great for regional advertisers who might have a multi-state area to cover, but don't want to waste banners on a larger audience, like cable companies and phone companies. And local advertisers, of course."

Mapquest geocoded almost two hundred Radisson hotels across the country. They have over twelve million businesses in their database from American Business Information and code them for longitude and latitude. Looking for a company? You can find it. What to advertise to people looking for geographic information? No problem. And when you look for anything within a five mile radius of a Radisson, lo and behold, there's a little Radisson logo where the hotel is. For the privilege, Radisson paid a premium. While untargeted ads on Mapquest cost $25 per thousand, geocentric ads run at a CPM of $40.

"The whole point is to make the site more useful," enthuses Sedgwick. "If you're looking at a map of Berlin and there's an add for Gateway Computers, you have to wonder how many impressions it takes to get a click. But the real issue, is that the site user looks at it as a waste of space. If there's an ad for a Berlin hotel, or 'Click Here for a guided tour of Checkpoint Charlie,' then it's no longer an ad—it's content. People will like our site better because it has such great content. They'll come back more so we'll be a more valuable site for advertisers." In the middle of 1997, they were getting twenty page views a month and it doesn't take much for them to tell you about pageviews per city.

If maps are good, how about the weather? The Weather Channel (**www.weather.com**) (see Figure 6.6) is happy to sell you a city-specific banner slot. They have 1,600 to choose from. Look at their home page and you might find an ad for Audi. Dig deeper and the picture changes.

If you're interested in the weather in a variety of towns in Pennsylvania, there's a page that lists all the cities they're keeping their eyes on—29 in all (see Figure 6.7). If you're looking at this page and wondering who on earth Lowe's Home Improvement is, then you live west of Texas.

Lowe's has more than 400 stores in the eastern part of the country. Eighteen of them are in Pennsylvania. You won't see their ads if you're looking for the weather in Bakersfield.

Internet Local Advertising & Commerce Association   Local advertising isn't just a good idea, it's a movement. The Internet Local Advertising & Commerce Association (ILAC) (**www. kelseygroup.com/ilac/index.html**) "is a not-for-profit organization designed to promote and facilitate local advertising and commerce between buyers and sellers on the Internet. The goal of ILAC is to help accelerate the development of the technology, the standards and the practices that will make the Internet local advertising medium more valuable to advertisers and consumers."

The organizers are from companies like Microsoft, The Kelsey Group (a national yellow pages company), BigBook (an online yellow pages company), Vicinity Corporation (an online mapping firm like Mapquest), GTE Directories, Times Mirror, and Reuben H. Donnelley.

Their purposes are all globally focused to support the local ad buyer. They want banner size and placement reporting standards to make it easy for advertisers to make buys across multiple sites. They want to promote the value of local advertising and facilitate advertising placement. They want to create common advertising categories and search criteria/methodology among advertisers. But primarily, they want to find a way to be a one-stop-shop for companies to place local ads.

In real life, most of the member firms do just that for a living. You can place your ad in a hundred newspapers or twenty yellowpage books with one phone call. These firms want you to be able to do the same thing with Internet advertising. But unless there are standards, they face an uphill battle.

FIG. 6.6
Audi is willing to sell to
anybody, anywhere.

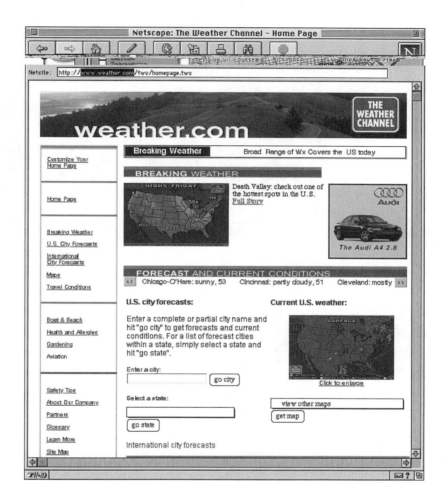

Some Out-of-the-Way Places

It's not a stretch to look at some sites less traveled and make the kind of choices you do when perusing magazines. Most of them have fairly small audiences, but they're fairly well identified. Despite this age of electronic communication, the magazine industry continues to blossom. Ink-on-paper has never had it so good. There are enough titles on the newsstands to cater to the most finely tuned interest.

Picture the modern newsstand with its thousand of titles. Imagine that the rack is a handful of sand. Each grain is unique. Each is a slightly different color. Each takes up its own space and each sells advertising. Now look up and admire the beach.

FIG. 6.7

Lowe's isn't wasting impressions on people west of Texas.

In April of 1997, it was announced that the one millionth .com had been registered. In the same month, *Advertising Age* put the number of sites selling ads at 1,000. Bear in mind that those are the ones that are officially selling ads. Those are the ones that showed up on *Ad Age*'s radar. Did they count Kim Baynes' site (**www.wolfbayne.com**), which is shown in Figure 6.8? It's the home of the High Tech Marketing Communicators List and wolfBayne Communications.

Baynes sold me a banner ad on her site in 1995, not too long after Hotwired showed how to do it. I put up a banner for my first book, *World Wide Web Marketing*. She isn't trying to make a living selling ad space, she just saw an opportunity.

Why would I pay for a banner on a site that only gets a handful of visitors a day? Because they are the kind of people I want to reach. They are my context. I doubt *Ad Age* has www.wolfbayne.com in its database. Their loss.

So who are you trying to reach?

If your tastes are more, shall we say, eclectic, you may want to look out on the fringes of the Internet. No, you don't need to go all the way to the Interspecies Telepathic Communication site (**www.cyberark.com/animal/telepath.htm**). Unless, of course, you feel that people who believe they can communicate with their pets via ESP are just the sort of clients you've been looking for. But there are some interesting alternatives for finding just the right sets of eye-balls.

FIG. 6.8
The wolfBayne Communications site will sell you an ad if you feel your target audience frequents it sufficiently.

Bull Feathers

The people at the BAR-G Feedyard are proud of their custom cattle feeding services. They can feed up to 75,000 head of your finest and even have financing available. But they're in Hereford, Texas. Where are they going to advertise on the Internet?

Elliott Cox, Jimmy Barton, and Tommy Craver know just about everything there is to know about farm and ranch truck needs. They work at Wilson Motors in Snyder, Texas, and they're not set up to deliver trucks to Trinidad. They want to attract local attention.

Down in San Angelo, Texas is that state's largest cattle market. It's the Producers Livestock Auction. They'd be pleased if somebody from Singapore came to bid on their stock, but they know better than to spend any money trying. They want to advertise locally as well.

And all of them want to find the cattle growers in their neck of the woods. That's why they all bought space in the online version of *Livestock Weekly* (**www.livestockweekly.com**). 'Tain't a purdy site, but's got a mess a' stuff that's custom made for the cowboy. This newspaper keeps up on the price of cattle in different markets, the public health of the livestock in the area and legislative moves. Perfect for BAR-G, Wilson Motors, and Producers Livestock Auction.

Cleaning Up Online

If you sell brushes, brooms, carpet chemicals, dusters, dust mops, environmental supplies, floor finish concentrates, floor pads, hand cleaners and soaps, matting, mops, safety supplies, soaps and soap dispensers, sponges, trash can liners, washroom/restroom accessories, waste receptacles, or wet mops, you should consider picking up some ad space on Jansan Online (**www.jansan.com**), which is shown in Figure 6.9. It has everything for the man who wants to clean up at work. If this is your target audience, they'll serve up thousands of impressions a day on their home page for only $1,500 a month, or $800 a month for internal pages.

Going Places

If you specialize in European tourism you need to look into the official World Wide Web site of the French Government Tourist Office (**www.fgtousa.org**). As stated on their site, "The FGTO World Wide Web site is the authority in providing timely and in-depth news and information about tourism in France. It is the essential resource for millions of visitors planning to travel to France each year. FGTO travel experts offer immediate and timely insight into the best ways to travel to France. Users around the world have instant access to the latest standings, news and professionals on France such as meetings and incentives planners, tour operators, travel agents, hotel representatives, rental agencies…"

Foreign Affairs at Home

Where do you go to advertise the first juried exhibition solely dedicated to representing Iranian and Iranian-American artists residing in the United States? It's a wonderful idea. First and second generation Americans from Iran explore their heritage and their newfound lives through art. The Evolving Perceptions 1997 exhibit in Washington, D.C. (to be held late fall of this year) wanted to let these artists know that there is a public place for their work to be seen. They turned to The Iranian, where their work can be seen at **www.iranian.com/Feb97/ Sponsors/EvolvingPerceptions.html** (see Figure 6.10). With 3,000 visitors a week, The Iranian is the right spot for a fledgling art show.

Et Cetera

If you want to reach Macintosh users in London, there's Mac Online (**uk.macworld.com**). For an entrée into the pulp and paper industry, **www.pulpandpaper.com** sells ads on their site full of news, archives, and links to the industry. Well, you get the idea. You can find a match between your product offering and your target audience and a Web site for both. Start surfing.

FIG. 6.9
Janitors will be attracted to this page like dirt to a freshly mopped floor.

Are You Ready for the Intranet?

On the edges of experimentation is a concept I find puzzling: intranet advertising.

Toward the end of 1996, the entire Internet industry switched gears in mid-click and started to dig into intranets. Why this narcissistic turn? Why this shift away from welcoming the world with open arms to contemplating the corporate navel? Because customers were getting demanding.

Customers saw the home page and the company brochure and they wanted more. They wanted access to the company. They wanted access to the people, the processes, and the data sequestered deep in the bowels of the corporate beast. Unfortunately, the beast wasn't endowed with decent access to its own people, processes, and data. How could they provide for the clamoring hoards when they, themselves were trapped in a Dilbertian nightmare?

FIG. 6.10

Reaching Iranians in America just got easier.

Turning the power of the Internet inward seemed like a potential solution. Taking advantage of Web tools and instant communication sounded like the right approach. Hundreds of success stories later, Forrester Research declared the end of the search for intranet project ROI. After interviewing dozens of project leaders, they determined that the average return on intranet investment was around 1000%. Within a few months. Mellanie Hills, author of *Intranet Business Strategies* and *Intranet As Groupware* (John Wiley & Sons), puts it flat on the table: "You can do business without an intranet, but for how long, and why would you want to? It's easy, cheap, and the returns are so great."

But advertising?

Okay, let's start with the view from the advertiser's side of the table. You start with a captive audience. They're attached to the intranet all day long to get their e-mail and go look at whatever needs looking at from time to time. They have their internal home page up on their screen most of the time. They all need screen savers so they can use something like the PointCast server internally. These people can be well identified as to department, position, income, gender, family status. Man! This is sounding good. I can target my low-cost checking account services to new hires, my home equity lines of credit to those with kids in college, and my super annuities package to senior management. I'm stoked!

Now let's take a look across the mahogany plane to the face of the intranet owner. She's the one who has to make it all work. The queen of infrastructure. What's her problem? Resources. Where is she going to get them? She's going to stay later, get in earlier in the morning, and dial in from home just before going to bed…just to make sure. She figures a handful of hot advertisers, rightly controlled, of course, would put several thousand dollars *back* in her budget every month. This could be good. This could spell more head count. Maybe even a handful of interns and hire somebody to manage them. This could be really good.

But now I put on my corporate management hat. The black one. The one that says "We're Number One!" on the outside and "fire the bastards" on the inside. Okay, maybe it only says "productivity über alles." My beef is crystal clear. I don't want my employees distracted. I know they need access to information. That's why I'm happy to buy video courses and lectures and seminars for viewing in the conference room but will not approve television to the desktop anytime in this millennium.

If I run a law firm, it's going to be hard to turn down a large pile of cash from West Publishing, which wants to promote its legal publications, its online legal research service, its CD-ROM libraries, its law-related news services, and its online legal directory.

ComputerWorld ran a quick poll that turned up 4% of infrastructure gurus saying they were already selling ads and another 10% saying they would consider it.

When companies work together to create a special offer for their employees, it makes sense to let those employees know about the benefits that await them. My local Big Brand Tire Company sent me six plastic cards for 10%. Permanent, reusable, and good on all items and services. They targeted my company as a potential hotbed of customers. If I had an intranet, I might have agreed to publish their largess and offer these cards on a first-come, first-served basis. I didn't have the heart to call and tell them I run a one-man shop.

So the issue isn't as clear and my hat turns from black to gray.

If your local travel agency wants to offer your entire company great discounts on last minute airfares…If you can manage your profiling so that only those people who travel will see the promotion…If the travel agency is willing to bear the cost of creating the ads and managing the customer service portion of the arrangement . . . If the savings are truly substantial . . . you'd be a fool not to remind your employees to lower the cost of their travel.

The inside of the hat now says, "And we can charge them for the privilege!"

Where Does Your Competition Hang Out?

You keep track of how much money your competitors spend on marketing, don't you? You keep track of where they place their magazine and television ads, don't you? Then how about the Web? That lets you know where you stand in the branding wars and it may provide some insight into where else you should be placing banners.

Maybe your competition is going for the tried and true. Maybe they're pouring big bucks into Yahoo! or Netscape. Maybe they're finding small, out of the way places you should know about. Why? Because it's a good indication of where they think their market is. That might give you a pointer as to where they think they're headed.

Not as Easy as It Might Seem

Tracking your competitors should be straightforward. This is the Internet, right? You can search for anything, right? Not quite.

You could do a search engine like AltaVista to search for links to your competitors pages. Type in link:www.toyota.com and you get about 6,000 matches. Why? Well, Toyota has a lot of pages that link to their home page. Toyota has a lot of dealers that point to Toyota's home page. There are lots of car enthusiasts who think the Toyota site is swell, and there are a lot of Web enthusiasts who think so, too.

Then, of course, there's the problem of dynamic Web pages. When you did your first search for links to Toyota on AltaVista, you got an ad for Isuzu (those sneaky guys—there are more on keywords in "The Search Engine Connection" section of this chapter). If you hit the Reload button, you might end up with an ad for the AutoVantage New Car buying program. Now how on earth do you track the number of pages Toyota is advertising on when banners are served dynamically? You get help.

Hired Help

There are several companies that can keep an eye on your competition for you. Lycos (**www.lycos.com**) offers Link Alert. Besides being valuable for finding holes in your own chain of links to drive more traffic to your own site, Link Alert can keep you posted on your competitors' efforts. "Monitor your competitors links and who is linking to them. View the competitive roadmap to easily identify where you and your competition have similar links and where they have links that you do not have. Develop marketing programs to contact these sites to establish links to your site and/or 'float' your link to the top of the list ahead of your competitors."

Digital Vision (**www.digitalvision.net**) has a service called Net AdTracker. Net AdTracker reports:

- How much your competitor is spending on the Internet
- Where your competitor is placing banner advertising
- What your competitor's banner and creative look like
- How much traffic their site is receiving
- When their Web site URL appears in television or radio commercials
- On what TV or radio stations their Web site URL appears
- Where your competitor is located in the search engines

The Search Engine Connection

The most often visited type of site on the Internet are the search engines. The first thing everybody wants to know about search engines is, "How can I get my company listed first?"

When you're searching for luggage on AltaVista, the first thing you see is:

> *Mori Luggage & Gifts*
>
> *Thanks for visiting our new web site!! Established in Atlanta, Georgia in 1971, Mori operates 26 retail stores in the Southeast U.S. and offers full . . .*
>
> *http://moriluggage.com/—size 4K—5 Feb 97*

On Lycos your first option is:

> *FixNet home page luggage luggage luggage luggage discount discount luggage luggage*
>
> *http://www.linkstar.com/h [100%]*

On Infoseek:

> *HandiLinks To Luggage & Accessories HandiLinks To Luggage & Accessories HandiLinks To Luggage & Accessories HandiLinks To Luggage & Accessories HandiLinks To Luggage & Accessories HandiLinks To Luggage & 63%*
>
> *http://ahandyguide.com/cat1/l/l47.htm   (Size 7.1K)*

AltaVista seems to be the most helpful. The others have fallen victim to keyword abuse.

You can load your home page with spider food: text for search engine agents and robots to find and catalog. The problem is, you devastate the value of the search tool. But there are some tricks that will help.

Learning to Work with Search Engines

There is a great deal of technically-specific knowledge required to get placed just so in the search engines of the world. This is a book on advertising. If you want to dig into all the best ways there are to get into search engines, you might look at some of these:

1. The Webmaster Guide to Search Engines and Directories

   By Danny Sullivan, Calafia Consulting

   http://calafia.com/webmasters

2. Creating Web Sites For The Search Engines

   www.digital-cafe.com/~webmaster/set01.html

3. META Tagging for Search Engines

   www.Stars.com/Search/Meta.html

4. A Practical Guide to Announcing Your World Wide Web Page

   www.toltbbs.com/~cmaher/cmsubmit.htm

5. FAQ: How To Announce Your New Web Site

   http://ep.com/faq/webannounce.html

The listed pointers were gleaned off a great page at the Netpost site (**www.netpost.com/ wa97**). Netpost is run by Eric Ward and the /wa97 page is based on his presentation, "Publicizing Your Web Site: Getting Free Publicity on the Internet…" given at the Web Advertising 97 conference (**www.thunderlizard.com**).

This page is the epitome of the gift-giving cultural imperative on the Net. Ward is one of those rare resources on the Internet. He knows about search engines, lists, directories, the Internet industry press, and all of the intricacies of netiquette. Ward gets it. Ward gives it away.

His presentation and, by definition, the /wa97 page, are no less than Ward explaining what he does for a living, telling you how to do it, and showing you where all the resources are that you might need. He is a master mentor. He is the journeyman and the world is his apprentice.

What's that? You say you don't have the time or the experience to pull it all off? That's okay, Netpost can do it for you for a modest fee.

So, if you want to know how to do Internet marketing using the search engines, you can do no better than starting with Eric Ward. (Of course, it wouldn't hurt you to read my first book first.)

General Banner Rotation

A Web site that gets multiple millions clicking through it on a daily basis is nothing to sneeze at. That much traffic means that some number of them are sure to be interested in your offer. Just put up a banner in front of enough of them and—presto!—you get clicks.

Rick Rickling was my very first sales teacher. The first day on the job, when he realized I knew just about nothing about selling, he told me there were two ways to make a sale. "You can stand in the middle of the freeway and wait for a car to run you over that happens to have a purchase order in the trunk, or you can use your head."

If you're into branding and branding only, there's nothing wrong with a billboard on the highway. There's nothing wrong with showing your message to everybody with a mouse and a browser. You can buy general rotation ads on search engines pretty cheaply.

General rotation means that your banner will be shown over and over again to whomever passes by until your money runs out. Hit the Reload button and up pops another general rotation banner. If you have a budget of $10,000 and you're paying $25 CPM, you can blow through 400,000 impressions in a day. Your ability to test different creative in a short period of time is wonderful. Your ability to zero in on your target audience is more wonderful.

Search Engine Segmentation

For a little bit higher CPM, you can specify where you'd like your ad to show up. You can buy categories from the sites that include directories like Yahoo!, Infoseek, and Lycos. The Lycos home page sports eighteen different category buttons. News, Sports, Money, Travel, Technology, Health, Science, and so on. If you click Business, you find that Charles Schwab & Company have staked this page out as their own private domain (see Figure 6.11).

To split hairs, Charles Schwab has split this page with the PC Financial Network. Hit the Reload button and half the time you get a Schwab banner and half the time you get a PCFN banner. PCFN seems to be a direct competitor. Lycos is happy to support them both.

AltaVista lets you segment geographically, by domain name, by computer or browser type, by SIC code, or even company size. They do it by performing IP (Internet Protocol) look-ups. Let's say you visit AltaVista from **www.ibm.com**. AltaVista sees the request as coming from an IP address such as 129.34.139.2, 192.35.232.34, 198.4.83.35, or 194.196.0.201, because the computer side of things is always numbers. Then it can look these numbers up and determine that they are either **watson.ibm.com**, **austin.ibm.com**, **almaden.ibm.com**, or **uk.ibm.com**. As a result, if you wanted to show a different banner to IBM in Texas as the one you show to London, the choice is yours. For smaller companies, AltaVista can look up the firm's physical address and SIC code.

Keyword Referred

Search engines shine where they match up what the visitor is looking for with the ad banner at the top of the results page. Knowing that on-topic ads are seen as content, the search folks are happy to charge almost double for the privilege. The resulting response makes the expenditure worth while.

If you're ham-fisted and type "cras" into the text box at Infoseek you end up with 1,456 pages found, including a bibliography of works by Patrick Cras, a list of the California Restaurant Association's publications, and the Centre for Remote Area Studies. You also get an ad for Infoseek's software and services—a general rotation ad.

FIG. 6.11

Schwab figures a Lycos visitor interested in Business will be interested in online trading.

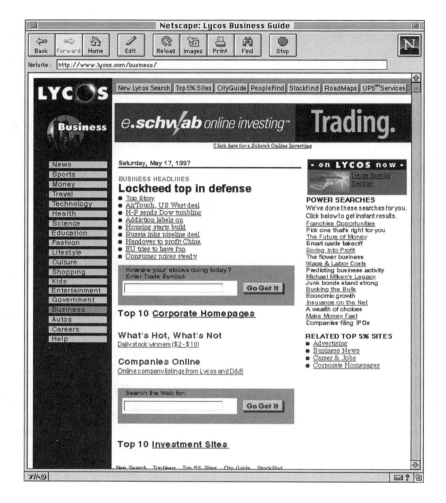

When you slow your typing a tad and manage to spell "cars" correctly, you end up with 773,676 matches and an ad for Lexus, Isuzu, AutoAdvantage, or Acura. Type in "Toyota" and end up with an ad offering "Virtually Everything @Toyota But That New Car Smell." If you're looking for them, they want to help.

Most Frequently Asked Searches   So how about going after the *most* people? You type in "flowers" and instead of getting the FlowerNet banner like you'd expect, what if Proctor & Gamble bought the word? You'd end up with a banner for Tide. Looking for "candy?" Tide. "Baseball?" Tide. If that were P&G's plan, what words should they pick up? The most commonly searched for terms are not the ones that are likely to make P&G execs in Cincinnati very happy. Often touted as more button down than IBM, these squeaky cleans are going to balk when they see the list.

Mark Grimes decided the list was worth publishing. He got the Yahoo! Top 200 list from a banner placement company and proudly displays it at **www.eyescream.com/yahootop200.html**. It's an eye opener. Table 6.1 shows (with a few deletions) a few of the search topics that made it into the top 25 ranked with the number of searches in October, 1996.

Table 6.1   Top 25 Searches in October 1996

Rank	Search Topic	Number Search Requests
1	sex	1,553,420
2	chat	414,320
3	XXX	397,640
4	Playboy	390,920
5	netscape software	350,320
6	nude	292,560
7	porno	257,860
8	games	217,440
9	porn	199,180
10	weather	190,900
11	Penthouse	186,980
12	Pamela Anderson	172,760
13	pornography	172,260
14	(even this word makes me blush)	169,840
15	persian kitty	163,620
16	maps	163,360
17	Halloween	155,680 (it *was* October, after all)
18	music	151,780
19	adult	148,960
20	chat rooms	139,960

Clearly, the value of spending the money on keywords is to match the expressed interests of the surfer to the message in your ad.

Choose Your Words Carefully   Tracking what comes after the click can make the buy even more valuable. John Wells of Movie Madness (**www.moviemadness.com**) sells movie and TV merchandise. Movie Madness is set up as a LiveStore hosted at ViaWeb (**www.viaweb.com**).

One of the tools LiveStore offers is the tracking of people on your site and a comparison against the search terms they used to get there. In a testimonial on the ViaWeb site, Wells signs its praises: "ViaWeb can show where every visitor came from and how much money visitors from each source spent. We can even show what they were searching for in search engines, and how much people searching for each phrase spent."

Those results are very interesting. ViaWeb lets you look at those reports for Movie Madness (**www.viaweb.com/cgi-bin/master/DEMOMGR**). John Wells is a happy store owner.

Wells could tell, for instance, that people coming to his site after searching for *Star Trek* spent far more than those searching for *Frasier*. Are Trekkie devotees more rabid about their collectibles than Frasier fanatics? Maybe. Doesn't matter. What does matter is that knowing which search terms bring in the most money (see Figure 6.12) and what the path through his store was (see Figure 6.13), means Wells can now plan his ad buys accordingly.

FIG. 6.12

How did they get there and what did they spend? Don't you wish you had reports like these?

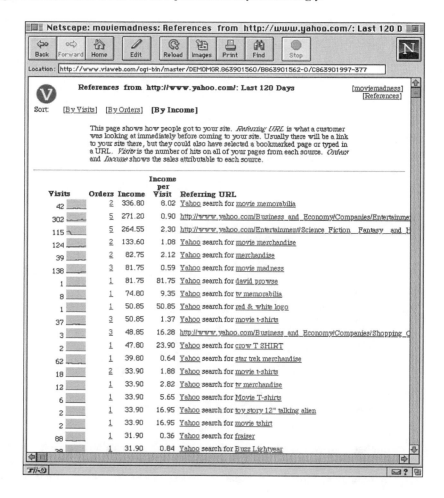

FIG. 6.13
Where did they wander
once they arrived?

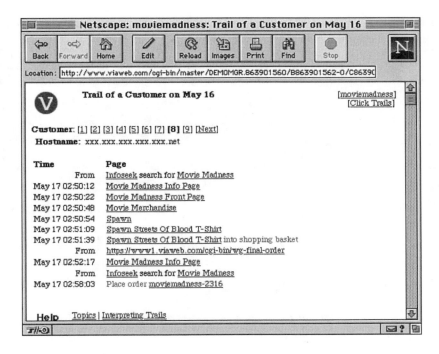

The Reference Oblique   On the brand-building side of the fence, there is a desire to move beyond the one-to-one correlation between what is being sought and what is being sold.

Search for "Toyota" at Infoseek and you get a Toyota banner. Sure. But Saatchi & Saatchi helped Toyota play the word association game. They picked up "cigar." Cigar? What do cigars have to do with cars? Were they looking for more bad typists? No, they were looking for lifestyle connections. Cigar hounds were shown an ad for Supras, the more upscale Toyota. Somebody searching for "baby carriages" found themselves looking at a banner for Corollas. Toyotas database showed 60% of Corolla owners have kids. Seemed like a good match.

Unfortunately for Toyota, they missed a beat at AltaVista.

Competitive Name Dropping   A search at AltaVista for "Toyota" turns up almost 150,000 page references. But it also turns up an animated banner (see Figure 6.14).

Panel #1: Looking for some fun?

Panel #2: A good time?

Panel #3: No, Not That . . . Try this:

Panel #4: Isuzu Rodeo—Click Here

FIG. 6.14

Isuzu bought Toyota from AltaVista.

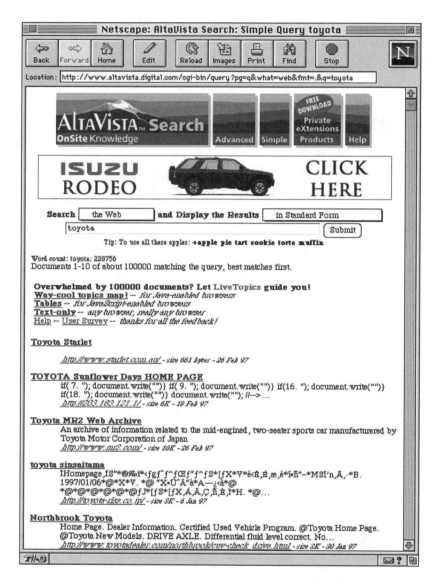

Is it a trademark infringement? Is it ethical? Is it right? Robert Bethge, at Venture Forward (**www.bethge.com**), took the competitive high ground in a post to the Online Advertising list:

```
Date:     Fri, 14 Mar 1997 01:17:40 -0800 (PST)
To:       online-ads@o-a.com
From:     R.O.B. Bethge (rob@bethge.com)
Subject: ONLINE-ADS>> Searching for St. Pete
```

One of the coups that made so much sense, and has since directed much of the advertising dollars I control, was when IBM and OS/2 bought the words "Microsoft" and "Windows" for a search engine. So, when a person types WINDOWS they get an OS/2 ad. The highest CTR's I enjoy (usually 11% or so) are when I buy a competitors name. And I feel good about it.

    a) the customer gets some competitive education (an educated consumer and all that

    b) My competitor didn't bother to get their name, so I might as well benefit.

Incidentally, I get _substantially_ lower CTR's on my client's name. Obviously they already know who we are, and they are looking for information ABOUT us. Great, an educated consumer and all that, again. They don't need to see our ad, or click on it, they already know more than the person I was trying to reach.

And I just feel so good about being one up on the competition.

-Robert Bethge
Venture Forward

It's Not Foolproof   No, it's not perfect. Ask Yahoo! for something about the Grateful Dead and no banner shows up at all. Seems there are enough corporate types who chose not to include that term in their general rotation pages.

Try "sport utility vehicle" at Infoseek and you are more likely to get the ad for the CBS SportsLine Web site than a rugged 4×4.

Narrowing the Search   Next to insufficient bandwidth, finding anything on the Internet is its most frustrating feature. Looking for something about a general subject and you're overwhelmed. Looking for a particular fact and you'd better have a fresh cup of Starbucks at hand.

In an attempt to solve this dilemma, new subject-specific search engines are showing up. Selecting a search tool in which to look saves the looker a great deal of time and trouble and offers more opportunities to more finely target your message. You probably want to send a different message to somebody at Yobes Chess Search Engine (**www.gams.at/~saj/chess**) looking up Deep Blue, versus somebody at MusicSearch (**www.musicsearch.com**) looking for Deep Purple.

Here's a handful of examples and how they describe themselves:

    80s Search (**www.80s.com/Search**)

    Having trouble finding certain 1980s-related information? Welcome to the first search engine that searches exclusively for 1980s information on the web! You can search just within The 80s Server or expand your search to include 80s-related websites worldwide!

    @queous (**www.aqueous.com**)

    You have found the only search engine dedicated to water related sites. Whether you are looking for a cruise ship, a master plumber, or a new bikini, this is the place to start.

    Internet Legal Resource Guide (**www.ilrg.com**)

    Welcome to the Internet Legal Resource Guide. A categorized index of 3100 select web sites in 238 nations, islands, and territories, as well as more than 850 locally stored web pages and other files, this site was established to serve as a comprehensive resource of the information available on the Internet concerning law and the legal profession, with an emphasis on the United States of America. Designed for everyone, lay persons and legal scholars alike, it is quality controlled to include only the most substantive legal resources online. The selection criteria are predicated on two principles: the extent to which the resource is unique, as well as the relative value of the information it provides. More than 1,600 percent growth in usership since November 1996 and growing!

MusicSearch (**www.musicsearch.com**)

MusicSearch is many things but, above all, it's simply the fastest and most precise way of finding music-related sites and groups on the world-wide Internet. For some it is a quick stopping point to find the latest Music News; for others it is an irreplaceable wealth of resources available world-wide on the topic of music; still others are able to find their favorite artists' sites on the Internet. There's just too many ways to use MusicSearch to list them here. But as you start to surf your way through our site, the reasons to start all your music searching here will be clear.

Neuroscience Web Search (**www.acsiom.org/nsr/neuroadv.html**)

This site contains a full-text index of over 121,000 web pages related to neuroscience. The object of this site is to make it easier to find information on the structure and function of invertebrate and vertebrate nervous systems. Although you could use a general-purpose search engine like Alta Vista, you'll be likely to get many links to irrelevant pages. Here, EVERYTHING is relevant by pre-selection. So you can search on a word like 'mushroom' and find out all about the mushroom bodies (and read one bad mushroom joke—'You're a fungi!').

Yobes Chess Search Engine (**www.gams.at/~saj/chess**)

The underlying database contains a lot of information from several chess related WWW pages. If you want to add your site, then fill the registration form. Tell me, [sic]*what you think about this service! This Broker was built using the Harvest system. You may access help for formulating queries.*

You should also check out The Internet Sleuth (**www.isleuth.com**), shown in Figure 6.15. This site lists over 1,000 different search engines and directories by subject. "The Internet Sleuth is a bit different from the other search engines you might have used. While AltaVista or Lycos attempt to index the entire Web, The Sleuth maintains an index of searchable databases, most of which can be searched directly from The Sleuth, simplifying the search for information."

Don't Forget the Directories

There are lots of different kinds of directories out there. The Internet mall (**www.internetmall.com**) (see Figure 6.16) is a directory of places on the Internet that sells things. This is the oldest and largest site of its kind, boasting some 27,000-plus merchants and stores and a range of products that would put any yellow pages to shame—and the $24 per year price tag is enough to send the yellow pages people into hiding.

FIG. 6.15
Think of The Internet Sleuth as the Yahoo! of search engines.

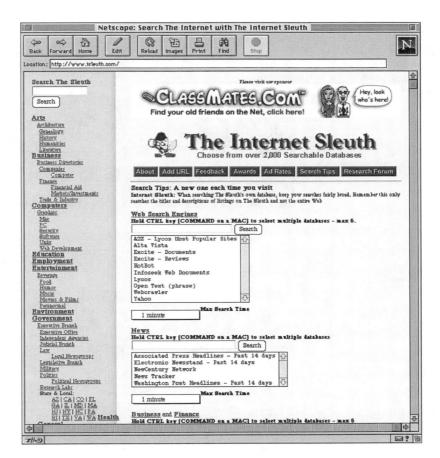

Started in 1994 by Dave Taylor, the mall itself is a directory. As such, it attracts almost a million people a month. People who are looking for electronic stores. People who are actively shopping. Obviously, it looks like the right place for Microsoft to promote their CarPoint site and for CDNOW to attract your attention.

The Middle-Man—Web Ad Reps

Buying a bunch of banners from Yahoo! is pretty easy. Writing a check to Netscape isn't that hard. Sending an e-mail to CNET asking to buy some banner slots on their site is the work of a moment. But what if your goal is to strategically place your ads on the two or three dozen sites that cater to your specific demographic target?

FIG. 6.16

If you're trying to sell something, how about advertising where people are buying?

If that's the case, get ready to buy a more ergonomically correct desk chair, a new wrist brace, and a new telephone headset. You're going to be at your keyboard for days looking for the right places to place your banners. You're going to be typing keywords over and over again at various search engines looking for those topic-specific sites that are most likely to draw your kind of audience. You're going to be on the phone to thirty or fifty sites trying to negotiate individual banner placement deals in order to find the fifteen or twenty that will work for you. Oh, and don't forget the cot for your office because it's going to take days on end and you have deadlines to meet. Sound like fun?

On the other hand, you could turn to banner advertising networks.

One Stop Shopping

More than just outsourcing, there are several other advantages of going to one place to do your ad shopping. For example, a content company running multiple sites is likely to have standardized their banner sizes across all sites. That means you can place the same ad format at a variety of sites.

Companies running multiple sites are probably using common ad server software. That means your ad goes into a database and is served in proper sequence to all of the sites under that content creator's control. As a result, you get one report detailing your ad activity at all of the sites.

But the real fun starts when you are able to take advantage of cross-site demographics. The power of targeting increases many fold when the information about people includes more and more Web sites. Before you get into that, you should look at the different kinds of networks out there.

Web Property Providers

This model began simply enough. It was a content-ownership thing. The people who run ESPN SportsZone also happen to run Outside Online, NFL.com, NASCAR Online, NBA.com, ABCNews.com, Mr. Showbiz, CelebSite, and Wall Of Sound. That means you could call one sales rep and make a buy across all of those sites. Simple. Time saving. Carpel tunnel syndrome-avoiding.

As Yahoo! creates regional properties and Infoseek and Excite branch out to add new titles to their stables of sites, they become another type of network. One placement purchase can put you on every MyYahoo!, on Yahooligans! made especially for kids, Yahoo! Net Events for Internet aficionados, all of the ten regional, and five national versions of Yahoo!

CNET has a variety of properties to attract surfers of all kinds and they describe them this way:

> *CNET.COM—the definitive online source for product reviews and information about computing and the Internet.*
>
> *NEWS.COM—the first, free 24-hour-a-day technology news service created exclusively for the Web.*

GAMECENTER.COM—the one-stop supersite for gaming news, reviews, tips, downloads, and more.

Mediadome^{sm}*—a joint-venture Web site from CNET and Intel that merges today's hottest media properties with cutting-edge technology to create a new form of Web-based entertainment.*

CNET's Software Download Services SHAREWARE.COM and DOWNLOAD.COM—the Internet's leading sources for downloadable software.

ACTIVEX.COM—a library of downloadable ActiveX controls.

SEARCH.COM—the broadest selection of Internet search tools in one comprehensive environment.

As successful companies expand their purviews into more and more subject categories, they offer more and more venues for ad placement with one purchase.

Radio Content Provider

It is true that the more things change, the more they stay the same. Television and radio have had an advertising business model in place for decades that spawned the word "network" as it pertains to advertising. Call it the Sell-Local, Sell-Global approach.

The basic premise is for a content company to offer its programming to geographically disparate affiliates, include some nationally placed ads, and leave room for the affiliate to sell local ads—simple.

One of the most straightforward examples of this model is ElectricVillage (**www.electricvillage.com**). John Felt is responsible for signing up radio stations around the country. His job is to go into a territory and offer an exclusive to any of the several radio station types a particular city supports. Quoting directly from the ElectricVillage site, rock stations, jazz stations, and country stations can choose:

■ *Crawl into the Web*

Earwig is geared toward users who prefer a New Rock, Alternative and/or Indie format. Content slants toward the offbeat tastes, attitude and live-on-the-edge orientation of this group.

■ *A Web Walk on the Wild Side*

Rock Village reflects the interests of Classic Rock listeners. Content includes interviews, reviews and news on classic artists, along with other features and activities designed to appeal to this audience.

■ *Country Music*

CountrySpotlight reflects the interests of Country listeners. Content includes interviews, reviews and news on country artists, along with other features and activities designed to appeal to this audience.

What does ElectricVillage offer? Content. Lots of content. The kind of content a radio station fan would enjoy but which no radio station has the wherewithal to create. So ElectricVillage is the creator, producer, publisher, and broadcaster on the Web for its affiliate stations. The station maintains its own site (see Figure 6.17), but that site includes a good-sized link to rich content including articles, interviews, reviews, polls, games, chat rooms, and more.

FIG. 6.17
ElectricVillage's Earwig lets radio stations expand their content and their identities.

While the content is plentiful, the local radio station's logo stays prominently displayed in the bottom center of the screen. Making use of HTML frames means visitors can participate in all the different Earwig offerings without losing site of who's paying for it.

The radio station gets to sell the ad space on the left of the logo and ElectricVillage gets to sell the space on the right. As a result, the actual cost to the station is negligible.

The Networks Try Their Hands at Networks

NBC and Time Warner are going to give it a go as well. But they add a new dimension to the fun. They can cut deals to promote their content on television as well.

NBC-IN (Interactive Neighborhood) will offer content to all their affiliates along the same lines as ElectricVillage: one ad for the network and one for the local station. The locals have the ability to sign up for a cut of the national advertising if they go for a long term contract. NBC is rounding up content from Microsoft's Sidewalk site and Infoseek. They're also looking at taking a cut of any transactions. Content providers such as Rent Net and Auto-By-Tel are out looking for online consumers. NBC wants a piece.

Warner Brothers announced CityWeb in January, 1997, saying it would include content from CNN Interactive and People Online. "CityWeb will allow each affiliate to offer its audience local, national and international news, local and national weather and sports, local and national television listings, local community affairs information, original programming for men, women, children and teens, local and national classified advertising, educational information and interactive educational support, as well as a special CityWeb version of the Lycos search engine—the Internet's only personal guide allowing multimedia searches."

Unlike NBC (or ABC and CBS, which have suggested they're going to follow suit), Warner Brothers isn't limited to just one television network to sell to. They can go out and compete directly with the big three.

Content Aggregators

What do you get when you cross the topic-specific directory concept with the advertising network concept? You get companies like Digital Music Network (DMN) (**www.dmnmedia .com**). DMN is on a mission to sign up as many music-oriented sites that sell advertising as they can, and represent them.

DMN is a classic ad-rep organization. Think of them as a banner space dealer. They can buy ads from a large number of sites and be the one stop shopping center for those selling punk rock CDs, classical concert tickets, or harmonicas. Why go to a consolidator in these times of disintermediation? Because they manage the relationship with the content sites. They managed the condensation of data from those sites into a comprehensible format so you can see whether your choices need tweaking.

Their business was born of necessity. Having created the popular Casbah site (**www.casbah .net**), they ran into the success trap. They oversold their available inventory of banner space. Desperate to keep their clients, they went out to find other music sites to host the over-sold ads. The first one they signed up was Pollstar, and a new income stream was born. Now the Digital Music Network includes:

IUMA (www.iuma.com)   The Internet Underground Music Archive is "the premiere independent music site on the World Wide Web. IUMA's mission is to bring the music and merchandise of independent artists directly to music fans and the music industry worldwide. IUMA hosts five times more independent bands than any other site in existence and averages well over 300,000 hits per day. IUMA generates significant advertising and band submission revenues and has consistently attracted top notch press exposure since it was founded in 1993."

POLLSTAR (www.pollstar.com)   "For over a decade, POLLSTAR has provided music concert industry professionals with the most reliable and accurate source of Route Book (concert tour schedules), box office results, industry directories, news and other industry-related data services."

Now, the tour concert information on the Web and is updated and verified every week. This U.K.-based site also offers mailing lists for purchases such as major concert venues, booking agents, record company executives and staff, not to mention a database of historical box office results.

Webnoize (www.webnoize.com)   "Webnoize is a cultural congregation of music, technology, and new media information. This online publication ushers in a new age for music reporting, delivering quality editorial from experienced music writers who examine the state of today's music scene through the prism of emerging media, communications, and Internet technologies. Offering daily news, feature articles, interviews, in-depth special reports, site/music/technology reviews, and much more, Webnoize is the first publication to exclusively devote itself to such an editorial mission."

CD Universe (www.cduniverse.com)   CD Universe is "the Internet's hottest online music store. Search our database of over 180,000 items and place your orders online. We offer fantastic service, low prices and carry a full line of Compact Discs, Cassette Tapes, CD Singles, Cassette Singles, VHS Music Videos, and Import CDs."

Adam Curry's The Metaverse (http://metaverse.com)   The Metaverse "is the patriarch of music/entertainment sites on the Internet. Since 1993, The Metaverse has featured exclusive celebrity interviews, album and concert reviews, and four private chat rooms. A photo gallery of 2000+ rock stars, original internet radio programming, and the hottest gossip column on the net, CyberSleaze. The Metaverse is also home to the Cybercast. Whether it's backstage at The Grammy Awards, on the Polar Beach in Tuktoyaktuk, Canada for a Metallica show, the Meadowlands for a Blues Traveler concert, or on the set of *Melrose Place* for a cast party, The Metaverse lets you be a part of the action."

Casbah (www.casbah.net)   Casbah "is a multi-faceted navigational directory and informational resource specifically structured as an open-architecture system to encourage traffic generation for music sites. Besides providing a standard URL-based directory, Casbah features a comprehensive music release and article index incorporating hyperlinks back to label and artist sites, specific release pages within those sites, to newsgroups, fan site and other related web locations."

Music Previews Network (www.previews.net)   "Music Previews Network is always first with Music Previews from today's hottest new releases. Purchase CD's [*sic*] online. Weekly giveaways. Updated constantly with new RealAudio, WAV and MPEG sound files."

Musi-Cal (www.musi-cal.com)   "Musi-Cal provides easy access to the most up-to-date worldwide live music information: concerts, festivals and other musical events."

Mass Music (www.mass-music.com)   "Mass Music carries over 185,000 titles discounted everyday. A free weekly eZine, music chat room, spelling tolerant music search engine, charts, simple navigation, overnight shipping, and domestic shipping as low as $1.49."

Worldcast Internet (www.worldcast.net)   "Worldcast Internet Music, books, health and more. Resources, information and shopping. Also featuring The Flow, a new listening experience featuring a tapestry of musical styles from many musical genres. The finest streaming audio content that can be found anywhere on the net, courtesy of Netscape LiveMedia."

MusicSearch (www.musicsearch.net),   "MusicSearch, a focused-search site, contains one of the largest resources of music-related Internet sites on the Internet today and growing daily. Using our search engine and directory-style database visitors can freely find sites based on over 200 topics covering all styles of music (genres, artists, groups, etc.), as well as music-related software, files, news, instruments, and by regional location. New features are built for the site weekly, which has been visited from over 90 different countries world-wide and gained over 14 Internet awards (including from NetGuide, Creative, and iWORLD) for design and use. Start MusicSearching today!"

TheDJ.com (www.thedj.com)   "TheDJ.com delivers over 50 channels of non-stop music to your desktop using RealAudio. When you hear a song you like, click 'Buy This CD' to place that CD in your shopping cart. Enjoy the music."

LiveUpdate (www.liveupdate.com)   "LiveUpdate is the web site for Crescendo, the leading MIDI music player on the Web. With Crescendo, LiveUpdate enables Web authors to add a new musical dimension to their sites. MIDI is extremely efficient—CD-quality music can be streamed using a 4800 bps connection. LiveUpdate invented technologies for streaming MIDI music on the Internet, and recently previewed tools for live MIDI concert broadcast."

EMusic (www.emusic.com)   EMusic has "Super Low Discount Prices on Over 100,000 Titles!"

This is just the network to look to when you want to promote something that you know appeals to those who like a given musical genre.

Doing It for Free

Keeping track of the numbers at LinkExchange (**www.linkexchange.com**) (see Figure 6.18) is heady work. Started in March, 1996, this banner exchange program has swelled to over 100,000 sites collectively delivering more than 5 million banner impressions a day, and growing at a rate of nearly 800 Web sites every day. What is making this banner ad network so popular?

It's free. That's right—it costs nothing.

The LinkExchange network includes commercial and non-commercial sites, all of which are in the medium, to the small, to the tiny size range. Some sites are serious Web endeavors and some are personal home pages ("Hey! Look at me!"). Each creates a banner promoting its site or its products and gets them shown on the other 999,999 sites. For free. What's the catch? All members have to be willing to show other member banners on their sites.

Do The Math   The math works like this—you put up a site and plug in the HTML that lets LinkExchange serve banners to your visitors. For every two banners that are served to your site, you get one of yours served somewhere on one of the other 999,999 sites. In other words, for every banner of yours LinkExchange serves on other sites, they get to put two on yours. One of them will be from the other 999,999, the other will be one that was paid for by an advertiser.

Why would you buy ads from a network that was free? Why would you buy ads from a network that includes college students' home pages and Web sites of companies that can't afford to buy banner space? One purchase order, 100,000 Web sites, 5 million impressions a day, and it's cheap. They like to be flexible about pricing, but you can expect to pay around $10 CPM.

FIG. 6.18

The LinkExchange serves over five million impressions each day.

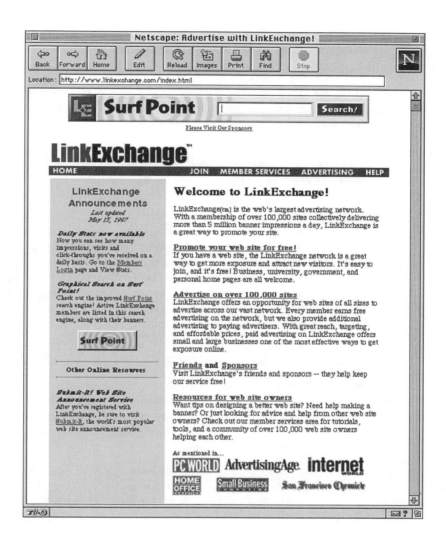

Where Have All the Banners Gone?   They also let you make some decisions about where your ad gets shown. Some of your decisions concern targeting (entertainment sites, Internet-related sites, business, computers, people, recreation, arts, hobbies, culture and society, education, health, politics). Each of these has subcatagories with 50 specific subjects in all.

Some of your decisions are about the appropriateness of the sites on which your ads appear. LinkExchange explains it this way:

The ratings system is meant to give you a degree of control over the types of sites you advertise for and advertise on. There are three ratings to choose from:

Level 1

These are sites intended for children. We will examine all Level 1 sites thoroughly to make sure that they are appropriate for children. Please do not classify yourself as a Level 1 site unless your site is intended for children.

Level 2

These are sites of general interest. Most LinkExchange sites come under this rating which roughly corresponds to 'PG.'

Level 3

This is the most inclusive rating and includes sites which contain language or subject matter which may be considered inappropriate or controversial to certain members. This rating does NOT include pornographic sites, sites with links to pornographic sites, sites encouraging illegal activity, racism, or other sites the administrators deem to be inappropriate. Such sites are NOT allowed to participate in the LinkExchange. Level 3 sites are merely sites whose appeal is not as general as those under the Level 2 rating. This rating roughly corresponds to 'PG-13.' Examples of sites that would probably fall under the Level 3 rating: Sites with swimsuit pictures, Sites relating to alcohol, Humor sites using strong language, etc.

The control may not be surgical and the sites you end up on are not the cream of the crop, but consider what they do offer—incredible reach out to people who are not passing through.

The search engines and directories that can sell you millions of impressions (and can deliver them in days instead of months) place your banner on sites that people are going *through* rather than *to*. LinkExchange offers sites that people found through the search engines. They went through the search engines in order to find Asian Food Net (**www.afn.com**) and California Menus (**www.californiamenus.com**).

Because you're advertising at the destination instead of on the highway, people are going to spend more time on those pages and be exposed to your message a lot longer. In his presentations at the Web Advertising conferences in 1996 and 1997, David Yoder, Media Director at Anderson & Lembke, advises Web advertisers to "Buy Wide, Not Deep." This is the place to do it.

Roadblock   Because LinkExchange includes 100,000 Web sites, it can perform one little trick that no one else can: the *roadblock*. It's a term derived from television and radio, where you buy up all of the available commercial slots for a given time period. ABC was the first client to put this model to the test for their May, 1997 Sweeps. LinkExchange was able to show the ABC banners for a U2 concert and *only* the ABC banners on all 100,000 sites for one hour prior to the airing of the concert on April 26, 1997.

Studies keep showing that people are taking time away from television in order to spend it online. We're still eating, we're still sleeping, and we're certainly working more now than before. But we're willing to give up a little TV time in order to be on the Internet. ABC decided it was the right tool for getting people back.

World Wide Reach Masters

You want massive exposure? You want millions of impressions? You want to deal with the cream-of-the-crop sites that get more than five million impressions a month? Time to talk to the big boys of Web sales.

Softbank Interactive Marketing (**www.simweb.com**) are the people who represent such megasites as Compuserve, Netscape, Playboy, TV Guide, and ZDNet. You would almost expect to see golden arches on the Softbank Web site because they claim to have sold over one billion Web advertising impressions in 1996. Judging by the numbers from Jupiter Communications and a Coopers & Lybrand study, Softbank also claims that they are responsible for 25% of the ads sold on the Web.

By definition, Softbank is a Web ad representative. Like their competitor, WebRep (**www.webrep.com**), Softbank is a broker. It makes deals on behalf of its clients. This sounds familiar to anybody who has done a large buy across a number of broadcasting firms. It's all a matter of representation. "You'll have to talk to our reps about that," say the sites, knowing that as a result, some or all of your advertising dollars will be spread to other sites represented by the reps.

WebRep has its own criteria to determine if a site is worthy of its representation:

Complimenting a site's unique, quality content and committed management, WebRep requires certain things from its Web site partners. Those sites must:

1. *offer at least 1,000,000 monthly page views/impressions*
2. *be up and running for at least three months*
3. *have the ability to serve or change banners within 24 hours of receiving notification*
4. *have a counting software package in place (such as Intersè, MarketWave, WebTrends)*
5. *offer real time, on-site confirmation of impressions and transfers per advertisement*
6. *have, although it is not required, an ad management system (such as AdServer from NetGravity, ClickWise from ClickOver, AdOptimizer by W3.com) or service (Focalink smartbanner, Globaltrack)*

WebRep offers one point of purchase, management of the relationships between the buyer and the seller, and consolidation of reporting from multiple sites. These are valuable services. Unless you have a large staff and want to do all of these non-core competency things yourself, ad representatives can be a good way to go. But these companies don't do something that a true ad network can: serve the ads themselves. Because of that, they can only provide for market segmentation, rather than real targeting.

Targeting

Besides being my domain name (**www.targeting.com**), targeting is today's tool for putting the right ad in front of the right person.

Targeting has to do with knowing who your site visitor is. So far, you've tried to match ads to eyeballs based on the type of computer and browser visitors use. You've tried to address them by company, by region, and by broad areas of interest. But you're still dealing with prevalent demographic guesswork.

The only way to get to know your audience on a more intimate basis is to get them to reveal themselves. If you can give them a reason to tell you a little about themselves, suddenly the sky's the limit and the 1:1 marketing relationship begins.

If you haven't read *The One To One Future* by Don Peppers and Martha Rogers (Doubleday, 1993), you should. If you haven't been to **www.1to1marketing.com**, make a point of it. The issue is dealing with your customers on an individual basis. I covered the relationship side of doing business on the Web extensively in *Customer Service on the Internet*. These days, that relationship is growing out of the customer realm and into the advertising world.

Getting to Know You

People tend to use the same search engines over and over again. Once you get to know how one works, you know how to get at the information you want as fast as possible. You go back. If that search engine starts asking questions about you and learning who you are, it can more tightly deliver banner ads you are more likely to click.

So how can a Web site in this stateless server world tell the difference between you and the next guy? If you're surfing the Web from your own private domain, then it's possible to say, "Ah, here's Fred! He's coming from the fred.com domain and he's the only one who ever does, so it *must* be Fred! Hi, Fred!" But so many people come from aol.com that we need some other way of knowing who's who.

Will Our Mystery Guest Log In, Please?   Getting people to log into a site is okay in three circumstances: they paid a subscription fee to become a member; the site contains personal information such as their credit card number and billing address, or it's their online bank site; they know there's valuable information and they're willing to trade some information about themselves in order to get it.

I willingly let Amazon.com know who I am. That way I can buy books. I'm happy to log into **www.wellsfargo.com** and give them my password. Same with **www.schwab.com**. I don't want just anybody paying my bills and trading my investments.

But these are private services. They're not public Web sites where millions of people show up every day. Millions of people would not show up at Yahoo! if they had to log in. The solution, then, lies in the magic cookie.

Cookies   Netscape created the cookie in order to get to know you better. The *cookie* is a text file on your hard drive that stores a server-given user identification number. Maybe it even adds some useful information, such as your name and address, if you happened to mention them. If the server doesn't recognize any of the cookies in your file, it gives you one. If it does, then it knows something about you. It knows that you are the same person that came to visit three days ago. It can also look into its database to see what you told it on previous visits. You told it your name? "Hi, Fred!"

The wonderful thing about cookies is that they are unobtrusive. I don't have to log in. I don't have to identify myself. I don't have to have references. It's just like going to the same gas station for the past twelve years. "Hi, Jim!"

Cookies have a couple of problems. They're not infallible. If you're interested in the technical dissertation, head over to the Netscape site and enjoy. If you want to know the skinny without the dry technical jargon, wander over to Andy's Netscape HTTP Cookie Notes (**www. illuminatus.com/cookie.fcgi**). But if you're only interested in the practical side of the issue, it boils down to this:

> It's a text file. Anybody can find it on their PC and delete it—Personality Deficiency.
>
> It's browser-dependent. If you use Netscape and Internet Explorer, you end up with two different cookies—Schizophrenia.
>
> It's computer-dependent. If you use a desktop, a laptop, and you use Netscape and Internet Explorer, you have four cookies—Multiple Personality Disorder.
>
> It can't tell the difference between you and your spouse if you both use the same browser on the same computer—Ambidextrous.
>
> Not all browsers are able to accept a cookie—Catatonia.

Yahoo! uses the cookie to good advantage. They don't make you fill out a form and reveal your most secret predilections. Instead, they offer a service. Yahoo! will display a custom home page made just for you (see Figure 6.19).

You select what kind of news you want to get headlines on. You select your favorite Web sites. You select the cities in which you want to watch the weather. You get what you want. Yahoo! gets to know a little bit about you. When a search site knows a bit more about you, it can use that information to sell targeted ad space.

Getting to Know all About You   *April 14, 1997—Framingham, Mass.—Lycos, Inc. (NASDAQ:LCOS) the premier navigation center on the Internet announced today it will soon have a new ability to dynamically target online ads and automate advertising management using AdManager, a highly sophisticated tool from Accipiter Inc., a provider of Internet advertising solutions.*

The move will greatly enhance Lycos' ability to provide highly sophisticated Internet target marketing benefits to the more than 300 companies that advertise on its site. Located at www.lycos.com, Lycos and its properties serve more than 6 million daily page viewings.

Dave Peterson, Vice President of Advertising Sales at Lycos, points out their targeting can include topic, keyword phrases, page specific, operating system, browser type, company, ISP, and more. Lycos automates the process of targeting, scheduling, rotating, and delivering ads on the Web. According to Peterson, "Advertisers get real-time on-line reporting enabling them to adjust their advertising campaigns in direct response to the activities and preferences of individual site visitors."

FIG. 6.19

Yahoo! learns about you by offering personalization.

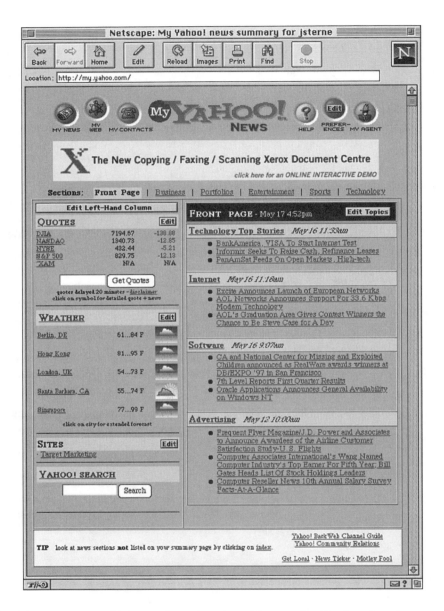

Lycos will be able to use personal interests in conjunction with page classification, domain type (.edu, .gov, .fr), time of day, day of week, and selected keywords. If the personal information includes a postal zip code, then all kinds of demographic information gets stirred into the mix. If the personal information includes favorite cuisine, movie genre, sport, vacation spot, and so on, it starts to get interesting.

I'm reminded of the ads IBM ran in computer journals for their technology to help you find women who like boating and science fiction; people who like seafood and motorbikes; and women who like classical music and home improvement projects. The first was accompanied by a photograph of a woman in a powerboat with four terrified extraterrestrials. The second showed a lobster riding a motorcycle. The third depicted a woman in an elegant evening dress playing a rather large chainsaw as if it were a bass cello.

We understand and have become used to database marketing. We just haven't gotten used to the idea that this data can be live, online, or real time. It can be information gathered at the moment the Web site visitor shows up and can be modified as he or she moves through the site.

The power of this kind of information is manifest. The task of managing an advertising campaign that takes this power into consideration can be daunting. There is help out there, however, in the form of ad networks.

From WebRep to Network

The DoubleClick (**www.doubleclick.com**) tag line is "Building one-to-one relationships, millions at a time." DoubleClick isn't kidding. Although it represents less than 100 sites, DoubleClick has something that other Web reps can't compete with. DoubleClick serves all of your banners itself.

All 70 of its client sites are set up to ask for a banner from DoubleClick whenever a page is requested. For example, the banner at the top of the AltaVista page does not come from the AltaVista server (see Figure 6.20).

FIG. 6.20

AltaVista gets its ads from DoubleClick.

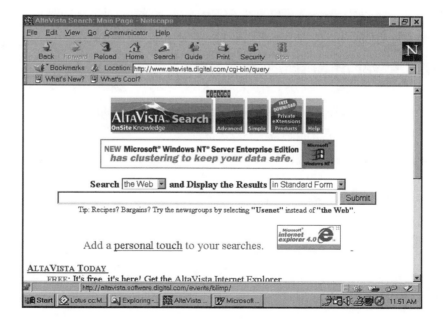

If you watch the "Connect:" comments at the bottom of your browser (and if you've had more than two cups of coffee—it goes by pretty quickly), you notice that the AltaVista page is coming from **altavista.digital.com**. Then you notice that the banner ad is being retrieved from **doubleclick.com**.

View the source and you see the HTML:

```
<center><a href="http://ad.doubleclick.net/jump/altavista.digital.com/">
<img ismap width=468 height=60 border=0
src="http://ad.doubleclick.net/ad/altavista.digital.com/"></a></center>
```

Not only is the banner coming from DoubleClick, but the link it takes you to if you click *goes* to DoubleClick. Shouldn't the link take you to the site being advertised? Well, it does. But it does so in a roundabout way. First, it sends a message to DoubleClick, which redirects the link to Web-Ignite (the "Targeted Internet Promotions" company).

In doing so, DoubleClick can keep absolute tabs on how many ads are being served on which sites.

In doing so, DoubleClick can keep absolute tabs on which ads should be served to which sites.

In doing so, DoubleClick can keep absolute tabs on which ads should be served to which people.

In doing so, DoubleClick can keep absolute tabs on which ads are being clicked.

It's nice to have all the reporting coming from the same server. If you select DoubleClick client's sites for your ads like Dilbert, Quicken, or IGolf, all of the stats about your impressions and clickthroughs are going to come hot off the press in the same format. You won't have to wait days or weeks for the Web Rep to consolidate the data and make it meaningful.

But that's nothing compared to the power of targeting a specific audience across multiple sites.

The Power of Network Targeting

Want to reach college kids in the Midwest between 6 and 10 P.M. the week before spring break?

Want to reach New York investment bankers who work Wall Street and are planning to travel?

From a DoubleClick magazine ad, May 1997

A network of sites multiplied by a database of demographic information, times a database of ads equals unprecedented advertising power. Let's take it one step at a time.

Time of Day/Day of Week   What time of day are they coming to the site? That's a no-brainer. If there are different ads for different times of day, the database need only look at the system clock to determine which banner to bestow.

If you are advertising a television concert, you want to stop showing the banner after it's over. It would make no sense to display banners intended for small children after evening turns into night. According to DoubleClick, "This is particularly helpful if you only wish to reach business users (who have access to the Internet only Monday-Friday during business hours), or if your banner is linked to a telemarketing campaign which only operates during set hours."

Operating System   Microsoft took advantage of the fact that all browsers report the operating system and version number when a surfer arrives at a site. They wanted to let Macintosh users know that a new version of Internet Explorer was available for them. If the surfer was using Windows 3.1, they have a different banner. Windows 95? Different again.

Anybody selling computer-related products or services would be wise to follow Microsoft's lead and pay attention to what sort of computer is on the other end of the modem. On their Web site, DoubleClick says it feels that "[e]ngineers, scientists and students tend to use UNIX systems. Creative, artists and graphic designers usually use Macintoshes. Software developers often use Microsoft NT. Professionals and business people tend to use Windows-based systems."

High Level Domain   Surveys and focus groups may have told you that people at work react to different messages than people at home. You would have guessed yourself that college students and teachers live a slightly different lifestyle than the rest of us. Government employees have different interests and needs. Non-profit organizations respond to different stimuli.

Thus, with a handful of banners in an ad network database, the proper communication can be made depending on whether the page viewer is coming from a .com or from a general Internet Service Provider (ISP) such as America Online or Netcom. You can tailor your message depending on whether they're coming from an .edu, a .gov, or an .org.

Specific Company   As mentioned, it's not too hard to keep a local database of IP addresses to determine exactly which company somebody is coming from if they're surfing from work. Cisco Systems, an Internet router manufacturer, uses this approach for recognizing anybody coming to Cisco customer service site from one of its competitors. If the server sees you're from Bay Networks, it hands back a picture of the customer service team smiling at you, with the words "Welcome to our Friends at Bay Networks!" If it works for them, it can work for banner ads as well.

Company Specifics   Looking up the IP address leads to the name of the company. Looking up the company can lead to the SIC code. Now that you know what they do for a living, you can determine which of your products you'd like to promote.

There are lots of services which provide databases which can tell you company locations and sizes. Is it a small firm in the Midwest? They react to different material than a billion dollar corporation in the Northwest.

According to their Web site, DoubleClick has "compiled an extensive database of every company currently on the Internet. Using reliable third-party data, we have compiled financial and size information on the majority of these companies. Targeting by Size or Revenue can be particularly helpful if you are marketing a business product to organizations or if you are offering a human resource service."

Editorial Content   There is also information to consider about the site on which your ad resides. You can catalog different content for each page if you like. That gives you a clue as to the viewers' interests.

At the moment, DoubleClick offers a number of "affinity groups":

Premium Sites (Quicken Financial Network, Dilbert, USA Today, Gamelan Java Directory, Travelocity)

Business and Finance

Entertainment

Sports, Travel & Leisure

Technology & The Internet

News/Information and Culture

Directories & Search Engines

In DoubleClick's own words, here's what happens when you click (**www.doubleclick.net/nf/ adinfo/bandeset.htm**):

How Does DoubleClick Do It?

Since the inception and launch of DoubleClick's targeted advertising network, one question keeps coming up again, and again. Even our most enthusiastic clients and customers are not satisfied with knowing that it works wonders for them,—they all want to know HOW?

In brief, DoubleClick reads the User IP address, extracts the network address, identifies the company, and then selects and delivers a targeted ad. That's it. It's that simple.

Here, in more detail, is how . . .

A user enters the name (URL) of a DoubleClick Network web site they wish to visit, usually by clicking on an icon or link;

The selected Web page is delivered from that Web site to the User, and the User's browser loads the requested page. Embedded in the page are Image Tags that link the browser to the DoubleClick server in New York. The User's browser initiates the HTTP Get request from the DoubleClick server, establishing a connection between the two, and a graphic file is requested from DoubleClick to fill the ad banner space on the Web page being loaded on the User's screen. (In most cases near the top of the loading page.)

DoubleClick then performs the following . . . :

The User's Internet Protocol (IP address) is referenced, and the series of numbers that make up a User's network address (ex. 199.25.206.5), is noted. These network addresses are referenced against the DoubleClick database of more that 400,000 mapped networks.

Each mapped network reveals the User's Domain (at&t.net, microsoft.com, etc.), and the following information about that Domain:

Country State Postal Code Area Code SIC*

(*SIC codes identify an organization type. This information is gathered from independent third party sources, is matched with identified domains, and becomes part of the DoubleClick database.)

DoubleClick assembles and reviews all the information it has collected to this point, including referencing the content (News, Sports, Weather, Financial . . .) of the DoubleClick Network site the User is visiting, and even pages within a site that contain words that an advertiser wishes to place a banner near, (example: 'auto,' 'highways,' 'tires' for a car maker's ad). DoubleClick also notes the time of day, and day of week relative to the User.

The DoubleClick server reads the HTTP header from the User and notes the User's Browser Type (Netscape, Microsoft, etc.) and Version (2.0 3.1, etc), Operating System (Unix, Mac, etc.) and Version, and Service Provider (AOL, Netcom, Pipeline, etc.). This information is sometimes used in targeting ad banners. As the User's browser permits, a cookie identification number is assigned to the User. DoubleClick assigns each individual User its own unique user ID number, primarily to track the number of times a User has seen each banner in order to control frequency, or deliver sequential banners to the same User.

Then DoubleClick scans the more than 1,000 ad banners waiting for delivery at any time, matching the ad and its targeting criteria with the User, and the information gathered. The appropriate ad banner is selected and delivered to the User.

All of this, every bit, takes place in the blink of an eye, the snap of a finger, . . . less than 20 milliseconds.

Then What . . .? When the User sees a highly targeted ad banner, they are more likely to be interested and respond. When they do, when they 'click-through,' DoubleClick receives a Get request and redirects the User's browser to the URL of the site that placed the ad banner. The advertiser's server delivers the page content, and DoubleClick records another successful targeted click-through.

If the user is from a network not previously identified, it is tagged as 'new' and DoubleClick performs an automatic search looking for this new network by sending a query to Internic, the central repository for network identities on the Internet. Internic provides the Domain (and the associated information submitted at time of registration) and the data is incorporated into DoubleClick's database.

All the information collected to this point is part of a running process that continually updates itself 24 hours a day, 365 days a year.

DoubleClick isn't the only one playing the network game. One contender, Matchlogic (**www.matchlogic.com**), uses their Web site to make a direct comparison between themselves and the senior DoubleClick:

> *MatchLogic is the only company providing advertisers with campaign management services across the entire Web with performance information available online within 60 seconds. This means that marketers can reliably compare performance of banners and sites, calculate their ROI, and make adjustments during the campaign to increase performance. Unlike DoubleClick and other networks, MatchLogic doesn't restrict marketers to specific sites. Instead, MatchLogic implements and manages campaigns across sites, including those within networks. And because the company serves ads across the breadth of the World Wide Web, MatchLogic provides the most comprehensive solution of any online advertising management service.*

Categorical Targeting

Petry Network is another DoubleClick competitor. They offer different types of targeting: Affinity; Geographic Location; High-Level Internet Domain Type; Internet Service Provider;

Operating System; Browser Type; Days and Times to Display Ad; and Demographic Profiling Targeting. In other words, pretty much what you'd expect. But then they get deep.

According to Mark Welch (more on Welch later in the section titled "Networks of the Future") in a presentation he gave at Web Advertising 97 (which has more information on ad networks than would fit in this book and is well worth your time. It's found at **www.ca-probate.com/ webadv97.htm**, the Petry Network requires that each URL it places an ad on be assigned one sub-category from the following list:

General Art (All, Art History, Artists, Arts Therapy, Children, Companies, Countries and Cultures, Design Arts, Education, Events, Forums, Humanities, Institutes, Libraries, Magazines, Museums and Galleries, Organizations, Performing Arts, Pictures, Publications, Real-Time Chat, Television Shows, Thematic, Tour Operators, Visual Arts)

Business (All, Business Schools, Classifieds, Companies, Consortia, Consumer Economy, Conventions and Conferences, Courses, Economics, Education, Electronic Commerce, Employment, History, Intellectual Property, International Economy, Labor, Magazines, Management Information Systems, Marketing, Markets and Investments, Miscellaneous, News, Organizations, Products and Services, Real Estate, Small Business Information, Taxes, Technology Policy, Trade, Transportation)

Computers (All, Art, Communications and Networking, Companies, Computer Science, Contests, Conventions and Conferences, Cyberculture, Desktop Publishing, Games, Graphics, Hardware, History, Humor, Information and Documentation, Internet, Magazines, Mobile Computing, Multimedia, Music, Operating Systems, Organizations, Personal Computers, Programming Languages, Security and Encryption, Semiconductors, Software, Standards, Supercomputing and Parallel Computing Systems, Telecommunications, Training, User Groups, World Wide Web)

Education (All, Academic Competitions, Adult and Continuing Education, Art, Career and Vocational, Companies, Conferences, Distance Learning, Educational Standards and Testing, Educational Theory and Methods, Financial Aid, Government Agencies, Guidance, Higher Education, Institutes, Instructional Technology, Journals, Languages, Lectures, Literacy, Magazines, Math and Science Education, Music, News, Online Forums, Organizations, Products, Programs, Resources, Special Education, Teaching)

Entertainment (All, Amusement/Theme Parks, Audio/Visual Equipment, Books, Comics and Animation, Contests, Cool Links, Drinks and Drinking, Events, Food and Eating, Hard to Believe, Humor, Internet, Magazines, Miscellaneous, Movies and Films, Multimedia, Music, News, Organizations, Paranormal Phenomena, People, Radio, Real-Time Chat, Reviews, Science Fiction, Horror, Television, Theater, Trivia, Useless Pages)

Government (All, Agencies, Citizenship, Conventions and Conferences, Countries, Documents, Embassies and Consulates, Executive Branch, Federal Employees, Institutes, Intelligence, International Organizations, Judicial Branch, Law, Legislative Branch, Military, News, Politics, Real-Time Chat, Reengineering, Research Labs, Student Government, Technology Policy, U.S. Budget, U.S. States)

Health (All, Alternative Medicine, Career and Employment, Children's Health, Companies, Conferences, Death and Dying, Dentistry, Disabilities, Diseases and Conditions, Education,

Emergency Services, Environmental Health, Fitness, General Health, Geriatrics and Aging, Health Administration, Health Care, Health Sciences, Hospitals, Institutes, Journals, Law, Magazines, Medicine, Men's Health, Mental Health, Nursing, Nutrition, Organizations, Pharmacology, Public Health and Safety, Public Interest Groups, Radio Programs, Real-Time Chat, Reproductive Health, Sexuality, Travel, Weight Issues, Women's Health, Workplace)

Internet (All, Business and Economics, Chat, Commercial Services, Commercial Software, Communications and Networking, Conferences and Events, Connectivity, Directory Services, Domain Registration, Education, Electronic Mail, Entertainment, FTP Sites, Gopher, History, Indices to Web Documents, Information and Documentation, Internet Fax Server, Internet Phone, Intranet, Magazines, Mailing Lists, Maps, Network Topology, Newsletters, Organizations, Policies, Resources, Searching the Net, Software, Statistics and Demographics, Usenet, User Groups, World Wide Web, Usenet)

Investing (All, Bonds, Brokerages, Commercial Financial Services, Commercial Investment Services, Corporate Reports, Currencies, Economic Indicators, Exchanges, Forums and Chats, Futures and Options, Hard Assets, Initial Public Offerings, Mutual Funds, News, Organizations, Quotes, Real Estate, Reference and Guides, Socially Responsible Investments, SRI, Software Products, Trading Games and Simulations, FAQs, Usenet Media/ news (All, Broadcasting, Business, Columns, Commercial News Services, Daily, Editorial, Entertainment, Events, Government, Health, Internet, Journalism, Legal, Magazines, Newspapers, Newswires, Personalized News, Politics, Radio, Real-Time Chat, Science, Sports, Technology, Television, Usenet, Weekly, World, WWW What's New)

Movies (All, Actors and Actresses, Awards, Box Office Reports, Columns, Companies, Contests, Events, Exhibits, Film Festivals, Film Making, Film Music, Film Schools, Genres, History, Home Video, Independent, Interactive Games, Journals, Laserdisc, Lists, Magazines, Mailing Lists, Multimedia, News, Organizations, Parodies, People, Personal Pages, Quotes, Real-Time Chat, Resources, Reviews, Screenplays, Studios, Theaters, Theory and Criticism, This Week's Releases, Titles, Trivia, Usenet)

Music (All, Artists, Awards, Band Naming, Bootlegs, Charts, Classifieds, Companies, Composition, Computer Generated, Consumer Information, Contests, Countries and Cultures, Cover Art, Discographies, Education, Events, Film Music, Games, Genres, Girl Bands, History, Humor, Independent Music, Instruments, Karaoke, Listening Booth, Lyrics and Notation, Magazines, Mailing Lists, Music Videos, Musicals, News, Organizations, Polls, Radio Programs, Real-Time Chat, Religious, Reviews, Software, Soundtracks, Trivia, Vocal, Usenet)

Recreation (All, Amusement/Theme Parks, Animals, Automotive, Aviation, Cooking, Dance, Dating, Drugs, Events, Fashion, Fishing, Games, Hobbies and Crafts, Home and Garden, Hovercraft, Motorcycles, Outdoors, Real-Time Chat, Sports, Toys, Travel)

Reference (All, Acronyms and Abbreviations, Almanacs, Atlases, Calendars, Codes, Dictionaries, Encyclopedia, English Language Usage, Etiquette, Flags, Interesting, Journals, Libraries, Maps, Parliamentary Procedure, Patents, Phone Numbers, Postal Information, Quotations, Searching the Net, Standards, Thesauri, Time, Weights and Measures, White Pages)

Science (All, Acoustics, Agriculture, Alternative, Amateur Science, Anthropology and Archaeology, Artificial Life, Astronomy, Aviation and Aeronautics, Biology, Chaos, Chemistry, Cognitive Science, Complex Systems, Computer Science, Earth Sciences, Ecology, Education, Energy, Engineering, Events, Forensics, Geography, Geology and Geophysics, History, Humor, Hydrology, Information Technology, Institutes, Journals, Life Sciences, Magazines, Mathematics, Medicine, Meteorology, Museums and Exhibits, Nanotechnology, News, Oceanography, Organizations, Paleontology, Paradoxes, Physics, Psychology, Real-Time Chat, Research, Space, Weights and Measures, Zoology, Usenet)

Society (All, Affirmative Action, Age, Alternative, Animal Rights, Birth, Charity, Children, Civil Rights, Crime, Cultures, Cyberculture, Death, Disabilities, Diversity, Environment and Nature, Etiquette, Families, Fashion, Firearms, Friendship, Gender, Holidays, Human Rights, Left-Handers, Lesbians, Magazines, Minorities, Museums and Exhibits, Mythology and Folklore, Nonviolence, Organizations, People, Poverty, Race Relations, Real-Time Chat, Relationships, Religion, Reunions, Royalty, Seniors, Sexuality, Singles, Size Issues, Veterans, Weddings)

Sports (All, Amateur, Archery, Art, Athletes, Auto Racing, Badminton, Baseball, Basketball, Baton Twirling, Billiards, Boat Racing, Boomerang, Bowling, Boxing, Bullfighting, Cable TV Networks, Canoe Polo, Canoe-Kayak Racing, Cheerleading, Coaching, Collectibles, College and University, Companies, Contests, Cricket, Croquet, Curling, Cycling, Danball, Disabilities, Dog Racing, Dogsledding, Education, Equestrian, Events, Fantasy Leagues, Fencing, Fishing, Flying Discs, Footbag Hacky Sack, Football American, Football Australian, Football Gaelic, Gambling, Golf, Gymnastics, Handball, High School, History, Hockey, Horse Racing, International Games, Jai-Alai, Jump Rope, Korfball, Lacrosse, Luge, Lumbering, Magazines, Martial Arts, Motorcycle Racing, Museums and Halls of Fame, News and Media, Officiating, Organizations, Orienteering, Paddling, Polo, Psychology, Racquetball, Ratings and Rankings, Real-Time Chat, Regional, Ringette, Rodeo, Rounders, Rowing, Rugby, Running, Sailing, Schedules, Sepak Takraw, Shooting, Shuffleboard, Skateboarding, Skating, Skiing, Skydiving, Snowboarding, Snowmobiles, Soccer, Softball, Software, Squash, Stadiums, Surfing, Swimming and Diving, Table Tennis, Technology, Tennis, Track and Field, Triathlon, Trivia, Tug-of-War, Volleyball, Wakeboarding, Walking, Water Polo, Waterskiing, Weightlifting, Windsurfing, Wrestling, Usenet)

Travel (All, Air Travel, Automotive, Backpacking, Boating, Books and Publications, Budget Travel, Convention and Visitors Bureaus, Cruises, Currency Exchange, General Information, Health, Honeymoons, Lodging, Magazines, Products, Resorts, Tour Operators, Train Travel, Transportation, Travel Agents, Travel Related Businesses, Travelogues, Virtual Field Trips)

Weather (All, Aviation Weather, Books, Climate Centers, Companies, Daily Weather News, Education, Events, Institutes, Maps and Data, Newsletters, Organizations, Real-Time Chat, Research, Software, Storm Chasing, Weather Phenomena, Usenet)

If you can't find an affinity group that matches up with the demographics or psychographics for your product, I'll be happy to offer my consulting services at my standard rate.

But Mark Welch, an attorney, doesn't think it's that easy. He offers himself as an example in a post to the Online Advertising List.

Date: Sat, 27 Jul 1996 12:55:02 -0700

To: online-ads@o-a.com

From: Mark J. Welch (markwelch@ca-probate.com)

Subject: ONLINE-ADS>> New Subscriber Intro: Mark J. Welch

I am an estate planning attorney in Pleasanton, California. I have created a wonderful web site about California estate planning, probate, and trust law. I would like to attract people to my web site, and of course ultimately I want people to hire me to represent them in their estate planning matters, or in probate administration proceedings.

Geography.

I am admitted to practice law only in California, and generally my clients live or work within about 15 miles from Pleasanton, California. There are probably about 1 million people in my geographic target area.

Wealth.

While everyone should have a will, poor people and those with modest incomes don't hire me. Most of my clients have a net worth of $250,000 or more (per married couple), and estate tax planning generally is important only for clients with a net worth over $600,000.

Age.

Young people do not do estate planning. Roughly 85% of my clients are over age 40, and 60% over age 50.

Sex.

In a married couple, it is the wife who most often provides the pressure to do estate planning, and more often than not she also selects the attorney.

Sexual Orientation.

Gay couples have more need for estate planning because 'interstate succession' rarely matches their goals.

Triggering Events & Behaviors.

Most clients seek out legal assistance for estate planning because of common triggering events:

Birth of second child (rare)

3-5 years after second marriage ('blended family')

Youngest child 'leaves the nest'

Pre-Retirement (age 57-62)

Retirement

Death of Friend or Relative (Not Spouse)

Death of Spouse (update plan 1-2 years later)

Of course, the other aspect of my practice—estate administration (probate or trust administration)—arises when someone dies.

Okay, let's try to design an Internet advertising program for me, based on the information. . .

We have some problems right off the bat: there is no way to target directly geographically or based on age, family status, or based on the triggering events specified. (Indeed, even designing a direct mail campaign would be difficult.) Certainly, we can provide some geographic targeting, based on the IP address of the visitor (that will probably result in acceptable accuracy for 60% to 80% of visitors, if I accept about a 30 to 40 mile radius).

But we could easily identify a list of possible web-site subjects that would be relevant and would target a relatively high percentage of people in my target audience: seniors, retirement, retirement planning, financial planning and investment, death, grief, obituaries, life insurance, investments, rental property management.

Unfortunately, if I wanted to place an advertising buy with most pooled advertising networks, I couldn't get categories even vaguely related to these subjects.

Even if the categories I want were available, I would want some assurance that the sites that checked that category were truly relevant. Indeed, I would almost certainly want to screen all the pages where my ad would appear, in advance, to insure that the ad would not appear on sites I found offensive or inappropriate for my ad. (Note that a web page that is acceptable one day might become unacceptable the next, if the content is changed.)

Is Welch hard to please? Is Welch asking too much? Actually, he's a pretty typical advertiser. But you'd be hard-pressed to find somebody that's thought about these issues as long and as hard.

The power of targeting specific editorial content and collecting such a wide variety of information across multiple Web sites is considerable. Knowing your audience is, after all, the name of the game. There is, however, a fly in the ointment. There's a little bit of a discussion about cookies.

The Cookie Conundrum

Cookies have been getting a bad rap up on Capitol Hill. It's a privacy issue.

The protectors of the realm in Congress feel that one-to-one marketing might be okay if it's done carefully. A server can write a cookie on a client's hard drive because there is an implicit relationship between the surfer and the surfee (Web site).

You come to my Web site and we can be said to have established something of a relationship. That's fine. No harm, no foul. But it's possible for a third party to place a cookie on your browser. Did you know that? Doesn't it bother you? Doesn't it seem like there's infinite room for abuse? Well, not really.

The only way a third party could plant a cookie on you is with the permission of the second party—that is, the content Web site operator. The content Web site has to put the hooks into his HTML that calls the third party.

So why is this a problem? Because DoubleClick and MatchLogic use cookie technology to keep track of people. You go to AltaVista and through them, DoubleClick is permitted to write something in your cookie file. It's a very powerful tool for advertisers because they can start to hand out banners based on information collected over time instead of information gathered and deciphered at the moment.

The Internet Engineering Task Force, which more or less sets the technical standards for the Internet, has offered up Request For Comment #2109 (**http://ds.internic.net/rfc/ rfc2109.txt**). This RFC would have all browsers automatically reject cookies from third parties.

The obvious solution is to let individuals decide if they want to accept cookies or not. Like most of what's wrong with the Internet, it's not a problem that needs to be legislated. If you start to feel your privacy is being violated, you can delete your cookie file after every session. Better yet, with Netscape version 4.0, we'll all have the ability to set our cookie preferences ourselves. This wasn't a decision made in the dark. In fact, Lou Montulli, protocol manager at Netscape, was one of the original authors of the RFC. The bit about the third-party Web sites got in there over his objections.

"I think we're doing the right think for the users," Montulli told Rick Bruner, of *Advertising Age*. "But it's a very fine line. If we were to unilaterally disable this feature, existing content on the Web would no longer work…[Also] sites that use [cookies] tend to use them in a way that generate revenue. If you take away revenue from the sites, then the users may lose their ability to go to these sites."

With Netscape 4.0, I'll be able to reject them out of hand if I choose. Chances are very likely that I'll immediately notice that the Internet if full of dumb ads for things I don't care about and would never buy. I'll notice that the longer my cookie file is in use, the more interesting the ads get. Sounds like a win-win situation to me.

Networks of the Future

Mark Welch is one of those Internet marvels. In addition to being a probate lawyer, Welch is a man deeply interested in advertising on the Internet. His magnum opus, Web Site Banner Advertising: Banner Ad Networks & Brokers, which can found at **www.ca-probate.com/ comm_net.htm**, is a resource not to be missed. It includes pointers to players and sound advice, not to mention a healthy helping of his own opinion. Take a look at it in Figure 6.21.

Some of Welch's advice from his Web site includes:

If it sounds too good to be true, it probably is. Note that several companies listed here have already defaulted on payment promises, and several companies have 'changed their rules' with little notice (at least one imposed new rules retroactively to refuse to pay sites).

Beware of strangers. Don't do business with a company that won't tell you its street address, telephone number, and the names of the principals. Check if the information you get matches the information in the company's domain name registration. Consider carefully whether you should do business with a company that's located in another country or even another state or city.

Contracts: Be sure to carefully read and print out any web site pages describing payment rules and policies. Some companies change their rules or don't define their policies clearly. Don't sign or otherwise accept a contract that includes unacceptable terms; if a vendor tells you the contract doesn't mean what it says, don't sign the contract until it's changed to say what you believe. Consult with an attorney (I do not provide legal advice to web publishers). . .

Don't count on payment. The entire advertising industry is famous for paying late, or not at all. Don't put yourself in a position where you can't pay your web hosting fees unless your royalty check arrives on time (or at all).

Warning to Advertisers, Ad Networks, and Web Publishers: Beware of 'web page pirates,' who copy successful web pages and then attempt to sign up with ad networks and exchange programs to unfairly generate profit from their copyright infringement. The page you are viewing has been copied three times in the past few months, and each time I have had to spend time, effort, and money to get the ISP to close down the offending web site. Don't do business with web pirates!

FIG. 6.21
Mark Welch's compendium of Internet advertising links and thoughts is well worth your time.

That's good advice for ad buyers. On a related page, The Ad Network of the Future (**http://www.ca-probate.com/adfuture.htm**), Welch offers some suggestions for network builders:

SmartClicks (still in 'beta' testing) designed software that allows each web page to be separately categorized; the software tracks the performance of each banner advertisement (based on the ratio of displays to click-throughs) in each category. An advertiser can then designate specific categories for their advertisement, or can instruct that SmartClicks automatically display ads more frequently in categories that it has 'learned' are more effective. My own experience, after two weeks of allowing random rotation of ads, was the discovery that my ad was performing well in an unexpected category; on reflection, I understood why, but I would never have selected that category without first seeing its success.

A vendor must devote substantial energy to creating, maintaining, adapting, and enforcing a system of categories for web pages. Each page must be separately registered, since many web sites include a variety of web pages often with unrelated content. And the vendor must adopt a system to verify the proper assignment of categories. For larger sites, this will entail actual review of the site or page and confirmation that the correct category or categories have been assigned. Ideally, the category system must allow for dynamic extension, with sub-categories added to distinguish sites and pages whenever possible.

The ad network must address the issue of content changes at a web site: some system must be created to insure [sic] that new content, or gradual changes to content, are reflected in the category assigned to the specific page. A system must also be adopted for web sites with "dynamic content" (such as newspapers with new articles each day, or sports sites whose primary sports theme shifts with the seasons).

There are a few more tricks beyond targeting that network builders can use. Some have been through the proof-of-concept stage and some are just now being put into practice.

The Real Me: The Fine Art of Profiling

Mark Gibbs, network consultant and contributing editor of *Network World* magazine, pinpointed the art of pinpointing during an e-mail discussion between the two of us:

With an Internet Marketing campaign, there is no idealized consumer—a sales message should be unique for each specific individual. The key to the future of Internet advertising is consumer information: the more you know about who is getting your message and the more that you tailor the content, the more effective your pitch will be.

The first I heard of profiling was at Firefly (**www.firefly.com**), when it offered to recommend a movie to me (see Figure 6.22).

I thought about the time and effort that would go into creating such a thing and shook my head. A huge database filled with all of the best movies, categorized by subject, genre, theme, actors, music, director, and a dozen other attributes. It was truly a task of epic proportions.

Furthermore, I couldn't see how it could really work based on the limited information it asked of me. I was presented with a list of movies and I was asked to rate them on a scale from nothing to 7, as follows:

> don't know
> 1: hate it!
> 2: pretty bad
> 3: not my thing
> 4: it's alright
> 5: I like that
> 6: great stuff
> 7: the best

FIG. 6.22
Firefly is smart enough to make movie recommendations without a direct pipeline to Siskel & Ebert.

Surely that's not enough to go on. But, to my surprise, it started recommending movies that I had not rated yet. And they were good movies. Well, I'm sure my wife would disagree and my mother would be appalled, but my brother would say, "Hey, that Firefly knows what you like!" And he'd be right.

Collaborative Filtering

That's when I looked under the covers and tripped over *collaborative filtering*. I had heard the phrase only once before, in association with Net Shepherd.

Net Shepherd (**www.netshpherd.com**) started life as a tool to help keep kids away from objectionable material on the Web. CyberSitter, Net Nanny, and Surf Watch were busy building databases of pornographic sites that they would block if you installed their software.

Net Shepherd took a different perspective. It understood the community nature of the Internet and wanted to create a filtering system that was in keeping with the idea that like-minded people like to share their opinions. So it created a database server that allows any database subscriber to vote on the Web sites they visited. If you subscribed to your state's elementary school database, you would rate sites based on their appropriateness to kids' ages: 4–6, 7–10, 11–13, 14–17, and 18–21. But not all by yourself.

Everybody who subscribed to that database would always have the opportunity to vote on whatever sites they wanted to. The result would be a communal collection of ratings based on community standards. Not legislated standards, but true community standards.

Youngsters would be blocked from seeing Web sites that talked about AIDS. Pre-teens would be blocked from sites that talked about romantic sex. Teenagers would be blocked from sites dealing with racial hatred. But the exciting thing that caught my attention was that it wasn't a small group of people in some Star Chamber deciding what was good and ill. It was up to the community.

Further, you could belong to more than one community in recognition of the fact that we all wear multiple hats. You could subscribe to your church database, which would bar sites that use foul language, and you could subscribe to the *Playboy* rating database that, as a community, felt nudity was okay, but violence was not.

And that's what I found under the covers at Firefly: collaborative filtering, but of a slightly different nature. This version was simpler. This version was so simple I marveled that it hadn't been done before and still can't figure out why everybody else isn't doing it yet.

Firefly didn't compare my taste to a database full of Oscar awards and actor nominations. It compared what I liked against what other people liked. I like science fiction. I like historical drama. I like action adventure. Firefly created a profile of me based on how I responded to specific movies. It then looked for comparable profiles. When it came across some that were the same, it looked for movies they liked that I hadn't rated yet. Simple. Brilliant.

May I See Your Passport, Please?

Moving this technology out of its own site and into others, Firefly created the Passport. Think of them as the Secretary of State. They know who's who and they keep all of the basic profile information in Firefly Central which they describe on their site as "a rapid cache of Firefly Passports which can be used by any site to recognize existing Passport holders and exchange Passport profiles with other sites." If somebody comes to a Starwave Web site and shows their Passport (logs in with their Firefly identification), then Starwave knows something about them right off the bat. Starwave can then start asking questions and build the profile over time.

Doug Weaver, Vice President of Advertising and Web Publishing for Firefly, explained during a hastily-grabbed lunch at Spring Internet World 1997 how this information could be shared. "Let's say I go to the Starwave site and it asks me some questions. Let's say it finds out that I like Willie Nelson. I'm cruising around the site and come across a banner for a Ford Explorer. I click. It takes me to a picture of the dashboard highlighting a killer sound system that has a streaming audio clip of a Willie song. If I agree to take a test drive, they'll give me a free Willie Nelson CD. Cooperative marketing at its best."

The drawback here is the need to log in, the need to be identified.

Proof Positive

The marketer in me says that what this world needs is a good five-cent ID number for every man, woman, and child. One number that identifies you, nails you beyond question. Assures us marketers that we know who you are. It borders on being something only the Borg from Star Trek could love. We know where you live. Resistance is futile, you will be assimilated.

Now I, of course, have nothing to hide. I'm as pure as the driven snow and have never looked for pornography on the Internet or parked in a red zone or driven over the speed limit—so such an identity number would never bother me. And Scully and Mulder were born in the Cardassian Sector.

But we're not that far off from having a universal ID. It's just that we're going to end up having several. Barnes & Noble, Yahoo!, AOL's Greenhouse Networks, Ziff Davis, and Reuters New Media are all using Firefly's Passport.

Netscape, Internet Shopping Network, Motley Fool, Switchboard, and Virtual Vineyards are all signed up to use VeriSign's Digital ID, which guarantees the identity of the visitor. Web traffic trackers and profilers like Affinicast, Broadvision, ClickOver, I/Pro, Netcount, and net.Genesis are in the process of altering their code to accommodate the Digital ID.

Microsoft has been pushing the idea of a Global User ID (guid) and Versit, made up of companies like IBM, Apple, AT&T, and Siemens are touting a virtual business card called a vCard. At **www.versit.com**, Versit suggests the vCard can be "used in applications such as Internet mail, voice mail, Web browsers, telephony applications, call centers, video conferencing, PIMs (Personal Information Managers), PDAs (Personal Data Assistants), pagers, fax, office equipment, and smart cards."

If you think about it, we really will need some sort of verified digital identification soon. Online buying and selling is going to move from being a child to an adult and we're going to have to be certain we know with whom we're dealing. These are the tempestuous teen years for secured communication. It will have to settle down and start making its own car payments any day now.

Behave Yourself

From the July, 1997, issue of *Webmaster* magazine (**www.web-master.com**) by Jim Sterne:

It's been a while since I felt my hair (what's left of it) stand on end. No, I didn't have my hands on a Tesla-coil. I was sitting in a micro-office in the middle of the Infoseek booth at Internet World, listening with rapt attention under non-disclosure to Peter Rip, vice president and general manager of Infoseek Network. He was talking about the very near future of advertising on the Internet.

Advertising has come of age on the World Wide Web. We've progressed from getting flamed for launching commercial Web sites to getting bombarded with offers to buy banner space. And while there are many effective ways to get your message out besides banners, banners are starting to get smart.

Yes, you can go to DoubleClick and buy space across a whole network of Web sites, targeting men in the 18-to-24 age range by zip code who are surfing in from .edu's and sell them condoms. You can also buy a banner on Women's Wire (www.women.com) promoting home pregnancy kits. If you do, your clickthrough response will go from the usual 1.5 percent up to 3 or even 5 percent.

You can also buy keywords on search engines. You want to advertise your marathon run on Maui? Buy the words 'marathon,' 'Hawaii,' 'Maui,' and so on. Doing so will increase clickthroughs significantly.

But what if the ads themselves were smart? What if a banner ad knew who might want to see it? In that case, you'd have a bit of a content/context revolution.

Infoseek Gets Ultra Smart

Rip talks with the urgency associated with a major discovery, tempered with the strain of having to explain it again before it's even announced. In a nutshell, Infoseek now knows what users like and what kinds of ads they are most likely to click without violating their privacy. That raises the same question asked of Napoleon when he described the thermos that could keep hot things hot and cold things cold: How does it know?

Infoseek's new feature—called Ultramatch—starts off with 300 Micro-Interests spread across 22 Behavior Segments. A Behavior Segment is a broad area of interest such as computers, entertainment, health, the outdoors, or real estate. Users are categorized according to which subjects they seek on the Web. Their interests are identified by actions, rather than by declaration. Infoseek watches while they surf.

Say a user goes to Infoseek and searches on 'airfare.' The engine then gives him or her a cookie that identifies that person as somebody interested in travel. He or she proceeds to one of Infoseek's partner sites—to which the company is delivering ad banners, and clicks an ad for a Hawaiian vacation. Sometime later, the user does a search on sporting events. At each step, his or her behavior pattern is crunched into a digital profile that Infoseek slips back into the user's cookie. The next time he or she goes to an Infoseek partner page, Infoseek reads the profile and selects a banner to show—on a marathon on Maui. In real time.

Before privacy hormones start coursing through your veins, rest assured that Infoseek is tracking the user's profile, not the user. The company knows what she is interested in, but not who she is. It doesn't know her name or e-mail address. It knows what sites she visited, but that information is recalculated into her profile and then discarded. Yet because it knows what she likes, it can give her a banner that she is more likely to click.

As a result, the user sees more ads that speak to her interests. Users will like going to the Infoseek site because it's sponsored by companies offering stuff that is right up their alleys. The other search tools just have regular, run-of-the-mill ads.

The result for the advertiser is less waste. You buy one million impressions and you get one million people who are likely to be interested in your products and services. The eight-year-old doing her homework on the Hawaiian Islands won't be one of the impressions you paid for.

Really Smart Ads

Now let's go one step further. Using collaborative filtering, the technique pioneered by Firefly, Infoseek can actually imbue an ad with intelligence.

Firefly recommends things like movies by comparing a user's stated likes and dislikes with the stated likes and dislikes of a database of others. Infoseek's innovation was to think: Why not do the same with the unstated but exhibited behavior of others? Lots of others?

A banner ad is thrown into the profiling machine. Based on the ad's content, Ultramatch makes some educated guesses about who might want to view it. The software then starts showing the ad around. Over a surprisingly short period of time, it builds a database of the profiles of people who have clicked that banner. The result? Ultramatch knows what types of behavioral profiles are most likely to click that ad. Not just that type of ad, or ads about that subject, or ads with that type of offer—that specific ad.

And once it knows, it takes action. When the next person with that profile calls up a page on the Infoseek network of sites, Ultramatch reads the cookie, matches the profile to the ad, and ships it off. In milliseconds.

The software that runs Ultramatch was adapted from the code that checks someone's credit card history when he makes an unusual purchase.

'Mr. Sterne? You don't usually spend $10,000 in a single month on air travel. Has your card been compromised?'

'No, I just have a lot of flight time ahead of me, and bought a bunch of tickets. But thanks for checking.'

This technology has been in place and working for years. It scales.

Value Ads

The bottom line is that exhibited behavior is a far more reliable gauge of future behavior than anything an individual might say on a profile form. Giving users an ad that people similar to them have clicked dramatically improves the chance that they will click it, too.

How dramatically? In a six-month trial on its site, Infoseek measured a split run. Users exposed to the usual rotation of banners clicked the usual number of times (1.5 percent for random ads and 3 percent for keyword-selected ads).

Those targeted by Ultramatch had a 25 percent higher clickthrough rate. When Ultramatch was coupled with the use of keywords, the results were even more impressive. In some campaigns, Infoseek experienced a 9 percent clickthrough rate—better than anything on the Web this side of 'Download naked pictures here!'

For example, those seeking information about teens, kids, college, and shopping enthusiastically clicked the Columbia House Records banner reading '7,000 Reasons To Stay Home Tonight.' People seeking information about entertainment, travel, science, and computers—presumably upscale types—were successfully tempted to 'Click here to check out over 100 beef recipes.'

This sort of tool points you toward people who have a demonstrated proclivity for clicking your offer but who don't hang out in the obvious places. With it, you can seriously test which banners work and which don't.

There are two problems with the Ultramatch approach. First, people who don't like cookies can blow them away. But this is a small threat to marketers: recent studies show that only 25% of the browsing public has ever even heard of cookies. (And once enough people do know about them, it won't take Madison Avenue long to kick off a 'Got Cookies?' campaign.)

The other concern is legislative. Some people worry that aggregated behavioral information could potentially invade the privacy of registered voters. Heaven help us as the government embarks on the long process of legislating technology that changes on a weekly basis. That cat, however, has already escaped its bag. Databases have been used by marketers for decades, and now they'll be able to talk to each other.

There is every expectation that Ultramatch technology will be applied to content as well as to ads. The ability of a search engine to learn about users' tastes and interests has interesting implications for finding things on the Net. In the hands of marketers, 'Where do you want to go today?' becomes 'Where you want to go today.'

The Future of Advertising

The time will come when we are well known for our inclinations, our predilections, our proclivities, and our wants. We will be classified, profiled, categorized, and our every click will be watched.

Eventually we will stop wondering "How did they know I'd need a new vacuum cleaner?" and start wondering, "Why didn't I get an ad reminding me it was time to change the oil in my car?" It'll be the next great excuse of the next decade. "I'm so sorry, but my mail server was down and your Hallmark birthday reminder bounced."

Now that You Know Where to Find Them. . .

You've set your budget for banners. You determined the goals of your campaign and you settled on which metrics will establish just how brilliant you are. You figured out where your potential customers hang out. You tracked them to their favorite places. You set up caller ID and profiling and voice-prints and DNA testing to know exactly who you wanted to advertise to and where they would be at any given moment.

Now that you know just where to find them, all you have to do is figure out what you're going to say. ●

CHAPTER 7

What Makes People Click?

The problem is the current marketing Web site model uses a banner-to-site device for attracting consumers. This approach will not work for all companies. What kind of banner could encourage any consumer to visit dentalfloss.com?

Martin Levin, Director of Sponsored Programming, Microsoft Network

Why did you click that banner? No, really. Think back to the last banner you clicked. Why did you do it? What was it that derailed you from your train of thought?

Was it the offer? You just couldn't pass up a great discount? Was it a joke to which you had to have the punch line? Was it some weird, cryptic image that piqued your curiosity? Or, like me, do you click ads in order to see what some other ad person put on the other end? If that's the case, count yourself out. The world is not like you and I. My wife cannot fathom why I want her to keep all the junk mail while I'm out of town or why I refuse to mute the TV during the commercials.

So what is it that gets the great, unwashed masses to click a banner? ■

Limitless Limitations

When Madison Avenue got its first glimpse of the Web they became giddy with their newfound freedom. Suddenly there were zero restrictions. No limits on the number of pages—the "paper" was free. No limit to the number of colors—the "ink" was free. No limit to the type of media—audio, video, text, you-name-it were all possible. Life was an open book again, filled with promises, hope, and unrestricted horizons.

Wrong.

Wrong, wrong, wrong.

At the International Design Festival 1996 in Glasgow, Peter Gillespie from VOICE Creative Engineering got up and told the highbrow audience of artists and engineers that he felt certain the World Wide Web would be the engine of the return of style. Pure style.

I had seen enough of the Web to wonder what on earth he'd been drinking so early in the morning. Most Web sites circa 1996 were dreadful affairs created by members of the MIS department in their spare time. Only a handful of marketing people were on the ball and creating anything that could even remotely be thought of as stylish.

"I rest my hopes on the fact that the Web is one of the most restrictive canvases ever offered to an artist," said Gillespie.

I cocked my head in attention.

"The Web's useable area for presentation is not much bigger than the span of your hand."

I sat up in my chair.

"The color palette is actually less than 256 colors if you want your work to be the same on all monitors."

He was speaking from experience.

"There are limitations to the nifty computer images you can create due to the need for the smallest file size you can manage."

He got it! He understood what Madison Avenue had missed by a mile.

"When you only have black ink and a twig to draw with, you tend to sharpen your sense of style. So it is my hope, that as this medium grows in popularity and attracts more and better designers, that they will recognize these limitations and work within them. Doing so can only result in a return to pure style."

He had convinced me. I'm now hopeful, too.

The restrictions Peter outlined are even more restrictive when applied to a banner. They're visually smaller, download time is more critical, and they serve a special and specific purpose.

Isolating the Issues

Getting people to buy is a question that gets answered after the fact. First, you've got to get their attention. You've got to generate interest. You've got to elicit a reaction. *You've got to get them to click.*

If your sole goal is brand and image awareness, you could follow the lead of Kodak's Digital Science unit. They put up an interstitial ad on Microsoft's MNS network in the Life section to draw attention to their c@pture digital camera.

Microsoft wasn't ready to push these ads at all of their customers at once. "It's not the most highly trafficked area on our site. We felt we should start out cautiously," said MSNBC general manager Jim Kinsella. The Kodak interstitials pop up and then go away of their own accord. And, most interesting, they don't click through to anything. They're there to let you know about the new camera. You can't learn more. You can't click through. You can't buy now. You can only become aware or become more aware.

So we'll leave the brand building to Kodak, Disney, Nike, and the like and take a long, hard look at what it takes to get people to actually click. What it takes to get them to take action.

When creating an ad for print publications, there are numerous topics to be discussed around the creative table. What format can we afford? Should it be a full page? A double-page spread? A quarter-page announcement? How about black and white? Color? How often do we run it? Will it go on the top of the page or at the bottom? What's the theme? What's the best way to express it? Should we use that word there? Doesn't that sound just like our competitor's ad from last year? Will that be misinterpreted in Canada? Do we want to include a coupon?

When it comes to creating Web banners, the choices are no easier. Some of them are obvious and some are not. We'll attack them in the following order:

> Where on the page should it reside?
>
> How long should it stay there?
>
> How often should it be seen?
>
> What verbiage is most effective?
>
> If it's not a standard size, then how big?
>
> Does animation help or hinder?

Obviously, your process of banner creation is not going to be as orderly as all of that. You may be handed predetermined decisions from the get-go. But whether you approach it from front to back or from the middle out, here are some guidelines to help along the way.

There are four ways to determine strategies for your banner ads:

> Use your common sense.
>
> Do what everybody else is doing.
>
> Try everything and measure your results.
>
> Look for those who have measured their own results.

The Adventurer

Common sense is often spoken of as not being common at all and is hard to come by in the best of times. It is spawned from the wisdom of time and experience. At this juncture, in this medium, we are lamentably in short supply of experience. The oldest and wisest among us go back less than a handful of years.

Common sense says to make your banners as big and bright and loud and animated as possible. Put it at the top where people can see it and show it to them so often that it becomes part of the landscape, engraved in their brains like the tune to "Happy Birthday." But these are assumptions based on your experiences with other media. They are valid—to a point.

Let's say you arrive in a new city for a weekend vacation. You know that generally the southeast side of most cities is not the best neighborhood so you avoid going there. You know that well-lighted, busy streets are usually the safest to walk at night. You know that if you get lost you can always ask somebody for directions. You decide that's all you need to know and you head out into the day. You obviously don't mind getting lost, wasting your time, and putting yourself at risk. Everything will be all right—after all, you have common sense.

Making those kinds of decisions with your advertising budget is a bit like blundering into a new city without so much as a compass to guide you. Making those kinds of decisions without seeing what the rest of the world is doing exhibits a certain lack of common sense.

The Guided Tour

Doing what everybody else is doing is the easiest. Just watch and imitate. No need to convince the boss it's the right thing to do. It's the norm. No need to investigate, calibrate, or calculate. You just do things the way they've been done by everybody else. Simple. Call it "best practices" and you won't get into trouble, as in, "It's not my fault," and, "Nobody ever got fired for buying IBM."

Imitating what everybody else is doing with their banners is akin to jumping on the tour bus and seeing the typical tourist attractions. Yes, you'll see all the things you are supposed to see. Yes, you'll learn a few facts. Yes, you'll get to stop and take pictures and buy postcards to prove that you were there. But you won't get to know this new city on personal terms. You won't get the chance to talk to the cab drivers and the shopkeepers and watch the people on the busses and subways. You might as well have stayed home and rented the video.

If we've learned anything on the Net, we've learned that it's the unusual that gets the attention. It's the abnormal that catches the imagination. It's that which falls outside the norm that gets the response. As Mark Grimes from Eyescream puts it, "I've found what's different gets noticed, what gets noticed gets clicked. When it's radically different (and relevant) zounds…step back, get a T3, it's a 'flash crowd.'"

People have an enormous capacity for curiosity when they're online that seems to stem from the fact that surfing is a personal activity. In a crowd, people tend to go with the flow. In small clusters, they yield their desires to the group. By themselves, they are free to go where they will and click whatever appeals to them at the moment.

Taking the tour bus in the city of Internet advertising is doubly risky because none of the tour leaders know much about the city themselves.

The Self-Guided Tour

Taking a map in hand and striking out toward the other side of town will certainly gain you the most exposure and help you create a very vivid impression of the new city you're exploring. It's the only way to get to know the territory up front and personally. With a map and a compass and a big breakfast, you're ready to take on the day. You will learn by doing. By the time your feet wear out you will know the quintessential qualities of the city, you will know where you have been, and you will be at home next time you come back.

Trying everything with your banner ads and measuring every response is the correct thing to do. It's the only way you'll know exactly what all of the variables are, up close and personally. It's the only way you'll be in control of enough of the elements, all at the same time, to make the measurements meaningful and the successes repeatable. It's also the only way you'll learn how the different factors effect your ads in your marketplace.

The only drawbacks are that it takes time and it takes money.

The Tour Book

But most of us who travel and enjoy seeing the sights stop off at the bookstore and pick up a book or two. And a map. And talk to some friends who have been there. We want to be armed with the knowledge that we can take the bus from the airport for two dollars instead of a taxi for forty. We want to know for sure where the seedier side of town is ahead of time. We want to know where the antique stores are in advance. We want to be prepared.

So, in an effort to give you a head start, here are some of the findings from those who have watched, counted, and reported back to the rest of us. There are not a lot of studies and evidence and proof out there yet, but at least we have some accounts of success and failure to help us on our way.

Location

You can work out any sort of deal imaginable for the type of ad you run with the content sites you sponsor. Your ad can be part of the story line, part of the background coloring, part of the border around the page, or even a whole page between content pages (interstitial). But banners, as such, have to live somewhere on the page and, for the sake of brevity, I'll stick to banners.

If you run your banner at the top of a Web page people see it first, right? Not always. If you put your banner at the bottom nobody will never see it, right? Not always. If you put your banner in the middle it will annoy people and they'll scroll right past it, right? Not always. In a nutshell, however, most people will tell you that it's always best to start at the top.

Top Dog

It's very easy to find a lot of advice on the Web about building Web sites. Dig just a little deeper and you'll find advice about banners, including where to put them. But it doesn't take too much digging to realize the advice is mostly the same and the research is fairly shallow. Until serious usability studies tell us otherwise, the following advice is the best there is.

Whit Andrews, Associate Editor of *Web Week* magazine, gave the following advice in an article on Meckler's Internet World site:

Put it at the top. If you are placing just one banner, put it at the top of the page. Banners down the sides are less successful. Discreet banners or banners squeezed across the page—while appealing to sites for aesthetic reasons or multiple-impression volume—are clickthrough losers.

"You want to be on top," says Bob Ivans, Vice President of market research at San Francisco-based I/Pro. "I think it has to do with screen size. I don't scroll sideways to see an ad."

"Banners squeezed across the page" and "scrolling sideways" refer to a serious design flaw perpetrated by Web site layout personnel who only think in terms of what the site looks like on his or her screen; that high-density, UNIX workstation screen that stretches from here to the next cubical in perfect clarity. He or she never considers that the majority of us are using a standard 14" monitor or laptops.

Real Media, the people who pioneered streaming audio (RealAudio) and are now into streaming anything and everything, say they always get a better response when their ads are placed at the top of the screen as opposed to down the side. They say the difference is three and a half or four percent higher clickthrough. Out of every 100 impressions, three and a half or four more people click it when it's at the top.

Because DoubleClick is the preeminent network on the Net, they have an unmatched view of the heart of the hurricane. Of their ten top tips (**http://www.doubleclick.net/frames/general/10tip.htm**), number five is location, location, location:

According to research, banners that appear when the page first loads are more likely to be clicked on. Negotiate ad placement at the top of the page when buying space. The best possible scenario is having banners placed both on the top and on the bottom of the page.

Other tales seem equally convincing. Leonid Deskin at the Sputnik Advertising Network (**www.kulichki.com/sputnik**) says that, depending on the banner, "the 'ad hoc' values for Russian sites are 3 to 10% for the top of the page and 1–1.5% for the bottom of the page." Deskin adds, "If a banner is placed at the top and also at the bottom, the top banner gets 80% of the clicks to the bottom banner's 20%."

Then we saw a formal, academic attempt to figure out what was going on.

Created in April, 1997, and updated in May, the "Banner Ad Placement Study" (**http://www-personal.umich.edu/~agrobbel/index.html** and **www.webreference.com/dev/banners**) was conducted by graduate students at the University of Michigan for Professor Sunil Gupta's "Marketing in Online Environments" class, in the winter of 1997.

Of the study, Professor Gupta says, "it is a student project, done by a group of MBA students (rather bright ones, I might add), as one part of the final grade, for one of the courses they took during the past semester. So, if it does not resolve all of the many uncertainties and unknowns about banner advertising, the reader ought not to be surprised."

While the good professor does not consider the study good enough to be published in an academic journal, he's pleased it showed that changes in placement on the page do, indeed, cause measurable differences in clickthroughs.

The students did three comparisons: the top versus the side, the top versus one-third of the way down the page, and the top alone versus the top and the bottom. In a nutshell, they concluded:

1. Ads next to the right scroll bar (in the lower-right corner of the first screen) generated a 228% higher clickthrough rate than ads at the top of the page.

2. Ads placed one-third of the way down a page, as opposed to the top, generated 77% higher clickthrough rates.

3. Results from placing two ads on a page (at top and bottom) were inconclusive.

The first test they ran compared a banner across the top of the page to an ad box at the lower-right corner next to the scroll bar (see Figure 7.1). While the top one was a typical enough banner at 468×60, the box at the lower right was 125×125. The content of the ads was kept as similar as possible and several different ads were used so that the measurements could be averaged.

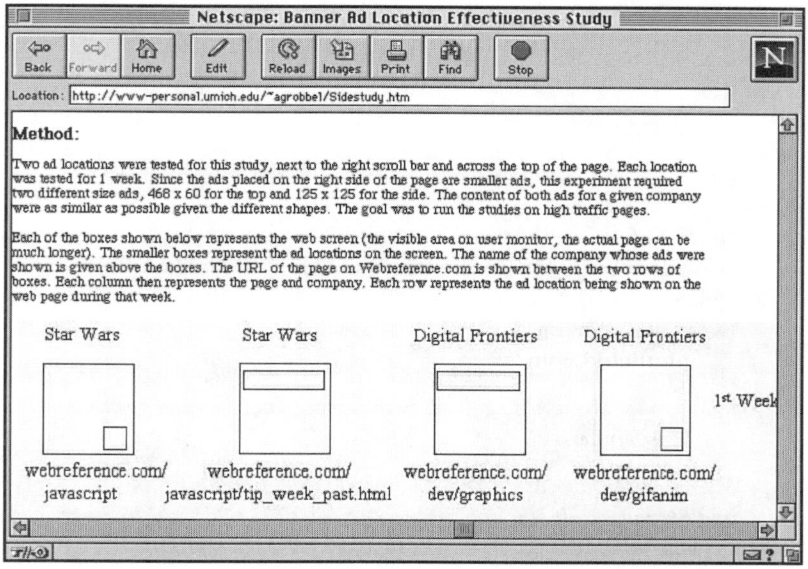

FIG. 7.1

The Webreference study found the lower-right corner to be the most effective place for an ad.

The bottom-right boxes got more clicks. In two cases, there were differences in click rates of 1.1% and 2%, and in the case of the Digital Frontiers ads, a difference in rate of 10.6%, and even 12.1%. (The banner on top got a clickthrough of 5.2%, while the one on the side got a clickthrough rate of 17.3%—a difference of 12.1%.)

In other words, putting it down and to the right got 228% *more* clicks than the straight banner at the top.

For the next test, they placed standard banners halfway down the page and compared those to the ones at the top (see Figure 7.2).

FIG. 7.2
Banners one-third of the way down the page increased clickthrough by 77%.

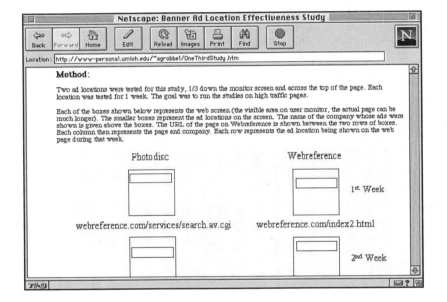

Never having been accused of keeping his opinion to himself (one of the reasons he's so valuable a member of the lists he frequents), the prolific Mark Welch (**www.ca-probate.com**) took a look and expressed his doubts. In part, Mark wrote to the Online Advertising list (**www.o-a.com**) on April 26:

Okay, I have been reading about the "Banner Ad Placement Study" for a week now, and I have finally taken the time to go look at the (scant) information posted at http://www.webreference. com/dev/banners/

My response: 'hogwash.' While the information from this study raises some important questions and the raw result (an improvement of 200%) should spark more serious study, this is NOT a scientific analysis and the results should NOT be accepted at face value.

The study is fundamentally flawed for several reasons. First, the 'experiment' was done on sites that have traditionally carried a 468×60 banner ad at the top of the page. Second, two major changes were combined: a change in ad size (from 468×60 to 125×125) and a change in placement (from top of the page to lower right corner of the first screen). Third, the study only measured a single out-come (clickthroughs), ignoring the single most likely reason for variation (user error) (see below).

1. *Any change is likely to result in increased user response. Measuring the effect of only ONE of many possible changes, and measuring for only one week or two, is unlikely to help establish whether the effect is due to the specific change, or only to "change in general."*

2. *Changing the banner size dramatically—in this case, reducing it from 468×60 (28,080 pixels) to 125×125 (15,625) is likely to have a significant effect because of the faster loading time for a smaller banner: it is more likely to be seen, period. Apparently, no effort was made to measure the change in click-through if a smaller ad (such as 400×40 or 16,000 pixels) were displayed at the top of the page (e.g. measuring ONLY a change in size), nor was any effort made to measure the effect of ONLY moving the ad (e.g. displaying the same 468×60 ad in the lower right corner of the screen).*

   Also, given the likely propensity of users to scroll down before a top-of-screen ad is fully loaded, it is obviously important to measure the effect of simply moving the ad down; indeed, the study's authors did examine this effect by measuring the effect of moving the ad from the top of the page to a position one-third of the way down the monitor screen (so that the ad appears below some "content" information on the page).

3. *Moving an ad to the lower right corner of the screen—as the study's author's note, "next to the right scroll bar"—is highly likely to result in unintended clickthroughs, as users who intended to scroll down accidentally click on the ad a few pixels to the left. These spurious and unintended clickthroughs COULD easily be measured in two ways: first, by using an "image map" in the ad and examining whether an unusual ratio of clicks occur in the right edge of the image; and second (and more important) by measuring something other than clickthroughs—specifically, the PERSISTENCE and DEPTH of the visit to the site being advertised.*

I am NOT suggesting that this study is useless or meaningless, nor am I suggesting that the authors did not provide a very useful service. Clearly, a lot of work was done and a very significant (even dramatic) change was discovered. However, the meaning of that change is open to substantial doubt, and therefore this study is best viewed as a reason to examine more thoroughly the effect of these changes.

I also note that the results of the study are based on a very small pool of advertising impressions, well under 10,000 impressions in each test and under 500 adviews in some tests. A handful of clicks, or a minor distraction (or hiccup in the Internet) could cause dramatic changes when the sample is so small. At the Web Advertising '97 conference, several speakers suggested that at least 100,000 and perhaps as many as 250,000 adviews are required before the results of a test cam-paign can be viewed as reliable. (Of course, one cannot fault the study's authors if they simply did not have access to larger sites to experiment with advertising—few publishers or advertisers will be willing to let students meddle with their primary source of operating revenue.)

Remember that Mark Welch is an attorney and the fine quillets of the law are his prime do-main. Of course he's picky! But he makes some good points. This study is more anecdotal than scientific. There were a lot of changing factors going on at the same time and that made it a bit difficult to determine what, exactly, caused the changes in clickthroughs.

But overall, Welch is right—these people gave us some insight into something we'd never seen before and that always deserves credit.

Professor Gupta harbors no illusions about the work his students have done:

The study DOES NOT provide any reasons for why this happened. Several people have suggested such possibilities as mistaken clicks, laziness, attention grabbing, change in size, downloading speed, etc., to explain the effect. Some, at least, of these are reasonable possibilities. My own takeaway (when looked at in conjunction with other ad banner studies that have been reported by others online) is that doing something different gets people's notice, and then a measurable impact on clickthroughs. But, this is mere conjecture. Systematic exploration of the many possibilities that have been mentioned, guided by a theoretically defensible framework is clearly needed.

About sample sizes. At least a few people have commented on the "small cell sizes" (the number of impressions measured for each experimental condition). Some have suggested a cell size of 200,000 as the minimum needed. I think this issue is misunderstood. 200,000 impressions measured on a very high traffic site might happen in a few hours. If the hours are not chosen carefully, the results could be seriously biased. The mere largeness of cell sizes does not alleviate this problem. On the other hand, well designed experiments, guided by appropriate theory, where the expected effect size is sufficiently large can be done with much smaller cell sizes (see medical journals). In general, the power of an experiment (the probability of getting a significant result), is a function of the sample size, the effect size, the standard deviation of the error, and the desired significance level.

My "takeaway" is that people who are interested in a subject enough to get down to the bottom of the page are more interested in the subject and more likely to be interested in a banner that advertises something that is related to that subject.

Maybe the lower-right corner discovery made by these students is indicative of a phenomenon happened upon by a couple of very different marketing professionals. Think of it as the click at the end of the rainbow.

He Who Is Last Shall Be First

It's tempting to agree with Mark Welch that the clicks on the banner at the lower-right corner of the screen may, indeed, be due to people missing the scroll bar. None of us is getting younger and hand-eye coordination isn't what it used to be. Yes, another round of research would clear this up once and for all. Somewhere out there, there are graduate students who want to be the first with a thesis, or there are banner ad sales organizations that want to prove a point and will do formal, controlled studies.

In the meantime, there are two compelling, illustrative incidents that would suggest it has nothing to do with mouse manipulation. One goes back to 1995 and the other is based on a Web site that's up and running now, and will remain so until the year 2,000, when all of the software in the world comes crashing down around our ears.

ResultsLab's Surprise   Ron Richards of ResultsLab has been tweaking advertising since Hector was a pup. He's a curious mix of creativity and scientific analysis. Imagine a genetic lab mixture that produced a clone from the DNA from David Ogilvy and Thomas Edison.

Richards is warm and charming. He's gregarious. He eschews pocket protectors, but he is absolutely meticulous when it comes to the selection of every word and the precise layout of every graphic element in a printed promotion. He has spent years working on ads, brochures, and direct mail promotions. He is creative, inventive, and prone to flights of imagination.

But you don't have to scratch Richards very deep to find an experimenter and statistician underneath. He loves tabulation, calculation and computation. He's been studying what makes people click for years. In the middle of 1994, he started focusing his intellectual microscope on the Web.

One of his first efforts, years ago, was a study with important implications for all Web advertisers. It was a study of classified ad titles on CompuServe. Not the ads themselves, just the titles. The titles are critical because, like e-mail or newsgroup posts, that's all you see as you try to decide which one to read next. As an advertiser, you get a set number of characters to speak your peace and that's it. You have to be evocative, informative and captivating because your ad can appear in a list that has dozens, and in some cases, hundreds of entries. Richards did his testing where there were 15 screens and some 300 little ads!

The CompuServe experiment turned up a startling result. It seemed best to be last.

When you place a classified ad on CompuServe, you submit it and wait. Within hours it shows up on the list. It seems to show up at random. The list is not alphabetic; it is not first-come-first-served, either. Richards would submit an ad, see where it ended up, and start tabulating the number of people who responded to the ad.

The first time one of the ads Richards placed showed up on the very bottom of the list, Richards was despondent at his random bad luck. This ad would never be seen. It would never be selected. It would be a waste of time and energy. But Richards had a surprise in store. The ad CompuServe placed at the bottom of the list got more responses than any other position—four times more.

In another e-mail to me, Richards speculated, "Being in last position resulted in white space being below the ad, giving it visual prominence. This advantage was further amplified by the fact that when people scrolled down and 'hit bottom' the eye had nowhere to rest but on the last item. It's really more a point about the power of visual prominence than about position on a screen. Anything that causes eye-grabbing can produce extraordinary multiples in response, so long as it doesn't trigger 'hype' defenses in the reader."

Since then, Richards says he's proven this principle several times. For example, he's made the "Subject" line in e-mail distributions to magazine subscribers so long it sticks out on the right, surrounded by white space.

www.Year2000.Com   Cliff Kurtzman is another one of those people who believes in and lives the Internet Gift Culture. He was quick to take over the task when Glenn Fleischman retired from the limelight of Internet Marketing List moderator. The Online Ads List (**www.o-a.com**) is hosted by Kurtzman's company, the Tenagra Corporation.

Besides creating and maintaining Web sites for others, Tenagra hosts a couple of content sites with considerable enthusiasm. The Tennis Server (**www.tennisserver.com**) has been going great guns and caused Kurtzman to excuse himself from a dinner he was hosting at Web Advertising 97 in Monterey, California. He had to phone in to report that Brooke Shields and Andre Agassi had just tied the knot not too far from where he was dining.

Another site he runs covers the issues involved with the pending software disaster known as the Year 2000 problem (**www.year2000.com**). The first time you see the sponsors for this site, they are listed down the left side of the home page (see Figure 2.11). If an effort to be fair to the sponsors and not list them according to amount paid or first-come-first-served, and in a tip of the hat to his site visitor who would be lost otherwise, Kurtzman lists these sponsors alphabetically.

Week after week, Kurtzman finds that no matter which new advertiser has the last slot due to its name, that's the one that gets the highest number of clicks. What's going on here?

It seems that when faced with indecision, people will settle for the last one. They know they want to click something. They know they want to know more. It's just that they can't make up their minds. They have a tough time choosing between the myriad of options and, when they reach the end of the line, they click.

In an e-mail to me, Kurtzman was quick to point out that it's not as easy as it looks:

There are a lot of factors that influence how many clicks a vendor gets, only one of which is placement. Certain company names seem to have quite a pull regardless of placement, either because of words in the name or because of the brand value in the names.

When the entry that used to be last on the list became second to last because a new vendor was added beneath it, it's monthly page accesses dropped from around 1200 a month to about 800 a month, which is purely a placement effect. Even at second to last, it still received more hits than any other vendor with a mini-homepage (a demi-site, located on the Year 2000 site), except for the one we recently added to the top of the list. The placement effect seems to work most on the few at the very top and at the very bottom. Obviously this is because it is where people look first and last as they scan the list. They are less likely to stop and click in the middle.

What it does tell us that is very important, is that a fair percentage of people are indeed looking through the list, rather than just looking at what they can see in the opening screen.

I went through last month's log file and pulled out the access data on the vendors that have mini-homepages on our site (about 50% of them do). I then filtered out all mini-homepage hits which did not have referral data, as well as those hits that appeared to come from links on pages other than our vendor listing. This gave me a clearer picture of clicks that come from our listing.

The entries near the beginning and end of the list seem to have the greatest click rate.

If your banner is going to be set among many others, Richards and Kurtzman would tell you to put it in last place. If your banner will be the only one on the page, even though the "Banner Ad Placement Study" found the difference "insignificant," others have suggested you get a better response when your ad appears at the top and the bottom. Most sites offer to place your ad at the top only. It's one of those issues that may be out of your hands, but shouldn't be off your mind. Remember, everything is negotiable.

Page Design Dilemma

If I had bought a banner slot on the results page of the Alta Vista search engine before the design change, I would not be a happy camper after the change. The difference between the old version (see Figure 7.3) and the new (see Figure 7.4) are not readily apparent.

FIG. 7.3
AltaVista before.

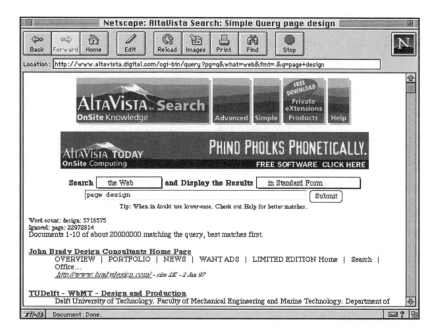

FIG. 7.4
AltaVista after.

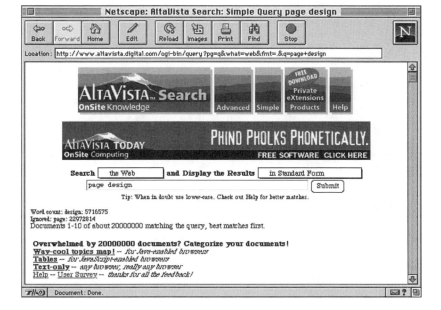

The difference is not in how they look. The difference is in how they act. I am a frequent Alta Vista user and I can tell you that I don't see the banners there anymore. Here's why:

When the old results page showed me what it had found, I saw the first couple of Web site choices and the banner. I would then scroll down the list looking for that all-elusive needle in a haystack.

With the new version, I do not see any of the search results. Instead, I wait until the text of the page is loaded and hit the scroll bar on the right side of the screen to jump down. Turns out, on my monitor, that one click at the bottom of the scroll bar jumps the page down to where the first foundling is listed. The kicker is that all of this happens before the banner loads.

The page loads, the text loads, the Alta Vista graphics are pulled up out of my local cache file and the banner is taking its sweet time, winding its way from DoubleClick, through the backbone to my ISP, and up the hill on a twisted copper wire to reach my desk. I hit the scroll bar and I'm off and surfing. I never saw the banner.

Oh yeah, AltaVista puts the banner at the bottom as well as the top. Does that solve the problem? Not quite. You see, the "Pages 1 2 3 4 5 6 7 8..." are above the banner. I scroll down to that page list and I'm off to the next page. Ad dollars wasted.

Length of Time

Web advertising is sold based on space. A full page interstitial ad is going to cost more than a simple banner. Then you calculate the number of impressions. If you want it shown to a lot of people, it'll cost you more.

Television commercials are sold based on time. Thirty seconds costs more than ten seconds and less than a full minute. Then you calculate the number of impressions. If you want it shown to a lot of people, it'll cost you more.

On the Web, you choose exactly how large an audience you want your ad to reach. On television, that is a function of how many people watch the show you are sponsoring.

TV doesn't give you a choice of size and the Web didn't give you a choice of time. Now it does. It makes a big difference. The longer an ad is in front of somebody, the more likely they are to click. Period. The trouble is, controlling how long the ad is in front of people is a tough nut to crack.

Pages show up and allow the surfer to move on at the click of a mouse. The only way you can make an ad stick is to put it in a frame.

Framing Your Ad

A page comes up on your screen with a banner at the top. The split second you scroll, the banner disappears off the top and is never seen again.

A page comes up on your screen with a banner at the top (or bottom, as shown in Figure 7.5) inside a frame. The split second you scroll, the banner stays right where it was, on your screen and in your face.

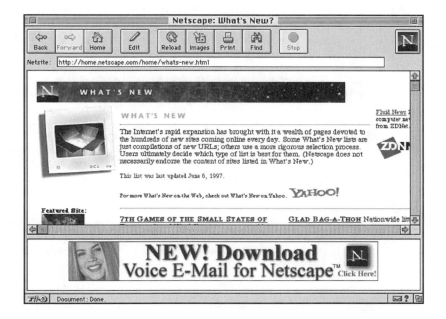

Even better, if you click an *interior link* (a link that takes you from one page on the site to another page on the same site), the ad still stays put, while the rest of the page changes. Imagine a billboard that followed you down the street or a radio commercial that was on all the channels you switched to.

Brian Cowley is vice president of sales at LookSmart, an Internet search tool and directory. He was at Netscape when the Netscape site decided to try frames for the first time. He says the response rate to the advertising ran up from a low of 1% clickthrough to a low of 7%. Instead of one person out of a hundred clicking, they were seeing seven people out of 100 clicking. The difference was even more prominent on the high side.

The best banners placed on the Netscape site were getting 4% clickthroughs. When they switched to showing the same ads in frames, the clicks went up to 30%. Almost one-third of the people who saw the ad within a frame were compelled to click.

When Cowley moved to LookSmart, he was so excited about the difference in response that he performed a formal study over a three-month period to test it again.

He measured static and animated ads. He used various message strategies such as direct response, curiosity generators, and sweepstakes. On the high-end ads (the most popular), the difference in clickthrough was 50%. Half as many more people clicked that ad that was in a frame and in their face longer than when it was on the page and could be scrolled or clicked away.

Flipping Out

One of the tricks used by a Web content site to get more impressions in a limited number of pages is to "flip" ads. This is the art of showing an ad on a page for a certain period of time and then flipping another ad in its place. Ad *rotation* is running through a database of ads, one page at a time. *Flipping* is running through a rotation of ads on the same page—as long as the page is up, new ads get flipped. Think of James Bond's Austin Healy with its changeable license plate, and you have a good picture of how ads can flip.

This practice has been a boon to the content site and a bane to the advertiser. It's pretty easy to use the HTML Meta tag "refresh" command so it's not hard to implement. It also can double or triple the amount of inventory a content site has to sell. However, from the advertiser's perspective, it doesn't matter how long a person looks at a page, your ad will only be seen for a set period of time, usually about thirty seconds.

Craig Swerdloff, at ClickNow, complains about sites that flip through ads every five or ten seconds. He recently lamented to the Online Advertising list:

I cannot imagine this is fair to the advertiser.

It's also not fair to the viewer. If you chance upon a page and glance upon a banner that catches your fancy, what do you do if it flips before you click? It's gone. You have no control over it. The Back button won't help. The Reload button won't help. You're frustrated and the advertiser missed an opportunity.

I think the best way to go about deciding what time interval to set your Meta refresh commands at," continues Swerdloff, "is to find out how much time on average a user spends on a single page within your site. If the average is fifty seconds then maybe that is where the Meta refresh should be set.

Swerdloff seems to believe that the refresh command can be useful, but setting it to flip an ad at the same interval as the average user is on the page is tantamount to having a static banner field—no refresh at all.

The frames tests indicate the longer a person is exposed to your ad, the more likely they are to click it. If you're going to buy an ad from a site that uses the refresh command to flip ads, you may want to negotiate a bit harder.

While longer is better and stands to reason and logic, it more often does seem to be a waste of resources.

It's Still Reach versus Frequency

It's the same question you ask about branding versus direct marketing in the broadcast media: Do you want to reach more people or do you want to reach people more often? With unlimited resources you have some choices.

You could simply inundate everybody with the same message over and over again until everybody knows that Coke Refreshes You Best or even the original, "Drink Coca-Cola." That would combine reach and frequency to the point where the entire planet would recognize your tag line as well as their own phone number.

Familiarity Breeds Contempt

George Parker is a freelance creative consultant and a columnist for *Marketing Computers* magazine. Parker opened his March, 1997, "Creative Impulse" column with a great example of one of the problems with frequency:

So, I'm watching one of the NFL playoff games and up pops an IBM sub-title commercial, the after-Christmas version of the Santa Claus spot, in which Santa and all his pointy-eared helpers loll around in a steaming hot tub, somewhere in the tropics. During the course of the chit-chat, they realize they can put their Christmas catalogue on the web and keep their business in the Caribbean (or wherever), thanks to the wonders of Lotus Notes.

Now, it's not a bad spot, but by the end of the game I was really annoyed. Because I'm a 49er fan and a glutton for punishment, I sat through to the bitter end, waiting for a miracle. So not only was I mad at my team for throwing the game away, I was mad at IBM for bombarding me with the spot at least 20 times.

By now, of course, we all know that was a mistake; Ogilvy and Mather fumbled the media buy by mislabeling some cassettes and the spot was shown at about double the frequency the agency intended. Too bad: O&M managed to turn a lot of people off with what is quite a good spot.

While annoying the very people you are trying to sell to is a disaster that we should all hope to avoid, the real problem with showing an ad too many times to the same person is the waste of money it represents. Parker was mad at IBM, while the rest of us would just have hit the mute button.

As Seen on TV

In *Advertising Reach and Frequency* (Association of National Advertisers, 1995), Colin McDonald pointed out that clutter in the media stream is the advertiser's biggest enemy:

Originally, television had followed the radio convention of a 60-second commercial as the norm. By 1979, however, almost 90 percent of the commercials on television were 30-seconds rather than 60. During the 1980s, the 15-second commercial appeared, and by 1993 it accounted for a third of all commercials. In addition to shorter commercials, the networks have tended to increase the time they occupy. By 1979, more non-programming announcements were being added by the networks, along with an additional minute of commercial time to movies and specials, and 10 seconds to newsbreak formats. Similar trends continued through the 1980s. Overall network clutter (the total number of announcements) is estimated to have increased more than 50% in the past 10 years.

Increasing clutter inevitably has an important bearing on the effective frequency of television advertising since it becomes harder to make an impact through the medium. The Newspaper Advertising Bureau has reported that in the 1960s 34 percent of all viewers could name one or more products they had just seen advertised on TV, but by 1990 only 8 percent of viewers could do so."

Advertising Reach and Frequency includes the results of numerous studies. Among them was a laboratory experiment to determine the effectiveness of TV commercials reported by Robert Glass at an Advertising Research Foundation conference in 1968. The conclusion was "attention (interest) increases and maximizes at two exposures, while the amount of learned information increases and maximizes at two or three exposures."

In other words, after the third time an individual has seen a specific television commercial, it ceases to add anything in the way of furthering the viewer's interest. It's a waste.

All the Ads that Are Fit to Print

The same year, Robert Glass published a study in *American Psychologist* that investigated print advertising. This study used eye movement information and determined that the optimal number of exposures were between two and three. Pattern or coincidence?

In *Advertising Reach and Frequency*, Glass explains what happens to people during these different exposures.

Well, first we have exposure number one. It is by definition unique. Like the first exposure of anything, the reaction is dominated by a 'What is it?' response, i.e., the first response is to understand the nature of the stimulus. Anything new or novel, however uninteresting on second exposure, has to elicit some response the first time if only for the mental classification required to discard the object as of no further interest. Thus the new stimulus, good or bad, has an initial attention-getting requirement, even if it is quickly blocked thereafter.

The second exposure to a stimulus has several implicit qualities. One is that the cognitive 'What is it?' response can be replaced by a more evaluative and personal 'What of it?' response. That is, having now fully appreciated just what is the nature of the new information, the viewer can now shift to a question of whether or not it has personal relevance. Some of this might occur during the first exposure if the respondent is absorbing the commercial with great interest, but more likely, especially on television where you can't rewind or reverse the film, there's enough missed first time around so that elements of the cognate reaction are still present on the second exposure.

Another element of the second exposure, and unique to the second exposure, is the startled recognition response: 'Ah ha, I've seen this before!' The virtue of such recognition is that it permits the viewer to pick up where he left off—without the necessity of doing the cognate thing ("What is it") all over again. So the second exposure is the one where personal responses and evaluations—the 'sale' so to speak—occurs. This 'What of it?' response completes the basic reaction to the commercial.

By the third exposure, the viewer knows he's been through his 'What is its' and 'What of its,' and the third becomes, then, the true reminder, that is, if there is some true consequence of the earlier evaluations yet to be fulfilled. But it is also the beginning of disengagement, of the withdrawal of attention of a completed task.

McDonald points out that the vast majority of people tune out after the initial recognition phase during exposure one. "Oh," they say to themselves, "I'm not interested in a new mortgage on my home. I don't care." From that point on, each additional exposure has no effect. The 'What of it' has equaled zero. That viewer could see the ad a hundred times, there is no interest in what's being offered.

However, months later, when the viewer *is* thinking about refinancing, the 101st viewing has the same effect as the second. He is attentive and interested and reevaluating his 'What of it' response to realize the subject is something he's interested in. On the third exposure, he has learned enough to be able to take a pro-active step toward contacting the advertiser.

Frequency Principles by the Baker's Dozen

Having looked over the results of studies by others and correlating them with his own work, McDonald finished up *Advertising Reach and Frequency* with 12 conclusions:

Conclusion 1: There is convincing evidence that advertising, when it is good enough to work at all, may have short term effects, including effects of purchase probability.

This verdict was created primarily to contradict the first conclusion of the first edition of Advertising *Reach and Frequency* in 1979, which stated in part that, "a single exposure provides no more than a nominal advertising effect." Twenty years ago they felt the first time you see an ad, the only value it had to offer was to prepare the viewer for the next exposure.

Conclusion 2: The weight of evidence suggests strongly that an exposure frequency of two within a purchase cycle is probably an effective level.

A purchase cycle is the time required for the purchaser to need to buy the product again. The purchase cycle for groceries is typically once a week and getting shorter as people's time is more and more at a premium. The purchase cycle on a candy bar can be daily. The purchase cycle on an automobile is measured in years and continues to get longer as cars become more dependable and conspicuous consumption diminishes.

McDonald points out that timing is important during the purchasing cycle. If the two exposures are closer together, they are much more powerful than spread apart.

He also mentions the importance of *share of voice*. "Two exposures for someone who is a heavy viewer, and sees many other advertisements for competing brands in the same period, is a very different matter from two exposures for a light viewer who sees relatively limited competing advertising; one exposure in the latter case may be worth very much more to the advertiser than several exposures in the former."

Conclusion 3: There is some quite good evidence that frequency, as defined as a clustering of exposures or opportunities to see shortly before a purchase occasion, may increase the probability of a desired response, including in purchase probability.

If the viewer is exposed to the message closer to the end of the purchase cycle, when the need for the purchase is greatest, it has the highest likelihood of having a positive impact.

Conclusion 4: There is good evidence that this effect tails off with larger frequencies above a certain level (a convex curve).

All of the studies indicate that level is four exposures and above. McDonald is just being careful to not add any confusion. It seems the level of purchasing probability is not increased by four-plus exposures, but it does stem the decline in probability.

Conclusion 5: There is no convincing evidence of a general rule which tells us what the optimum frequency should be. The biggest effect will often be at one exposure/OTS (opportunity to see), especially if we are looking at large and familiar brands; in those cases, two, three, etc., will often add to one, but at a lessening rate.

Conclusion 6: The shape and steepness of the response curve, and whether or not there is a threshold, are effected by a large range of variables. These include:

> *The brand's share and status.*
>
> *What the competition is doing.*
>
> *The quality of the advertising (bad advertising will not work whatever the frequency).*
>
> *The degree of clustering of the exposures on OTS.*
>
> *The timing of the exposures/OTS in relation to the purchase cycle, their 'propinquity' to it.*
>
> *Share of voice, and whether the group being advertised to is a heavy or light consumer of media (because it may require more frequency/clustering to get a new message heard through a higher clutter of competing noise).*
>
> *Etc.*

Conclusion 7: The frequency-of-exposure data from this review strongly suggest that wear-out is not a function of too much frequency per se. Indeed, wear-out is a copy or content problem.

Bad advertising cannot wear out because it never had the chance to "wear in." On the other hand, "We have not really proved that too much frequency per se, over short periods, may not be counter productive." I think George Parker may disagree on this one. Even though he liked the IBM/Lotus Notes ad, seeing it too often during one football game caused him to lambaste it in print. Some ads can make you laugh and some cry. But even in the face of a lack of evidence from McDonald's studies, I agree with Parker. Too much of a good thing is too much.

Conclusion 8: Very large and well known brands—and/or those with dominant market shares in their categories and dominant shares of category advertising weight—appear to differ markedly from smaller or more average brands in response to frequency of exposures.

Simply put, the well-known brand has it made and the new, rival brands have a much harder row to hoe to raise awareness and have an impact on people's buying propensities. Brand building is difficult and expensive. Momentum is important to a brand. The one with momentum can climb the hill easier than the one starting at a standstill.

Conclusion 9: Frequency of exposure has a differential effect on advertising response by daypart.

Because television sells time, rather than space, one of the issues to consider is what time of day your ad shows up—the *daypart*. Advertising between 6:00 A.M. and 8:00 A.M. will work when targeting the business person on her way to the office. Between 8:00 A.M. and noon, the houseperson. If you're selling office supplies or computer systems on television during the soap opera and talk show hours, you're missing your audience.

Conclusion 10: The greater the share of category exposures, the more positive the effects of frequency.

This is the big fish in the small pond effect. If you're the only one on the tube in your daypart advertising breath mints, you're going to be much more successful. Even if you are one of hundreds of other ads, the fact that you are alone in your category will make you a stand-out.

Conclusion 11: Nothing we have seen suggests that frequency response principles or generalizations vary by medium.

TV is pretty much like print. Print is pretty much like radio. The biggest differences are that it is much easier to plan clustered advertising on a time-based medium like broadcast. In print, you are limited to the period of the publication. If the magazine comes out once a month or once a week, that's the highest clustering you can hope for.

Conclusion 12: Although there are general principles with respect to frequency of exposure and its relationship to advertising effectiveness, differential effects by brand are equally important.

Brand building is powerful and cannot be left out of the equation. "Therefore, each brand should be examined to establish its own response function and how this varies in different circumstances, including good versus less good advertising."

Conclusion 13: The leverage of different equal-expenditure media plans in terms of frequency response can be substantial.

This one is just sort of thrown in to summarize the others. Given the same amount of money, you can have a significant impact on your results even if the only thing you change is frequency. The same ad, same length, same daypart, or publication will produce substantially different results if you plan your exposures wisely.

Banner Burnout

McDonald's eleventh conclusion suggests that the medium didn't matter. Given all other things being equal, the stimulus-response model was pretty much unchanged. When we turn to the Internet, we note the similarities and the differences between the differing media, and the fact that the three-exposure model holds up pretty well.

Like TV, we experience the World Wide Web on a flickering screen. This makes the text harder to read and gives us the feeling that whatever we're looking at is going to go away any second, lost forever, unless we capture it on tape. That the text is harder to read than print is not contested. That we have the feeling it's short-lived is a matter of training; it's something we can be trained out of once we get used to the idea of the Back button.

Like print, the Web is (for the most part) static. We can turn the page forward and backward. We can linger over the content. We can go back and revisit the same page anytime.

But the Web has its ephemeral aspects as well. Pages get moved. Content gets updated. Banner ads get rotated. Domain names change. In time, we'll see the vast majority of content on the Net coming from dynamic servers: pages that are created for us on-the-fly. Instead of living in frozen HTML on a server, they'll be served up for us each time we visit, depending on time of day and whether the site knows who we are.

Even in light of the differences, the principles of frequency seem more similar than not.

DoubleClick Study: First Is Best

Because DoubleClick is an ad-serving network, it has a great deal of data it can sift through. The company looked through their database of hundreds of thousands of banners and decided there was a "sweet spot" in response:

DoubleClick's Top Ten Tips:

#9 is: Avoid Banner Burnout:

After what number of targeted impressions does click-through rate significantly drop off? After how many impressions do people start ignoring your banner? Our study concluded that there indeed is a "sweet spot" for user response. After the fourth impression, average response rates dropped to under 1%. We call this banner burnout, the point at which a banner stops delivering a good Return on Investment. These findings are incredibly significant. Controlling your frequency extends your reach and maximizes your ad dollar.

In their study, dated July, 1996, they found that, on average, the first banner got a 2.7% response. Out of every 1,000 impressions, 270 people clicked the first time they saw the banner. The second banner exposure yielded 1.9%, the third 1.4%, and the fourth pulled in 1%. Thereafter, the response dwindled (**http://www.doubleclick.net/frames/general/frequset.htm**) (see Figure 7.6).

DoubleClick felt that a response below 1% was a poor ROI. If your marketing plan number suggests that half a percent will achieve your goals and that's just fine with you, you might be happy holding at the response rate through ten or twelve exposures. But the ease with which you can come up with a new banner with a new message that will kick the rate back up into the 2%–3% range means that DoubleClick is right on the money. Why waste the exposures for half a percent when you can do five to six times that with a fresh banner?

The fact is, people can ignore banners easier than they can ignore TV ads. As you're watching your favorite TV show, it takes a second to realize that the new scene is not the next one of the program you're watching, but an ad. Then you reach for the remote control. Then you push the mute button and then the sound dies out. In the meantime, the advertiser has had at least two seconds to put the product name in your ear. With three or four seconds (you had to wrest the remote away from your significant other), the advertiser has a chance to hit you with the product name and its main benefit. At the very least they had the chance to get you hooked or intrigued or managed to pique your curiosity.

Print is a little harder and here is where it is similar to the Web. While you're reading the morning paper, it's pretty easy to ignore the ads. The eye is trained to scan the headlines and work in coordination with the hands which are turning the pages, drinking the coffee, and scratching the dog's head. The eye is trained to ignore the ads. You know what they look like and how they are formatted. You can tell without even glancing at them that they are not articles.

FIG. 7.6
DoubleClick determined that the frequency/response model on the Web was not much different from TV or print.

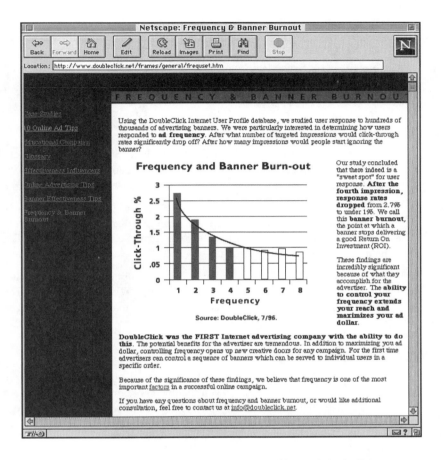

Banners on the Web train the eye the same way. On the sites you like to visit, the banners are always in the same position and they are always the same size. Ignoring them is the easiest thing in the world.

Maximize Reach, Minimize Frequency

This has been the conclusion reached by David Yoder, Media Director at Anderson and Lembke, at two consecutive Web Advertising conferences (1996 and 1997). According to David, the numbers point to the Web as being too expensive for brand building. Compared to print, in the case of ZD Net and a host of Ziff Davis magazines, the Web called for a CPM of $54, where the magazines were asking $28. USA Today Online wanted $33 per thousand impressions and *USA Today* newspaper wanted only $28.

But when Yoder looked at the effectiveness of these two publishers, the difference was even more pronounced. Calculating the cost of unduplicated impressions by the cost revealed a significant CPM variance.

Medium	CPM
ZD Net Online	$195
Ziff Magazines	$44
USA Today Online	$175
USA Today	$28

Yoder's conclusion was not surprising. "Print delivers more gross and net impressions for similar prospects per dollar with a more communicative ad unit (page versus banner) than online." He recommends against using online for awareness as a primary *or even secondary* objective.

On the other hand, he is a staunch supporter of using the Web for direct response. His studies showed how much more effective the Web is for clickthroughs versus direct response in direct mail or print.

In support of these numbers, Yoder points to the diminishing return issue. He pegs the optimal number at three. Not because of the 'What is it,?' 'What of it,?' and true reminder, but because the third exposure still gets sufficient response to make it worthwhile. Yoder is a numbers kind of guy.

Common Knowledge

If you have a large content site that draws a crowd, you can measure impressions differently. The folks over at Yahoo! will tell you that banners burn out after two weeks. Infoseek says banners lose their luster after 200,000 to 400,000 impressions. Obviously, on smaller sites with more repeat visitors, these types of figures will change.

In recognition of the need to keep frequency to a minimum, DoubleClick has implemented their Dart system, Hotwired has started offering "reach-frequency management," and all makers of serve-your-own-ads tools like NetGravity's Adserver are adding this capability to their products.

Regardless of the scale or who is doing the delivering, the message is the same: overexposure is a waste and familiarity breeds contempt. Or, as the philosophers put it so wisely, the only thing worse than hate is indifference.

Creating Better Banners

Colin McDonald spent a good deal of time trying to figure out how frequency varies the response, all other things being equal. To him, this included "good versus less good advertising."

If ever there were a case for "I can't define it, but I know it when I see it," good advertising is certainly a nominee. All of us can react in an instant and tell you if the ad we're subjected to is a good one or a bad one. It's easy.

Fine art requires an open mind and heart and a touch of historical knowledge and artistic education to boot. But advertising holds no mystery. It has no charm beyond the immediate impression it makes. It's art for the masses.

As a child, I would tell my father at the dinner table about a great ad I saw on TV. It captured my imagination. It said something interesting about humanity. It stretched the limits of good taste without crossing the line. His reaction was invariably the same: "What was the name of the product or the company?"

After having this question repeated to me time and again, I learned that great ads were not just the ones that made you feel good or were entertaining. They weren't even the ones that made you want to buy a new whatsit. They were the ones that made you want to buy a particular whatsit and *remember* which one it was.

So how do you make an ad work? How do you make it attention-getting and persuasive? How do you make great ads?

Philip Ward Burton's and Scott C. Purvis's *Which Ad Pulled Best* offers six "Guidelines for Copy Revealed by Copy Testing":

1. *Offer a major benefit.*

   So what's the big deal? What is it that makes your product or service shine? What do you have that's so special? Do you have features people have been clamoring for? Do you have a great price? Better delivery? Can offer a wider variety?

2. *Make it easy to see and read.*

   Burton and Ward warn that this is the one that most ad professionals miss. They're interested in arresting design and startling imagery. They're interested in winning that next award. You have a major benefit and a small amount of time and space to promote yourself so don't get carried away on the drawing board by making it too complex and artsy that you sacrifice readability.

3. *Establish audience identity.*

   Can the audience see themselves in your imagery? Does your ad show men on the moon eating your product? That's okay if you're targeting astronauts. But if you're after Mom, Dad and the kids, you'd be better served with a picture of the family car, the family room, or the family itself.

4. *Attract by being new.*

   "New" is one of the most powerful words in the advertising lexicon. New product, new feature, new benefit—doesn't matter. If what you're offering is so new it's newsworthy, you're onto something. Present tense and action words get the point across better.

5. *Be believable.*

   Advertising people share the bottom of the list with used car salespeople when it comes to the question of believability. Puffery, hype, and general aggrandizement are the adman's stock-in-trade. Avoid it. State your claim and prove it. "Actual size" and real results are better than over-promising and under-delivering.

6. *Stress what is unique.*

This is the USP, the unique selling proposition. It's the differentiator. Some refer to it as the positioning. What makes yours so much better than the others? What makes yours stand out?

Then Burton and Purvis get into some serious directives:

1. *Name the benefit; be specific about it.*

Regardless of the publication, the audience, or the product, Burton and Ward say the more specific ads are the more successful ones. One example they cite is a headline that reads, "Low-cost steam-shop assembled and ready to use." It pulled twice as many responses as the one that read, "Steam That Satisfies." Being clear about the benefit is critical. "8 square feet of dynamic display" for a folding table for use in retail stores was out shined to the tune of 3 times more sales by, "Move up to $100 in iced watermelons in 8 [square feet] of space."

The U.S. Envelope Company tried eight different headlines to sell self-sealing envelopes. They included;

So sanitary

Novel

Different

Better

Humid weather never affects

The winner by a landslide was the headline that said, "Avoid licking glue." It offered the most immediate benefit.

2. *The product is the big benefit; tell them what it will do.*

Here, Burton and Ward exhort the reader to explain the benefit and show the product. Ads where the happy buyers were shown being happy didn't do as well as the ones where the product was prominently displayed. "How to get good pictures for sure" did much better with a large picture of a camera, than the one with a picture of a couple smiling at the camera in their hands.

3. *Make it easy for consumers to visualize the benefit; keep your advertisements simple.*

Connect with the target audience on a personal basis and make it as easy as possible to respond. Give them a number to call, a coupon to send in, or both. The ad promoting health insurance did far better than the one advertising health, disability, and hospital coverage. Too much to think about. Too many choices to make.

Two ads for Welches Grape Juice brought the simplicity point home. One showed a jar and talked about a new low price in honor of their anniversary. The other added children in party hats and spoke of hosting an anniversary party with a great reduction in price. The simple, straightforward version was a clear winner. It didn't try to mix too many messages together.

4. *Emphasize the benefit as much as possible; use large space.*

   Tests showed that larger is better. A bad ad is still a bad ad and a larger piece of real estate won't help it. But a good ad can be much improved through enlargement.

5. *Don't obscure the benefit; the cute, the catchy, or the tricky may not work.*

   This works for the truly gifted, but not for the rest of us. Overall, humor, plays on words, and clever headlines simply don't pull as well as the straightforward. Too many people with too different an upbringing just don't get it. Not everybody laughs at the same jokes.

6. *Get personal about the benefit, but don't get personal without a purpose.*

   Be as personal as you can as long as it supports the product or service you're offering. There's no sense suggesting personal achievement as the benefit of an accounting service or an industrial pipeline service. The benefits in these ads are accuracy, delivery, and maybe low cost. Those are things of more value to the business than the individual.

Some of these bits are valuable and some simply do not apply. Some will work on the Web, but the only way you're going to make your banner larger is by making it not a banner. If that's important to you, by all means, talk them into creating a demi-site or an interstitial page for you.

But the advice offered has value in as much as it sets the ground rules for what follows.

Here, then, is advice from people out there on the Web who are making a go of it. Advice about what to say, how to say it, what color to paint it, and whether it should move. All in the name of figuring out what will make people click.

Choose Your Words Wisely

Simplicity must be the first watch word. There is no question that the amount of room you have to work with is infinitely, aggravatingly, and stiflingly small. With only so many pixels to work with, your work had better be to-the-point and easy to read. But what should you say?

If there is one thing that everybody in Internet marketing hates but agrees has a huge impact, it is the words, "Click Here."

Click Here   I was lucky when the discussion came up on the marketing lists online. I was busy. I was creating new presentations, writing articles, reviewing Web sites and, as usual, traveling all over God's creation and racking up the frequent fliers' miles. I only posted a few messages about how stupid the words "Click Here" really are.

Imagine printing an ad that said, "Read This!" Or a radio spot that started, "Listen Up!" How rude.

The Hippocratic oath in a nutshell is based on a principle known as "First, Do No Harm." Whatever you're going to do to that patient, don't make him worse. In marketing, my oath has always been, "Don't Annoy The Prospect." That's why I am so vehement in discussions about unsolicited e-mail.

"Click Here," it seemed to me, was an insult. Well, of course I'm supposed to click there! What do I look like, an idiot? Why waste what little space is available on such an obvious instruction?

Then I started looking at other successful advertising. They didn't say "Listen Up!" they said, "Call Now, operators are standing by." They said, "Mail away for yours today!" They said, RSVP—please respond. They were all calls to action. Then I started reading the opinions of people in the trenches.

The research done by Doubleclick and I/Pro says, "As in traditional direct response, telling consumers what to do helps raise response rates. Simple phrases such as 'Click Here', 'Visit Now' and 'Enter Here' tend to improve response rates by 15%. These phrases should be strategically placed in the ad, preferably on the right side. This is where the eye will be drawn."

Scott Rabschunk at Anderson & Lembke says "Click Here" doubles the response rate.

Wendy Marx, writing in *Advertising Age*'s supplement *NETMarketing* (December, 1996) says, "'Click here' may be the two most powerful words in cyberspace."

Toshiba not only used the words "Click Here," but added a bright red arrow pointing to the button. Michelle Rennert at Outfitters, who created the banner, says it pulled a 5.7% click-through.

Jeremy Ring, eastern sales manager at Yahoo!, suggests that using "Click Here" can dramatically improve response.

Infoseek's Ten Quick Tips to Make Your Banners More Effective put this as number one: "Click Here. The easiest way to increase clickthrough is to ask for it. A recent study by Infoseek found a 44% improvement in clickthrough rates just from providing visual or text cues that this banner leads to more information. There are many ways to remind the viewer besides the two simple words, 'Click Here.' Put buttons or arrows in the banner. Tell the viewer more information is available. Just do something that tells the viewer that they can interact with the offer."

I am now a firm believer and a staunch advocate. A call to action is never out of place.

Offer   You just want me to click? Is that it? Is that all? Okay, I'll click. But what do I get in return? You have to make me an offer. After all, I'm quietly surfing away, minding my own business, and you want to drag me away from what I'm doing. What's in it for me?

Free   It's possible that, after "Click Here," the next most powerful thing you can put on a banner is the word "Free."

Part of the charm, the mystique, and popularity of the Net is that it is free. Okay, so you have to buy a $3,000 computer, a $200 modem, and pay for the phone line and the Internet access and the electricity, but besides all that, it's free.

It started out essentially free. The university said I could run a wire from my business to the campus and they'd let me run packets through their routers, gratis. You asked if you could run a wire to my computer room across our shared parking lot. Fine. No problem. It won't cost me anything to have your incremental traffic going through my system. No charge.

The software that runs the Internet? Free. Advice on the newsgroups that help me figure out how to make my routers sing? Free. So now that you actually want to sell me something, there better be something in it for me and it better be free.

I don't care what it is. A T-shirt. A game. A report based on studies you conducted. Maybe a poster of your CEO riding a camel—but it has to be free.

Infoseek will tell you that free is the best price. The I/Pro-DoubleClick study indicated that free hardware and software offers resulted in a response rate 35% above those banners without the magic word. You are left to wonder, however, why free travel offers cause a 10% drop in response.

Contest   The next best thing to delivering something for free is giving somebody a chance to win something for free. Contests and sweepstakes have been on the Net since Web sites first began. Win a car, disk drive, trip, or T-shirt. The point, as always, is to drive more people to your site or into your marketing database.

But the trade show problem crops up again. You end up with a database of people who like ice cream. Rob Frankel at Frankel-Anderson (**www.frankel-anderson.com**) who does "Advertising, Marketing & Killer Creative," has been doing online advertising longer than most. In a January, 1997 post to the Online Ads list, Frankel said contests are a fallacy. "Our experience is that when you sponsor contests, what you get initially might be great traffic, but over time, all you get are contestants. If you want qualified traffic, you must attract them with that which qualifies them."

Spot on. If your banner says "Win a Drill Press Tune-Up" you don't have to worry too much about people without drill presses bothering to enter.

If you're going to run a contest to boost traffic to your site or raise awareness about your product, there are a couple of places on the Web you should take a look at.

The first is an article by Carl Klein about using contests for promotion (**www.referrals.com/articles**). Next, take a look at a list of contest listing sites at **www.181-4.com/promotions/sweeps.html** (see Figure 7.7).

Finally, check out a place that will aggregate contest players for you: Contestworld (**www.contestworld.com**) (see Figure 7.8). Jim Kulakoski will list your contest at his site for all who are interested in such things to see. He charges for the privilege, but at $25 per month, you could pay for it out of petty cash. Kulakoski does something a lot of contest sites don't do. He links to your home page. As he puts it, "The problem with contests on the web is that there are contest listing sites which are sending the traffic directly to the contest entry page."

Kulakoski goes on:

Here is an analogy. A furniture store is giving away [a] bedroom set...to enter the contest you have to go to the back of the store to find the contest 'entry box.' As the customer makes his way through the store he is exposed to all the furniture the vendor has to offer and maybe sees something he likes.

Then someone leaves the back door open and the word gets out. It's easy to enter the drawing for a bedroom set. Just pull up in the alley behind the store jump out of your car and fill out an entry... you don't even have to turn the car off! The vendor gets tons of contest entries but no sales.

That is what is happening on the net. I am in the contest listing business. I noticed that in fact contests were not providing websites with 'bona fide' traffic. Just contestants. If visitors enter a contest because they are already at a site and they notice the contest it does not help that site gener-ate new traffic (although it may help increase return traffic). And more importantly if traffic is directed by a third party to the contest entry page this does not expose the visitor to what the site has to offer.

FIG. 7.7
Promoting a contest?
Don't miss this list.

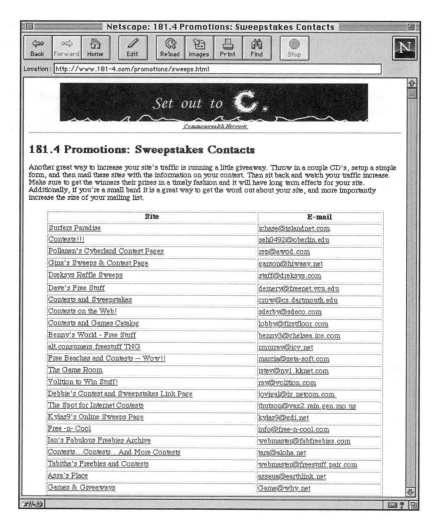

FIG. 7.8
Contestworld is one
of the contest listing
services that won't take
people into your back
door.

Do contests work? Anecdotally, yes. Tim Gayda of Discover Canada Online
(**www.dicovercanada.com**) says so. After promoting a $1,500 heli-skiing holiday as actively as
it could, Discover Canada Online got some traffic at their site. Now, Gayda figures the word is
out, because their second contest, a five-day ski trip to Banff, doubled the traffic to their site.
And it's a pretty sure bet that people who are interested in winning a ski trip to Banff are going
to be interested in other Canadian travel information and services.

But not all banners promoting sweepstakes are winners. Like everything else in life, it's not a sure
bet. As I said before, the I/Pro-DoubleClick study found free hardware and software offers resulted
in a response rate 35% above those banners without the magic word "Free." Hardware is something
specific that fits your machine that you know you want. Software is something you can download
now. But travel means serious planning. The I/Pro-DoubleClick study determined that offers for
free travel caused a 10% drop in response. They didn't say what other factors were involved, but it
certainly makes one wonder if everybody on the Web it just too busy to take a vacation.

Infoseek doesn't think the disinterest in winning is particular to travel and disagrees with DoubleClick. Number seven on Infoseek's Top Ten list says "Don't Waste Time/Money on Contests." The mere offer of large payoff does not impact clickthrough. An Infoseek analysis of over 2,000 banners and 500,000,000 impressions found no significant improvement in response rate for banners offering a contest. Given the cost and legal complexity of doing contests on the Internet (more on that in Chapter 8, "Real Life Stories: The Good, the Bad, and the Unexplainable," this is one marketing idea that you can comfortably avoid.

Works for some. Not for others.

Now!   The "limited time offer" is ubiquitous in all other forms of advertising. "Today Only," "Until Supplies Last," and the ever-popular, "Going Out of Business Sale."

The day after Thanksgiving is the busiest retail shopping day of the year in the United States. Getting the whole family together to eat too much and watch football is a perfect time to go out shopping together and see what everybody might like toward Christmas.

Last year my wife and I spent Thanksgiving with my parents and joined the throngs in San Francisco. The streets were packed, the decorations were up, the air was crisp and everybody was getting into the spirit. We wandered into Macy's. Okay, we elbowed our way into Macy's and found numerous sales tables with signs that said "Three Hour Sale!"

From 9:00 A.M. until noon, certain tables were blessed with an additional 25% off. The result was near pandemonium. The excitement in the air was palpable and my father and I tried to stick to the walls.

As I watched, it occurred to me that such an approach would not work as well on the Web. This was a situation that you had to take advantage of at the moment. This was a group dynamic, mod-psychology kind of thing. You could smell the avarice pheromone in the air.

The Web is more of a personal endeavor. It's not done in a herd. It's not a competition. A Web site that offered a "GREAT DEAL!" was fine, but one that suggested you had to buy now or the offer would expire in 10...9...8...7... just didn't hold water.

Banners may be different. There are some who say limited time offers on the Web are the way to go and some who say they are not.

Jim Gleason at Pacific Digital (**www.pacdigital.com**) says creating urgency is a good thing. "'Last chance' or other time dependent phrase[s] will prompt users to click now or forever hold their peace." Jeremy Ring from Yahoo! thinks urgency helps (**www.whitepalm.com/ fourcorners/yahoobannertips.shtml**).

But the I/Pro-DoubleClick study says that the limited time offer performed below average. "Statements creating a psychological sense of urgency actually seem to DECREASE average response rates."

This is one you'll have to test on your own banner, in your own marketplace.

Humor   If you're good, you can get away with humor. There are enough bad joke banners out there that they are not worth repeating. But the online bookstore, Amazon.com, has banner ads that make a real point in a very humorous way. They are short, sweet, and let you know that they have a huge selection of books. Their banners include a click button over on the far right that says, "Click here to enter www.amazon.com Earth's Biggest Bookstore." The majority of the space is taken up with funny couplets:

16 books on male pattern baldness.
And, fortunately, 128 on hats.

662 books on golf.
And, what do you know, 800 on divorce.

460 books for Marxists.
Including 33 on Groucho.

They're simple. They're fun. They're informative. They work. Now, mix that sort of copywriting with some real content/subject targeting and you're going places.

Ask a Question   The I/Pro-DoubleClick report also suggests posing a question. "Using questions ('Looking for a bargain?') can raise click-through by 16% over average." An improvement of 16% isn't bad. That's a change that will take you from 862 responses to 1,000. DoubleClick thought highly enough of the idea they made it #2 in their list of tips. "Don't just make statements or show pretty pictures. Use questions ('Looking for free software?', 'Have you seen?'). They initiate an interaction with the banner by acting as a teaser. They entice people to click on your banner."

They also act as a decent qualifier if you pose the question the right way. "Want To Save Money?" would be a bust. Everybody wants to save money. Nobody is interested in a generic offer.

Be Specific   Kate Margolese is vice president of marketing at Nets, a provider of Internet business-to-business services. In an article in *NET Marketing* (December, 1996) she says forget the graphics and go for the offer. Margolese says she'd prefer to stay away from the flashy colors and the moving graphics gimmicks. As far as she's concerned, it's all about being straightforward and interesting.

Because there's such a small amount of space on a Web page, it's a matter of turning to conciseness and brevity as your guides. Be clear. Be up-front. Don't make people guess what you're getting at. Make a fair offer in a direct way and the people you are looking to attract will click. If you're too "attractive," you end up attracting all kinds of people.

In the same article that quoted Kate, Jim Savage, Vice President of Z DNet, was quoted as saying "You want good, strong copy, a clear call to action and an emphasis on impact over design beauty." Savage isn't looking to be cute, clever, or win awards for spiffy graphics. He just wants meaningful results.

U S Robotics learned the same lesson while selling 28.8 modems. "Time Is Money : USRobotics : Mobile modem Rebate : $25–Click Here" got 1.02% clickthrough while "Go from 14.4 to 28.8 and get $25 : USRobotics : Mobile modem Rebate : $25–Click Here" got 1.66% and "Upgrade your modem and Download $25 : USRobotics : Mobile modem Rebate : $25–Click Here" got 1.67%. The lesson is go for the straightforward. Sell the benefit. Make it obvious.

While this advice sounds like it's straight from Colin McDonald, it's worth emphasizing to encourage you from going for the all-to-common practice of invoking a response with the enigmatic, the weird, and the obscure.

Be Cryptic   The DoubleClick tips put cryptic messages as tip number 7 in their tip sheet. However, while "Cryptic messages typically increase click-through 18%," there are a couple of problems with this approach.

DoubleClick points out the first one. "Cryptic ad banners can help involve a user in the message. Because the 'sponsor' of the message is not revealed, cryptic messages can be very intriguing. But there is a downside. Branding is forfeited on the ad. This may not be an issue if branding is not your main objective."

If your main objective is branding, you want the name of the company or the product to show up as often as possible. If you're Nike or Mercedes, you can even get away with just your logo showing up. A cryptic banner doesn't remind the surfing population of your image. A cryptic banner counts on being secretive.

The second problem is one of qualification.

The crew at Site Specific (**www.sitespecific.com**) has produced some of the best promotional programs on the Web. Some have been contests, some have been demi-sites that tell a story, some have been simple banners. This group understands unleashing the power of creative skills on the one hand and harnessing them with the available technology on the other. One simple banner they did was for 3M.

3M wanted to promote a new high-intensity projector in a market teaming with competitors and overflowing with messages. They needed something catchy. Something that would stop people in their tracks and make them click. They turned to Site Specific.

They spread their media buy across a variety of sites and the biggest pull came from a banner that read, "Do it with the lights on," which was placed at the Dilbert site.

Being a professional presenter, and knowing the subject of this promotion, I find the hook clever, to-the-point, and delivering a singular benefit I can relate to immediately. But if I had seen this banner in a vacuum, if I had chanced upon it, I'd have assumed it would have clicked through to a site more true to its ribald nature than to a site talking about business equipment.

It was cute, but did it draw qualified prospects? Wouldn't it attract more people interested in doing it than in buying it?

Sex Sells   Infoseek's Ten Quick Tips counsels us with item number eight that "Certain Truisms Remain True." This is the same one that said the best price was "free" and that special offers feel special. This is the place they remind us that "Sex appeal sells."

You get to decide how far you want to go vis-à-vis taste. But then you face the sites themselves who will also decide how far you can go. If you thought TV censors were tough, listen to Cindy Alpers lament her efforts to advertise a contest for her tropical travel site (**www.tropi-ties.com**) on a banner exchange (posted to Online Advertising, May 2, 1997):

I recently submitted a banner ad for my site to a banner exchange organization which was rejected because they feared that other members and viewers might not like it. The banner consisted of a small, tasteful picture of a young woman, in a bikini, sunning on the bow of a boat while the caption read, 'Bikini Photo Contest! Enter to win! Click here.' We are running the ad to kick off our 'family oriented,' bikini photo contest on our site. I was dismayed and saddened to see that this harmless ad had been censored. There was nothing pornographic about it, we were not selling anything obscene on our site, yet someone's ultra-conservative opinion had tried to quiet our ad campaign. I have since sent them more prudish versions of the ad, only to be rejected.

Have we over-policed ourselves in hopes of acceptance by the other, more established forms of media? Will the internet ad agencies and banner organizations make our decisions on what is suitable and proper for the entire internet community? Your comments please.

Alpers followed up on this several days later:

After my ad was refused two or three times by a banner exchange for having a girl in a bikini on it, I finally took off the photo and just ran the text on the banner that read "Bikini Photo Contest, Enter to Win! Click here." I also found another banner exchange that was willing to run my ad as I originally designed it, bikini clad girl and all. Both of the exchanges' banners are placed on my home page, one just below the other.

I have been tracking the ads for about a week now and have noticed that both ads pull about the same click-through ratio, about 22:1. This is much higher than any other ads I have ever run. However, I find it even more interesting to note that even without the picture, the text-only ad pulls just as well as the picture ad. It just goes to show that the power of the word and a little imagination goes a long ways in advertising!

Alpers' lament isn't particular to the Internet, as we all learned over the uproar caused when Ellen came out of the closet. Olympia tours, which promotes cruise vacations for female couples, was turned down by the TV network. Their ad depicted two women in lounge chairs holding hands. Provocative? Hardly. The network folks said they had trouble with the "editorial content," and so declined to run the ad. Olympia, recognizing the potential number of lesbian eyes on the fabulously hyped, two-hour-long *Ellen* "coming out" special, said they'd be happy to change whatever the TV gods found objectionable. The answer came back that there was nothing that could be changed to alleviate the problem.

Does sex sell? You bet. Cindy Alpers' clickthrough rate of 22% is nothing to sneeze at by anybody's measure. Like Alpers, however, you will have to get used to the idea of working with people who have not been in the advertising business long enough to have a clear idea about what is acceptable and what is not. They're simply trying to please as many people as possible.

Color

In the beginning, the telephone yellow pages were in black and white. Okay, black and yellow. If you wanted an ad in the yellow pages, you could have any color you wanted as long as it was black. The ads that pulled well were the biggest.

Then they added red. Ads which used black and red did really well. They stood out. They were different. They caught the eye. Then they added full blue. Eventually, almost all of the ads were in color. The thinking was that if your ad wasn't in color, it gave the same impression as if your ad was the smallest on the page. "Oh, that company has a small ad. They must not be successful enough to afford a real ad in the phone book."

But something odd happened. When the majority of ads went to color, the black and white ones started pulling better. Why? They were different. They stood out. Think about television. A black and white ad is unusual and captures your attention. But colors can do a great deal more than merely catching the eye, they can also set the tone.

There is a very interesting essay on the use of color in selling called "Potemkin's Village" (**http://www.mcp.com/general/news5/pearl.html**) by Pearl Lau, which is well worth a short diversion here.

"Potemkin's Village" by Pearl Lau

It is the last half of the eighteenth century. Field Marshal Grigori Alexandrovitch Potemkin must maintain order in an impoverished, over-taxed kingdom, while flattering the ego of his sovereign. One day, Catherine the Great, Empress of All the Russias, demands that he must arrange for her to tour the lands. Potemkin can't possibly let Catherine see how deplorable conditions are—he'd lose not only his job but his head as well!

Potemkin is forced to ask himself the critical question: "What can I do?" And from the depth of his soul comes the reply, "Packaging!"

He hammered up false fronts to hide decrepit buildings. As soon as the town is out of Catherine's sight, his minions frantically tore down the glittering scenery, raced ahead to the next village, and set it all up again.

Catherine, one of the most worldly monarchs of her time, was convinced that what she saw was what she got.

Today, many big-thinking people have spent years on the discourse of color. Companies spend tens of thousands of dollars researching the right color for a new product. Yet one of the world's most successful foods, Campbell's, adopted red and white because they were the colors of the leader's favorite team.

Colors surely influence our lives. Maybe it doesn't revive remembrances of things past as strongly as aroma does, but with the exception of 1 man in 24 and 1 woman in 286, we are born with a sense of color. Not only can color enhance the communication process, it can accelerate learning. Retention and recall are increased by 55 to 78%. Legibility and the willingness to read goes up by 80%.

And here's the best part: it can sell more effectively by 50 to 85%. Companies like the Wagner Institute for Color Research distributed four boxes of identical laundry detergent. The consumers felt neutral about the soap in the green/white and orange/green boxes, and questioned whether the "mild stuff" in the blue/white box contained any soap at all. The product they thought worked the hardest and cleaned the best was in the orange/blue box—one consumer was sure it took out tar stains.

Is such a reaction psychological or physiological? How do colors make you feel? Are you happier and more cheerful on a sunny yellow day, or a gray rainy one? Responses to colors are emotional, not logical.

It's been said there are two types of color people. One group prefers clear, distinct hues, the second group prefers hues of less saturation. There is also the phenomena of "after-image." Snow blindness is when, after seeing so much white, the eye needs to relax and seeks the complementary color, black. Next time you're in the meat or fish market, notice how parsley, or fake green plastic stuff, is used as decoration. Green is the complementary color of the red, and helps enhance the meat and fish to make it look fresher.

Pepsi-Cola installed light blue vending machines in southeast Asia. Sales plummeted. No one would buy soda from a machine in a "bad-luck" color. Pepsi changed the machines to yellow. Yellow and saffron are the religious colors, who's going to buy soda from a god? Finally someone did some research, and found that red is not only a "good luck" color in Asia, but it also stands out well.

In my last position before Macmillan, my books were in the global arena. We made design decisions to save money, when converting from English to Italian, for instance. Nothing was in alphabetical order, so that only the type would have to change and color didn't have to be stripped in again. We tried using the same covers, just changing the title. We never had a global disaster, but the mistake was in not taking other cultures, and their color sense, into consideration. I passed out a color quiz at one of the international meetings. I asked them about idioms. For weddings, white dresses in the western world, red in China. (The Chinese reserve white for funeral wear.) You know how the in-laws would feel in Connecticut if the bride walked down the aisle in a red dress.

To "make blue" in Germany is to have a day off. Blue is used in Portugal to paint around window ledges to keep out evil spirits. In America, blue connotes authority and respect—it's the average American's favorite color. "Big Blue" is IBM's nickname. And, according to industrial psychologist Dr. Kerry Johnson, blue is one of the three top colors that urges you to buy, the other two are gray and hunter green.

Colors change their personalities in the different socio-economic and age groups. Those in lower strata groups prefer simple, two-word colors, "grass green," "sky-blue". Higher income people prefer more complex colors, with more complex descriptions: "grayish-green with a hint of blue." Younger people gravitate toward colors with longer wavelengths—red and orange. As people age, their attraction to colors, and shorter wavelengths change. College students will go toward blue, green, and violet.

When an acquaintance of mine drove her new maroon Mercedes to her mother's house, the mother wondered why she didn't get it in orange, like her Gremlin.

Everyone loves to quote data. Culled from dozens of articles and books on color, here they are:

RED: Action, associated with violence, hypertension, and hysteria. Can increase the appetite (red interiors for restaurants). A cola color. When Canada Dry ginger ale switched from the red (cola color) container to green, sales went up 27% in 6 months. Your drink is much more refreshing with a little red cherry in it. Not a good text type color, 76 percent of a group found high chroma colors hard to read, and decreased comprehension. The Maori can see hundreds of reds.

YELLOW: Eyes see it fastest, it can be masculine or feminine. A small amount of yellow can be cheerful, large doses can cause anxiety. Crying babies and explosive people do poorly in yellow rooms. It can stick in the mind. Black type on yellow ground has been rated by most to be the easiest color combination to read. Black on white comes second. Direct mail packages in the goldenrod, buff, cream area increase response.

BLUE: Commands respect. Generally conservative. Sparks freshness. Cooler blues are more passive. Career counselors suggest blue, a non-threatening suit color for interviews. Blue is also associated with club soda, and low-cal foods. At a county fair, the first prize was changed to a red ribbon, the second prize was blue. Judges were amazed at the reluctance of the winner to take the red ribbon. Blue ribbons are symbolic of excellence. A direct-mail advertiser changed his package, aimed at males, from red/black to blue/black and increased response significantly.

GREEN: Freshness incarnate. Good for gum and vegetables, not for packaging for meat or fish, suggests mold. Good for nature, peace, and safety. Considered recessive and thus a good background color.

WHITE: Purity. Egyptians and Jews had their priests dress in white. Suggests diet foods, lightness, and elegance. The use of black and white photos has made new advertising stand out more, in the sea of color. Eskimos see seven types of white.

BLACK: Power. Drama. Stability. A color with a split personality. It can stand for the affluence of a black limo, or widow's weeds. A person who wears black in normal circumstances sees themselves as an individual, hipper than the average joe. The strongman's barbells at the circus are painted black so they look heavier.

ORANGE: This color can anger the reader! It draws attention quickly, indicates informality. It never says "expensive." With black it says Halloween, by itself it says autumn, or root vegetables.

PURPLE/PINK : Ever since purple was the most expensive color to produce, and therefore used only by Roman royalty, it's been a rich color. Never a good color to use as text type. In modern times it's been considered a "gay" color.

Pastries from pink boxes taste better. People will pay more for cosmetics when packaged in pink, they tip people more who wear pink. Men don't want to have people see them buying packages in pink, they prefer brown or blue.

We recently asked some of our sales representatives how certain colors made them feel. These are the majority's results:

Red = Powerful

Yellow = Eager

Green = Relaxed

Blue = Relaxed

White = Relaxed

Black = Powerful

If you're now trying to figure out how colors affect people on your own, you're in good company. Newton tried in 1704; he created a foundation for a scientific view of colors "with solid and coherent theory..." In 1671, Jean-Baptiste Colbert set a code of standards: "All visible things are distinguished and made desirable through color." Goethe said "the only thing that philosophers agree on in color...is that they all see red when discussing it."

But for people who must put aside philosophy to sell a product, what does it mean? Simply pay attention not only to your market's desires, but the colors of their desires as well. Know the emotional values they place on color—your color preferences don't matter, unless you represent all those who buy the product.

Will it sell better in the correct color?

Bottom line: Yeah.

Today, most banners use the standard PC palette of colors in order to maintain control over what their banner looks like from one monitor on one operating system to the next. For the moment, loud colors are rare and stand out.

The DoubleClick Top Ten Lessons lists Bright Colors as number three. "Colors effect [*sic*] the eye differently. Using bright colors can help attract a user's eye, contributing to higher response rates. Research has shown that blue, green and yellow work best, while white, red, and black are less effective."

Kate Margolese from Nets told *NetMarketing* that using eye-catching colors may be okay for consumer promotions. But in her world of business-to-business promotions, she'd rather focus on the offer and the branding. In her book, loud colors don't make sense for serious business offers.

The final issue to consider about color is the blue border around your banner. The blue border it a visual indicator that the banner is clickable. It's the visual equivalent of using the words "Click Here." Jeremy Ring from Yahoo! thinks this is the right approach.

But some say that the blue border is passe. They feel that so few people use it anymore and there are so many new users who have logged on for the first time since the blue border went out of style, that it has lost its intrinsic value. This is yet another case where we'll have to wait for some enterprising ad company, advertising association, or graduate student to step forward and do some serious research.

Animation

Everybody agrees that animation makes a difference.

DoubleClick talks about it as number six on the Ten Quick Tips page. "Animation can help you catch a user's eye. Strategic use of movement grabs attention more effectively than static banners. Using simple Java or gif animation can increase response rates by 25%."

ZD Net did their own study of some 30 ads in a five month period. While 25% may be a good measure as an average, ZD Net found a range in clickthrough improvements from 15% to as much as 40%.

As far as Infoseek is concerned, "Catch Their Attention" immediately follows "Click Here" in importance. "Animation increases the likelihood that your ad will draw the user's attention.

Animation also generates more 'clicks' than static banners, all else being equal. However, it may not increase the number of 'qualified clicks.' If the objective is generating qualified clicks, eye-popping animation probably doesn't help. However, animation can also tell a story—Feature/Benefit, Problem/Solution. Using animation in this way can be very effective at both capturing attention and inspiring action from the right viewers."

Animation has also been seen as a way to stem the banner burnout factor. The burnout factor seems to work with McDonald's "What is it?" stage of banner impression. Having already gone through the "What of it?" stage and determining it's of no importance, the eye acclimatizes to that specific banner and can recognize it and discount it in less than a split second.

A sudden movement in the rear-view mirror is alarming. That is, unless you frequently have a hyperactive six-year-old in the back seat. If that's the case, your eyes are so accustomed to quick, random movements back there, they no longer trigger the adrenaline glands. It would take a red flashing light from the Highway Patrol or the ravenous glare from the eye of a Tyrannosaurus Rex to get your attention.

My personal reaction to animation was exactly the same as it was to "Click Here." I was annoyed, felt all others would be annoyed, and wrote it off as a cheap trick with little true marketing value.

When I was working on something and out pawing through the Web in search of just the right tidbit or for fact-checking, I found I cringed every time I came across an animation. They took forever to download. The larger ones lived in my cache file and were read over and over as the image played again and again. No matter what I was concentrating on, I got distracted by the sounds of unnecessary I/Os and the feeling that my disk was getting a little hole worn into it.

As a result, I read them as quickly as possible (hindering retention) and then hit the Back button before I headed back to my spreadsheet or word processing document. The animated page never sat on my screen like wallpaper.

Even though new animation techniques stopped the disk-reading problem, I still find animation annoying. Does this prove I'm an over forty, post-MTV, getting-conservative-since-I-cut-my-hair-in-the-70s, hip-less wonder? Or is there a real reason to avoid gratuitous animation?

Perhaps the thing that is most disturbing about animation in banners is exactly the thing that makes it so powerful; it is distracting. As I am trying to read a page to extract information from it, my eye is repeatedly pulled up to the flashing, winking, blinking banner. It's involuntary. It's infuriating. And that's why it works. People look at it.

But people like me are also learning to scroll it just out of reach so as not to be confronted by it. Just move it underneath another window. Just hit the Back button.

So I agree with Infoseek. If you use an animated banner to tell a story and make a strong impression, you have a much better chance at selling me your product. If you use it to announce "New!" and "Improved!" and "New!" and "Improved!" I will hit Reload, hoping something else replaces it.

Size

Most people who have tried any number of shapes and sizes agree that bigger is better. The bigger the ad, the more intrusive, the more attention, the more clickthrough.

If you have the budget and the need, by all means cut a deal for a full-page interstitial. But the most important size issue to keep in mind is the issue of file size.

Number nine on the Infoseek Ten Quick Tip sheet is "Less Is More." "The best way to get a response is to make sure the message is delivered. Many sites limit the size of ad banners to 10KB to 15KB. The fact is that the likelihood of the image being displayed decreases exponentially as the size increases. Although it flies in the face of response-enhancing methods like animation, the simpler banner (few colors, fewer images) load faster. If the viewer moves to the next page before your ad can load, it doesn't matter how great the message or creatives are."

Remember the problem with the new configuration of the AltaVista pages? The banner takes so long to load that I am always able to scroll down to the answers to my search without seeing it.

Remember, text loads first and then graphics. Links are found in the text. It's easy to spot a blue word and click it before your banner shows up. One thing Infoseek forgot to mention: you get billed either way. The server sent the image. Period. Whether the browser painted that image on the surfer's screen is an unknown. But don't lose any sleep over it. It's certainly no worse than paying for ads in magazines that go straight into the recycling bin without having their pages see the light of day.

So you have to balance your desire for unusual colors, animation, and Java applets with the need for the smallest file size you can manage. If your ad pops up right away, it gets seen. Otherwise, you're wasting your time.

Don't Forget the <ALT> Tag

Depending on the source, as many as 15% of surfers wander their way through the Web with images turned off. That means they are not going to see your banner, no matter what. If the content site you sponsor has good tracking software, it will note that the browser did not ask for the image and they will not charge you for it.

If your banner takes too long to load, it will not be seen, but you will be charged for it. In either case, you're facing a missed opportunity. The solution is the HTML <ALT> tag.

The <ALT> tag tells the browser what to display in case your banner doesn't show up. If your banner is in a non-standard format, it won't display. That's non-standard as far as the individual browser is concerned. You have an animated banner and the surfer is using an old version of Navigator? You have a Java applet you're trying to show to an AOL user who refuses to upgrade? You'd better offer an <ALT>.

The ALT text that shows can duplicate your banner text or can (and should) be more explicit. "Click here for a higher return on mutual funds." "Click now and you could win a new BMW."

Some advertisers are submitting banners with additional text hanging off the bottom in the same vein as these examples. The result is a banner plus text. The reason is to get around generic banner burnout. People know where not to look on the page. Usually the banner is the first thing. So the eye is trained not to look at the first rectangle of advertising, but at the first bit of text that comes after it. Bingo!

When?

When should ad banners be run? This is a natural question when planning television and radio spots because the time will determine the audience. You think in terms of day parts. The same might apply to banner placement if your audience is children. They are less likely to click during school hours because they are otherwise engaged.

But a large percentage of people do their surfing at the office. Yes, most do it from home, but not by a wide margin. So does that mean you should advertise office supplies in the daytime and vacation travel at night? Some of us don't have time to think about paper clips and pencils during the middle of the day. And when we do get a break, visiting **www.tropi-ties.com** is much more compelling. I'd much rather spend my coffee break contemplating a Caribbean vacation than ordering toner cartridges.

When placing ads in the newspaper, one thinks not in terms of time of day, but day of the week. Bob Ivins at I/Pro discovered that while Web usage is 25% lower on weekends, banner clicking was higher, by a hair. The average banner, according to Ivins, gets 2.11% clickthrough. On Sunday it gets 2.20% and on Saturday it gets 2.28%. Not much of a difference to be sure. Mondays seem to be the bottom of the barrel, at 2.01%. Only the clergy and barbers like Mondays.

If you're planning monthly magazine advertising, you think in terms of which month to advertise. The rules are the same regardless of the medium for a time frame this large. Mark Welch pondered the seasonal issue in a January 28, 1997 post to Online Advertising.

Before it is possible to suggest what are the best times to sell ads, the obvious question is, "ads for what?" Each advertised commodity has its own schedule. Political campaigns peak in October; toys & games in November/December. Car ads peak in the months when cars sell best. But note that you can see car ads year round.

To quote Glenn Barr's posting in this forum:

'People drink soft drinks all the time but drink more in hot weather.

People buy car insurance (mostly) once a year.

People buy lawn mowers when the grass is growing.

People buy refrigerators when the old one has had it. (Summer seems to help.)'

As an estate planning attorney, I hired a marketing consultant to advise me regarding the best months to run seminars, and the best days to advertise them. The seminar 'market' peaks in March and October, and bottoms out in the summer months and December. Hence, you only operate them, and advertise them, in the better months.

Copy Meister

Ron Richards' San Francisco company, ResultsLab, has studied more than just what makes headlines grab the eye in cluttered settings like CompuServe's classified ads. He's also helped Web publishers improve their readership. One of his projects was helping Web Publishing, a division of IDG, that publishes four advertiser-sponsored, online-only magazines for technical/professional readers: *NetscapeWorld*, *JavaWorld*, *SunWorld*, and *NC World*.

They sought Richards's help after several months of stalled readership growth in *NetscapeWorld*. Ron increased their pageviews by two and a half times—an increase that's been sustained and increased since. This represented a serious financial improvement for the magazine because they suddenly had more than two and a half more pageviews/impressions to deliver to advertisers.

According to Michael McCarthy, president of Web Publishing, Richards redesigned the cover, which caused an immediate 50% jump in the number of articles read per visit.

"He re-wrote cover lines, table of contents language, headlines, and summaries with highly effective 'grabber' language," says McCarthy. "He found ways to measure the cause-and-effect relationships, track incremental results, and uncover what works best.

"He developed new advertising to drive traffic to our site from search-engine ads, finding clever ways to triple the clickthrough rate. As a result of his efforts, NetscapeWorld doubled, then doubled again in the course of only a few months, the number of monthly pageviews delivered to readers."

Here's a simple example. Simple from the standpoint of easy to tell and easy to understand. But not so easy to conceive in the first place.

NetscapeWorld has a pointer to a list of their most-read stories. This was the cream of the crop from past issues and acted as a sort of a gateway into the archives. The link read, "Reader's Choice Of Twelve Must-Read Articles From Past Issues." Ron was losing sleep worrying about that phrase he had written, specifically the word "Past" which he decided to change to "Recent." He got seventeen percent more readers clicking the Must-Read link by changing the word "Past" to "Recent." It's one of those things that seem like a nit. Then it seems obvious. But most people gloss over fine-tuning to that degree.

They shouldn't, because as Ron is fond of pointing out, sometimes finding many such "little" things can give a compounded improvement of from two- to fivefold.

"Many advertising and marketing executives don't seem to believe that the creative or the treatment of the ad is as important as the other variables. They focus on the share of voice relative to competitors. They tend to think that frequency and reach are more important than content. They want to be sure they stand out as the major player rather than optimize the contents of the ad."

Ron likes to show them that multiplying the results from creative is a giant missed bet.

"The difference between the ads I see in the magazines and the ones I see online is that online ads contain more poison and missed bets. They are even more inept, even more inane, even more hypey, even more cutesy; they're based on less substance. With so many people creating mediocre ads with low response, it's very easy to believe that the treatment doesn't matter. But I disagree with all my heart and so that's where I spend my energy. I'm very unhappy if I can't improve an ad's response, or a content site's pull, by two to five fold in the first project."

Ron is so committed to consistently achieving those kind of compounded gains, he even puts it in his e-mail signature. (Another example of grabber language.):

```
=================================================================

   Ron Richards, President                      ResultsLab

   voice:   415-563-5300                    2175 Green Street

   fax:     415-563-0897               San Francisco, CA 94123

   ronr@resultslab.com                http://www.resultslab.com

Goal: Multiply results 2-5 fold for WWW advertisers/publishers

=================================================================
```

It's Harder to Get Attention on the Web

Ron calls the Internet "the most awesome promotional clutter that ever existed in history. A fifteen second television commercial is at least some very carefully sequenced linear concepts. In contrast, a Web ad is one of 15 things calling for your attention at once."

That, combined with the fact that banner ads are almost always in the same place near the top or edge of the page, means that they are very easy to ignore. Ron makes his point in the restaurant where we're having lunch by asking me if, without looking, I could tell him anything about the art on the wall on my left. I remembered that they were large and dark. That was about it.

"If you glanced at those paintings as we sat down, somewhere in your mind you registered that they weren't particularly interesting to you. So from then on, you could ignore that whole wall. If you're at all anti-commercial or anti-capitalistic or anti-hype or just busy looking for something in particular on the Web, you're going to be able to ignore those rectangular shapes. from the very beginning. There are dozens of techniques one must use to break through the clutter. Our tests prove that attention grabbing alone can yield as much as a three times increase in clickthrough rate."

Fundamental Desires

When Ron starts talking about what kind of copy belongs in an ad, it doesn't matter if it's print or online, you'll tend to forget about your lunch and your soup will get cold. He's very energized by the whole thing and it's infectious. His first premise is to find a fundamental desire that is satisfied by your product or service, or a disaster that it can be used to avoid. Fundamental issues are those things that all of us relate to, beginning with Maslow's Hierarchy of Needs and including love, wealth, security, learning, beauty, and the like. The disasters are the loss of those desires. Fear of losing your spouse, your job, your self esteem.

Find that central goodness in your offering and a whole new way to describe what you're selling falls out of it. Key ideas that can be used in ads, brochures, packaging, banners, and so on.

When Ron goes to work with a client, he starts with the basic, underlying truth or the value of the product as perceived by the "rational evangelist" customers—not the company. The company may know about making and selling, but those customers know about buying and using. They know why they bought and why it produced a breakthrough or avoided a disaster.

If your customers maintain that your main claim to fame is that your product works faster, you can build on that central theme to create a brand identity and each of your subsequent advertising instruments. If they think what you really offer is furnishing a commodity at a low price, then you have a different set of premises to work with. If your customers say your product tastes, smells, cleans, lubricates, sounds, feels, illuminates better, you have a different peg to hang your hat on. But if you try to convince the public that your product is faster, cheaper, *and* better, you have your work cut out for you.

Finding the issues that make up the breakthroughs and disasters is far from enough—if you only express them in abstract concepts. The key, Ron says, is getting highly evocative, to tap those fundamental human desires. "So, the real persuasion power is not in abstract benefits, but finding the more specific way in which they change the experience of one's work life, and create a breakthrough or disaster that matters. For example, for a subhead in an ad, don't use: 'The fastest Software in its class.' Not even: 'Software that will let you finish the project in half the time.' Instead, use: 'What happens to your company's competitive position, and your career, if you start finishing projects in half the time it takes other people?'"

Grabbers and Qualms

Grabbers are compelling. They are turn-ons. Qualms are the opposite. "Great grabbers capture the attention of your target audience and compel them to continue reading, or to click to find out more," Ron explains. "They break through the reader's lack of focus and urgency about the subject and drive them to learn more."

The best banners make the best headlines for a full-page ad, but the reverse isn't necessarily true. Clicking a banner is a far more committed act than glancing at the opening paragraph or scanning the subheads on a page. Clicking means you see something so promising, something that makes you so curious that you feel compelled to go off the engrossing path you're on, and take the side trip.

Richards stands by four major imperatives when creating banners. These are the things that make all the difference in the "What of it?" battle for attention:

1. Announce a news story, signal a hot issue or disaster, and offer a breakthrough or extraordinary results.
2. Reset the standard that the buyer should expect, demonstrate uniqueness, or make an offer or guarantee.
3. Offer the gift of critical learning.
4. Create urgency.

Use evocative language to make the surfer create a mental picture. Describe your product in such a way that the competition must play at a disadvantage on your field. You have to move people from the "I don't care" stage through the "Gee, that's interesting" stage and into the "Wow, I need to learn more about this right away!" stage. If you're really good, says Ron, you can move them all the way to "I've got to tell my family/friends/colleagues!"

Richards always shoots for the goal of "resetting the standard, and disqualifying all competitors."

These are things Richards has proven work in print and is now proving also work on the Web. But if he has one overarching personal characteristic, it's curiosity. What is different about Web advertising? What really makes the biggest differences in click rates? And why are the results, such as those shown in the next chapter (Chapter 8, "Real life Stories: The Good, the Bad, and the Unexplainable"), still so unobvious?

I've watched Richards turn out success after success by amending something the rest of us would gloss over. Publishers and advertisers are well advised to use his ideas, and adopt his experimental approach to increasing clicks. ●

Real Life Stories:
The Good, the Bad,
and the Unexplainable

To really get a handle on banners and the like, the best thing to do is look at a bunch of them. Look at bad ones. Look at good ones. Look at weird ones. It's also helpful if during all this looking, you know if you are looking at successful ones.

A small but growing number of people have published their response numbers. In light of everything you've read so far, you'd think it would be easy to look at two banners and select the one that worked better. If it were that easy, you wouldn't be looking in books to help explain it, you'd just be doing it.

So, here are a slew of examples from near and far, from the great, the near-great, and the great unwashed. There are comparisons, testimonials, a site that shows what they like, and a database of banners to sift through. I present you with what information there is (which is scant) and leave you to wonder at the success, the failure, and the imaginations of the people who created each banner and each campaign. ■

WhitePalm Four Corners Shows a Wide Range

Sandwiched between software that lets you print your picture on your label and cartoons for real estate publications on the White Palm Web site (**www.whitepalm.com**) is a healthy amount of information about banner ad performance.

Whitepalm's Four Corners offers a plethora of banner examples, including those that just broke through the 1% clickthrough barrier (**http://www.whitepalm.com/fourcorners/ctrcomp80.shtml**) See Figures 8.1 through Figure 8.3) to get an idea of what not to do.

Four Corners' winners stayed below the 8% clickthrough ceiling. Considering, however, that they were being displayed on the LinkExchange network for free, and the targeting is not optimal, they can still be held up as examples of what works and what doesn't.

On the White Palm Best CTRs Of All Time page (**www.whitepalm.com/fourcorners/bestbanners.shtml**), they point you to The Best CTRs For Non-Picture Sites (see Figure 8.4) and The Best CTRs For Picture Sites (see Figure 8.5), offering more examples on who got how many clicks.

Five Million Banner Impressions a Day

When you serve as many banners as LinkExchange, you start to keep track of what works. LinkExchange is kind enough to share what they've learned by showing example banners and their clickthrough results (**www.linkexchange.com/members/banners.html**) (see Figure 8.6).

How much of a difference can a banner make in terms of click-thru ratios?

Plenty!

The banner ads below were shown over 16,000 times each, and they all advertise the same thing: our service, the LinkExchange advertising network. Can you guess which banner has the best click-thru ratio? Which one has the worst? How much more effective do you think the best banner is?

The answers may surprise you....

The sober mind, filled with common sense and years of experience in other marketing media, might look at this bunch of banners and come up with the following thoughts…

The first banner, "You're one click away from the COOLEST thing," is banking on curiosity. There is no benefit stated beyond the promise of something cool. This would probably not score very high.

The next one, offering more hits for free, has a hint of hype about it. "Do you want more hits for only $10" lets you know it's a serious offer and not a scam, but the colors make it very hard to read. "100's Of Sites" is also hard to read.

My vote is on the flags. The graphics are colorful, recognizable, and professional. They carry the weight of the nations for which they stand. The text is clear and the action word "Linked" looks like a link. The visual backing of the word greatly increases its power.

Now, it's time for the truth.

FIG. 8.1

Four Corners' hall of shame.

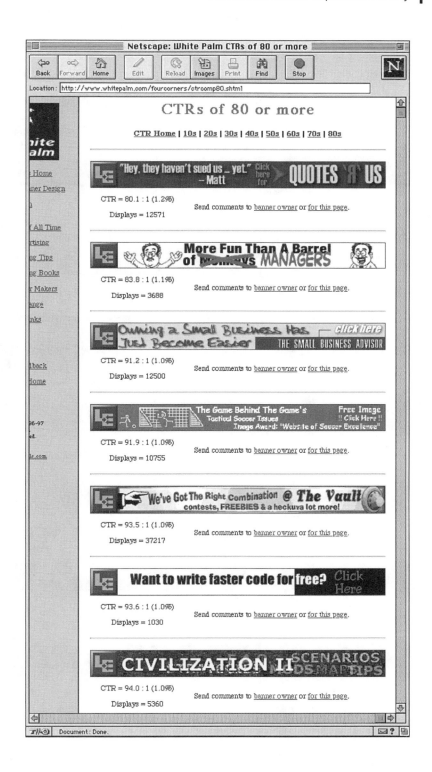

FIG. 8.2
Four Corners shows the middle of the road.

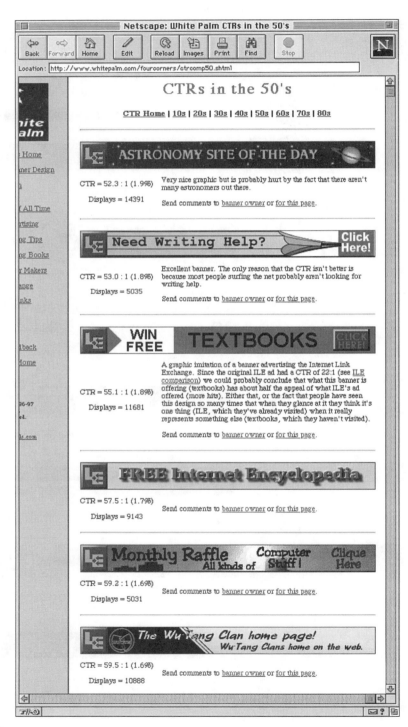

FIG. 8.3
Four Corners' winners.

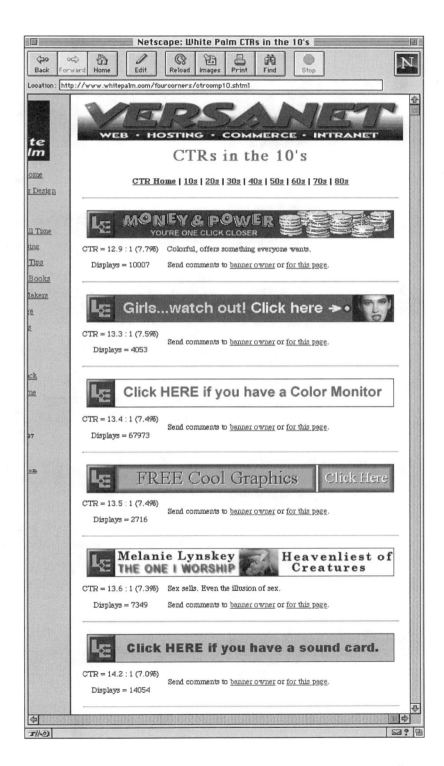

FIG. 8.4
Here are some of the best clickthrough rates for non-picture sites.

FIG. 8.5
Here are some of the best clickthroughs for sites selling pictures.

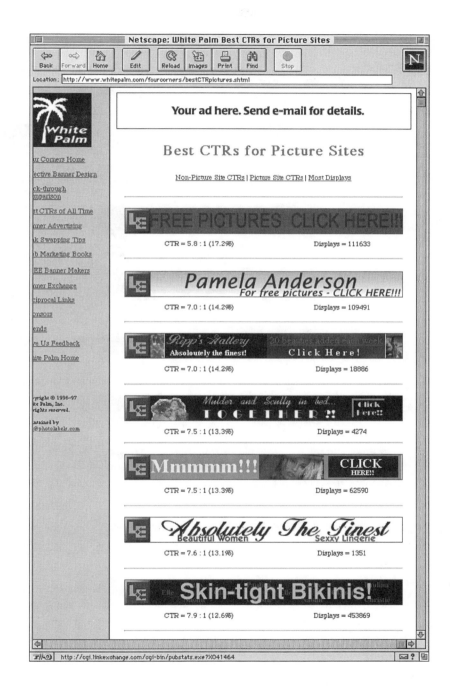

FIG. 8.6
LinkExchange tests your ability to spot the winner.

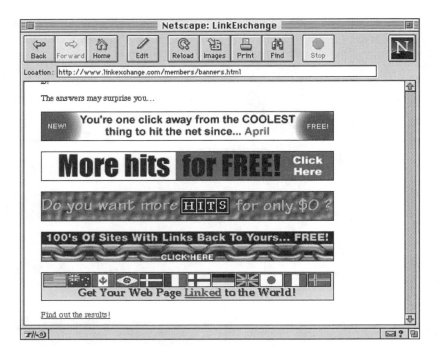

With my opinions worn proudly on my sleeve, I see that my favorite banner is not the choice of the public. Indeed, my favorite only beat out the worst by 5%, while the winner, "More hits for Free!" beat out the worst by 58%.

Why? Brighter colors? Fewer words? People thought they could get free CDs? Or was it the placement on the page, the page itself, the time of day, or a multi-million dollar television campaign run at the same time? There are a lot of factors to consider when trying to guess what will make more people click.

Improving on the Best

LinkExchange took the next step in tweaking the best banner to see how it could improve the results.

On the same page as the banners (see Figure 8.7 through Figure 8.9), LinkExchange admits it's a bit of a mystery. But they did prove a point. A very important point. "The point of this was to show that it is important to test out different banners before going out and spending thousands of dollars on banner advertising."

Crowing Reports

If you want to know who's doing the right things and getting the right responses, it's just a matter of asking the agencies and the networks, rather than the advertisers. Advertisers don't know if their results are good, bad, or indifferent compared to the rest. If the advertisers feel the results are good, then they want to hang on to their competitive advantage, and keep mum. If the results aren't so good, they like to keep it to themselves. So, it's up to the vendors to convince them that they have a good story to tell. First stop—DoubleClick.

FIG. 8.7
Look at the answers to
see how well you
guessed.

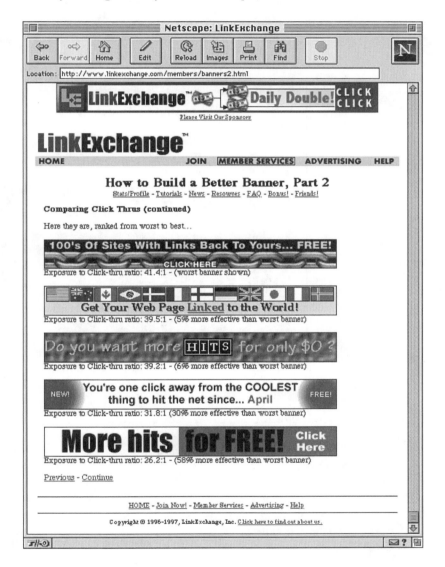

Over 1.5 Billion Served

DoubleClick set out to help brand Heineken as hip and sophisticated by generating traffic to the Heineken site and delivering a Heineken Valentine's Day E-Card. They offer up this report from **www.doubleclick.net/nf/general/casesset.htm**:

FIG. 8.8

Once you know what works best, it's time to try to improve on it.

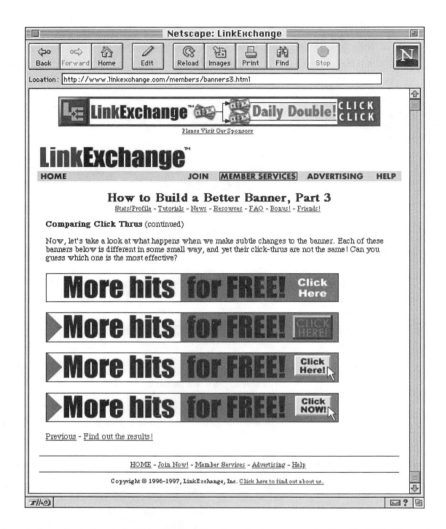

Campaign Description: An animated ad (with a beating heart) ran across the DoubleClick Network the week before Valentines' Day to drive people to Heineken's site which contains virtual bars, jazz music, and chat rooms. To avoid underage drinkers, DoubleClick's DART technology excluded all users from the .edu domain (students), and was only on sites that have a primarily adult audience.

Results: 15,000 downloads of the Heineken Valentine's Day E-Card in only one week's time. 1,010,510 banners were delivered during the one week run. 50% increase in entries to Heineken Quest game which appeared on the entry form of the Valentine's Day E-Card. Since you can play the game for a month, the site generated many repeat visitors. 8.77% click-through rate from the 321,408 unique users who saw the ad. "The Valentine's campaign was a complete success. We have been able to take the numbers from this campaign and use them to plan our future online campaigns. It was also nice to work with a sales staff and customer support group that was so helpful with such great service," Dirk Willem, Heineken Corporate Marketing Client Comments.

FIG. 8.9
LinkExchange increased the draw by another 26%.

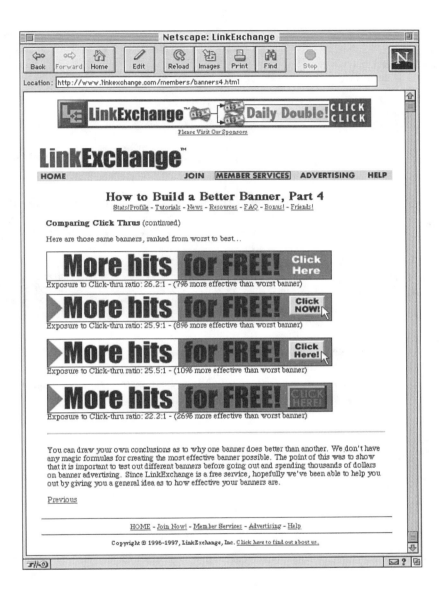

SiteSpecific

Recently Acquired by the CKS Group, SiteSpecific (**www.sitespecific.com**) has been responsible for more than the normal number of breakthrough type advertising campaigns.

One campaign for The Mining Company started with an animated banner. This series of figures (see Figure 8.10 through Figure 8.13) shows them interrupting themselves to get your attention.

FIG. 8.10

SiteSpecific created this animation for The Mining Company #1.

FIG. 8.11

The Mining Company #2.

FIG. 8.12

The Mining Company #3.

FIG. 8.13

The Mining Company #4.

That animation drew people to a bridge page (see Figure 8.14), rather than the company's home page. This is a practice strongly recommended to one and all. If somebody goes to the trouble, makes the investment of time in clicking your banner, you stand to lose a great number of them unless you use a bridge page. Don't make them start at index.html and try to find the information you referred to in your banner. Instead, take them to a page that deals directly with the banner content.

Was it successful? Did it work?

According to the SiteSpecific case study (**www.sitespecific.com/Site/CaseStudies/Brand/Mining/index.html**): "The goal: Launch the Mining Company brand to online consumers and drive traffic to the Mining Company network. Online advertising is coordinated with offline print, outdoor, and radio campaign.

"The result: In week one of the campaign (ending 4/27), 60% of all Mining Company page views were directly generated by SiteSpecific's advertising."

Not bad.

SiteSpecific was also responsible for one of the most interesting ad campaigns on the Web to date, which went well beyond banners and home pages. It included direct participation by the site on which the banner appeared. It included a world famous cartoon character. It lead the clicker on a wild chase through cyberspace. It taught clickers how to use a search engine while they were trying to win a vacation for two. It was the Yahoo! "Missing Y" campaign (see Figure 8.15 through Figure 8.18).

FIG. 8.14
SiteSpecific wisely used a bridge page for The Mining Company's banner campaign.

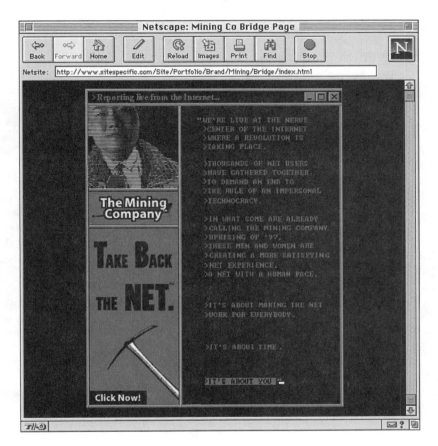

Pizza Eaters Delivered to Pizza Hut

The Domino's Web site is a destination. The Pizza Hut site (**www.pizzahut.com**) is owned by one of Pizza Hut's franchisers. Pizza Hut realized it didn't want to be in the publishing business. It wanted to sell pizza. It doesn't want to produce television programs, it just wants to advertise. On the Web, that means paying for advertising instead of creating the ultimate pizza-consumer's Web site.

Given its largest identifiable block of consumers and its television and print campaigns, Pizza Hut opted to place its eggs in the sports basket. It intended to keep its message the same across all media for branding purposes, but the jocks are its target. Visitors to the ESPN SportsZone are the object of the Hut's attention. Sports buffs. Men. Younger ones. Prone to consuming mass quantities of pizza.

They started by scattering banners around the SportsZone. With no corporate Pizza Hut Web site to take people to, they didn't even want a demi-site. Instead, they opted for a single page (see Figure 8.19). Check out the newest pizza and then get right back to sports.

FIG. 8.15
The Yahoo! Home page
had been vandalized!

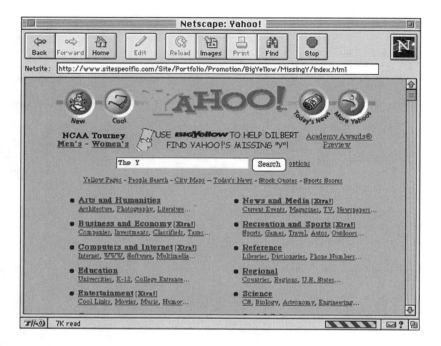

Then they took the gloves off with games like Pigskin Pick'em. They unleashed the marketing machine. Armed with the names and e-mail addresses of 327,000 gamers, Pizza Hut braved the waters and sent a message. Unsolicited? Yes. Promotional? Yes. But it came with a reward:

Pizza Hut thanks you for playing our sponsored games on ESPN SportsZone during the past year. As a reward, we're extending to you a special offer to try our new pizzas.

The message contained the address of another single page that offered a coupon for the totally new pizza as seen on TV, in the newspapers, and online. The results?

Starwave, which runs the ESPN SportsZone, did the production and maintenance of the banners, pages, and games based on the creative work of BBDO, one of the world's top ad agencies. Starwave reported 14.4% of the e-mail recipients went to the coupon page within three days. Almost 19,000 people filled out a form saying they wanted more offers sent to them for pizza. That's a 5.75% positive action response in three days.

After ten days the numbers had grown to 79,000—24% of people who received an e-mail had ventured to the coupon page. That was triple the surfers that were enticed by the banners. The entire campaign was estimated at $500,000 per year, all inclusive. Did they sell pizza? Too soon to tell. Did they let a lot of people know—really know—they had a new pizza to offer?
You bet.

FIG. 8.16

As Dilbert, it's up to you to save the day—or just the "Y."

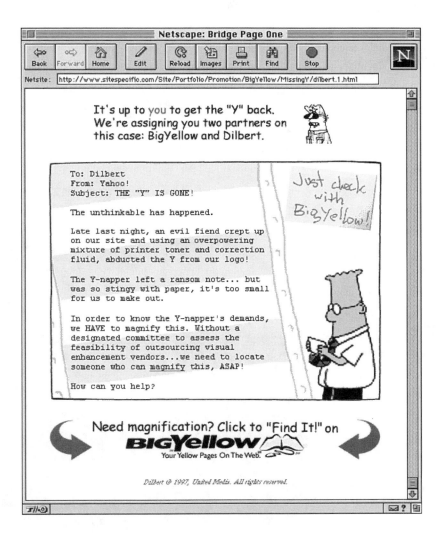

Scope Out the Competition

There are two sites well worth a visit for a look at a lot of banners all at once. They don't show statistics on the number of clicks, but they do offer a good look at what's out there.

The first one was mentioned before in Chapter 3, "The Buck Spangled Banner": The Microscope (**www.pscentral.com**). Dedicated to keeping an eye on the best ads, this weekly update is a must-see. This site does a fine job of keeping abreast for you. Take a look at Figure 8.20.

When animated GIF banners hit the scene in early 1996, Rich Paschall started noticing a drastic improvement in the quality of Web ads. People seemed to be putting more thought and effort into creating the banners. The ads got more creative. Some were even quite entertaining. Paschall spotted an opportunity. He told me about it in an e-mail in March, 1997:

FIG. 8.17
Dogbert shows how to track the thief.

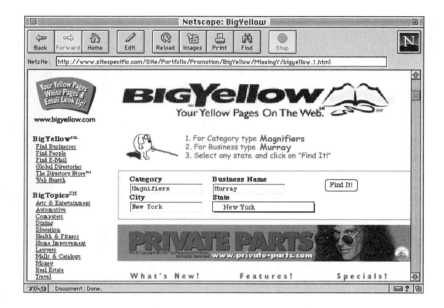

FIG. 8.18
The results of the search lead to a clue.

I thought it might make an interesting subject for a web site: a zine that singled out the best ads on the web. I searched the web to see if the idea was being done by someone else, and, much to my surprise, it wasn't. So, in September of 1996 I posted the first issue...

FIG. 8.19

Pizza Hut offered one page of information, instead of a whole site.

My biggest fear and concern about the future of the site has always been the supply of creatively driven banners on the web. It can take hours and hours of surfing just to find something above average. During the first three months we only had one submitted ad that was worthy of posting on the page. But things have improved greatly over the past two or three months. I would say that half of the ads on Microscope are the result of submissions. The other half we go out and find.

The second site worth a visit is hosted in France. But don't worry, it's bilingual. ZAW (**www.zaw.tm.fr/intro.html**) touts itself as The Only Database of Web Advertising Banners. Take a look at it in Figure 8.21.

FIG. 8.20
The Microscope should be on your list of sites to visit weekly.

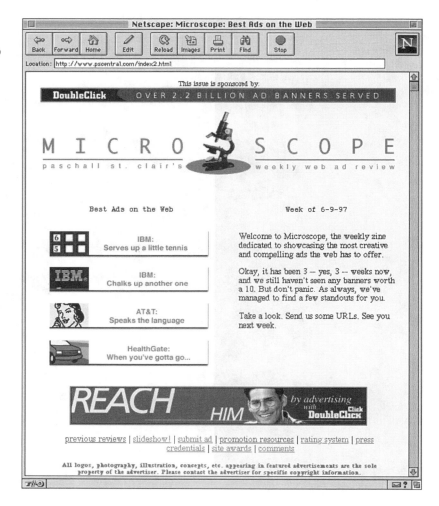

This site is handy because it offers a chance to review banners by subject:

Food

Online

Automobile

Divers

Loisirs

Compute

Services

Shopping

Frenchy

World

Food

Okay, so it's almost bilingual. Nevertheless, it is one-stop shopping for when you want to see a lot of ads at once. Sure beats hitting the Reload button all day.

FIG. 8.21
The French ZAW
database of banners
is worth a look.

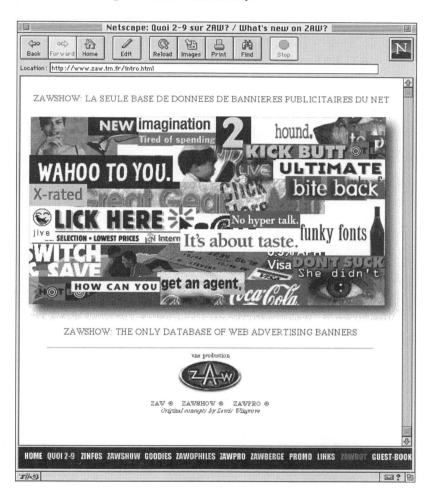

I'm Not Sure but I'll Click It when I See It

Judging your own banner efforts based on the campaigns shown here may make sense and it may not. Your banners may be intended for different goals.

But as hard as it is to know what makes people click, the point LinkExchange made is well worth repeating: "It is important to test out different banners before going out and spending thousands of dollars on banner advertising."

The Internet is one of the most forgiving places to try ads. Unless, of course, you're spamming newsgroups and sending unsolicited e-mail. In those cases, you're just as likely to find a dead squirrel in your shorts as you are to get somebody to answer your ad. The forgiveness on the Net relates to the lack of the same on television. The costs of production and testing are astronomical compared to a trial balloon on the Web.

Now all that's left is getting out there and giving it a shot. ●

CHAPTER 9

Creating a Web Advertising Strategy

That's it. That's all there is to know. Simple, right? Ready to jump right in and take control? Well, if you're feeling a little lightheaded, it's no surprise. Advertising on the Web is just like anywhere else, only different. You're going to set different goals and make different decisions and use different procedures. Maybe this chapter can help a bit.

This chapter is not intended to be a blueprint or a cookbook. It just has a few things you need to think about and a suggested order in which to do your thinking. Real life never lets you plan something from start to finish and then calmly and coolly execute your plan.

While sitting in a café in Berlin, waiting out a rain storm we simply had not planned for, Rob Raisch, the original holder of the internet.com domain, told me that there are certain benefits to getting older and wiser. One of them was recognizing that plans, proposals, blueprints, and designs were always works in progress. There's no way you can expect your expectations to be met with anything but surprise and adjustment.

If you follow the advice here, you may be better off, but you will not necessarily succeed. That takes guile, guts, flexibility, and a good eye for taking advantage when you can and backing off when you can't. ■

Tips for Any Project

There are some things you need to do for any large undertaking because they're necessary. No matter how many times you go to the airport, you still need to make sure everything is packed and that you have your tickets. Forget just once and you're toast. So here's a little common sense before you head off without your toothbrush.

Get Management Support

The best laid plans of mice and men often go astray. One of the main reasons is that mice and men are generally happy with a lukewarm nod from the powers that be, rather than a fully considered plan, before rushing into things.

My wife has a theory about why men don't prepare as well as women. She says men use their lack of preparation as a combination of competitive prowess and built-in excuse. If they win, they can gloat that they did it without even bothering to properly prepare. They can feel the rush of self assurance that they have what it takes. If they lose, well, they hadn't really taken the time to prepare—they weren't trying all that hard anyway.

My theory is that every seven-year-old boy has learned that if you ask Mom for a cookie you might not get one. It might be too close to dinner. She might be on the phone. She might have just given you one five minutes ago. It's better to just go take one. Later in life men learn how to say, "It's easier to get forgiveness than permission." Same thing.

The idea here is not that you need to get all of your ducks in a row and have your boss, and his boss, and her boss approve every detail. The idea is to get somebody sufficiently near the top of the ladder to fall in love with the concept, the approach, and the intention. You're after support from above.

Management wisdom tells us to tell our staff what to do, but not how to do it. They'll figure it out on their own. Their way will be the best way for them. It might even be the best way for anybody. If it's not, it's better to reassign a few people than stick our noses into the details and really screw things up. We are managers, not parents.

So, when going up the food chain to the folks who have a firm hold on the budgets, the aim is to get them hooked on the what, not deep into the details of how. That's your job. If you can hook them on the what, then they are much more willing to tolerate the occasional setback. They will allow for a little on-the-job learning. In other words, they won't pull the plug out from under you at the drop of a clickthrough rate.

So, here is the Jim Sterne method of convincing upper management that you deserve their unwavering support and continued funding: Quote The Experts, Hire A Consultant, Round Up The Troops, enjoy a Breakfast Of Champions.

Quote the Experts   Go grab the latest Jupiter report that shows how fast Web banner spending is growing. Visit the banner broker and banner network sites and quote their testimonials. Show the big dogs at your company just how much Bill Gates is spending on online advertising and imply that they better start following the leader if they ever expect to get invited to William Buffett's ranch.

Internet advertising has more potential to offer more return on effort and return on the dollar than any other marketing medium to date. It opens the doors to electronic commerce and electronic relationships with thousands upon thousands of customers with never before imagined accuracy and personal attention.

Jim Sterne, Target Marketing of Santa Barbara

The idea is to get them excited.

On the other hand, if you don't believe that statement, you may not be the right one for this job. The fact is that we have just located the surface and just discovered that we have fingernails at the same time. It's up to you to start scratching.

Hire a Consultant   You know the definition of an expert, don't you? It's somebody who has to get on an airplane to come to a meeting. I don't have any clients in Santa Barbara because I'm a local boy. "He can't know any more than we do, he's from around here!"

So go get somebody who won't fill upper-management full of unobtainable dreams, but also won't be afraid to get in their faces and tell them it's time to get with the program. Find a consultant who will lay it on the line and who doesn't have to worry about saying what the brass wants to hear in order to keep his or her job.

Round up the Troops   Support the experts from afar you've found with a few from inside. Locate the corporate visionary. Maybe it's the Chief Scientist or that guy with no real title who is forever going out to lunch with the CEO, meeting with important visitors, and talking to the press. Those types are deep thinkers and have top management's ear. The bosses listen to these highly educated, finger-on-the-pulse people. That's why they were hired—to think deep thoughts.

These deep thinkers are also very interested in new things. You call up and tell some deep thinkers you'd like to run some ideas about Internet advertising by them and they might even offer to pay for lunch. To these people, this stuff is fun!

Find those among the middle managers who just aren't sure. These are the mugwumps who need a little extra convincing. They're important to get to before going all the way upstairs because a momentary, "Gosh, I'm not sure" in the elevator from more than two of these people sounds, to all the world, like a consensus to the big cheeses.

Then, step-by-step, you build your powerbase. It's the grass roots approach. Figure out what motivates each blade of grass and explain how this project can provide them with what they need. Then, when the winds of change start to blow, they'll stand tall together and be bolstered by the company they keep.

Machiavellian?

You do want this project to get a long green light, don't you?

Breakfast of Champions   Now it's time to call a meeting with the big dogs. No, not a formal, board room, too-many-PowerPoint-slides-and-cold-coffee meeting. A *breakfast* meeting.

Why breakfast? Because the powers that be are rested in the morning, they are up, they are ready to take another stab at this game they're playing called business. They're sharp. They're attentive. They're not full of a thousand slings and arrows of outrageous fortune that usually hit them between the eyes before 10:30 a.m.

Feed them well. Feed them croissants with honey. Feed them visions of grandeur. Feed them strong coffee. Feed them a little competitive angst. For dessert, show them how they will be seen as the visionaries they truly are. Go ahead, lay it on just a little.

Then remind them that visionaries march in where more common captains of industry fear to tread. The results may not be instant; there are no guarantees in this life. But the spoils will go to other winners if they don't let their remarkable insight and keen astuteness shine forth. They stand not only to reap the rewards of electronic promotion, but will be seen as fearless guides into a brave new world!

Then go wash your mouth out with soap.

Assemble the Team

If you could do it all yourself, it would be a different story. But you can't. There are too many responsibilities and to much to do and not enough time to do it. Like most projects, the trick is getting the right people with the right skills working together. The trick is getting them to work together well. More about the necessary skills later, when it's time to hand out the responsibilities.

For now, gather the people in your immediate area who will be working with you. Then, reach out to other departments with whom you are not used to working. Get to know your legal people a little better; their input will be important.

Find out who the movers and shakers are in your information technology department. Get them to participate a bit in the brainstorming phase. That way they'll be more receptive when you need their help down the line.

Reach out beyond the walls of your company and create a board of advisors. People like being asked for their opinion and if you gather a diverse group, you are certain to have the power of the richly divergent feedback you need when you get puzzled. And you will get puzzled.

Nobody has been doing this for years and years. We don't have a river of MBAs flowing out of our universities who have been pouring over decades of case histories and gigabytes of statistical samples. We have some people who have tried a few things. You're going to have to be one of those who tries things. You're going to have to make some of it up as you go along. For that, it's nice to have a variety of minds off of which you can bounce ideas.

Here's a short list of the types of people you need:

- Marketing managers who have a perspective on corporate goals
- Business line managers whose promotional budgets will pay for it

- Product marketing managers who know what audience to target
- Web marketing connoisseurs who know what the options are
- Media planners who can find and negotiate with the right sites
- Technology savants who can tell you what's feasible and what's not
- Creative types who can breath life into a campaign
- Art directors who know their way around a Windows monitor
- Bean-counters who can track and adjust based on numerical success
- Public relations mouthpieces to tell the world what a visionary your boss is
- Legal eagles to watch your backside
- Science fiction writers who can look into the future

If you have all those people working for you already, you're off to a good start and I'd like to know where you work; it's a rare company. You'll simply have to mold that crew into a well-oiled machine that can move like lightning, turn 180 degrees on a moment's notice, and stop on a dime if need be. Pick up a few books on personal motivation and practice that look in the mirror that says, "I really sympathize with your dilemma, but if you don't figure it out yourself I'll find somebody who will."

If you don't have dozens of people at your beck and call, you need to go out into the world and find them. If you're like the rest of us, it's often easier to get project and expense funding out of the powers that be than it is to get additional headcount. Trying to add a bunch of people to your staff is a nice way to build an empire, but it's no way to get the job done. The wisest move may be to call on some people who have already been in your position, people who have been there and done that—and find out what outside firms they're working with.

You saw a banner you liked? Call 'em up and see if you click. You read about a one-shot promotion that brought in oodles of customers? Take the responsible party to lunch and grill them. You read an interview with somebody that is doing it right? Start exchanging e-mail.

Having a clear idea of what you want to accomplish with this whole Web advertising thing becomes important here. If your corporate culture thrives on suspicion and power struggles and closed doors, it would be best not to let that trash roll downhill. Create your own project culture and give your team the benefit of a stated goal, a clarity of purpose, and a feeling of responsibility. Make it crystal-clear what the goals are, what their responsibilities will be, and how success will be measured and let them get to work.

Or you could threaten them with pink slips.

Get Educated

This book is a good start. You have the right idea. But there are two things that are not in this book. They can't be. The first is the latest information about what the Web advertising industry is up to and the other is anything about what your industry is up to.

Take a few days to surf the Web looking for reports, articles, newsgroup postings, and list discussions that might give you some insight into what is passing for Web advertising right now, as you're reading this. Appendix B, "Advertising Resources on the Web," can give you some ideas about where to look, but the best practice you can pick up is to ask people questions.

- What periodicals do you read?
- What lists do you subscribe to?
- Who do you think is doing an outstanding job?
- What have you heard?
- What do you like?
- If you could do it all over again, what would you do differently?

The best place to find a whole bunch of people who know a whole bunch about this stuff is by going to the conferences. There are lots to choose from: Internet World, Internet Expo, Web Advertising, and more, too numerous to mention.

Descend on the speakers you like and pick up some free consulting on the spot. It always surprises me when thousands of people come to hear a few experts speak on a subject and then only a handful are brave enough to talk to the presenters after the presentations. I have news for you, they're just people, too, and they love having folks ask them questions.

Be a sponge about what's going on in the online world and then do exactly the same in your particular industry. Who is spending money in your business? Who is hiring? Who is touting their latest campaign?

One of the best sources for industry-specific information like this is the trade press in your business sector. No, not just reading them, but calling up the writers and talking to them. As any PR professional knows, these people are story eating machines. They are desperate for good, solid information they can turn into copy and surround by display ads. It's their business. But what people tend to forget is that they are also a font of knowledge. Editors (reports and writers) often end up in the ranks of the industry analysts because they know so much. Try this one tomorrow: pick a writer you like in one of the trade journals you read and invite him or her to lunch.

No, you don't want to pitch them a story. No, you don't want to pre-announce some earth-shattering new product. You want their opinion and their advice and you want to feed them. Flattery and food is a fabulous combination. Now, if you do happen to have a tidbit of gossip, a rumor overheard in the locker room, or a heads up on a new political battle about to hit the streets, your lunch date is a shoo-in.

The other way to keep up on what's happening in your sector is to watch your competitors like a hawk.

Heed the Competition

Is your competition advertising online? On which sites? How much are they spending? Are their campaigns tied tightly into the rest of their marketing, or are they just running hit and miss spots? Are they hiring electronic marketing and advertising people? Are they switching agencies?

Without a firm grasp of what they are up to, it would be foolish to jump into anything. Would you float an ad through a dozen magazines without looking to see how your competitors are positioning their products? Nope.

This problem becomes more insidious on the Web because the medium is so new. It's so hard to know what to track. In print, you can look at the style of the ads. Same on the Web. In print, you can look at the type of language used to entice people. Same on the Web. In print, you can count the number of pages of advertising they buy. Same on the Web.

But the Internet starts taking on a different look when the business models change on a daily basis. Is it a banner or is it an interstitial page? Is it a simple impression deal or is it a pay-per-clickthrough contract? Is it a simple banner or is it a pointer to a game? Is it an ad or is it content?

Is the opposition just placing banners or are they creating content as well? Are you competing against simple banner ads, or animated, 3-D, order-taking Java applets? Or entire Web sites? Have they mounted a Dalmatian-spot background campaign? Are they working hand-in-glove with content sites to sponsor sections? Are they giving away charter memberships to some buying club? Are they offering software downloads of an application that make it easier to buy their products?

Get a handle on how high the bar has been raised by others so you know how high you have to jump just to get started.

But before you get started, it's really worth your time to sit down and figure out why you want to jump. What is it you're trying to get out of this Internet-based promotion? Just what are you trying to accomplish?

Determine Your Goals

Getting started means knowing where you're going.

To start, it helps to know what the options are. Essentially, there are two. You can make a name for a company and forever tie it to the Internet in the minds of the public by taking the branding path, or you can do whatever it takes to get people to respond.

So here are your choices:

> Branding
>
> Direct Response

The rest of your time will be spent differently, depending on which selection you make. To whom you advertise, where you buy banner space, and whether you use banners at all are decided after you know your general goal.

Which of these you pick is based on your current corporate/division/department/product line goals. This is the place where you need to be well in synch with the people holding the purse strings. If they balk, you'll be able to point to the corporate mission statement, the last memo from headquarters, or the major bullet points from the briefing they gave last Wednesday.

Your selection is also based on your own objectives. Think for a minute about what you are trying to accomplish for yourself. Your personal goals are an important part of the mix here. Be your goals financial, political, career, or personal, if you don't have a stake in this effort, its chances of success are severely compromised. If the only goal you can come up with for this project is "Because the boss told me to," you need to go back to the boss and start over. Find out why it's important and what it can mean to the company and to you.

Same for the people who will be working with you. Make sure that you know your team well enough to understand their hopes and dreams. Figure out a way to accommodate them and they'll bend over backward to deliver.

Promote the Brand

Our goal is to (select all that apply):

Increase awareness about the company

Increase awareness about our product, _____.

Change the impression of our company from _____ to _____.

Change the impression of our product from _____ to _____.

Gain market share from (competitor) _____.

Get written up in the press.

Who says you can't have big goals?

Just remember that the more choices you check above, the more you'll be torn trying to satisfy multiple masters. Clear and concise goals are always the best. They're easy to explain, easy to administrate, and easy to measure.

Get a Response

Site Specific wanted to get a lot of clickthroughs with the "Do It In The Dark" banner for 3M. They succeeded. But is that what 3M really wanted? A lot of clicks? You can achieve that with a banner that says, "Answer this one question survey and we'll send you $500," but it does nothing for sales.

Michael Skaff runs a Web site that helps small businesses. He calls it "Virtual Human Resources." Skaff spent a healthy chunk of change to put a banner up in the "Web Releases" section of Yahoo!. That's where announcements of new Web sites get listed and a banner there can attract a lot of attention. Skaff says it did. In one week they got 22,000 clickthroughs. He was thrilled. But then he noticed that there were no sales. Not one. He was no longer thrilled. He raised awareness. He promoted his brand. But he didn't achieve his goal.

Levi Strauss put up banners that weren't intended to make sales. They were intended to get people to play a game. They wanted a response, but it was for branding purposes only.

So what sort of response are you looking for?

We want people to…

> Come to our site so they know we're on the Web.
>
> Come to our site and learn about our products.
>
> Fill out a survey so we can do some market research.
>
> Sign up on our mailing list.
>
> Buy something.
>
> Write a testimonial.
>
> Learn how to use our product.

One of the best Web promotions I've ever seen was another Site Specific production, this time for Big Yellow (**www.bigyellow.com**). It was a banner placed on Yahoo! with a major twist. For a couple of weeks in March, 1997, the letter "Y" in Yahoo! was a faint outline. It was "missing." Having licensed Scott Adams' Dilbert and Dogbert cartoon characters, the banner enticed the surfer to click now, in an effort to help our hapless friends find the missing consonant/some-time-vowel.

That was cute, and the fact that Dilbert is truly the iconic character of the Internet helped a lot. The licensing was a solid success, but the best was yet to come. A click brought you to a full page describing the heinous crime. Somebody had stolen the Y. It went on to describe the method for following the clues. You had to "click here" to get to Big Yellow, a yellow-pages-on-the-Web, where you could enter the clues Dogbert provided and see what Big Yellow came up with by way of a link. The links lead you, as a virtual detective, from site to site and finally back to My Yahoo!, where you could register to win a vacation for two.

What were the goals? One was to get more people registered in My Yahoo!. That paid off nicely. But the other goal was to teach people how to use Big Yellow. After following three clues through the Big Yellow search engine, players were well-versed in its purpose, capabilities, and use. A major win all around.

So do limit your thinking when you're dreaming up goals. Before you start worrying about where you're going to advertise and what the creative should look like, stretch your mind to include the kind of goals you just can't get through direct mail and telemarketing.

Select a Target

Now that you know what you want people to do, it's time to decide who you want to bend to your will. That's nice that you have a shiny new cannon that you can use to blow giant holes in the competition, but it won't do you a lick of good unless you know which way to aim it. Then it would be a significant help if you could fine tune it a bit. Let's see if you can't hone it down from a cannon to a shotgun, and then, from a shotgun to a rifle. The rifle you end up with will be very powerful and capable of hitting a very small target at a very great distance. If you can afford a nuclear device, hey, go for it, but if you want to make every shot count, use a rifle and target with precision.

Housewives? Mothers? Business travelers? People who like French food? Frequent fliers? SOHO owners with copy machines? Elderly shut-ins with pets? Children between four and seven-years-old? (Don't laugh, they're out there in huge numbers and they take to the Internet like ducks to water.) The ability to slice and dice your audience is unlike any other medium. Choose them wisely.

Aside from making every ad dollar more effective, targeting is absolutely necessary in order to select the proper advertising methods and locations.

Select Tactics

How do you want to reach your audience? Straight banner? A Site Specific special? A promotion in cooperation with a major movie release? Combined with a scavenger hunt in Milwaukee?

Here's a quick checklist of some standard techniques to see which way you're leaning:

Newsgroup Announcement Posting

Newsgroup Discussion Participation

Creating a New Public Newsgroup

E-Mail Update Lists

E-Mail Newsletters

E-Mail Signature Block Ads

Listserver Sponsorship

List Discussion Participation

Creating a Public List

Creating a Private List

Game Sponsorship

Classified Ads

Link Trading

Link Placement

Banner Ads—Static

Banner Ads—Animated

Banner Ads—Interactive

Banner Ad Exchange

Site Sponsorship

Event Sponsorship

Content Development (your own, special site)

Interstitial Ads

Product Placement

Push Channel Sponsorship

Chat Sponsorship

Virtual World Sponsorship

Integrated Advertising Event

Something Else Altogether

Well? Are you feeling adventurous?

One of the most celebrated integrated marketing events at the beginning of 1997 was an IBM affair aimed at geophysicists. If this is your target audience, gather 'round and listen up. If not, pay close attention anyway because this is the way Internet advertising is going to be done in the future by those with the smarts to do it. That is, those not in a vacuum.

One of the many, many vertical markets IBM earmarks for special attention is the petroleum industry. A sale in this category runs between $100,000 and $250,000, so it's worth spending a little money to get their individual attention. Truth be told, it's worth a lot of money to reach these people and IBM has been known to spend $20,000 for all of the effort required for a personal sales call to one of these people. That includes the advertising, the marketing, and getting on the airplane to go visit. A tidy sum. I'm sure many a petroleum engineer would love to forgo IBM's attention in lieu of the cash.

IBM decided that because half of its target audience was using e-mail already, it was time to bring the power of the Web to bear on this market. They set up a site, they sent out direct mail offering CD-ROMs that would connect the engineers to the site, and for six months they bought specific keywords on eight search engines.

The results were good. They sent out 15,000 direct mail pieces offering the CD-ROM and 2,250 said "Yes, please." Over 550 of those CD recipients showed up at the site within two weeks. Another 500 showed up through the banners on the search engines. Another 4,000 moused over due to that all-encompassing *combination of factors*. A combination of factors is marketing speak for "we don't know." It would be safe to assume it was because this e-mail literate market place was busy spreading the word. The only thing that spreads faster than bad news on the Internet is news of a new Web site that has some valuable content.

All in all, IBM says they spent $500 per prospect compared to $20,000. That made them very happy. You can be sure it was the banner ads and the word of mouth that got the greatest bang for the buck. Proof that targeting, site selection, and combining the right elements into a marketing event can pay off far better than you're used to.

Assign Responsibilities

The team you've assembled may be the best and the brightest. On the other hand, they may be simply what's available. Or they may be that trustworthy trio of you, yourself, and that person in the mirror.

However large or small your team, there are some things that need to get done and you are the one who has to decide how to divvy up the assignments. If you have lots of help, count your blessings. If you have a hole in your project plan under the heading, "Staff," then you need some outside help.

Either way, now is the time to do the really tough assessment of what your core competencies are. To begin with, it's a corporate question. I am always astonished at bright, responsible managers who would never think to buy a printing press and get into the magazine business, think nothing of buying a server and hiring people to produce a Web site full of nifty things to attract the attention of Web surfers. The term "core competencies" seems to have fallen from their lexicon.

This issue is a personal one as well. At what are you really good? How about the people on your team? The corollary to that includes asking what do you do that's the most fun? One of the reasons you like it may be because you're good at it.

Now it's time for you to do the same sort of inventory of your team. What do they like to do? At what do they excel? What would they like to learn how to do? Tally it all up and look at the leftover tasks that still need to be done. That's the list of tasks that should be outsourced.

No, we don't know just the right ways to ensure success. We simply haven't been at it long enough. But we have been at it long enough that a lot of service companies have sprung up to help do the things that the team doesn't have the skills, desire, or time to do themselves.

In her immensely useful book, *The Internet Marketing Plan* (John Wiley & Sons, 1997), Kim Bayne is "glad to shoulder the role of devil's advocate" by offering up a wonderful list of considerations to remember when looking for help from the outside (Table 9.1). While Bayne's book is directed at those creating an entire, overall marketing plan, all of these issues are either spot-on or have a close corollary to advertising.

Table 9.1   Kim Bayne's List of Using In-House Resources for Development versus Outsourcing

For In-House Development	For Outsourcing
On-site employees are easier to manage.	Outside agencies require less supervision.
Outside agencies cost more money.	Employees have other responsibilities.
Outside agencies have no respect for budget.	Employees have no concept of cost overruns.

For In-House Development	For Outsourcing
The company doesn't have a big budget.	The agency is willing to negotiate.
Using current employees will save money.	Using outside agencies will save time.
Employee salaries and wages are already a given.	Agencies use fewer people for the same work.
Employees already know the company and products.	Outside agencies already have the skill set.
The market is full of HTML tools.	A software package doesn't make you a designer.
Employees can be trained in HTML.	Novices can make embarrassing mistakes.
In-house employees are more trustworthy.	In-house employees never meet deadlines.
Management wants us to hire and promote within.	Outside consultants can offer on-site training.
If anything goes wrong, agency is responsible.	If anything goes wrong, the employee is responsible.
If anything goes wrong, marketing is to blame.	If anything goes wrong, the agency is to blame.
Hiring a vendor requires bids and paper work.	Using an in-house employee requires staff hours.
Our last outsourcing project was a disaster.	You hired the wrong agency or consultant.
Employees respect the chain of command.	Agencies know who to talk with to get things done.
Temporary personnel services can solve this.	All the best people are employed.
Outsourcing makes the marketing staff obsolete.	Outsourcing makes the marketing staff look good.

If you do go off to find outside help, you want to interview them to see if there's a personality match. You want to look at their work to see that they have a reasonable portfolio and aren't a couple of fresh-faced graduate students. You want to satisfy yourself that they know something about the business you're in.

Most of all however, you want to check their references. And you want to check more than a few. Anybody who has been in business for more than a year can pull three names and numbers out of their Rolodex of people who will give them a glowing report. Everybody has fans.

Everybody has a booster out there. You want to talk to enough people to find out some of the less flattering things about the company you're about to entrust with your company's image and your project's budget. Check their references.

Set Standards

Standards in the world of the Internet are somewhat oxymoronic. Things move fast. But the value of company standards is manifest. With so much going on, so many choices to make, and a marketing need for consistency, standards offer a firm place to stand after a turbulent voyage. Standards can be strict or they can merely be suggestions. Either way, they offer signposts in an uncharted territory.

> The company logo should always be used in online promotions to take advantage of the large number of impressions to be purchased.
>
> The color scheme for banners should use the intersection of the Windows 95, Netscape, and Internet Explorer palettes to ensure common representation across the most common browsers.
>
> All online advertising will be approved by the legal department.
>
> Banners will be kept to the CASIE standard sizes to ensure ease of placement across multiple content sites.

These don't have to be enforced with an iron fist, but they do provide two important benefits. First, they act as the corporate common sense. They are a means of reigning in the outrageous and controlling the "great idea" that's not such a great idea at all.

Corporate standards also provide a point of reference. They act as a helping hand for the first timer who isn't sure how to stay out of trouble. They are the compendium of corporate lessons learned and passed on to subsequent generations. You are operating a "learning enterprise," aren't you? Then don't keep your lessons to yourself.

Establish Procedures

The Internet has always been a fun place to hang out. It was created for the geeks, by the geeks, and of the geeks. Then the researchers and the students got involved and immediately understood the inherent joy found in the lack of control. Anybody and everybody can publish whatever they want. There are no rules. There are numerous ways to communicate with people too numerous to fathom. You can make friends around the world and there's nobody to tell you it's illegal, immoral, or fattening. You learn your cultural lessons by getting flamed and everybody is equal in the eyes of the Net.

Then the business people discovered the Web. For a while it was all done on the side by cowboys and experimenters and visionaries in their spare time. Management didn't know about it. When management found out, they didn't understand it well enough to know what to tolerate, what to regulate, and what to terminate.

Today it's a little different. Today it's your job to make sure things go well. That means it's your job to rein in the cowboys and set up some step-by-step instructions so everybody is singing off the same sheet. Fun and innovation and experimentation are all well and good, but this is business and we have to show serious value. That old ROI is forever at our heels.

You must assume that advertising on the Web is not a one-shot production. It's an ongoing operation. Each department that wants to promote its goods and services to the outside world will eventually want to publish on the Web. A set of procedures makes it easier for them to do so. How to create a Web ad, what issues to consider, and what the approval process looks like should be predefined.

There's no need to get a stonemason to write your rules in granite. In fact, you'll be much better served by writing them in Swiss cheese. They should be ductile, flexible, slightly soft. There should be sufficient holes to allow for creativity and invention. That's not to say they should be written in baked Brie, either. Rules that ooze, stretch, and drip are worse than no rules at all.

Provide some guidelines so people know what makes sense and then let them find their own way. In time, they will suggest alterations to the rules as experience makes them wiser. Listen to them. Encourage them. Even Swiss cheese has a tendency to harden over time.

The Process

All great projects (and all others, as well) start off with the Great Idea. It may be found in a book, it may come in a dream, or it may come after too many beers at the bowling alley. It's hard to say. Somebody is going to come up with a Great Idea. When they do, there has to be a logical process in place to determine if it really is a good idea, or whether it's time to trade in the bowling shoes for some cross-trainers.

At first cut, the usual hierarchy comes into play. The Great Idea has to move high enough in the organization for the money to be approved. Left to its own devices, it will move up from level to level until it finds a plateau where it is not understood and is left languishing in the inbox. That's why a formal process is necessary. The right people looking at the right information can make the right decisions in subgeological spans of time.

The Internet is a complicated enough place to do business that those who approve an advertising project are depending on others to help work out the fine details. But before it gets to the person with the hand on the corporate coffers, it needs to be vetted by people in the know.

Who Approves?   There are technical issues, cultural issues, timing issues, brand management issues, logistical issues, and political issues. Each needs to be addressed, explained, and satisfied before seeking final approval.

In each case, somebody who knows enough about the question to pass judgment has to be selected—somebody who can bring to bear experience and common sense. Does this project violate any Internet cultural mores? Does it violate any state, national, or international laws? Does it violate any corporate standards? Does it violate boundaries of good taste?

Given the different approvals to be considered, identifying the players is your first step. As you read "The Proposal" outline that follows, think about who in your organization is the right one to judge whether the answer to each question has merit.

What's the Sequence?   The Proposal was laid out with an eye toward the order in which things should be decided. Without knowing the target audience, you can't determine if the site selection is meaningful. Without a clear idea of the technologies involved, you can't make a decent guess about the cost or the schedule.

And before you figure out the schedule for a specific project, there should be some agreement, some standard approach that determines the schedule of the project approval cycle.

What's the Schedule?   The bank down on the corner will tell you how long it will take to approve your loan. They worked it out. They listed the steps and assigned a given amount of time to get each step completed and then they sharpened their knives and started carving. In the financial world, a quick decision can be a serious competitive edge. Your turnaround for the approval of advertising on the Web is no different.

Things change on the Web at blinding speed. There aren't too many set ways and strict rules. There's "Don't Spam." There's "Add Value." Then there's just a lot of heartfelt advice and a modicum of common sense, but the rest is philosophy and experimentation.

As a result, you have to be fast on your feet. Spend some time outlining the approval process with an eye toward streamlining it. Figure out how to create parallel permission paths to speed things along. The legal department doesn't care what color is used on the background of your pages. Let them review the text while the art department plays with the palette.

A Great Idea is usually time-dependent in the advertising world. Don't turn a good idea into a bad idea through neglect.

The Proposal

Here's the heart of the matter. Here are a series of questions that should be answered to kick off an online advertising project. You get the answers to these questions, and the rest pretty much makes itself clear.

Project Name   What does the proposing group call this project? This should be a name that is easy to remember, easy to use in discussion as well as on paper, and somewhat descriptive. "50% Off Banner" works much better than "Bobby's" or "Project 27." You're going to be using this name internally and externally, and should you be so lucky, your marketing brilliance will be written up in trade journals. When that happens, you don't want to be associated with a project moniker like "Brown 25."

Project Identification   Assigned by review committee for future reference, this is where cryptic is just fine. This is the project ID, rather than its name. Figure out a naming convention that ties to the department, the date, the type of media, or all of these.

If you give the 50% Off Banner project an ID like CI50%BYIE2/698, then you can programmatically sort and search and compare project results depending on the product (Creamy Italian dressing), the promotion (50% Off Banner), the media (Yahoo!, Infoseek, Excite), and the date (February through June of 1998).

Project Description   Describe this project in 30 words or less. What is the intent of this particular promotion? What form will it take—Banner? Interstitial? Demi-site? Other? Make it as clear and concise as possible. The people reviewing this proposal may not remember the name, so give them a clue. Something that will remind them of your conversation last week at lunch.

What is the life expectancy of this project? Is this a good-until-canceled type project that should live forever in the minds of the public? Or is it a limited-time offer meant to be as fleeting as a Lollapalooza concert?

Purpose   What do you hope to accomplish? The more specific you can be the better. " Announce new service offerings," may be accurate, but it's not specific enough to be useful. You want to announce new service offerings in order to increase awareness, or to make sales? The thrust of the project will be very different depending on your answer,

> Increase brand awareness in the target audience by 10%.
>
> Unload excess inventory of Cabbage Patch Dolls in two months.
>
> Raise store traffic in targeted locations by 20% by March.
>
> Counter competitive claims of superiority.

Without a clearly defined purpose, it's better to leave the wheelbarrow full of money in the office. If you don't have a specific purpose, your creative people will have nothing to work with, your media planner won't know where to place your banners, and if they're worth their salt, your head of online projects will never approve your plan.

The Intended Audience   Who is the target for this project? As detailed as you can, describe the ideal person you want to respond to this project. Use demographics (location, age, income, and so on), use psychographics (left-wing, right-wing, political party, sports fan, environmentalist, NRA member), compugraphics (runs Windows 95 and uses Netscape 3.0), and whatever other descriptor you can think of to clearly identify the type of person you want in the cross hairs. Now describe the outside limits: how far away from the ideal do you get before you are attracting the wrong kind of person? Where do you draw the line?

How large is this market segment? Given the ideal and the brackets around that ideal, how many people fit the description who are also online? How about offline? (IBM did pretty well sending out CD-ROMs to geophysicists.) Just how big is the universe you're after?

How is this project directed toward them? What are you going to do in particular to attract the interest of the people you've described? A special offer? A certain use of language? Color? Celebrity? What are you going to do in particular that is going to make them click?

Response Mechanism   What sort of customer response is expected?

There's an ad that runs every spring on Los Angeles radio stations for a company that sells a home sealing product/service that's "twenty times thicker than paint." The spring promotion is for ten homeowners to take advantage of a seasonal discount. This company knows that people start thinking about painting their houses after the winter weather is over and they want to be one of the options people have on their lists. They only need ten jobs to make the promotion cost effective and, of course, they can offer the discount to as many people as they want while waiting for the summer rush to start.

Are you looking for ten customers? Are you looking for ten thousand customers? Are you looking for them to call? To click? To register? Be clear about the response device you want to employ because that determines the means by which you collect that response and the cost.

If you want surfers to sign up for a contest, how will the contestant data be recorded? If the goal is to have people send in personal stories to win a prize, who is going to be assigned to read the stories and make the selection? If one person is assigned and 5,000 three-page personal tales show up, how will the judging be completed by the award date?

This is the logistical portion of the project proposal and it's the one with the most potential for underplanning. The key thing you're looking for from your Great Idea people in this section is an aptitude for contingency.

When Hewlett Packard first put up its Web site, it shied away from listing the toll-free number. Why? They were afraid of the massive response they might get. They cowered before the impending threat of thousands of people calling and asking thousands of questions. Did they not want to talk to people? Did they want to keep their distance and let the poor public blunder its way through a mountain of technical information? Not at all. HP simply couldn't figure out who was going to pay for the extra people and phone lines that would be necessary. They fell down on the contingency planning.

Automate as much as you can. But be forewarned, if you advertise, people will e-mail you. Better have a plan in place to manage the response to that e-mail. That plan had better include standard, boiler-plate answers and training on handling the typical, the unusual, and the abusive.

You will also cause people to call you. Humans are rather funny when it comes to contacting a company. Sometimes they simply dial the number that is closest at hand, like that on your Web site. Sometimes they look in the phone book. Sometimes they look on the box you shipped them, or on the packaging of the item they picked up at the store. Sometimes they call the store.

Do you have a plan in place to educate all of the employees and cooperative marketing partners who might be on the receiving end of one of those calls? There's nothing worse to a potential customer than calling up and finding out that no one knows anything.

"You saw this offer on a banner on a Web site?"

"Whose Web site was it?"

"Was it our banner?"

"What's a banner?"

"Oh, no, you'd need to talk to our Webmaster about that."

"I don't know anything about advertising banners, man, I'm a Webmaster!"

Competitive Analysis Who is doing anything similar? Are you in a contest for mind share and want to use the same tactics they are using?

Why is this project better? What have you learned from your competitors' efforts that you can use? Have they been wildly successful and you merely want to cash in on it? Can you improve upon it? Did you see them do something dumb and you want to do it better?

Media Selection Which sites are being considered for placement of this project? What makes each one uniquely suited to this project? How does the variety of the sites selected increase the reach of this project to improve the response beyond just the sum of the sites?

Heather Anderson, Senior Media Planner at J. Walter Thompson, finds FocaLink's MarketMatch a valuable tool for planning when looking for the right sites for her clients to sponsor. She searches on everything from target audience characteristics (Web developers, for example) to site characteristics (such as news sites in the Bay Area). She also uses it to get specific information about a site such as monthly traffic numbers, production specs, and ad sales contacts.

While MarketMatch helps the media planning process, Anderson knows better than to rely on it completely. She always talks to the reps before making a final decision.

The Players Who is involved in this project and what are their responsibilities? It's a good idea to know who's going to be on the hook for what. A simple form, like that shown in Table 9.2 can go a long way toward letting the players know what their roles are going to be and how to play well with others.

Table 9.2   The People You'll Need and What They'll Do

Role	Responsibility	
Project Manager	Primary stakeholder	
e-mail address	phone number	direct manager
Response Manager	Responds to incoming data	
e-mail address	phone number	direct manager
Creative Manager	Devises the theme and the form	
e-mail address	phone number	direct manager
Design Manager	Produces the art	
e-mail address	phone number	direct manager
Processing Manager	Designs the back-end processing	
e-mail address	phone number	direct manager

The Tools   What graphics and coding tools are used for authoring?

What new software are required?

What tools are used to manage response?

What training is required to use these tools?

Who provides the training?

What special services are required of the site being sponsored?

Guideline/Standard Deviations   How will this project vary from the guidelines and standards?

What is the expected benefit of these deviations?

How will the evaluation of this project be different due to these changes?

Is this a request for a waver or should the guidelines be changed?

How Will the Project Be Tested Prior to Going Live?   If newer technologies are being used, or if a new response mechanism or procedure is being employed, some kind of testing is necessary. A simple banner created by following corporate standards always displays on all browsers. That's what standards are for. But new technology comes out of the Internet at a breathtaking rate.

If the Great Idea revolves around the publicity value of being the first to offer 3-D, all-singing, all-dancing, tele-smell technology into a banner, then there has to be a test plan. Remember, this is a software program, not a brochure. It needs to be assayed in the lab where it won't do any harm to the Internet, the customer's computer, or the company's reputation.

The Cost   Define the funds required for:

> Training
> Design
> Copywriting
> Graphics creation
> Back-end development
> Integration
> Testing
> Fixes
> Documentation
> Updates

From where will the funds come?

When will funding be required?

An Outfront Marketing study by *Business Marketing* showed 1995 spending for business-to-business marketing (Table 9.3). (Figures exclude compensation and commissions.)

Table 9.3   Spending Broken Down by Segment

Segment	Total $ (billions)	% of Total
Sales force automation	$11.9	22.9%
Advertising	11.3	21.9%
Direct marketing	6.3	12.3%
Sales promotions	6.3	12.2%
Trade shows	5.5	10.7%
Public relations	2.6	5.1%
Other	2.0	3.9%
Premiums/Incentives	1.9	3.7%
Online	1.4	2.6%

Will your firm spend 2.6% of your marketing dollar on online marketing? If so, you're behind the times. This chart was published in *Business Marketing* in the January/February, 1997 issue. It's the latest information. Rest assured that the percentage of marketing budget for online marketing is not going down.

The Timeline   Define the time required for:

> Approval
> Training
> Design
> Copywriting
> Graphics creation
> Back-end programming and development
> Systems integration
> Testing
> Fixes
> Documentation
> Updates
> Success determination

Potential Risks   Define the risks associated with this project: technical, financial, political, competitive.

How can these risks be minimized?

Why is this project worth subjecting the company to these risks?

What contingency plans are in place to respond to these risks should varying degrees of disaster strike?

The Alternatives   How else might this project's objectives be met, both online and offline?

Why is this approach the best alternative?

What is the next best alternative?

The Lost Opportunity Cost   What is the risk of not producing this project? Will you fall behind your competitors? Will you lose some of the goodwill you've created with your best customers? Will you face a larger challenge down the line when a quick effort now will stem the tide?

Measuring Success   How will you know this project was worthwhile? The number of impressions? Of surveys? Of T-shirts given away? Of visits to the home page? Are you looking to increase market share? Share of customer? Do you want people to download and print out coupons? Fill out a survey?

> What specific metrics will be used to calculate success?
>
> How will they be collected?
>
> How often will they be collected?
>
> How often will they be reviewed?
>
> How will a no-go decision be made?
>
> At what intervals will a no-go decision be made?

That's enough to get started. Now the laboriously documented project has to be approved. So, who's going to do the approving? Just how long are you going to give them? Be vigilant to the prospect of cutting the time necessary to approve a project. Internet and advertising wait for no man.

Automation Is Your Friend

When it comes to internal processes and procedures, there's nothing like turning to the technology you are looking to exploit for help.

Can you spell *intranet*?

If you can define the steps, identify the players, and have browser and server gadgets at your disposal, there is every reason to believe that you can improve the speed of the approval process by automating it.

Need help writing a proposal? Build an internal Web page that's a proposal template. Fill in the blanks, hit the Submit button, and it's on its way. Who sees it first? How much of it do they really need to see? Oh, sure, the entire document should be available to any of the decision makers who care to delve, but those very same people will be delighted to tell you they only really need to see certain bits. The rest is for somebody else down the line.

A Matter of Perspective   The customer service manager is primarily interested in the parts that deal with the response mechanism, the tools, the testing, the risks, and the metrics. Like everybody else, he or she will be interested in the costs and the training plans as well. The creative becomes important down the line, when it is further refined and schedules for training need to be worked out.

The lawyers are particularly interested in the creative. They need to scrutinize what is going to be said, where it will be said, and how the company plans to defend itself...er, respond...to customers.

Each player has different interests and these can be accommodated via differing views of the proposal.

Going with the Flow   Each view of the proposal, meant for each stage of approval, comes complete with two buttons. One says, "Approved," and the other, "Not On Your Life," or words to that effect. Hit the "Approved" button and the whole thing is forwarded onto the next in line. It then falls on their shoulders to render an opinion.

Hit the other button and a new page appears, asking for details on what you found objectionable, why you feel you know more than everybody else, and just what on earth is your problem, anyway?

In this manner, with the addition of automatic e-mail to let you know it is your turn to be judge, it's possible for a project to get propagated through the approval process in record time. Just be sure to consider the secondary and tertiary routings when people are out sick or on vacation. Web access being what it is today, simply being on the road is an insufficient excuse for not paying attention to the intranet.

Construct the Creative

This is the magic part. This is also known as the fun part. It's brainstorming time.

Whether you use an agency or you do it yourself, that task is to match the brand, the offer, and the technology to the target audience.

This is the point where you have to think outside the box. Can you create something that reaches into the heart of the product and pulls out its Unique Selling Proposition? Can you then turn that USP into something that is brilliantly clear, instantly recognizable, and personally meaningful to your audience?

Can you come up with something like "Just Do It?"

Maybe you can. The process for being creative is not at all understood. I leave it to the masters to outline how it's done. Suffice it to say that this is the point in your project where it is finally time to come up with the magic. It's time to come up with the magic several times over.

You're not going to create just one ad. You're going to create several ads. Why? Because the Web has a way of eating banners alive. Remember our optimal frequency is only three? Well, after that, you need to have something else to show them. Otherwise, you're a one-trick pony with no momentum.

Oh, and you're going to create several versions of each banner. Why? Because before you launch it on the unsuspecting masses, you want to run tests and see which version pulls best. You might be as creative as they come, but when it comes time to show your creations to the world, you have to be ready to tally the response and react accordingly.

Be Systematic

"Be Systematic" is tip number ten from Infoseek's "Ten Quick Tips to Make Your Banners More Effective."

The power of the Net is its adaptability. You can try lots of creatives, flightings, sites, messages, etc. The best advice is to set a systematic set of variations of campaign variables so you can understand why banners vary in response. While most advertisers use multiple banners to find the one with the best response, very few actually design their campaigns with an up-front set of experimental variations to actually know why the banners were different. In the long run, this is the most valuable "clickthrough tip," because the knowledge you gain will be unique to your product and a proprietary advantage in the market place.

Jerry W. Thomas runs an Arlington, Texas, market research company called Decision Analyst. He's in agreement with tip number ten. Thomas laments that marketing and advertising are the most inefficient of all purchases the average company makes.

In an editorial in *Business Marketing* (April, 1997) that talks about television commercials (which apply rather well to Web advertising), Thomas listed the three reasons for his lamentations:

First, few companies do basic strategy research to develop a creative ad blueprint.

Second, few pretest creative to make sure it has a chance to work.

Third, even fewer companies track their ad once it's on the air to measure its effectiveness over time.

With the advent of tracking the way we can, it borders on sinful to carry these missteps over from TV to the Web.

Testing One, Two, Three

Three kinds of tests are called for when preparing a Web ad campaign: the client, the server, and the content. The first two are absolutely critical or your banner will not be displayed—or will be HOA (hideous on arrival). The latter is only necessary if you care about being successful.

Client-Side Testing

A Gateway Computer banner that showed up for a little over a week on AltaVista said something like, "Brace yourself for this," and depicted their emblematic black and white cow leaning into the force from a television screen. It was a takeoff of that wonderful black and white ad with the leather- and sunglasses-clad, long haired guy slumped in a chair, getting blasted by his stereo system while the curtains were billowing and the lamp was being knocked over.

So Gateway started with a great premise and then fell flat on the delivery due to a technical problem. The banner was an animated .gif file that did *something*. I'm just not sure what it was. The effect of that something was that the color on some monitors went haywire—and only on that banner.

I was running on a Macintosh with a 15" Sony monitor that was set to millions of colors. It was a *Mac*! It's pretty tough to screw up the colors on a Mac. Somebody had neglected to test the client side of the street when they were whipping up their nifty banners.

Server-Side Up

Technically, you're probably not going to run into much trouble. Any banner network or serious content site is going to be using a database and server software that can handle a variety of file types. Text files, .gif files, Java applets, and others are common enough that those who want to make money selling space had better keep up with the times.

But it will be worth your while to work out a test run with the sites you choose just to be absolutely sure your banners don't end up in the bit bucket. A couple of quick tests will keep you out of the dog house, off the carpet in your boss's office, and out of harm's way when the trade journals run their annual, "Ten Dumbest Advertising Mistakes of the Year" articles.

Your content is the other thing you should test with the sites you sponsor.

The Message Is the Message

Here's where the rubber meets the road. This is where you separate the talented from the rest. Here's where the methodical can win the day over the lucky.

Somebody needs to be responsible for checking and rechecking the combination of your message and your medium. Are you putting up an ad for gun control support that might end up on the National Rifle Association's Web site? Better safe than sorry.

Is It Okay with the Sponsored Site?   Pacific Bell decided to get into the content business. They put up a site called At Hand (**www.athand.com**) as a reference for all things California, including a complete yellow pages. Pacific Bell is a phone company after all, they have lots of yellow pages content.

However, their banner business was refused by the *Los Angeles Times* because the *Times* felt the At Hand data was in direct conflict with the classifieds found on the *Times'* site. Just goes to show that it's hard to tell the players without a program. These days newspapers are competing with phone companies, and computer firms are competing with delivery services (IBM and Federal Express both offer high-level Web site hosting and transaction services).

As discovered in the Bikini Photo Contest case, the site that accepts advertising may not always accept your advertising. It's best to ask for approval from the sites you plan to sponsor before you get too far down the road.

Is It Okay with the Legal Beagles? Ah yes, the lawyers. Will they never get any respect? On a *Tonight Show*, Jay Leno suggested running "Jurassic Park" backwards on your VCR just so you could see T. Rex run into the bathroom in order to throw up a lawyer.

No matter what your feelings about lawyers, your lawyers are necessary to protect you from dangers, both real and imagined. Copyright, liable, infringement, false advertising: the list goes on. For more, see Chapter 11, "A Few Words About the Law."

In the meantime, be sure your legal people are in the loop. Make sure they are part of the approval process, just like you do with brochures and press releases.

Which One Is More Okay than the Others? Here's where the Internet shines.

In most media, you run an ad or drop a mail piece and you wait. Then you try to attribute changes in consumer behavior to your brilliant marketing maneuvers. Sometimes you can measure direct response. You can count the number of people who called the toll-free number that appeared in the ad and nowhere else. You can count how many people clipped the coupon and went to the store to redeem it. But on the Web, you have a much faster ruler: the click.

Want to test your banner on 5,000 people prior to a roll out? Fine—are you willing to wait a few minutes?

Want to know if Banner A gets a better response than Banner B? You know before your coffee gets cold.

With that sort of power, that kind of feedback, in that short a time frame, you'd be foolish to run a banner on a big scale without doing your own side-by-sides, like the people in Chapter 8, "Real Life Stories: The Good, the Bad, and the Unexplainable."

In the long run, it would be nice to know why B pulled better than A. It would be nice to know that it was the copy or the color or the frequency or the offer. But the most important thing is that B is the one you want to run.

During these tests, you also get to test your response mechanism. Are you getting more e-mails than you thought you would? Now is the time to make corrections. Selling those widgets better than you thought? Time to upgrade production.

The small test can be an absolute life saver preceding a big run.

Let 'Er Rip

Now it's time to open the floodgates. It's time to let the cat out of the bag and run a million impressions. Keep your finger on the pulse. Keep your eyes on the real-time reports. Keep a watch on the customer service department. Keep your fingers crossed.

And get ready for the other response your efforts engender: the opinion of the people, vox populi.

Act on Feedback

Everybody talks about the weather but nobody does anything about it. Everybody has an opinion about how the world is going to hell in a hand basket and nobody knows how to do it better. In the same vein, everybody has an opinion about your banner. At least it seems like everybody.

Let's say you do run a million impressions. If your banner is a middle of the road crowd pleaser, you should get about two-point-something clicks. That's 200,000 clicks. Typical. Now let's say that the surfing public, safe behind their terminals, wants to tell you a few things about your banner.

Maybe you pulled a Gateway and people want you to know you screwed up. That could generate a good deal of e-mail. Let's say your banner says, "Click Here for a Free Hawaiian Vacation!" and it takes people to a form where they might be able to win a vacation. A healthy number of people are going to want to explain truth in advertising to you.

Now let's say there is nothing in particular about your ad that is inciting or provocative, it's just an ad. Nevertheless, it's not too hard to imagine that one person out of, say every 10,000 who see your ad, wants to give you a piece of his or her mind. One out of 10,000 is easy to fathom. However, the result is 100 e-mails critiquing your advertising efforts.

A suggestion? Read them very carefully. Never mind that half of them are wackos. Half of the rest are trying to sell you something. That leaves you with 25 people who felt compelled to give you some advice. Some of those oysters have pearls in them. Make sure you thank each and every one of them, and then go diving for pearls.

Do It Again

In *Soul Of A New Machine*, Tracy Kidman describes the pinball theory of building computers. If you were really, really good at it, if you worked yourself into a frenzy, if you put your work before your family, before your friends, before your love of the outdoors, indeed, if you put it ahead of your health, and you put your nose to the grindstone on a 24-7 basis, *and if you were successful*, then the reward was that you got to keep your job and do it again.

Guess what…

You've done direct mail. You've organized trade shows. You've mounted media blitzes. You know that the same rules apply here.

Heed the Competition

Every time the earth turns on its axis, your competition is up to something else. While you were busy deciding, planning, creating, and executing, well, they were, too. It's time to revisit their efforts. It's time to re-evaluate their strengths and weaknesses. It's time to get reacquainted with the types of technology they're using, the sites they're sponsoring, and the current message they're sending.

Determine Your Goals

How long has it been since you dusted off that notebook, re-read that memo, and unfolded the flip-chart pages from that strategy meeting you had? What has changed since then? It's only been a few months? Here's news for you: it's already been a few months!

The thing that's changing the fastest in the business world is the rate of change. If three months have gone by and your goals have not changed, then either your goals are too broad, your industry moves at a comparative snail's pace, or you're dead in the water and you just don't know it yet.

You've learned a lot about your customers and your prospective customers over the past few months. They have clicked. They have avoided clicking. They have answered survey questions and they have purchased or not purchased.

Are you sure you're going after the right people? Yes? Well then, it's time to broaden your horizons and expand your ambitions.

Time to re-think, re-plan, and re-launch. ●

CHAPTER 10

Selling Space on Your Web Site

This book has heretofore focused on placing ads on other sites. If you are inclined to place other companies' ads on your site, this chapter is for you. This chapter looks into what the selling side of Internet advertising looks like so you know what you're selling when you approach a potential client. It discusses finding clients, what to charge them, and how to help them be successful. Finally, there are a few ideas on how to make your site stand out and provide superior customer service to your advertising clients.

When only a few had the technical skills and the money to produce books, only the richest and politically-strongest organizations (the church) could afford it. When only a few had the technical skills and the money to produce television, there were only a few places one could buy advertising time. To a much greater extent, today's Web resembles the early days of radio.

When radio was young, the technical skills and the money required to put out a local broadcast were minimal. Ham radio operators are still at it; it doesn't take much. But advertising dollars flowed to where the transmitters were strong enough to reach the largest numbers of people, and the content was good enough to make those people want to be reached.

So, as in the early days of radio, you can simply put up your own Web site if you want, and, like the early days of radio, if you attract enough people, if you have a powerful enough site, you can sell ad space. The first question is whether the ad-selling game is the right business for you. ▇

There's No Business Like Show Business

Is your Web site an ad for your company or is it a company in itself? If you're thinking that you could use a little extra income by selling ad space on a site designed for marketing your own company, think again. If you're not dedicated to the business of selling ad space, you should probably stick to your knitting.

A Web site is a great place for marketing, sales, and customer service. Marketing means educating people. Sales means transaction. Customer service means solving customer problems.

The only way you're going to be successful turning your company Web site into an advertising money-maker is by deciding that advertising is the business you're in. If you're selling widgets and think you're getting enough traffic to help defray the cost of your widget site, you haven't thought about the cost of selling ad space. It is not a part-time job.

Advertising Profitability Is Newsworthy

It was front page news when Yahoo! went into the black. On January 15, 1997, Yahoo! stock (YHOO) went up from 20 7/8 to 25 3/8 when they announced that they had actually turned a profit for the second time. For the fourth quarter of 1996, they posted a profit of $96,000. Before you think that $96 grand is a nice, tidy sum, remember that Yahoo! made this profit on revenues of $8.5 million and their total 1996 results were a loss of $2.3 million.

Must one spend $8.5 million to see a return of less than $100,000? No. Some smaller sites are profitable. But it's not easy. It's not cheap. It's not simply selling banner space.

Web sites selling banner space are a commodity. They are a dime a dozen. The media rep is overrun with e-mail, phone calls, and faxes from sites looking for representation. Media planners for sizable companies are similarly inundated with offers to advertise. Satisfying their needs is central to successful ad selling.

If you want to be a major Internet advertising force and you aren't already, you may have missed your window. The Internet advertising industry is now old enough that jumping into the game in a big way with a large investment is a dangerous way to participate. A better approach would be to quietly acquire sites that are doing the right things and build your empire that way. Starting a big site that's looking to sell big time advertising has a big job ahead of it—spending big bucks on branding.

If you're a small- or medium-sized Web site, the recommendation is to start off slowly, conquer the problems, and learn the lessons one by one.

Get Started Slowly

You want to see if your site is ripe for advertising? Go out and find ads like the ones from The Midi Zone. The Midi Zone isn't looking to buy ad space on your site, they're looking for clickthroughs. Negotiating a contract? Convincing them to buy from you? You won't be bothered with these issues. Instead, just wander over to their site and read about their offer to pay you per click (**www.midizone.com/sponsor/welcome.html**) (see Figure 10.1).

FIG. 10.1

The simplest way to get started is with ads that pay you per click.

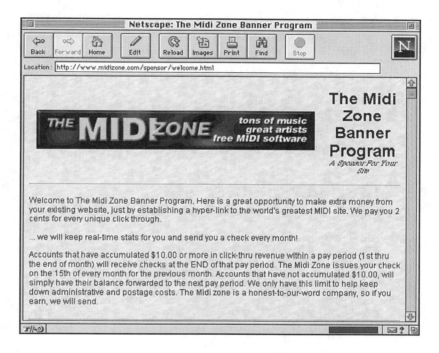

You'll get a check every month, they say, if you can produce more than 500 clickthroughs. If you can, you get a whopping $10.00 in the mail. If you wanted to go into The Midi Zone clickthrough business, you could put up a site that does nothing but get people to click to The Midi Zone. Get a million people to go to The Midi Zone every month for 12 months and earn $240,000 for the year. There have to be easier ways to make a living.

One alternative is to set yourself up as another The Midi Zone–style site. They sell ad space on their Web site. In other words, somebody pays them for traffic that they try to get from you. That makes them a traffic broker. Sounds like hard work to me.

Another get-started approach calls for you to do your own advertising on your own site. Create some banners that point people to other sections of your site or to other sites you own. Or even to friend's site. Do it for free. Do it until you get a feel for what it takes to serve multiple ads.

You're not going to get rich in this getting-started phase. The goal is to try it for a while and see if you

1. Have enough traffic on your site that a significant number of people will click a banner ad now and again.
2. Understand banner ads well enough to create a banner that will attract attention to another site.
3. Can manage the ad-serving and ad-tracking mechanisms advertisers will demand.
4. Realize that it takes a lot of effort to get a million people a month to go to The Midi Zone site.
5. Wouldn't really rather be doing something else for a living.

No? You think selling banner ads is just the ticket? Okay, then, it's time to get down to cases.

You are now officially a seller of space on your Web site, and it's time to take a cold, hard look at just what you're selling. After all, you have to know the product if you want to convince people to buy it.

What Are You Selling?

Describe what you are selling in 15 words or less:

> We sell banner space on our Web site.

Wrong, try again.

> We sell Opportunities To See on our Web site.

No, but you're getting warmer.

> We sell access to people who might be interested in a client's products.

You're getting even warmer…

> We sell specific types of people for you to put your ad banner in front of.

That's pretty good, except for it being 16 words and ends with a preposition. Try this:

> We sell specific quantities of identifiable types of viewers in a given time period.

Bingo. You are selling eyeballs. Very specifically identified, classified, and itemized types of eyeballs. And lots of them. This is the first decision you need to make about the kind of people you want to attract to your site; are you looking for a very specific type of surfer or lots and lots of all kinds of surfers.?

What Kind of Site Is It, Anyway?

Is yours a content site or a transition site? Is it a directory that people are going through or a destination site people are going to?

The mass-media, mass-interest site gathers masses of people and has masses of pageviews on which to sell lots of ad space. It also spends a massive amount of money letting the world know that it exists and that the world should beat a path to its door.

These sites are usually directories. They are the portal through which people pass on their way to something worth looking at. They are the Yahoo!s and Infoseeks of the Net.

The narrowly-focused, topic-specific sites are the destination sites. These are the places people are looking for when they pass through a portal. They are destinations.

The logic of an advertiser wanting to put a banner on either type of site is a bit convoluted and there are no hard numbers to back up the assumptions. But see which of these conflicting ideas makes the most sense to you.

Either:

> You shouldn't put ads on directories because people are on their way somewhere else. They're looking for something in particular. It's too hard to distract them.

> or

> You should put ads on directory sites because people are there in search of places to go, and your site might be just the sort of place they're looking for.

The non-directory logic is equally as diametric:

> You shouldn't place a banner on a destination site because people are there to see what's there and distracting them is very hard.

> or

> You should advertise on destination sites because people are interested in the topic and spend more time there; thus, they'll be exposed to your ad longer.

Here's some advice from the sidelines: the more tightly focused you are on a particular subject, the easier it is to draw a crowd of people interested in that subject and the easier it is to convince advertisers that your site is right for them.

Want to be on the cutting edge? Follow the lead of those topic-specific search engines and directories described in "Narrowing The Search" in Chapter 6, "Looking for Space in All the Right Places."

Real Estate

Now that you've decided what your Web site is going to be when it grows up, it's time to think about the actual space you're going to devote to advertising. You have to come up with a description of your pages that lets media planners know how many places there are to place a banner on your site and how they differ.

Just as there are differences between directories and destination sites, there are differences between the traffic you get on your home page (the highest percentage), the intermediate menu pages (transitory), and the meat-and-potatoes pages (concentrated attention).

How many of each do you have? Do you charge different prices for banners on these different pages? Do you rotate ads throughout the site? Do you create special packages that would appeal to different advertising goals?

Package 1:

> Your banner is rotated between the five most often seen pages to provide the most exposures in the least amount of time.

Package 2:

> Your banner is rotated on the pages that are viewed the longest in order to provide the longest amount of visibility per viewer.

Package 3:

> Your banner is shown on specific pages that are topic-specific to your offering, providing the highest likelihood of interest from each viewer.

Make sure you have a clearly defined map of your site and advertisers know what to expect in the way of exposure if they place a banner on different pages.

With that in place, the big question is this: How many impressions do you serve?

How Many Come to Your Site?

If you want to compete with, or at least play in the same ball park, as Yahoo!, Infoseek, AltaVista, and the like, you're going to have to attract millions of surfers a day. Every day. If you're running a destination site, you're going to attract only thousands per day. If you run the Knappers Anonymous site (**www.ucs.mun.ca/~t64tr/knap.html**) shown in Figure 10.2, then even a handful of viewers a day would be enough to entice somebody selling instructional knapping videotapes.

Because Web site banner space is a commodity, the numbers matter, and the percentages matter more. Are you the only site on the Web that's designed to attract people interested in high-altitude running? Are you sure? Is your site getting 100% of the people who want to know more about window-box gardening in the Bronx? That's good. Producers of small cartons of potting soil who have retail outlets between Manhattan and Long Island will certainly want to buy an ad from you. Unless you have competition.

A potting soil packager might find other sites that attract the same kind of people you do. Even if those sites are not about gardening, they are still your competitors. If that's the case, the numbers are important. But the change in the numbers over time will carry more weight than the raw numbers themselves.

It's been said that the best way to go out of business is to own a larger and larger share of a dying market. You end up spending more and more supporting a market whose needs and interests are dwindling. Advertisers don't want to fall victim to the same problem.

FIG. 10.2
The Knappers Anonymous site is so finely focused that small numbers of visitors are still impressive—and valuable.

If your site is the new kid on the block and you can show that your site's visitation numbers are increasing, advertisers are going to smell opportunity. The first probability is that they will be able to lock in a decent price now, in hopes of keeping their costs stable as your popularity grows. Think of it as a charter member deal.

The second possibility is that they will benefit from association. The longer they sponsor your site, and the better your site does, it's no longer as much a matter of response rate as it is a matter of branding. Mobil Corporation has sponsored Masterpiece Theatre for years. Those of us who watch have the Mobil name forever linked to quality television.

As important as the numbers and the percentages are, the critical issue is being able to identify your visitors.

Who Are They?

Television is pretty good at guessing whether the viewers of a particular show are 18–34 or 35–50 years of age and are high, medium, or low income. But Web site ad buyers expect a lot more detail from you than that. Nike wants 18–34 year old females who work out three times a week and spend more than 10% of their disposable income on recreation (for one banner they want to run) and 35–50 year old males with incomes over $45,000 who are health conscious and like to play competitive sports on the weekends (for another banner they want to run).

Can you deliver? How well do you know your audience?

Remote Control Identification　With nothing but a standard server you can at least report back to advertisers how many unique IP addresses were used to reach your site. The value of this number is soft at best. If I look at your site from my desk, your server records whatever temporary IP address my access provider gave me when I dialed in. If I look at your site from inside a large corporation, your server records the address of the firewall gateway that thousands of fellow employees pass through on their way to the rest of the world. If I visit through my account at CompuServe, then your server can't tell me apart from millions of other CompuServe customers.

So what can you tell your clients? What do you know for sure?

The time of day, for starters. You know exactly when the traffic at your site is high and when it is low. You know the day of the week and the hour of the day that things pick up. If your advertiser wants to promote a time-sensitive offer, this can be valuable information.

You can also make broad generalizations about whether people are business types, students, government workers, or foreigners. By analyzing visitors' high-level domains, you can at least give your clients a general idea about who might be popping in. If they're selling products to students, they'll be reassured to see that the vast majority of visitors come from .edu domains.

You might also provide advertisers with some insight into how these visitors use your site. Do they show up, run a search, and take off? Do they come and wander around for a while? Do they always zero in on the one or two central pages of your site? Maybe you're doing well in the world of online chat and people come back often and stay for hours.

But if you really want to get to know them, it's time to use the cookies and the logins.

Hands-On Identification　As an advertiser, I want to know who visits your site. I want to know where they live, how much money they make, and how many kids they have. I want to know when they last bought a car and whether they buy medical insurance and if their friends' kids have had their teeth straightened. I want to know everything.

It's your job, if you want to be competitive, to find out and tell me as much as you can.

So don't just keep track of visitors' movements through your site, taking note of the search words they use and the pages they view. Ask a question every now and then. Build a profile. Make the aggregated information available to me to help me pick out who I want to target with my message.

Can You Guarantee Delivery?

Once the individuals have been identified, you better be sure you can deliver the type of people I want, in the quantities I want, and when I want.

My advertising campaign depends on split-second timing. It wasn't always that way. I used to be able to set some goals, make a plan, and carefully, cautiously, and thoughtfully execute. But with the immediacy of the Web, my press release, my Web site, my contest, my trade show press conference, my print ads, my direct mail pieces, and my banner advertising all have to hit at the same time. Which always seems to be at the end of next week.

It is important to my success as a marketer to narrow down the delivery of my banners to specific hours. If you can't deliver a set number of impressions to a select category of people within a half-day period, I may not be willing to do business with you. I may not have the luxury of time to be able to work with you.

That means you have to know not just when the majority of people show up and what kind of people show up, you need to know when specific types of people show up. Sound like it's getting complicated? We've only just begun. Because now you have to prove it.

Can You Prove It?

As if you haven't spent enough time and money getting everything ready, now you have to be able to prove that the numbers you're reporting are actual and factual. Just like television and print media, I expect you to show me the reports.

Use the Tools   Don't waste another minute writing a quick Perl script to make your server logs meaningful. There are plenty of tools out there now that can help you do it. And besides saving you the time and trouble of writing, testing, and maintaining your own programming, advertisers feel a lot better about numbers produced by software they've heard of before. They will also appreciate that your reports come in a format they've seen before.

I won't even try to list the available tools here. There are too many. Besides, with the server technology being updated so frequently, the tools simply change too fast. You can keep up with the industry periodicals and tune in to places like CNET (**www.cnet.com/Content/Reviews/ Compare/Webservers**) that run product comparisons on lots of different tools. They're worth keeping an eye on. Take a look at Figure 10.3 for a preview of CNET.

FIG. 10.3
CNET offers up-to-date comparisons on server software for tracking visitors.

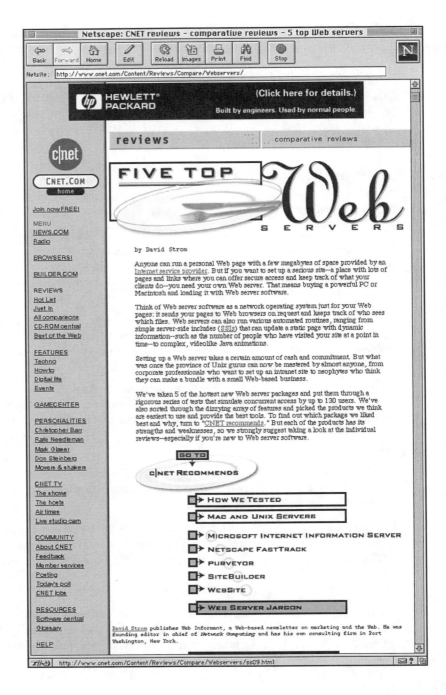

Okay. You've paid good hard cash and installed a respected piece of software and learned how to use it. You're generating detailed reports on all aspects of your site. You're finished, right? Nope.

All you did was implement a reporting system. You still have to prove that your numbers are correct. You have to prove that you didn't jimmy the logs, didn't write an automated Web site reader, or hire an infinite number of high school students. For proof, you have to go to an outside agency.

Get Audited   The "Independent Verification and Validation" section in Chapter 5, "Measure for Measure," describes the need for audits and the types of companies that can do them. Since you're selling ad space, you'll be on the underside of the magnifying glass.

Yes, it's a pain. Yes, it's going to cost you something. But it gives you two things you cannot survive without: credibility and comparability.

I like your site. I like your style. Heck, I even like you. But I don't know that I can trust you. Builders are bonded, stock brokers are licensed, doctors hold degrees. Banks are audited and so are companies that sell ad space or time. Having that little stamp of approval isn't going to bring in more sales. It isn't going to suddenly make doubting advertisers jump on board your list of happy clients, but it will remove one of the obstacles between you and a sale. It will also either set you apart from competitors who are not audited or keep you from being dropped from the short list because you're not.

The other value an audit brings to your prospective clients is a standard report they can use to compare your site to the others they are considering.

When the whole site measurement thing began, it was all a matter of comparing apples to kumquats. Netscape said they got so many visits per day. Yahoo! reported so many page views. ESPN had so many sessions. Playboy had visitors. How could an advertiser know the difference and know which was best?

If I can easily compare your site to the others I'm considering, it makes my life easier and you will be able to close the sale faster.

Another reason I'll tip my decision in your favor is if you can show me a primo plan for promoting your site.

Your Site Promotion Plans

I'm elated that you were sighted by Glen Davis from Project Cool (**www.projectcool.com**) as one of the coolest sites on the Web. Really. That's just swell. I'm glad it caused a twofold spike in your traffic. Really. But what about next week? What are you going to do to improve traffic once my banner is waving on your site?

The criteria is the same as I use when deciding whether to put up a booth at one of the never-ending streams of trade shows. Each one tells me how theirs is the biggest and the best and attracts the best audience. But if one tells me they're going to send out direct mail to 30,000 people in the local metropolitan area and the other talks about a 100,000 mailing and radio spots and magazine inserts and the Goodyear Blimp, my choice is obvious.

Are you putting up banners of your own? Are you sending direct mail to every other dwelling in the Bronx about your window-box gardening site? Where do you start?

Start with your referrer logs. These are the traces left in the fabric of the Internet that tell you where your current visitors come from. Do they all come from Yahoo!? Then it's time to buy a banner there and increase the daily numbers. Do the majority of them come from the Small Flowering Plant Seed Company Web site? Time to figure out a joint-marketing program with them.

Aside from actively spending money to make your site more visible to window ledge horticulturists, it's time to pay another visit to the Netpost site (**www.netpost.com/wa97**). Eric Ward tells you exactly what to do to get noticed. Follow his advice. Even better, hire him to help you.

Whatever you do, two things are important here. One is that you continually look for ways to improve your traffic. The other is that you have a way of communicating to potential clients that you are continually finding and implementing ways to increase your traffic. That's where the proposal comes in.

The Proposal

I write proposals all the time. I'm careful not to use too much boilerplate. Some is absolutely necessary, but too much gets too dull, too fast. A good proposal gives a very solid impression of you and your work, no matter if you're on the 78th floor or in your basement. It's an impression that lasts.

The one thing I've learned from many proposals I have written is the surprising importance of paper.

Commit It to Paper   I have created the proposal that had to get there today when I was flying all day. The e-mail proposal has some real pluses:

> It's easy to create because it's made of plain text—you don't get sidetracked by desktop publishing.
>
> Delivery is in moments.
>
> It's easy to copy to multiple people.
>
> It's easy for prospects to mark it up and return for revision.

It's also quite dull. It's downright boring. In fact, it's a bit disrespectful.

So, to overcome the minuses, I print out a copy with lovely graphic elements on fine bond and I FedEx it as soon as I can after the e-mail has been sent. The response has always been positive.

The team doing the real evaluation can print the e-mail just fine. But if they like what they see, they need to show their decision to upper management. If what they show is a printed e-mail, there is a serious unprofessional air attached to it, like turning in a draft with cross-outs and marginalia.

Once, in a fit of creativity, I put my fabulous proposal up on a private Web page, sent an e-mail with the URL in it to my contact, and waited for the praise to come pouring in. This was, of course, in March of 1997, when the Internic domain registry was turning off domains for non-payment, whether you had paid or not. I had paid. They didn't notice.

"Jim, are you sure we've got it right? It *is* www.targeting.com, right?"

"Yes...."

"Well it's not there anymore. 'No DNS entry.' Not only that, but my e-mail is bouncing with an 'Unknown Host' error."

"Grrrrr."

Within two days targeting.com was back online. Yes, it was wonderful, they said, but could I please send them a printout? When they tried to print it, the page breaks were all messed up. I had neglected to take into account that they were in London and printing on A4-sized sheets. And they had to have paper. They couldn't get their manager to review it on a terminal. He didn't have a terminal at his desk and he wanted good old paper.

Make It Complete   You get the same advice for a proposal that you get for a Web site: Make sure that anybody who stumbles upon it has enough information to make a buying decision, and make it so easy to read that somebody looking for something in particular can get right to it. You know: table of contents and an index?

Your proposal should have the usual in it:

Who are you?

How long have you been on the Net?

What is your Web site all about?

How long has it been up?

Who comes to your site?

How long do they stay?

How often do they come back?

Who else advertises on this site?

What other sites compete for your audience?

How much do you charge?

But it should also have a good deal in it about your prospective client: Why are all the facts and figures of particular importance to them? How does the combination of traffic and audience and pricing fit their needs at the moment? Make it personal.

The Price of Admission

The one item they are going to be most interested in seeing in your proposal is your pricing. You can select pricing one of three ways. One won't work at all, one is okay if you must, and the other takes a lot more time and trouble but will be worth it in the long run.

Set your price based on your costs

Set your price based on your competitors

Set your price based on what the market will bear

It's common for companies with little or no experience and no touchstone in the market to figure their pricing on what they'd like their profits to be. You ad up the rent, the electricity, the labor, the phone lines, and the server maintenance costs and you ad 20% percent or so just to give you a ball-park.

Wrong answer. Your costs are very different from others. Your price will be so far out of step that it will make the rest of your proposal suspect. It may be way over the moon. You may have incurred some costs you shouldn't have. It may be rock bottom. You may have forgotten to add in the cost of the copy machine, or you may simply have forgotten to add in the value of having created a site that attracts a lot of people. Don't forget that your ability to attract a specific type of person has a serious value to advertisers.

Liberal borrowing of prices from your competitors will assure that you won't have to work very hard at inventing one yourself. It also means that your potential client has an easy way to compare the two of you. But what if they used the previous pricing method? Then you're both wrong.

The right choice is to scour the landscape and see what banners are selling for these days— over all. Take a look at Interactive Publishing Alert's Advertising Index (**www.netcreations.com/ipa/adindex**), shown in Figure 10.4, and get a feeling for today's banner rates.

You can search this database by:

Name of Publication/Web site

Location of Site

General Category of Site

Description/Keywords

Normalized Advertising Rate (U.S. dollars per month)

Names of Current Advertisers/Sponsors

Traffic Statistics

For a picture of the most well-known sites, take a look at the lengthy listing at **www.adresource.com/whatitco.htm** that discusses specific site traffic and pricing.

Then try to compare your site to the sites you find there. Which ones have about the same traffic you have? Which have about the same level of subject matter focus? Which ones offer about the same level of detailed visitor information? This will give you an idea of what the market will bear at the moment.

Then it's time to thoroughly check out your competition. No, not just the other Web sites that cover exactly the same things you do, but the sites that cover things that would attract exactly the same audience your prospective client is looking for. Your competition may be in far flung subject matter but still threaten to steal your client's limited budget.

Oh—and be ready to negotiate. Be very ready.

FIG. 10.4

The Advertising Index keeps track of who advertises where and what the rate cards say.

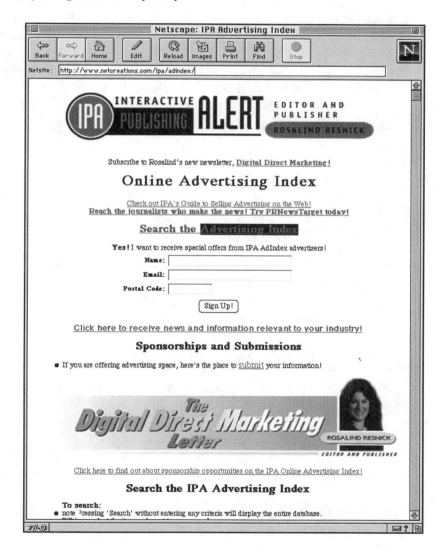

Trail Balloons

Here we are again at the statement that we haven't been doing this long enough to know what the right price is. Yahoo! thought selling clickthroughs to Proctor & Gamble was the right thing to do at the time because they wanted P&G's business.

You're going to have to float some prices in front of prospects and see if they bite. They are going to know you're doing it. They're going to look at your site and see how many different advertisers you have on board and make some assumptions. Fortunately, they don't have to know how much those others are paying for the privilege.

Make an offer. Ask them how much they're spending at other sites. Ask them if they're willing to be flexible and consider alternative plans, packages, and sponsorships. Talk to them. Negotiate. Be prepared for them to offer you only half of what you ask.

And expect them to ask for a free sample.

The Free Ride

They will ask for the free sample. "Yeah, it looks good all right, but we don't really know how your audience will respond to our banner. We'd like to try in for a week until we get tired and can make up our minds. If it brings in more traffic than some of the other sites we're working on, we'll cut a deal."

You can talk quality. You can talk value. You can talk references. This is probably the best way to convince prospective buyers that freebies are old news. Have them call your other clients and hear about the wonderful response they're getting and how they're delighted with how easy and inexpensive it is to do business with you.

You have no clients yet? Hand out some freebies.

What Do You Find Acceptable?

After toiling and sweating and proposing and pleading and begging, you have finally bagged an account. Somebody is willing to give you money. Break out the aspirin.

Now comes the make-it-or-break-it side of customer service. The best way to limit the number of problems you have is to develop some policies up front and publish them in an obvious place. Your proposal, your contract, and your Web site come to mind. Make those policies easy to understand and easy to regulate. Just make up your mind which are important for you.

Geometric Size Standards

What size banners will you accept? All kinds, as long as it's a paying customer? Do yourself and your customers a favor and standardize. They don't want to have to create a special sized ad for you, and you don't want to have to cater to the creative idiosyncrasies of dozens of different client's agencies' graphic artists.

Go with the CASIE standard to begin with and be done with it. Then, read the following section on the need to improvise.

File Size Standards

Now that your clients know how big the banner can be, how about the file? If I want to place a 150K banner on your pages, your whole site looks like it's trying to serve overhead slams under water. Not pretty. If you place ads with huge banner file sizes, they will slow your site down. If your site slows down, people will stop coming. If people stop coming, you can't sell ad space. Vicious cycle.

Set a size limitation and post it in a conspicuous place. Make it obvious that you run a lean, mean, serving machine.

Whose Serve Is It?

Some advertisers desire to assuredly control and verifiably count how many banners are served and when. The option under consideration is to serve their banners from their server onto your pages themselves. Don't fall for it.

The success of your site depends on your ability to keep it as fast as possible. If the client serves banners slowly, even if they're small files, you're in the same pickle as if the banners are big, fat, slow ones.

File Type Standards

A banner is a banner is a banner, right? By any other name it would serve as sweet? If it's a GIF it would. But what if it's an animated GIF? A JPEG? A JavaScript or a Java applet? What if it's a Vtag order form?

This issue is worth considering for three reasons: technical requirements, download requirements, and administration requirements.

Can your server handle the new, weird types of files that pop up daily? Are you willing to accommodate a server push banner? Are you willing to stay on the cutting edge? Maybe your visitors expect it of you. Maybe they're after the type of audience that expects it. On the other hand, your entire audience may be coming to your site with the oldest of browsers and can't handle anything beyond an animated GIF.

The amount of time it takes to download somebody else's banner is another consideration. If it's a big file, you just say no. But if the banner is an applet that wants to call on servers scattered far and wide, is that okay with you? Would you even know what to look for? If it's only 10K, no problem—until you test it out through an America Online connection and find that a 10K banner calls other files from other servers and slows the whole page load to a crawl. Worse, whatever files it goes to get are incompatible with some older browsers and your page doesn't load at all.

What if a client was willing to pay extra—a lot extra—for a streaming video banner? At some point, somebody will ask. What will you say?

The administrative issue comes to play when your client decides they need to have control over what banner you're serving at the moment. Create a client-only Web page that allows clients to place their own banners in your database at will. That works fine as long as they adhere to your previously-defined standards and understand the financial penalties you will impose if they "forget" or simply ignore your wishes.

If your client decides to update their banner at your peak traffic hour and your database is busy serving ads, their update may bring your entire server to a crawl. Consider putting your banner database on a different machine. Consider having a nice, friendly chat with the folks who run the gear and gently inquire about potential bottlenecks. Then let them come up with brilliant technical solutions. You have more things to worry about, like what the banner says, shows, and implies.

Ad Content

Are you okay with a banner promoting a Bikini Photo Contest? How about a concert by a band whose name could never appear in a family newspaper? It's certainly not for me to tell you what is decent and what is indecent. That's for you to decide. That's the point.

Let prospective clients know what your measure of decency, applicability, and acceptability are. Put it in writing right up front. "Sorry, but that's against our policy as stated in section 5.6, Acceptable Advertising, in our proposal and contracts." That sounds much better than, "Sorry, buddy, but I think that banner is beneath our dignity."

Would you accept a banner from a competitive Web site? Would you accept a banner from a political organization? How about one that was an appeal for donations to a religious group? Your personal beliefs definitely come to play, but your first responsibility is to your visitors. If they get uncomfortable when faced with a social issue from United Colors of Benetton, if they feel uneasy about The Body Shop's stand on animal testing, if they balk at Sally Struthers' ongoing crusade, it's up to you to maintain the tenor of your site.

You didn't forget about your lawyers, did you? Somebody has to take care when publishing a periodical (like a Web site) that whatever gets published doesn't defame or encroach on somebody else's copyright.

Finding Clients

You know you have a killer Web site. All the people who write to your Webmaster say so. So where are the advertisers? Why aren't they beating your door down? How do you find people to give you money?

Check the Directories

The first stop is the directories of Web sites willing to sell ads. Check out **www.ca-probate.com/comm_net.htm#_reg** and start calling, mailing, and sending e-mail.

Make sure your description is appropriately compelling without stretching things too far. It's flattering to have a dozen people a day send e-mail asking about the specifics, but it's a waste of time if they discover you weren't as accurate as you might have been. Make your directory listing as factual as possible, and you won't have to spend an inordinate amount of your time being unproductive with non-buyers.

Be sure to put these Web advertising registers on your calendar and keep them updated. Your traffic will grow, your content will increase, your focus may change. Keep the directories up-to-date, and you'll attract advertisers who didn't know about you before because of the key-words they were using.

Drop In on the Competition

Is somebody else running a site on the same, or a similar, subject? Maybe a different subject but one that caters to the clients you cater to? Stop by once a week and see who's buying banner space from them. Then pick up the phone.

This is not a situation for a casual e-mail. That's too close to spamming for comfort. This is a job for personal contact. "Are you getting the response you're hoping for from that site? Is it the right demographic for you? If you're looking for surfers who are younger/older/richer/poorer/more this/less that, I may have the solution."

Getting Others to Sell for You

You don't have to do all the work yourself. You could get others to go out and sell your space for you—for a price.

Those same Web representatives and networks described in Chapter 6, "Looking for Space in all the Right Places," as places to buy ad space are in need of ad space to sell. If you have enough traffic and if it's identifiable traffic, then you can solicit their help in selling the space. You might also turn to the Adbots of the world and see if your site appeals to the auction crowd. Just be prepared to share the income. It's called commission, and it can range anywhere from 10% to 50%.

Offline Collaboration

Let's say you have a wonderful site about all of the joys of sewing your own clothes. You pulled out all the stops and are offering patterns people can download and print out at home. You have a database filled with them and a friend in the fabric business who scans the latest print material for you, so sewers can pick a pattern and then see what it would look like in their size in a variety of shades. You are uncompromising in your zeal to provide the latest news from fashion runways around the world. So where do you find banner buyers?

There you are, pondering your financial future while pawing through ads in the latest *Sewing Today* magazine and wondering if you should contact each of the print advertisers: companies selling sewing machines, material, thread, lace, elastic. It's a fairly long list and you see the task stretch out before you like a trip to the dentist. Then it hits you. Of course, you should contact them! But you're wily enough to let somebody else do your leg work for you.

Sewing Today, Modern Tailor, and *Lifestyles of the Stitch and Seamstress* are not just potential advertisers for your Web site; they are also potential sellers of advertising on your Web site.

Do they have sites? Not yet? Wouldn't they like to offer their clients a chance to have banner space on the Internet? Wouldn't they like to bundle your banner space with their magazine space? Wouldn't they like to pocket a little extra money from the clients they know and love and have been selling to for years?

Yes, you'll have to spend a day with their sales people explaining what they should and shouldn't say about online advertising, but the result is worth it. You'll have many more feet on the street than you can afford to hire. You'll be associated with the top magazines in your niche. You'll be able to spend every waking minute improving your site instead of trying to feed it.

Keep your mind open and every now and then a good idea or two can drop in.

Help Your Clients Be Successful

Good ideas are one of the reasons people stick with you as a client. It's not just that your Web site attracts people who might buy from them, it's that you make an active effort to understand what your clients are trying to accomplish and figure out ways to help them.

The place to start is a standard presentation leveraged over multiple media. You don't need to create a CD-ROM with flashy graphics; I didn't mean multimedia, I meant multiple media. If your client is a good old-fashioned type, go meet with him, ready to make use of the overhead projector. If it's just the two of you, show the paper version of your charts, graphs, and bullet points. If you're meeting with a room full of slightly more technically-oriented types, be ready to plug your laptop into the projector and give them the full PowerPoint drill.

If your prospect is too far away to visit in person and is excited about the technology, it's time to translate your presentation into HTML. Get them on the speakerphone and have somebody on their end be the designated clicker. That way you can talk them through the whole thing and they can ask questions along the way.

As with all dealings with prospects, your main job is putting on the customer-colored glasses and thinking like them. They don't want to hear what they already know. They also don't want to get inundated with technical jargon they don't understand. They want to know:

> What is it?
>
> What does it require?
>
> What will they get out of it?

What is banner advertising on the Web? Can you explain it in English? Can you spell it out? If they already know, then you have a different objective. You have to prove to them that *you* know what it is, and you have to do it quickly.

How much effort and how much money will it take them to do business with you? Will they have to devote a full-time person to create, maintain, update, and track their ads? Will they have to take raw statistics from you and try to format meaningful reports, or will they be able to rely on you for some of that? Just what are they paying for, anyway? Then, of course, they'll want to know how much they're paying.

Reconnaissance

Most of this is dependent on you in advance knowing what they know. You've never been there before or met with them before, so how can you in advance know what they know? It's called homework and it's critical.

Talk to as many people in the organization as you can ahead of time. Find out who creates their print ads and chat them up. Find out who negotiates their contracts and make a few discrete inquires. Talk to the administrative assistants and learn what the approval process and acquisition procedures look like at their firm. The more you know, the smarter you are, and the more impressive you'll be.

Creativity Counseling

If you have a Web site that attracts millions of people, chances are you deal with banner buyers who have been around the virtual block a few times. They can tell a hawk from a handsaw and they'll want to talk numbers.

But if they're new to the banner game, they might well look to you for advice on making a banner that works. You're the one who produces the reports on which banner gets the most clicks. They're going to assume you know why. Might I suggest you suggest some light reading for them? How about a recent tome titled *What Makes People Click*? It makes a great leave-behind on sales calls.

One Step Beyond—Adding Value

There are more Web sites popping up every day than there are tourists in Paris. A healthy portion of those sites sell banner space. The hardest thing for a potential buyer of ad space to do is figure out, beyond the sheer numbers, why they should put their ad on your site rather than one of a dozen others.

How many visitors your site has is a critical issue. Exactly who they are is everything. If you only get two people coming to your site each day, but they are the right people, then I'll buy banner space from you. But it seems the traffic on your site and the next are pretty much equal. And, with all things being equal, a decision to buy space on your site over the next one is tough. You can make it easier.

Try to take an extra step. Try to come up with another idea, another service, another way to promote your site that the others aren't doing yet.

Periodic Table of Banners

I hate it when I go back to a site because I saw a banner and it's gone. I don't know why I expect it to be there. I never look for an ad on television based on the show during which I last saw it. I do, however, look in the same magazine for an ad I saw in last week's or last month's issue.

So give me an index to your advertisers just like it's done in trade magazines. List them alphabetically. List them by product. List them by product category. List them by date. Then let me click through to the banner itself to see if it's the one I remember and then let me clickthrough to the advertiser's site. Your clients will end up with more traffic and your site visitors will appreciate it.

Advanced Intelligence

Every now and again, ask your visitors a question or two. The occasional survey will help further identify your visitors. You might also offer pre- and post surveys. Ask your visitors if they've ever heard of StayGlo Luminescent Strips first. Then place the ad, and then do a follow-up quiz to see if they remember who StayGlo is.

Offer some sort of extra privilege to people who are willing to be on your Question of the Month list. The first of every month, you send out an e-mail asking something about your site or your sponsors. Keep it short. Don't hit them with a fifteen-page inquisition. Just ask one or two multiple choice questions that can be answered in no time. Then start another Question of the Month list that goes out on the fifteenth of the month. Find out even more about your audience.

Start an insiders' discussion list about your site. The "advisory council" can be very helpful in telling you what works and what doesn't. That type of information is invaluable to your clients and may be the deciding factor in sending the business your way.

Spring for the time and money and have a real focus group. Fly people in, feed them lunch, and ask them in person how they feel about the site and the advertisers.

Now you're offering more information back to your clients than your competitors.

Accommodate, Adapt, Improvise

The times, they are changing. Go with the flow. Don't create processes and procedures and automation techniques that are set in stone. Keep things light and be willing to turn on a dime.

There's nothing a client likes better than to come up with an idea and be told it's a great idea. Go ahead and try things. You might be surprised. Your customers will end up a lot happier that they are working with somebody who respects their creativity and is willing to implement their ideas to see if they work.

The bottom line is that we have only just begun. We're not sure where we're headed. If you believe Bill Gates, and the man has made a dollar or two in his time, then we'll look back on the past twenty years as the time when everybody could have a computer but you couldn't talk to them. If your Web site is going to start talking soon, then the kind of ads you place will change dramatically. Who knows what type of ads will work and which will bomb? Where will the great ideas for new types of advertising come from?

They might come from discussion groups like the Online Advertising List. They might come from after-hours meetings with your sales team. They might come from your customers.

So listen to your clients. They don't live and breathe the Web like you do, so when they come up with an idea, it's from an entirely different perspective. That can be just the extra ingredient required to invent the next great advertising method.

Keep your mind open. ●

CHAPTER 11

A Few Words About the Law

It's nice to have an understanding of a subject. It's advisable to have a plan of action. It's good to set a proper level of expectation. In addition, it's very important to stay out of trouble along the way. There are some things you shouldn't do online and forewarned is forearmed.

This appendix is not intended to mete out morality. That should be entirely unnecessary. There's pretty much one rule to live and work by in that regard: If you think it pushes the boundaries of morality, for goodness' sake, don't do it. That's as much as you need from me on right and wrong.

What you do need is a feel for the tripwires. Some are obvious, some are not. Most will only be set by law when they are brought to the courts dressed up in suits. If you've been in business for more than a few years, you've come to learn that right or wrong, lawsuits are a drain on all resources: financial, temporal, and emotional.

The best approach is to know enough about the law to know when to bring in an attorney. If you let a wound fester long enough, it can reach the point of amputation. If you ignore a legal issue long enough, it can put you out of business.

There are a couple of twists to the world of online advertising that need special attention. The first is privacy. While we are just starting to come to terms with database marketing, those databases are now accessible. The second is jurisdiction. If ever there were a medium that could cross borders, the Internet is it.

Before delving into those, it's worth a moment to review the laws that don't change much. All of the laws of the land apply to the Net. The rules for advertising in print and on the air still have meaning on the wire. You're not permitted to advertise medical products or drugs that have not been approved by the FDA—period. It doesn't matter if it's TV, radio, blimps, or hand-bills. If you're in the medical field, you know how strict the FDA can be. When Claratin put up the Allergy Relief Site, the FDA made them take it down until they changed the name to the Allergy Symptom Relief Site.

For the rest of us, the rules of advertising apply and the Federal Trade Commission is the judge. ▪

Traditional Advertising Issues

Don't lie, cheat, or steal. Sounds straightforward, but there are those who feel the best way to describe their products is simply a matter of taste and style. The government doesn't agree. In the eyes of the Federal Trade Commission (FTC), it's a matter of being able to substantiate your claims, a matter of not deceiving your prospects, and a matter of fairness.

Ad Substantiation

You just said your new fountain pen can write underwater—even in whip cream. You just said your house coating is ten times thicker than paint. You just claimed that your airline has the best on-time record in the industry. Can you back that up? Can you prove it? Have you got the test results handy?

The FTC Policy Statement Regarding Advertising Substantiation Program from August 2, 1984 (**www.webcom.com/~lewrose/adsubpol.html**) reads in part:

> *[There is a] legal requirement pursuant to section 5 of the Federal Trade Commission Act that advertisers and ad agencies have a reasonable basis for their objective claims before their initial dissemination.*
>
> *Many ads contain express or implied statements regarding the amount of support the advertiser has for the product claim. When the substantiation claim is express (e.g., 'tests prove,' 'doctors recommend,' and 'studies show'), the Commission expects the firm to have at least the advertised level of substantiation. Of course, an ad may imply more substantiation than it expressly claims or may imply to consumers that the firm has a certain type of support; in such cases, the advertiser must possess the amount and type of substantiation the ad actually communicates to consumers.*
>
> *Absent an express or implied reference to a certain level of support, and absent other evidence indicating what consumer expectations would be, the Commission assumes that consumers expect a 'reasonable basis' for claims.*

If you promote your products anywhere by claiming that four out of five doctors recommend rubbing it on your toes after each meal, that's fine—as long as you can prove that you interviewed enough doctors and they did, indeed, make such a recommendation. If you don't make a claim with proof, but just make a claim, that's fine. As long as the claim can be considered reasonable. "Will keep you alive and well underwater for days," is a little tough to swallow without some kind of clinical tests to back it up. "These four strong legs will ensure your table stays where you put it," doesn't really require a battery of tests. We expect things to generally stay where we put them and since the matter of strength is not comparative (stronger than what?), there's nothing to substantiate.

Deception

The FTC Deception Policy Statement, from October 14, 1983 (**www.webcom.com/~lewrose/ deceptionpol.html**) says in part:

> Certain elements undergird all deception cases. First, there must be a representation, omission or practice that is likely to mislead the consumer. Practices that have been found misleading or deceptive in specific cases include false oral or written representations, misleading price claims, sales of hazardous or systematically defective products or services without adequate disclosures, failure to disclose information regarding pyramid sales, use of bait and switch techniques, failure to perform promised services, and failure to meet warranty obligations.

Sounds like a nervous shopper's nightmare. Makes you want never to buy a used car again. These are the problems people run into when they have a shoddy product to start with. This sort of malfeasance is perpetrated by those who operate under more pressure than their integrity or common sense can bear. Try this stuff on the Internet and the phrase, "Oh, what a tangled web we weave, when first we practice to deceive," takes on a whole new meaning.

Unfairness

"That's not fair!" If you have children, you know that phrase very well. The Supreme Court knew that there was no way to properly define unfair business practices in a meaningful way that would stand the test of time. Instead, they put their trust in the courts to keep up-to-date.

Federal Trade Commission Unfairness Policy Statement, December 17, 1980:

> By 1964 enough cases had been decided to enable the Commission to identify three factors that it considered when applying the prohibition against consumer unfairness. These were: (1) whether the practice injures consumers; (2) whether it violates established public policy; (3) whether it is unethical or unscrupulous.

Injury Did the ad cause you to buy something unwanted or defective, or harm you by leaving off some important bit of information? Billboards for cigarettes in London loudly proclaim, "Smoking Kills." It's a little more in-your-face than the quiet Surgeon General's statement in American advertisements. The first test is that the injury be of substance. You see an ad that injures your sense of style? Upsets your delicate sensibilities? Ruffles your predisposition toward the socially acceptable? Sorry, not substantial.

The second test is the "net effect" issue. If the harm done is outweighed by the good provided, the net effect is not an injury. This one is a bit squishy but stands to reason. "A seller's failure to present complex technical data on his product may lessen a consumer's ability to choose, for example," says the Unfairness Policy Statement, "but may also reduce the initial price he must pay for the article."

It's just not fair that my new laptop isn't documented well enough for me to get it to print through the nifty infrared port without spending an hour on hold waiting for tech support to explain how. On the other hand, if it were documented that well, it would cost twice as much and the manuals would take up a significant portion of my book shelf. The net effect is a non-injury.

The third test of an injury is that it "must be one which the consumer could not reasonably avoid." If you bought the broken lamp that was marked down, when there plenty of others to choose from, that's not an injury. If you were not told the lamp was broken, or if you were told that all of the others were, it would be a different story. If the media owner has a financial interest in an advertiser's success and secretly blocks other ads from being seen, then your injury as a space buyer could not be reasonably avoided and, well, that's just not fair.

Public Policy   Were there any local laws or established industry practices violated by the ad? Sometimes this test is used to determine that the advertising methods were unfair, but most often it's used to help determine the validity of the supposed injury. "The Commission wishes to emphasize the importance of examining outside statutory policies and established judicial principles for assistance in helping the agency ascertain whether a particular form of conduct does in fact tend to harm consumers."

If the community has determined that the practice is unfair, then the Commission needn't waste additional time trying to prove it.

Unethical and Unscrupulous   Here the Commission uses words usually brought to bear on cartoon characters or men in melodramas with black top hats and long waxed mustaches—words like immoral and oppressive.

This was added to be sure there was a way for the Commission to catch bad guys even if they squirmed around the first two issues. However, "Conduct that is truly unethical or unscrupulous will almost always injure consumers or violate public policy as well. The Commission has therefore never relied on the third element…an independent basis for finding of unfairness, and it will act on the basis of the first two."

Who knows, maybe the Internet will provide the unique circumstances necessary for the Commission to change its tune on this one.

Trademark and Copyright

The church was up in arms when the printing press made it possible to easily make multiple copies of a document or a book. They were afraid they would lose control over the dissemination of thought and the total rule of government. They were right.

The literary world was up in arms when the copy machine made it possible to easily make multiple copies of a document or a book. They were afraid they would lose control over the financial return on their efforts. The impact has not been significant.

The music industry was up in arms when the tape recorder/cassette recorder/digital recorder made it possible to easily make multiple copies of a piece of music. They were sure they would lose control over their ability to profit from copyrights. They had a bit more to worry about.

Today, they are all afraid of the Internet. Ideas can spread far and wide. A book can be posted to a newsgroup and downloaded by the thousands. A music sample can be put up on a Web site for all to hear.

But the law hasn't changed. It's still illegal to profit from somebody else's creation without permission. It's just that it's so much easier than before. In fact, instantly making copies of things on the Net is how the whole thing works.

Copies by Necessity   When you come to my Web site, you're not logged onto my computer. You're not "at" my computer. Instead, you made a request for a page. My server sent you that page, your computer stored it in your cache file, and displayed it on your screen. You can hang up the phone, pull the modem out of your computer, and be completely disconnected from my machine, and you're still looking at my home page. You made an electronic copy. And we won't even get into the issue of proxy servers that keep the copy for showing to other people.

The issue here is, what are you going to do with it? There's no problem if I check out the United Airlines home page and view their corporate logo. But if I "Save Image As…" and decide to put it up on my Web site as if they're endorsing my company, we have a problem.

Covering Your Assets   Trademarks and copyrights revolve around ownership and ownership revolves around protection. You are not permitted to call your tissues Kleenex or your copier a Xerox. These are not generic terms. Yes, they're used in modern day vernacular, but they are the respective properties of their owners. To satisfy the courts, owners must exhibit an active program of protecting their possessions.

If somebody calls their tissues Kleenex and Kimberly-Clark doesn't go after them, the courts figure Kimberly-Clark doesn't care. Once enough people have used the term, it is considered to be part of everyday speech and, bingo, no more ownership. The owner let their proprietorship lapse.

Fair Use   The fair use doctrine covers the use of others' materials for the purposes of education. This book is filled with pictures of Web sites. Because this book is intended as an educational tool and I'm showing these sites for the purposes of example or criticism, it's okay. If I were to create a coffee table book of all the nifty sites out there and offered no critique, I could expect to hear from some lawyers. Half would be there defending their clients' copyrights and half would be there arguing that their clients deserved a share of the profits.

In May, 1997, the Council on Fair Use adjourned for the year having agreed to disagree. A conclave of software developers, musicians, book publishers, academics, and video producers, this gathering conceded a lack of consensus. Even so, fourteen academic groups like the

American Council on Education, the American Library Association, and the National Humanities Alliance issued a statement opposing the proposals that the Council on Fair Use did publish. The digital world has made the issues a bit fuzzy.

There are a number of companies, however, that are looking at providing a technical solution to digital ownership: the digital watermark. This is a string of bits that would become part of the picture or the music that would be ingrained in the file like DNA. (There's a good paper on digital watermarks by Hal Berghel, University of Arkansas and Lawrence O'Gorman, Bell Laboratories at **www.acm.org/~hlb/publications/dig_wtr/dig_watr.html**.) Once fingerprinted, a daily search of the Web for that particular string of DNA would provide the first level of proof that you were trying to protect your mark. The next level is going after the perpetrators.

All in all, you still own the rights to your creations. It's still a crime for somebody to copy your work and use it as their own. It's just that it's so much easier to do.

Contests

Contests and sweepstakes are a big draw in the world of advertising. They're a big draw all by themselves. I freely admit to buying a lottery ticket or two when the jackpot climbs above $20 million. A million dollars a year for a buck? Go ahead and laugh, but I'll be writing my next book from my own little island in the Bahamas. Move over, James Martin.

But the rules and regulations about gaming are many and varied and can get you into a lot of hot water very quickly if you don't pay strict attention. The best place to start is with a definition of the one game that will get you into trouble the fastest.

A *lottery* is a contest that awards a prize, is determined by chance, and requires a player to pay something of value to participate. Operating a lottery is also illegal, except by certain states like California and Florida.

If it requires any kind of skill, like writing an essay or submitting a photograph for judging, it's not a lottery. If it can be played for free (no purchase required), it's not a lottery. If you eliminate the element of chance, it's not a lottery. That is, if it requires some skill to win. It is amusing, however, to see how close to the line contests in Canada come. Their idea of skill is, "Answer the following question: 7+3-6 = ?"

Be sure to make it clear who is permitted to participate in your contest. "Only open to residents of California." A simple "Void Where Prohibited" should keep you out of trouble. But remember, we live in changing times. The state of Florida figures that Internet access is a cost of entry for your "free" contest and they may, therefore, consider it a lottery.

One of the best introductions to the legalities of contests in general was written by Margo Block, Esquire, and can be found at the Arent Fox Web site (**www.calivin.arentfox.com/features/sweepstakes/articles/sweep.html**).

Unique to the Internet

There are some issues that are being decided as we surf. They are open for interpretation and are food for thought. The legality of unsolicited e-mail is being tested in our courts. The issues surrounding privacy are exaggerated online and are causing a great deal of discussion. The biggest conundrum of all, however, may be the puzzle of jurisdiction. Let's take the easy one first.

Unsolicited E-Mail

Love it or hate it, sending e-mail to a mass list of people who did not specifically sign up for it is bad marketing. But is it illegal?

That question seems to rest solely in the hands of Sanford Wallace of Cyber Promotions, Inc. Wallace is the self-proclaimed Spam King and makes a living helping others send out unsolicited e-mail. To the tune of four million each day.

He has been sued by America Online. He has been sued by CompuServe. He had been sued by Web Systems, a Web site developer in Houston, Texas. AOL and CompuServe wanted him to stop sending mail to their customers. They settled. Web Systems has a different gripe.

Web Systems was getting an avalanche of e-mail from people all around the Net complaining about the spam they received, seemingly from Web Systems. Web Systems didn't do it. Web Systems points to the King of Spam and says he was using Web Systems as a spurious return address. Cyber Promotions sent out hundreds of thousands of e-mails and made it look like they all came from Web Systems.

Why? Because anybody who spams can expect an avalanche of angry e-mail. So, in an effort to stay in business and not have their servers inundated with hate mail, Cyber Promotions and their ilk forged the return address. How often do you try to reply to a message that offers to remove you from their list, only to have your request bounce back as a non-address?

If the return address really belongs to another company, we start dealing with issues of copyright as well. It'll get very interesting before it's over. And it's only just begun.

Frank Murkowski, a Republican Congressman from Alabama, has proposed the Unsolicited Electronic Mail Choice Act of 1997. It would require spammers to identify their spams by putting "ad" or "advertisement" as the first word in the subject line. That way, e-mail programs could filter them all to the trash basket.

A nice idea, but not a solution. When I'm in a hotel in Hong Kong and being charged two US dollars per minute for using the phone, I don't want to wait for ten minutes while spammers fill my hard drive with trash.

If there is any legislation that comes out of it, I'm hoping it's not a restriction on what one is allowed to send, but on the necessity of signing your work. That way, if I get spammed, I can simply ask 10,000 of my closest friends to send the offending company an e-mail with a copy of the operating system attached.

Privacy

The copyright problem on the Internet is that it's so easy to make copies. The privacy problem on the Internet is that it's so easy to collect and access information.

When you consider the amount of information there is out there about you, it's, well, more than you can remember. Do you recall how many speeding tickets you got in the past seven years? The DMV knows. How about the number of times your mortgage check got to the bank a day late? (Hey, I forgot it was Memorial Day and the Post Office was closed!) The bank remembers. Your affinity card at the grocery store means they know every item you bought and when. American Express knows how much you spend on airline tickets. City Hall knows if you bought or sold a business.

This doesn't really become an issue if each of those entities keeps it to themselves. But now, it's so easy for different organizations to share information that your whole life story is bobbing around out there on the sea of consumer database marketing.

On the one hand, I'm all for data sharing. When I have to fill out a medical history questionnaire, I always have to scratch my head. Did I have the eye operation when I was four or five years old? Was I a freshman or a sophomore when I had mononucleosis? Why can't they just access that great big database in the sky and be done with it?

The problem comes when people know too much about you. Just ask the expectant mother a week after she's found out she's an expectant mother. The mail box fills with offers for diaper services and pregnancy-exercise video tapes. The phone rings with people selling all flavors of insurance, investments, and nutritional supplements.

In June, 1997, Lexis-Nexis joined seven other large personal information companies and announced an agreement to voluntarily limit the privacy intrusions their services could cause. Too little, too late says the Electronic Privacy Information Center. Marc Rotenburg, EPIC's director, says the law simply has not kept up with the changing times. "We are selling information today that ten years ago would not be bought and sold," he told a Senate hearing on the subject on June 26, 1996.

At the Privacy & American Business National Conference in October, 1996, FTC Commissioner Christine Varney wondered about the hundreds of other companies that collect and sell personal information. How would we get them to sign the self-limitation agreement? And, as the technology becomes more widely used, how do you get each company in the U.S. to agree to the limits of their personal data collection and dissemination over the Internet? "In short," said Varney, "the time has come for us to consider whether the existing arrangement properly balances individual personal privacy values with competing information flow benefits."

The FTC has to decide if rules and regulations are in order, or if the efforts of organizations such as TRUSTe (**www.truste.org**) will be enough. TRUSTe is asking Web sites to voluntarily label the level of care they take with information about visitors. Will the Web site simply not record the information? Will it keep the information strictly confidential? Will it share the information with third-party marketers? Can the Internet police itself, or is Big Brother required to step in and control potential privacy infringements by a burgeoning host of little brothers?

In the meantime, the Consumer Internet Privacy Protection Act of 1997 is bouncing around the halls of Congress. This bill is intended to prevent the disclosure of personal information without prior written approval. It would provide the subscriber of an interactive computer service the ability to review and correct information about themselves. It would require the sellers of the private information to tell subscribers to whom the information was being sold.

This bill is pretty narrowly focused. It offers up guidelines and remedies for access providers: ISPs. Presumably, ISPs are the only ones on the Internet who know—who really know—if you're a dog. You could describe yourself as just about anything you wanted to the rest of the world, but your ISP knows where you live. Your ISP knows when you log on and assigns the temporary IP address to you each time. That means they know where you surf.

"Oh look, there goes Jim Sterne again, reading the Advertising Age site and Interactive-Week.com. Pretty boring."

"Yeah, maybe, but we got calls just yesterday from Marketing Books Of The World and the Global Database Of Advertising Executives. They both wanted to get the postal addresses of everybody who showed an interest in Internet marketing information. What's our policy on that?"

"Well, that sort of depends on our cash-flow situation."

The issues are many and tend toward the philosophical. Are cookies the greatest thing since baked bread or are they a tool of the devil and should not be foisted off onto unsuspecting users of the Internet?

In June, 1997, the Open Profiling Standard (OPS) was put forward by a co-op that included Netscape, VeriSign, and Firefly. The OPS would let surfers prepare a Personal Profile containing the frequently asked consumer questions:

> Name
>
> Address
>
> Phone number
>
> ZIP code
>
> Age
>
> Marital status
>
> Interests
>
> Hobbies
>
> User ID and password

This profile could then be given out at the touch of a button. That keeps the user in control, it keeps the marketing world mollified, and it even keeps the FTC happy. Christine Varney was quoted in the press release (**www11.netscape.com/newsref/pr/newsrelease411.html**) as saying "OPS brings us one step closer to market-based solutions for privacy protection." We'll see.

The proper answer lies in self-determination. Individuals should have the right to participate in Web activities that collect and store and analyze information about them. If the payback is high enough, enough people will participate to make the venture worthwhile. If they don't feel they are getting value for the information they divulge, they won't. The market can decide.

Jurisdiction

PERSONS OUTSIDE OF MINNESOTA WHO TRANSMIT INFORMATION VIA THE INTERNET KNOWING THAT INFORMATION WILL BE DISSEMINATED IN MINNESOTA ARE SUBJECT TO JURISDICTION IN MINNESOTA COURTS FOR VIOLATIONS OF STATE CRIMINAL AND CIVIL LAWS.

Pursuant to Minnesota Statute Section 609.025 (1994)

And all because of a dispute with Indians. American Indians. It seems that a rifle was fired from inside an Indian reservation across the boundary line at somebody outside the reservation. The intention, said the State Supreme Court, was to cause harm in the state of Minnesota. Fair enough. But what if it's not your intention to cause harm there?

In 1994, Robert and Carleen Thomas, from northern California, were extradited to Tennessee and found guilty of obscenity. They ran a bulletin board from their home that charged money to download dirty pictures. A postmaster in Tennessee was able to download a few that may have been questionable in California but were clearly beyond the scope of decency according to local community standards. Two years in jail for him, thirty months for her.

But what if the couple had run their computer from a country that had no extradition treaty with Minnesota? What if the server were 100 miles off the coast of nowhere? How do you pass laws that govern a communication network that knows no bounds? Web sites updated from the top of Mount Everest, the bottom of the ocean, and the occasional space shuttle are no longer big news. They are simply part of the Net. And the Net is not simply part of any nation on Earth.

International Incident   It's not just time to get more familiar with the law of the land. It's time to get familiar with the laws of the lands.

If you choose to compare your products to those of your competitors, you are very likely to be breaking the law in Germany, France, and Belgium. Offering coupons or discounts? Special offers? Austria, Belgium, and Italy may have a legal bone to pick with you. Putting up a site offering short skirts and see-through blouses? Don't plan on visiting the Middle East very soon.

If you plan on selling products in France, better beware of the Loi Toubon. This is a 1994 law passed by the French government to preserve and protect the mother tongue. A $5,000 fine awaits those bold enough to advertise or label their products in a single language and that language is not French.

The Georgia Institute of Technology was brought up on these very charges for putting up a Web site about their school branch in France. They got off by the skin of their teeth on a technicality, but the issue about Web sites remains open. By the time you read this, the Defense of the French Language and the Future of the French Language groups may have been successful in their appeal of the decision.

CompuServe seems to be forever in trouble in Germany for allowing customers there access to some 200 different sexually-oriented newsgroups. The talk is dirty, the pictures are dirtier, and the German courts hold CompuServe responsible as a publisher. No, the argument goes, we're not the publisher, just the printer. Tell it to Herr Judge.

Virgin Atlantic came afoul of the U.S. Department of Transportation over taxes. They weren't behind in their payments, they were behind in their disclosure. Virgin announced a special advanced purchase fare between the U.S. and the UK and advised customers to check with their travel agent or the reservation desk for availability, restrictions, charges, and taxes. By not disclosing a $38.91 per ticket tax on their Web site, Virgin found themselves on the receiving end of a $14,000 fine. Did the ad meet advertising rules and regulations in Britain? The DOT didn't care. It didn't pass muster in the U.S. and U.S. customers were seeing the ad.

Benetton Group S.p.A. ran its "H.I.V. Positive" tattoo ad in France and had to pay $32,000 because the ad was "a provocative exploitation of suffering." That was in print, but lots of companies like to put their print ads on their Web sites. Beware.

Some of these examples are found in "Internet Marketing: Practical Suggestions for International Advertising and Promotions," written by Lewis Rose and John Feldman of Arent Fox. It can be found at **www.webcom.com/lewrose/article/intl.html**. It also contains some steps to take when preparing an international campaign, such as:

> Make sure you comply with U.S. law first.
>
> Clear your ads in the key foreign markets for the brand by consulting counsel in each country.
>
> Prepare instructions for foreign counsel that includes your advertising, a cover letter about timing, fees, and correspondence, and a questionnaire asking if the ad can be run and what changes would make it acceptable.

Rose and Feldman caution that the law there may be treated differently than the law here. Here, if it's not identified as illegal, give it a try. There, if it is not identified as legal, don't try it.

In summation, there are two rules to live by. First, if you don't plan on doing business in a country that finds your ad objectionable (and you don't have any assets there), don't worry about it. Next, sprinkle your banners, bridge pages, and Web sites with disclaimers.

Disclaimers Are Your Friends

> Void Where Prohibited
>
> Must Be 21 Years Old
>
> Not Valid Outside the United States and Canada
>
> Some Restrictions Apply
>
> Your Mileage May Vary

While these phrases seem to permeate our lives, there's good reason for them. They can protect you and your company. The best protection, however, is not to be stingy with them. It's one thing to have a disclaimer on your home page, but it's far more meaningful (and protectively powerful) if that disclaimer lives on each page that make a potentially offending offer. And don't settle for a link to a common disclaimer, either. The courts may not feel the expressed intent of a linked disclaimer is sufficiently intuitive.

I am not a lawyer, nor do I play one on TV. The information here may be incomplete, out-of-date, or misleading. Always check with your own attorneys in these matters. Some restrictions apply. Your mileage may vary. ●

CHAPTER 12

Conspicuous Conjectures

Advertising is changing. It's going to be different.

Oh, it's still going to have the same purpose, the same goals, and the same intent. It's still going to be measured based on building brands and bringing in responses—but it's going to be different.

Thinkers are going to come up with new thoughts. Tinkerers are going to come up with new technologies. The new technologies are going to cause new tools to be invented. Implementers to come will use those new tools in new ways. And in the midst of all of it is the population of Web surfers doing the inexplicable. We'll have to take them into account as well. ■

New Trends

It's easy creating new technology in a vacuum. It happens all the time. The problem is when those great inventions reach the real world. The real world is starting to react to the World Wide Web and the World Wide Web has started reacting back. It's not the same Web it was last year. It's not even the same one as six months ago. In fact, what day of the week is this?

Women Are Different than Men

We've known for over a year now that women like the Internet because it opens up new channels of communication. They like the collaboration aspect and that has a net effect.

Peter Grunwald is President of Grunwald Associates in Santa Barbara, California, which provides strategic counsel on the education content market for clients including major telephone, cable, and electronic publishing companies. His firm also provides competitive analysis, research, and new media industry tracking services. Grunwald thinks women are very interested in affairs on the Internet. No, not personal affairs—public affairs.

In a recent survey, "one of the things we found out," reports Grunwald, "is that women on the Net are disproportionally more interested than males in using the Internet for political expression. The way you're going to be able to reach women on the Net more effectively with sponsorship, with advertising dollars, is going to be through public affairs sponsorships."

It's not technology that's driving these sorts of changes, it's real people.

The Average Surfer Is Getting Older

They don't have a lot of money. They don't have a lot of friends. They don't have a lot of mobility. But they do have computers and modems and they are jumping online with a vengeance. That's half the picture.

The other half is that the Boomers are in their 50s now. The Boomers watch their kids leaving college and getting off the parental dole. The Boomers are discovering the computer that Junior left behind is pretty interesting, especially when it comes to banking and personal finance.

Their numbers are growing. The Internet is no longer about Gen Xers or nerds. It's more about a typical cross section of (slightly more affluent) Americans. We'll know more about how the rest of the world views the Internet when surveys are conducted and published.

The Bigger Picture

The 1997 American Internet User Survey completed in April of 1997 by Find/SVP (**www.findsvp.com**) was a random dial phone survey of business, personal, and academic Internet users and nonusers. Researchers found only 27% felt the Internet was not at all indispensable. They were beat out by 28%, who felt it was very indispensable and the remaining 45% figured the Net was somewhat indispensable. That means 3 out of 4 adult users are dependent on the Internet. Almost half of the adult Web users use it every day.

The Advertising Picture

That same Find/SVP study determined that 27% of users made online purchases in the previous 12 months. Of those, 39% said they did so after clicking ads. Furthermore, the longer they had been on the Web, the higher the amount of purchasing.

When they turned their attentions to the non-Internet user community, they extrapolated that some 55 million Americans are "poised to become users." Twenty million have plans to get on the Web and the other 30 million would like to learn more.

Major growth is ahead of us.

New Ideas

Whenever I have a conversation with somebody about life on the Internet, a new business model comes to mind. On my last cross-country plane ride, the gentleman sitting next to me was moving from Australia to California to help sort out the half-hourly exchange of settlements required by the upcoming deregulation of the electrical utilities.

"What I could really use," said my flying companion to me, "is a Web site that spelled out what to expect when I move to San Francisco."

Reaching for the Airphone and plugging in my laptop, Yahoo! lead me to **www.crl.com/ ~alfredo/helpstuff/sf/sfmain.htm**, where Alfredo Jacobo Perez Gomez has a wonderful list of what to do, see, and know—and he's not even selling ad space. In fact, he admonishes right up front that "[t]hese totally and completely non-commercial pages are for regular people to use, for free. Please report any profiteering from these pages to alfredo@crl.com."

"What I could really use," said I to my flying companion, "is a Web site that would keep track of the lowest priced electricity for me and let me switch from one to the other online."

"Why not just let it select for you and switch you automatically?" says he.

Why not, indeed. Yet another new business is born. It's one of the reasons I like traveling.

New ideas of how to use the Net that are going to affect the way we advertise are many. In fact, they are starting to flow like the Red River in the Midwest. It's overwhelming. Here are just a few.

URL Finder

Here's the premise: If you go to **www.intel.com** looking for the annual report, you face an abundance of choices. Aside from the cavorting, neon, cleanroom dancers, there are news articles of the week (BunnyPeople characters are in the house! See Intel at E3, where you might WIN your very own bunnysuit!—The Uniquely Intel Shop Intel T-shirts, mousepads, keychains, fanny packs, and more!—Electrify Your Eyes. Enter State of the Art, the exciting new 3-D virtual gallery featuring the Web's best artwork designed for Intel MMX technology.) This is news?

Then there are buttons to click for Business Computing, Product Information, Home Computing, Software Showcase, and—Ah!—Company Information. Now we're getting somewhere.

Among the many choices on *this* page is, indeed, "Intel's 1996 Annual Report." Now that's better than going to, say, AltaVista where entering "intel annual report" will get you:

> Word count: intel: 531775; annual: 1923650; report: 4378742
>
> Documents 1-10 of about 400000 matching the query, best matches first.

Then you get to scroll a while to find the one listing that is an annual report, instead of a page that merely talks about Intel's report and the one that is the 1996 report.

The people at Arlington, Virginia-based Netword (**www.netword.com**) think they have a better idea.

What if you had a browser add-on that let you type in the words "intel annual report" and took you straight to **www.intel.com/intel/annual96/index.htm**? Wouldn't that be handy? Wouldn't they be able to charge $5 a month for keeping the cross-reference directory?

No more bookmarking. No more Web site wandering. No more search engine overload.

Maybe they're not going to be the next directory of the Internet, but think about putting a Netword in your print ads that said "Netword: Free Ice Cream!" rather than trying to get people to surf over to **www.dreyers.com/cgi-bin/signup.cgi**. If they don't remember or have trouble typing it in, they might go searching and end up at the Stump the Missionaries Prize Winners Page (**www.new-jerusalem.com/ice-cream/homepage.html**).

Help for the Typographically Challenged

Okay, let's say you have good navigation on your site and paying $5 per month is not on your list of expenditures for that sort of thing. But what about people who are looking for your home page and not spelling it quite the way you do? Are there common mistakes people make? Then maybe you want to register with typo.net. Here's what it says at **www.typo.net**:

What is typo.net?

typo.net is the first World Wide Web URL spell checker.

When you make a mistake typing a domain name you ordinarily see an error message on your screen. This is frustrating: it takes a lot of time and energy to read the error message so you know what went wrong, then you have to dismiss the error message which requires a click of the mouse, and, as if that isn't enough work, you have to retype the URL all over again—what a pain!

typo.net ends all that by looking at the spelling of the URL you typed in your browser and comparing it to our large library of typos. If we find a domain name that closely matches what we typed, we assume that's where you wanted to go, and typo.net automatically sends you there.

Instead of an annoying and confusing error message, you see a brief announcement telling you what went wrong, and what correction was made so that you don't get lost. These error messages are sponsored by advertisers to help pay for the costs of maintaining our service.

Want to sponsor a typo or a group of typos? E-mail us to find out how to become a typo.net sponsor and contribute to making the World Wide Web a friendlier, easier, and more convenient place.

Find out more about typo.net at info@typo.net Copyright © 1997 NERDS Incorporated All Rights Reserved

You don't believe people mistype your domain name? Fine. Pick somebody else's. That's right. Go to your browser right now, select Open Location, or just inside the URL box type in "micorsoft." Interesting place to advertise, isn't it?

Pay Them to Read Your Ad

That's right, give them cash.

CyberGold (**www.cybergold.com**) "pays attention." They offer cash rewards to people who respond to Web ads and promotions. They even pay people to get their friends to sign up.

The concept is "pay-for-performance" ads. If you really want direct response to your ad, you pay for direct response and that's all. CyberGold advertisers offer incentives ranging from 50 cents to several dollars for such activities as visiting Web sites, taking surveys, filling out application and registration forms, downloading software, and making purchases.

The premise is that you'd normally pay $1.00 apiece to create a direct mail piece, rent the list, and pay the postage. But all you get is a 2% return if you know what you're doing. Who knows how many looked at it and decided against responding, versus the vast majority who simply threw it away?

So why not pay $1.00 apiece for each time somebody actually reads your promotion? The reader gets 50 cents, CyberGold gets 50 cents. You get 100% readership. Interesting.

Random House is experimenting with CyberGold rebates to book purchasers; prospective bidders can earn CyberGold for visiting ONSALE, Incorporated's online auction (**www.onsale.com**). U.S. Interactive ran a campaign paying CyberGold to people who downloaded software for Digital Bindery, a service that e-mails subscribers updates of their favorite Web sites. New interactive ads, like the one featuring an interactive game and quiz for Portrait Displays' pivoting computer monitors, are being added weekly.

A New Idea Is Born Every Minute

Every day brings a new perspective and your next Internet idea may be one the venture capitalists like. The point is that people are going to come up with new concepts for attracting attention on the Internet. Your job is to keep track of them and see which fit your goals.

While you're at it, try to keep track of new technologies as well.

New Technologies

The Dilbert dilemma is creating new gizmos because they're interesting, not necessarily because they're useful. A solar powered flashlight sounds like a good idea unless they left out the battery and it only works in the sun. We're back to the problem of trying to sell what you make instead of making what people want to buy.

But it's clear that new Internet gadgets, the latest in Web thingamajigs, and the most up-to-date interactive doodads may have an impact on how you go about advertising your goods and services. Keep your eyes on **www.cnet.com**. Keep reading *Webmaster* magazine. Watch *The Site* on MSNBC and stay tuned.

Animated E-Mail

How about an all-singing, all-dancing e-mail? That's what you'll find at **www.mediasyn.com**. Their product, @loha, lets you add animation and sound to your messages. At their Web site, Media Synergy encourages you to, "Impress your friends, colleagues and loved ones with multimedia greeting cards, announcements, memos, and much more!"

@loha's attachments are tiny! (10-20kB) super fast downloading!

Expand your @loha possibilities by importing your own characters, captions, backdrops, sound clips even your own voice!

@loha's extensive gallery of over 650 ready-made images and sounds allows you to create and send thousands of different messages.

Of course, all those friends, colleagues, and loved ones also have to shell out $49.95 to see and hear your marvelous message. Sounds to me like free player software, like a small self-loading Java applet, would be just the batteries this flashlight needs.

Audio Ads

AudioNet (**www.audionet.com**) has been netcasting speeches, sports, music, you name it, for a couple of years now. When you want to listen to a particular program, it starts with the equivalent of a radio ad. The user is attentive, the message is short, the advertiser is happy.

With more people using streaming audio, it seems very likely that this type of advertising is going to grow. One warning: Offer listeners a chance to pay a small sum in order to *not* hear the ads. That way you can keep your listenership high and your income stable.

Ad-Friendly Video

One of the holy grails of the Internet is figuring out how to compress video into small enough files that it can actually be transmitted and viewed at seemingly normal speeds. We have a way to go. But one company is so pleased with its approach that it's calling its services "Ad-Friendly" video.

InterVU (**www.intervu.net**) is not only tracking the most common and the best in compression, they're also offering to manage all of the video headaches for you. A content site can accept video ads provided by you, the advertiser, through the InterVU service.

Until now, video on the Net was not friendly to advertising: it was too risky, expensive, and unreliable. In addition, it could only be seen by a limited number of users. Not any more. With InterVU's breakthrough service, you can add video to your Web site or clickthrough advertisement with no up-front costs, no investment in file server technology or software, and no hassles.

Then they destroy the illusion by blathering about reaching nearly 40 million Web users. Why do these people insist on thinking of the Web as a broadcast medium?

Aside from their promotional copy, they are a harbinger of a trend. Video is coming to the Web. It's not pretty at the moment, but companies like InterVU are worth watching.

Who Knows What's Next?

When I turned seven years old, I remember being more delighted with a birthday card than any of my birthday presents. It talked. That was 1962. It didn't have a chip in it. It didn't have a battery. It was a strip of plastic that you pulled through a slot in the back of the card. A needle in the slot acted like it was playing a vinyl record and the tiny, tinny, scratchy voice said, "Happy Birthday!" It said it about a thousand times before it wore out. It took about an hour and a half. My mother was very relieved she wasn't going to have to burn the card before the rest of my family ripped it to shreds.

Fast forward to the beginning of 1997. Open up *Rolling Stone* magazine to the Twix ad from M&M/Mars and you are treated to an electronic voice that called out their new slogan, "Two for me, none for you."

With that sort of creativity loose in the world, there are sure to be more interesting developments on the Internet in the next ten minutes.

New Tools

The pace of change continues to increase, especially when it comes to data processing. There was a time when marketing and advertising practitioners didn't need to know about data processing. It was enough to get reports from the MIS department every now and then. Along came spreadsheets and we were suddenly responsible for our own numbers.

But now, with advertising being done on the computer, by the computer, and for the computer, we can expect some of the sophisticated software that's been created on behalf of nuclear physicists, urban planning engineers, and weather-prediction scientists will be focused on advertising.

Modern Solutions to Complex Problems

One of the mysteries that has stumped computer scientists for decades, bothered mathematicians for centuries, and sales managers since the dawn of time is known as the traveling salesman problem. The other mysteries have been why cats think you'd enjoy half a lizard in the morning and why the dry cleaners always hang your shirts facing right while all hotel hangers face left.

The traveling salesman problem is finding the most efficient path for a salesperson to take in order to visit multiple prospects in multiple cities with the least amount of backtracking. High powered computers and complex software are starting to make some progress on it, and there are other conundrums that make this one look like child's play.

Ever thought about keeping airplanes in the air? It's really a rather intriguing problem.

A modern jet aircraft is made up of hundreds of thousands of parts, all flying in tight formation. Each part is a highly specialized piece of equipment created with very precise tolerances and in need of periodic maintenance. Unfortunately, the periods of these parts vary. When it's time for one part to be overhauled, the entire craft must make its way to the hanger for service.

Okay, that's fairly straightforward. A simple calendar could manage the task. But it's not quite that easy.

Let's start with one part. If that one part needs routine maintenance, the plane has to make it to the hanger. That means the crew that flies the plane has to be available to do so, as they are only allowed to fly so many hours before getting a break. The plane has to make it to the hanger that is equipped to deal with that part. The hanger has to have the replacement components in stock. It has to have the staff who knows how to deal with that available part.

Okay, now it's a little more sophisticated. At this point, you remember that a modern jet aircraft is made up of hundreds of thousands of parts. You also think about the cost of downtime and how nice it would be if a lot of maintenance could get done at the same time. You don't want to perform unnecessary maintenance, but you do have government regulations, manufacturer's recommendations, and warranty requirements, and, of course you don't want your planes falling out of the sky.

The answer is artificial intelligence. Software rules. If this part needs maintenance within 20% of its allotted flight hours, classify it grade C. If this part can be worked on at the same time as any two other parts that are grade C, bump it up to a B. Oh, and that's about the time the system should spit out a purchase order for replacement components and start worrying about gathering together the proper work force.

When there are enough B parts in a plane, the whole plane gets an A and it's time to find the right hanger that's going to have the right parts, the right tools, and the right mechanics in time for that plane to get there and not have to spend too much time waiting on the ground. Airplanes don't earn any money while they are on the ground. Stockholders don't like it.

What if that sort of software power were applied to advertising on the Internet?

The Road at Hand

You're about to go into a meeting and explain all of this to the keepers of the budget. They're the ones whose job it is to say "You want *how* much for that advertising campaign/color printer/coffee pot?"

You have to make it clear to them that placing banners on Web sites is different than doing it in magazines. Lots different. So let's give them something familiar that they can get their minds around. Let's give them an analogy.

Billboard Control from on High   Today's analogy is the automobile and the billboard. If there are members of your senior management who are still happier riding a horse to work than driving, well, at least you know why they're called senior managers. This should even be easy enough for them to understand.

Let's set the scene and create some assumptions. First up: size of automobile. In this hypothetical world:

> People between the ages of 16 and 24 drive very small cars.
>
> People between the ages of 25 and 40 drive station wagons.
>
> People between the ages of 41 and 55 drive larger cars.
>
> People between the ages of 56 and 65 drive very big cars.

Next up: the color of vehicle:

> People who like fine dining drive green cars.
>
> People who like sports drive red cars.
>
> People who like music drive white cars.
>
> People who like camping drive blue cars.

Now we'll assume you're in control of the display of one billboard on the highway and you're sitting on a hill overlooking the traffic. You're trying to sell a vacation getaway to an island resort.

At certain times of day, certain sizes and types of cars go by. When the traffic is predominantly made up of very small, blue cars you pop up the billboard that says:

> Over A Hundred Campgrounds
>
> Under A Hundred Dollars

When the traffic seems to swell with green station wagons you hit the button to show the sign that says:

> Tropical Breezes
>
> Candlelight Supper
>
> Free Babysitting

When there are more large red cars than anything else, you pop up the sign that says:

> All The Sun, All The Fun
>
> Masseuse On Call

Billboard Network   But it's not you on that hillside, it's a media planner working on your behalf. And it's not just one media planner, but hundreds of them, scattered all across the city, watching the traffic and showing the right billboards.

They use their cell phones to talk to each other and tell the next one down the line what sort of traffic is headed their way. You start to create serial sign campaigns to play in sequence, similar to Burma Shave ads.

As a contingent of large, white cars cruises down the highway, four billboards in a row address them.

> Here's A Holiday That'll Help You Save
>
> We Have The Music That You Crave
>
> An Island Vacation, With All Its Charms
>
> Discounts For Mozart, Handel, and Brahms

Unfortunately, the normal state of affairs on the road is that the size and color of the cars are usually pretty well mixed. It's time to switch gears from human hilltop control monitors to electronic billboard-top control monitors.

Customized Billboards   As each car comes around the corner, each billboard spots the color and size and sends a signal. Only the occupants of that car can see the sign being displayed toward it. All other cars see signs designed for them, based on their ages and interests. Then billboards get smarter and start looking at license plates to see what state the cars are from.

Personalized Billboards   But so far, we've only described what's been available on the Net for a while now.

To be as current as possible, we give each billboard the ability to read each license plate, check with a central database, and show specific signs specifically created for specific cars. Not just size and color, but individual cars with known drivers.

> Alexis:
>
> Picture Yourself Playing Piano
>
> Overlooking the Beach in St Tropez

You make sure she is shown that message three or four times before you switch.

> Alexis:
>
> Discount Airfare to Europe
>
> Music By the Sea

The clincher, then, is the billboard that wraps it up with a picture of a young woman sitting at a piano on the balcony of an old, private villa, looking down on the crystal blue water of the port town. And a phone number, of course.

Now we begin to get a picture of the state of the art—today. By now your budget keepers are either convinced that this is some of the most exciting stuff they've seen in years, or they are so confused that they give you the amount you want just to make you go away. They've had enough modern technology for one day. And we're still not talking about the future yet. This analogy is based on what's available today.

Today's Tools   Infoseek's UltraMatch keeps track of what your interests are.

FlyCast Communications (**www.flycast.com**) lets you identify the target you're after, the sites or pages you want to sponsor, the number of impressions you want, and the price you're willing to pay. It then dumps your requests into their arbitration engine, which acts like a real-time auction house to determine whose ad gets shown to which people on which pages.

Watch for more activity along these lines from Adsmart (**www.adsmart.net**) and Narrowline (**www.narrowline.com**).

The point is that these approaches give you hands-on control the likes of which you've never seen before. Think the number of impressions is too low? Raise your price and broaden your target. Think the response rate is too low? Tweak your target and change your message.

If you can get people to log in and identify themselves, you can keep track and deliver. That's today.

What about tomorrow?

The Future of Advertising

The time will come when we are well known for our inclinations, our predilections, our proclivities, and our wants. We will be classified, profiled, categorized, and our every click will be watched.

Eventually we will stop wondering "How did they know I'd need a new vacuum cleaner?" and start wondering, "Why didn't I get an ad reminding me it was time to change the oil in my car?" It'll be the next great excuse of the next decade.

"I'm so sorry, but my mail server was down and your Hallmark Birthday Reminder bounced."

"Well, the Mobil Web site let me down. It didn't alert me to get more gasoline, so I guess we are sort of stuck here for a while…alone…together."

From the Surfer's Perspective

I was looking forward to writing this last bit about the far reaches of collaborative profiling. It's the fun part. I get to put on my science fiction hat and play Asimov. Unfortunately, I came across the *Backspin* column in that back of *Network World* (May 12, 1997) by journalist and networking consultant Mark Gibbs and that blew the whole thing. Since he did such a good job at it, I relinquish my inventiveness to him.

Just think of the impact the medium will have on your child when he or she visits virtual Disneyland. Mickey will walk up to your child's avatar and say in his irritating, squeaky voice, "Hi, want to buy my latest book, Johnny?" Then he'll open it to reveal animated contents that respond specifically to your child.

This will make today's, "Daddy, can I have…" look trivial compared with the screaming wants created by finely targeted marketing to the audience of one—in this case, your child.

Most importantly, the vendor won't actually have to know who any child actually is when they visit the vendor's site. All it needs to know is the behavior of a given ID. Then, using explicit knowledge, heuristics and careful trial-and-error, the vendor can refine its pitch.

For example, ID 40198763 goes (90% of the time) to the latest Batman story rather than the Barbie soap opera or the Star Wars episode when they visit BurgerWorld, so we can conclude that the child is probably male (probability of 95%).

Wait, that's a confirmed male, as we just noted his conversation with another visitor (we're obligated to monitor chats for legal reasons).

Further, we can estimate that the child's age is between 3 and 4 years old, given the style of the story narrative and the fact that 90% of the time ID 40198763 leaves before the story is complete.

Now we can present the Johnny (we just overheard ID 40198763 talking to his pal) with age-, gender- and interest-appropriate content. This is a whole new style of marketing, and it will [be] driven by content that is truly sophisticated.

And don't you dare treat these diminutive consumers statistically. If you fail to build a relationship with them very quickly, your competition won't miss the opportunity.

This will be the real drive of interactive media. And it won't be restricted to pitching to children. Oh no, you'll be a target just as we all will. And I bet we'll like it, because it will be personal.

And that's what, in the long run, will see to it that the marketers outpace the privacy pundits. Yes, as Gibbs so eloquently points out, there need to be some ground rules for marketing to children.

The Children's Advertising Review Unit of the Council of Better Business Bureau has revised its "Self-Regulatory Guidelines for Children's Advertising," on voluntary standards for online marketing to children. Privacy issues and the fine line between editorial and advertising are discussed in what is hoped will be voluntary policing and it's well worth a look, at **www.bbb.org/advertising/caruguid.html**.

The Associated Press reported in the middle of June that a presidential task force is demanding assurances from the FTC that children will not be allowed to give out their names, ages, or other personal information unless it can be verified that they have obtained parental permission to do. Ira Magaziner, the task force head (though better known as architect of the Clinton health care plan), says: "If the industry doesn't do it, we may have to legislate."

So we learn to control ourselves or get controlled. But Gibbs is right on the money when he says, "We'll like it, because it will be personal."

When the content is news and the ads are personal, the sites we visit become more important to us. I occasionally check my stock portfolio because I want to know my momentary net worth. If the advertising gremlins are watching me and reminding me it's time to fund my SEP-IRA account, it's not so much an ad as it is a service.

I'm waiting for the ad that pops up and says, "Hey Jim, you haven't had lunch with Mark Gibbs in a long time. Come by the Cliff House in the next two weeks and we'll give you a two-for-one lunch deal." And then I can pick up the tab and show Mark how magnanimous I am.

Online Real-Time Datastream Control

Looking through an eyeglass-weight display, barking out instructions and waving data glove-encased hands, tomorrow's ad maestro manipulates the reach, the frequency, and message delivered to millions of surfers in real time.

Our maestro sits at the virtual command center located anywhere a phone cell can hear her. The display shows levels of response across multiple sites to multiple banners from multiple profile types. With a push of a virtual button, a literal blink of an eye, the promotion balance is adjusted.

The image of the control panel resembles the angled table of an old analog recording studio. Dozens of knobs line up across a field of vertical slots, waiting for a touch to send them higher or lower. But these do not control the amplitude of the signal coming in. They control the types of people the message is going out to.

Each has a label floating over it that grows in brightness the higher the knob is set. The labels include auto, business, college, computer, education, entertainment, health, home, and more.

In the background, where musicians would have played and sang, hovers a mathematical grid, a rubber sheet, waiting to be pulled and stretched by generated results. It is black and at rest.

The product for this session is WebSim business gaming software. It simulates a Web site and puts the player in the Webmaster hot seat. Can you make your navigation easy enough? Can you keep it updated frequently enough to keep return visitors returning on the stingy budget you had to spread over servers, artists, Net connectivity, and Java programmers?

The maestro reaches for the sliders. As she sets each knob, a chart on the far side of the rubber sheet duplicates her choices with vertical, colored bars indicating the selected profile. She sets Computers to 80, Internet to 100, and Business to 40. Then she reaches for Entertainment and slides the knob up to the 60 mark, watching the blue bar on the far wall to follow her movement exactly.

She selects from a quiver of banners; a cross-segment marketing message aimed at everybody—the baseline. She tosses the banner toward the rubber sheet and nods as it rises and comes to rest up above, hanging motionless.

WebSim......You're the Webmaster......Click

Compete for Prizes......The Perfect Learning Environment......

Above and to the left, three gray zeros linger—the banners to be displayed yet, the clickthroughs received, and the response rate as a percent of exposures. To the right, she dials in a gray 10,000—the number of images to be shown in this first test run. At the lower-right, the session budget of $82,800 challenges her to deliver.

At the bottom-left are the figures that show the degree to which the average clicker follows the banner's path to the final goal of downloading the software.

She is set. It is time.

She runs through the numbers one more time and decides she really needs to net $5,000 for this session. It would only take a day, but with all the prep time she put into it, the banner art-work she envisioned and paid for, and the fact that the non-complete penalty was going to come out of her pocket meant she was at risk. She deserved the reward, but it wouldn't come easily.

Why had she said she could double the response they got through direct mail? She had still been glowing after her big win with the bond-fund company. She had read the *Wall Street Journal* cover to cover for three weeks and just knew Alan Greenspan was going to make a move. She had that one wired. She walked away with a big smile on her face and hefty commission.

This one didn't have that kind of background to it. It was just another new software package in a sea of new software packages. Their mailing numbers were pretty good and that made them harder to beat.

They had sent out 90,000 pieces over three runs at a cost of $69,300. They got a 3% response rate and followed up by sending a package costing $5 to each of the 2,700 responders. The data entry, the diskette, the quick-start guide, the postage. It added up. All told, they spent $82,800 at a cost of $31.66 each. Not bad as far as the cost of leads goes.

"I'll take the same budget and return twice the response. You make your software and docu-mentation available on your Web site and I'll get people to download it. I'll create all the promo-tional materials, and personally place the banners. And my fee will be included."

They took her up on her offer.

The maestro gives one last look at the budget counter and prays for a break. She is set. It is time.

A handle to her left resembles the brake lever on a San Francisco cable car. She moves it for-ward without hesitation and watches the impressions counter ratchet down to zero. On the ad banner network she's using, 10,000 impressions is but the work of a moment.

The results of her efforts gleam from the meters.

Impressions	10,000
Clicks	200
Downloads	1

Only a half a percent who clicked bothered to get the software!? She had successfully ignored the knot in the pit of her stomach up until now. Then she spots the telling number. Average level of depth: 1. It takes three clicks to download.

She snaps her fingers and the entire display is gone, replaced by the bridge page on the client's Web site, the page to which a clickthrough takes you. It looks fine. It's not the problem.

She flips the goggles up onto her head and looks into her own, physical monitor on her desk. She types in the URL for the bridge page and waits. The wait stretches.

She clicks a picture of her client and settles herself while she waits again, this time for him to answer the call.

"Well, if it isn't the bionic woman! Nice hat. When are you going to start the banners rolling?"

"I thought I had. When are you going to free up the load on your server?"

"What are you talking about? Our server's fine."

"Wrong. Check it out on an outside line and see what the rest of the world is seeing."

"Okay, Okay, give me…a…second…to…switch…to. Oh, my."

"Oh, your."

"Hang on. Okay, I killed it. It was a backup!"

"At two in the afternoon? What's the matter, can't you tell your AM and your PM?"

"That's very strange. Why would somebody be messing with the time of day?"

"The same people who are fixing your Millennium Bug?"

"Damn!"

"Please, there's a lady telepresent."

She flips the goggles back down and waves her colleague adieu. Another snap of the fingers reconstitutes the controls. With a quick glance at the interest levels of clickers, she makes a small adjustment to the sliders and gives the lever another full-throttle shove.

This time she listens more carefully to the telltale pitch. The clickrate pitch is a tad higher—that's good—but in the several minutes it takes to run through another 10,000 impressions, she only hears that sweet little bell ding three times. The numbers tell the story. Three percent clickthrough, of which only one percent downloaded.

She gives herself one more test run before opening the floodgates and some work is needed. The bridge page loads fine. The license agreement page loads fine. The download page loads fine. But you have to scroll two clicks down to the download button. Why hadn't she caught that before?

She grabs at the helpful, friendly, warm, and charming top paragraph and shoves it to below the precious download buttons. She smiles and runs the third round. The software retrieval rate goes up to 1.5%. She smiles. The clickthrough rate is still at 3%. She frowns.

A quick calculation. She has used up a half of one percent of her budget and realized a tenth of a percent of her target. This is not good. The knot makes itself known. She studies the surfer interest profiles with all of her attention.

The rubber sheet is now distended into a shape like the Matterhorn after too many martinis. There are two of them. She has a large enough sample to spot the problem. Those interested in computers responded nicely. Those interested in the Internet responded very well. Those with a thing for business were abysmally indifferent and the entertainment crowd was stretched up to where the black sheet had gone through all of the other colors and reached a white snowy peak at the top.

It is time to adjust, and to let out the throttle a little. She sets the interest sliders accordingly and re-dials the impressions to 200,000. She rummages through her quiver of banners.

> Master The Web......Quake2......Click
>
> WebSim—Puts YOU In The Master's Seat......Here!

She eases the trolley car lever forward. She wants to feel the response levels.

It takes longer to run through these banners. She listens as the response rate resonance turns melodious and the sweet download bell sounds more like a telephone than a tentative patron at an empty bakery. When it's over, she starts to relax a bit. A four percent clickthrough with a two percent download.

She realizes she didn't trust her gut. They told her this game was for older folks. Business people looking for a tutorial. They said the gaming crowd as defined by most banner networks were kids. Teeny boppers who wanted to play shoot 'em up, blast 'em, and watch 'em bleed games.

She knew better. Kids are savvy. Now is the time to prove it. She reaches in her quiver and grabs a bright orange, animated, in-your-face-ad and tosses it into position.

> Quake Is For Flakes......WebSim......Click
>
> Show 'em What You're Made Of......Master The Web......NOW!
>
> YOU run the server YOU design the pages YOU win the prizes

Time for the big guns. She steadies herself, dials the impressions to one-point-five million and eases the level into play. A smile dances cautiously across her face. The timbre rises. The sweet bells of the telephone ringing settle into a steady tone. The sound of the emergency broadcast network on the radio that signals all is well.

The noise finally quiets and the results are good. She's burned through 42% of her cash and only brought in 36% of the downloads, but she has a secret weapon on her side: frequency.

She dials up two million banners. She hits the full repeat button for full frequency and knows she has the numbers she needs, even before she starts. At the 5,400 download mark a small light blinks and the music halts. There's no need to buy any more banner space. She met the contract. The rest goes into her pocket.

The next morning she doesn't need to report to her client, they'll know when they look at their server logs. She need only e-mail the invoice.

There was even enough left over to fix up her own Web site a little. She could hire some outside help. Maybe she'd wait until the WebSim contest was over and make the winner an offer.

Final Words of Advice

While waiting for just the right tools to become available, there is one thing you can do to make your Web advertising more successful: keep an open mind.

The industry is young. Everybody in this industry is trying to make it fit the mold of the industry they were in. If you know TV, you think about the Web as clickable TV with still pictures. If your background is the publishing business, you want the Web to act like a magazine.

It's not a phone or a fax or a radio. We don't know if it's fish or fowl. We have an ailing alien visitor and we don't know if we need a surgeon or a vet.

> —Doug Weaver, Firefly Network

The whole thing is evolving. The novelty is starting to wear off but at the same time the usability is really well established. You just have to stay flexible, because you know it's going to change.

> —Randy Kawahara, American Honda Motor Co., Inc.

Surf a lot. Go out and see for yourself. Watch how other people use it. Use traditional media objectives and strategy and positioning and matching the creative to the environment. But remember that it's new. That's exciting and you should make sure it stays exciting.

> —Carolyn Doll, Hal Riney & Partners

Rule #1 Invest in knowledge about brands.

Rule #2 In a relationship-driven world, the key ingredient to successful media will be interactivity.

Rule #3 Creativity will continue to be key in breaking through an increasingly cluttered environment and reaching an increasingly sophisticated consumer.

Rule #4 We must have multiple communications pathways at our disposal—so as to find the most effective route to the consumer, so as to deliver the right message, in the right format, at the right time.

Rule #5 Become an aggressive supporter of measurement.

> —Peter Georgescu, CEO Young & Rubicam, *Advertising Age*, April 14, 1997

The only way to change the culture internally is to experiment, to succeed occasionally, to fail often, and to learn from our experiences. The same applies to advertisers.

> —Martin Sorrell & Eric Salama, *Harvard Business Review*, Nov/Dec, 1996

Marketers should keep three things in mind when considering using the Internet in any form as part of their marketing mix. First, using it requires the same goal-setting clarity as using any other marketing technique. Second, the dynamics of the Internet are changing daily, and therefore, today's perfect solution will be outdated tomorrow. Third, because of the rate of change, merely reading about this stuff is useless. You have to be a pioneer.

—Denis Carter, Vice President & Director of the Corporate Marketing Group, Intel, *Harvard Business Review*, Nov/Dec, 1996 ●

Glossary

A very complete dictionary of advertising terms (although not including Internet ad terms at last look) can be found at the Department of Advertising, The University of Texas at Austin site (**www.utexas.edu/coc/adv/research/ terms**). ■

Advertising Network   A group of Web sites which share a common banner server. Typically a sales organization which manages the commerce and reporting. An ad network has the ability to deliver unique combinations of targeted audiences because they serve your banner across multiple sites.

Affinity Group   A group of people with common interests. A special interest group identified for purposes of targeting specific ads.

Agents

1. Representatives who broker Web advertising space.
2. Software programs. See *Spider*.

Animated GIF   An animation created by combining multiple GIF images in one file. The result is multiple images, displayed one after another, that give the appearance of movement. Very useful for attracting/distracting Web surfers.

Avatar   A digital representative that identifies you in a virtual world, giving you the ability to "be" in a space where others can see you and you them. Often an avatar is a cartoon-like character or object.

Backbone   The primary conduit of electronic traffic in a network. Frequently used to describe the major information arteries between networks around the world.

Bandwidth   The amount of information that can be transmitted over communications lines at one time. The higher the bandwidth, the faster the Web page loads. Limited bandwidth is the main reason for keeping pictures small. Just as it seems we will never have fast enough computers, it feels like we will never have enough bandwidth. The amount of R&D money being thrown at this problem should yield surprising results before long.

Banner   A typically rectangular graphic element which acts as an advertisement and entices the viewer to click it for further information, typically on the advertiser's Web site.

Banner Network   See *Advertising Network*.

Browser   A software program used for accessing the World Wide Web. The most common are Netscape's Navigator and Microsoft's Internet Explorer.

Cache   A file on the client computer that stores temporary text and graphics for display in the browser. This speeds page viewing when you hit the Back button. Institutional cache helps speed viewing when many people use a common gateway to look at the same pages on the Internet.

CGI   Common Gateway Interface. A relatively simple programming language that aids communication between the browser and the server. Most commonly used to store information sent from the browser and to automate the generation of dynamic pages.

Clickstreams   The electronic path a user takes while navigating from site to site, and within a site, from page to page.

Clickthrough The act of clicking a banner, which takes you through to the advertiser's Web site. Used as a counter point to impressions to judge the response-inducing power of the banner.

Client/Server A type of computing that divides programs between machines. The browser runs on a PC as the client and interacts with the Web server.

CPM Cost Per Thousand (Roman Numeral) impressions. The price paid by an advertiser for a content site displaying their banner a thousand times.

Collaborative Filtering Estimating the tastes of an individual based on the comparison of that individual's profile to the profiles of other individuals in a database. Originally used by Firefly (**www.firefly.com**) to recommend movies and music.

Cookies Client-side text file that is used by Web servers to store information about the site visitor. Information pertaining to a site can only be read by the side that wrote the information. Used to identify repeat visitors.

Copy The printed text or spoken words in an advertisement.

Creative The concept, design, and artwork that go into a given ad.

Domain Name The naming convention for computers on the Internet. Examples of highest level domains include .com for company, .edu for universities, .fr for France, and .se for Sweden. The next level is your company domain name. IBM is ibm.com. Target Marketing is targeting.com.

Demographics Common characteristics that allow for population segmentation. Typical demographic data points include age, gender, postal code, and income.

Effective Frequency The number of times an ad should be shown to one person to realize the highest impact of the ad without wasting impressions on that individual.

Effective Reach The number of people who will see an ad the most effective number of times. The most effective frequency.

Elasticity The relationship between a change in advertising budget and a supposedly connected change in revenues.

Exposures See *Impression*.

FAQ Frequently Asked Questions. A list of the most common inquiries on a given subject.

Firewall Used to keep unwanted visitors from looking at, modifying, or copying proprietary information.

Flame A vituperative e-mail or newsgroup posting of an especially acrimonious nature. Emotional, ad homonym, and usually way out of line.

Frames The ability to divide up a browser window into multiple windows, which scroll separately. This is controlled by the HTML from the server.

Frequency   The number of times a given person will see an ad in a given time period.

FTP   File Transfer Protocol. Used to convey a computer file from one machine to another.

Geek   A person absolutely fascinated by technology for technology's sake. Will take apart a computer or a software package to see what's inside.

GIF   Graphic Interchange Format. The most common file compression format for banner ads and most other pictures on the Web.

Gross Exposures/Gross Impressions   Total number of times an ad is shown, including duplicate showings to the same person.

Hits   Every time a file is sent by a server, be it text, graphic, video, and so on, it is recorded as a hit. Not a reliable gauge to compare different sites, as one page with five graphic elements will register six hits when viewed, while a page with no graphics will only register one hit.

Host   Any machine can be a host. The machine you log into is your "login host," the machine you read news from is a "news host," and so on.

HTML   Hypertext Markup Language. A subset of the Special Graphics Markup Language that allows the remote display of Web pages on browsers and connects them via hyperlinks.

HTTP   Hypertext Transport Protocol. The system a browser uses for requesting and a server uses for delivering HTML documents on the Web.

Hypertext   Text which is electronically linked to other documents that can be accessed by clicking the linked word.

Impression   The Opportunity To See (OTS) a banner by a surfer. When a page that includes a banner is viewed, it is considered an impression, much like a billboard on the highway.

Intranet   The use of Web technology for internal communications within a particular organization.

Interstitial Ads   Web pages that pop up between what the view is looking at and what they are expecting to get. More like a TV commercial than anything else on the Web (at the moment).

Inventory   The amount of available space for banners on a Web site that can be delivered in a given time period.

IP Address   Internet Protocol Address—a unique number assigned to every computer on the Internet, even if only temporarily.

Java   An object-oriented programming language, developed by Sun Microsystems, allowing small programs (applets) to be downloaded on demand for execution on the client computer when needed.

Link   A hypertext connection between two documents, image maps, graphics, and the like.

Listserver   Software that allows many people to participate in an e-mail discussion. Similar to newsgroups, but with listserver, the messages are sent directly to subscribers. Most lists are offered to the public at no cost. The number of private lists cannot be known by their very nature. A great tool for an electronic focus group.

Nerd   Somebody who is fascinated by technology for the sake of what it can allow one to accomplish. While a Geek will take a video camera apart, a Nerd will figure out how to get a live video feed from the pet iguana's bed onto the Web.

Netiquette   The cultural and social rules on the Internet. Ignoring them may result in being flamed or castigated in public.

Newsgroup   An electronic bulletin board open to everybody and divided into tens of thousands of subjects. Only a handful of newsgroups permit the posting of advertising.

Opportunity To See (OTS)   A pageview is an OTS, but not necessarily an impression. The page can be downloaded but if the banner is located at the bottom to the page and the visitor doesn't scroll down, the banner is not seen.

Packet   All information on the Internet is broken down into packets for transmission. Each packet contains the address of the computer it's going to and the one from which it came. On the receiving end, after all the packets have been received, the packets are re-assembled into a readable or viewable file.

Pageview   When a Web page is requested by somebody through a browser. Pageviews are often used to track the number of impressions a banner gets.

Proxy   A proxy server acts as a cache file for an organization. It is also used where firewalls protect the internal network from the external Internet, while continuing to serve Web pages from the inside.

Psychographics   Common psychological characteristics that allow for population segmentation. Typical psychographic data points include opinions, attitudes, and beliefs about various aspects relating to lifestyle and purchasing behavior.

Push   While e-mail is the quintessential "push" technology, the phrase refers to tools that send information to a user's browser rather than wait for the viewer to reach into the Web and "pull" the information. Primary examples are PointCast, BackWeb, and Marimba.

Reach   The total number of people who will see a given ad.

Robot   See *Spider*.

Sell-Through Rate   The percentage of banner ads sold as opposed to traded or bartered in an ad network.

Server   The publishing side of the client/server couple. This is the computer and software combination that sends out the pages and pictures to the browser or the client.

Session   A completed visit to a Web site by a surfer/viewer/visitor. A session can start at the home page and last anywhere from mere moments to hours, depending on the interest the visitor has in the information, games, and so on, at the site.

Shockwave   A file format from Macromedia (**www.macromedia.com**) that allows animated and interactive graphics (Director movies) on a Web page.

Spam   Originally posting an ad to multiple newsgroups, now used to describe unsolicited e-mail advertising. Named after a skit by Monty Python, spam is one marketing and advertising technique to avoid at all costs.

Spider   Software that crawls around the Web to find, catalog, and report information it has been told to search for. Used more visibly by search engines like AltaVista and Lycos to gather text from Web sites in order to allow anybody to search for anything in particular. Also known as 'bots (robots), wanderers, and agents.

Streaming Audio/Video   The ability for an audio or video file to begin playing on the browser as it is being downloaded, instead of having to wait until it has completely arrived to begin.

Traffic   The number and types of people who come to a Web site. Measured in many different ways.

Universe   The total population in a given market segment used as the baseline from which reach, frequency, and response figures are calculated.

URL   Uniform Resource Locator. The address of any particular page on the World Wide Web, seen as: www.company.com/page.html.

Visit   See *Session*.

Wander   See *Spider*.

Advertising Resources on the Web

Things do change fast and there is no better source for information about the Web than the Web itself. I was going to create a long list of various places to find various things, but I find it unnecessary. Others have done a much better job than I could.

So, here for your edification and perusal, is a list of the best resources on the Web for finding the best information about advertising online. ■

Banner Vault

Zawshow: The Only Database of Web Advertising Banners

www.zaw.tm.fr/intro.html

Discussion

I-Advertising Discussion

www.exposure-usa.com/i-advertising

Kim Bayne's Marketing Lists on the Internet

www.bayne.com/wolfBayne/lists/default.html

Online Advertising Discussion List

www.o-a.com

Insightful Commentary

Microscope

www.pscentral.com

Webmaster magazine

www.web-master.com

Wilson Internet Services, Using Ads on other Web Sites

www.wilsonweb.com/rfwilson/webmarket/ad.htm

Internet Advertising Law

Advertising Law Internet Site (A fine resource from Lew Rose)

www.advertisinglaw.com

Mammoth Compendiums

Ad Resource Presents The One-Stop Directory Of Web Advertising, Promotion, Marketing, Sales And E-Mail Web Resources

www.adresource.com/silink2.htm

Internet Advertising Resource Guide
www.admedia.org/internet

Web Site Banner Advertising: Banner Ad Networks & Brokers (Mark J. Welch's incredible Web effort)
www.ca-probate.com/comm_net.htm

News

Advertising Age Interactive Daily
http://adage.com/interactive/daily/index.html

CyberAtlas
www.cyberatlas.com

Internet Advertising Report
www.internetnews.com/IAR

Pricing

Web Ad Rates—What It Costs And What You Get
www.adresource.com/whatitco.htm

Publicity

Internet Publicity Resources (Steve O'Keefe's online pointers from his book, *Publicity on the Internet*)
www.olympus.net/okeefe/pubnet

Web Technology

The Web Developer's Virtual Library
www.wdvl.com

Index

Complete and Return this Card
for a *FREE* Computer Book Catalog

Thank you for purchasing this book! You have purchased a superior computer book written expressly for your needs. To continue to provide the kind of up-to-date, pertinent coverage you've come to expect from us, we need to hear from you. Please take a minute to complete and return this self-addressed, postage-paid form. In return, we'll send you a free catalog of all our computer books on topics ranging from word processing to programming and the internet.

Mr. ☐   Mrs. ☐   Ms. ☐   Dr. ☐

Name (first) [ ][ ][ ][ ][ ][ ][ ][ ][ ][ ][ ] (M.I.) ☐ (last) [ ][ ][ ][ ][ ][ ][ ][ ][ ][ ][ ][ ][ ]

Address [ ]

[ ]

City [ ][ ][ ][ ][ ][ ][ ][ ][ ][ ][ ] State [ ][ ] Zip [ ][ ][ ][ ][ ] [ ][ ][ ][ ]

Phone [ ][ ][ ] [ ][ ][ ] [ ][ ][ ][ ] Fax [ ][ ][ ] [ ][ ][ ] [ ][ ][ ][ ]

Company Name [ ]

E-mail address [ ]

1. Please check at least (3) influencing factors for purchasing this book.

Front or back cover information on book .... ☐
Special approach to the content .... ☐
Completeness of content .... ☐
Author's reputation .... ☐
Publisher's reputation .... ☐
Book cover design or layout .... ☐
Index or table of contents of book .... ☐
Price of book .... ☐
Special effects, graphics, illustrations .... ☐
Other (Please specify): _____ ☐

2. How did you first learn about this book?

Saw in Macmillan Computer Publishing catalog .... ☐
Recommended by store personnel .... ☐
Saw the book on bookshelf at store .... ☐
Recommended by a friend .... ☐
Received advertisement in the mail .... ☐
Saw an advertisement in: _____ ☐
Read book review in: _____ ☐
Other (Please specify): _____ ☐

3. How many computer books have you purchased in the last six months?

This book only .... ☐   3 to 5 books .... ☐
2 books .... ☐   More than 5 .... ☐

4. Where did you purchase this book?

Bookstore .... ☐
Computer Store .... ☐
Consumer Electronics Store .... ☐
Department Store .... ☐
Office Club .... ☐
Warehouse Club .... ☐
Mail Order .... ☐
Direct from Publisher .... ☐
Internet site .... ☐
Other (Please specify): _____ ☐

5. How long have you been using a computer?

☐ Less than 6 months   ☐ 6 months to a year
☐ 1 to 3 years   ☐ More than 3 years

6. What is your level of experience with personal computers and with the subject of this book?

	With PCs	With subject of book
New	☐	☐
Casual	☐	☐
Accomplished	☐	☐
Expert	☐	☐

Source Code ISBN: 0-7897-1235-0

**7. Which of the following best describes your
    job title?**

Administrative Assistant .... ☐
Coordinator .... ☐
Manager/Supervisor .... ☐
Director .... ☐
Vice President .... ☐
President/CEO/COO.. ☐
Lawyer/Doctor/Medical Professional .... ☐
Teacher/Educator/Trainer .... ☐
Engineer/Technician .... ☐
Consultant .... ☐
Not employed/Student/Retired .... ☐
Other (Please specify): _____ ☐

**8. Which of the following best describes the area of
    the company your job title falls under?**

Accounting .... ☐
Engineering.. ☐
Manufacturing .... ☐
Operations... ☐
Marketing .... ☐
Sales .... ☐
Other (Please specify): _____ ☐

9. What is your age?

Under 20 .... ☐
21-29 .... ☐
30-39 .... ☐
40-49 .... ☐
50-59 .... ☐
60-over .... ☐

10. Are you:

Male .... ☐
Female .... ☐

**11. Which computer publications do you read
     regularly? (Please list)**

_____
_____
_____
_____
_____
_____
_____
_____
_____
_____

Comments: _____
_____
_____

Fold here and scotch-tape to mail.

Check out Que® Books on the World Wide Web
http://www.mcp.com/que

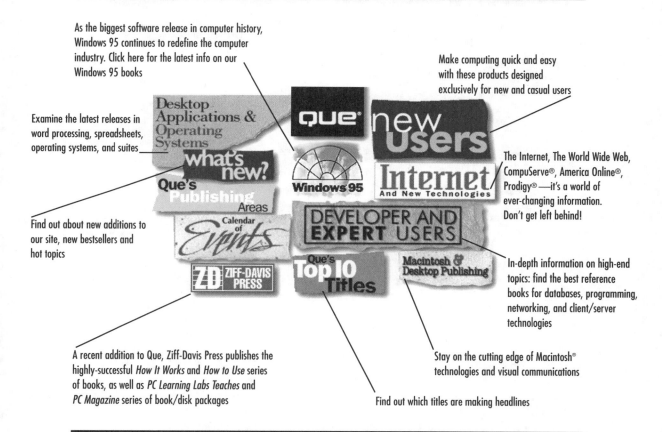

As the biggest software release in computer history, Windows 95 continues to redefine the computer industry. Click here for the latest info on our Windows 95 books

Make computing quick and easy with these products designed exclusively for new and casual users

Examine the latest releases in word processing, spreadsheets, operating systems, and suites

The Internet, The World Wide Web, CompuServe®, America Online®, Prodigy® —it's a world of ever-changing information. Don't get left behind!

Find out about new additions to our site, new bestsellers and hot topics

In-depth information on high-end topics: find the best reference books for databases, programming, networking, and client/server technologies

A recent addition to Que, Ziff-Davis Press publishes the highly-successful *How It Works* and *How to Use* series of books, as well as *PC Learning Labs Teaches* and *PC Magazine* series of book/disk packages

Stay on the cutting edge of Macintosh® technologies and visual communications

Find out which titles are making headlines

With 6 separate publishing groups, Que develops products for many specific market segments and areas of computer technology. Explore our Web Site and you'll find information on best-selling titles, newly published titles, upcoming products, authors, and much more.

- Stay informed on the latest industry trends and products available
- Visit our online bookstore for the latest information and editions
- Download software from Que's library of the best shareware and freeware

MACMILLAN COMPUTER PUBLISHING USA

A VIACOM COMPANY

If you need assistance with the information in this book or with a CD/Disk accompanying the book, please access the Knowledge Base on our Web site at **http://www.superlibrary.com/general/support**. Our most Frequently Asked Questions are answered there. If you do not find the answer to your questions on our Web site, you may contact Macmillan Technical Support **(317) 581-3833** or e-mail us at **support@mcp.com**.